# PHYSICAL DISABILITY IN BRITISH ROMANTIC LITERATURE

The modern concept of disability did not exist in the Romantic period. This study addresses the anachronistic use of 'disability' in scholarship of the Romantic era, providing a disability studies theorized account of British literature that explores the relationship between ideas of function and aesthetics. Unpacking the politics of ability, the book reveals the centrality of capacity and weakness concepts to the egalitarian politics of the 1790s, and the importance of desert theory to debates about sentiment and the charitable relief of impaired soldiers. Treating the aesthetics of deformity as distinct from discussions of ability, Essaka Joshua uncovers a controversy in picturesque aesthetics, offers accounts of deformity that anticipate recent disability studies theory, and discusses deformity and monstrosity as a blended category in *Frankenstein*. Setting aside the modern concept of disability, Joshua argues for the historical and critical value of period-specific terms.

ESSAKA JOSHUA is Associate Professor of English at the University of Notre Dame, Indiana. She is the author of *Pygmalion and Galatea* (2001) and *The Romantics and the May Day Tradition* (2007). She won the Tyler Rigg Award for Disability Studies Scholarship in Literature and Literary Analysis in 2012.

T0364228

# CAMBRIDGE STUDIES IN ROMANTICISM

This series aims to foster the best new work in one of the most challenging fields within English literary studies. From the early 1780s to the early 1830s, a formidable array of talented men and women took to literary composition, not just in poetry, which some of them famously transformed, but in many modes of writing. The expansion of publishing created new opportunities for writers, and the political stakes of what they wrote were raised again by what Wordsworth called those 'great national events' that were 'almost daily taking place': the French Revolution, the Napoleonic and American wars, urbanization, industrialization, religious revival, an expanded empire abroad, and the reform movement at home. This was an enormous ambition, even when it pretended otherwise. The relations between science, philosophy, religion, and literature were reworked in texts such as *Frankenstein* and *Biographia Literaria*; gender relations in *A Vindication of the Rights of Woman* and *Don Juan*; journalism by Cobbett and Hazlitt; and poetic form, content, and style by the Lake School and the Cockney School. Outside Shakespeare studies, probably no body of writing has produced such a wealth of commentary or done so much to shape the responses of modern criticism. This indeed is the period that saw the emergence of those notions of literature and of literary history, especially national literary history, on which modern scholarship in English has been founded.

The categories produced by Romanticism have also been challenged by recent historicist arguments. The task of the series is to engage both with a challenging corpus of Romantic writings and with the changing field of criticism they have helped to shape. As with other literary series published by Cambridge University Press, this one will represent the work of both younger and more established scholars on either side of the Atlantic and elsewhere.

See the end of the book for a complete list of published titles.

# PHYSICAL DISABILITY IN BRITISH ROMANTIC LITERATURE

### ESSAKA JOSHUA

*University of Notre Dame*

CAMBRIDGE
UNIVERSITY PRESS

# CAMBRIDGE
## UNIVERSITY PRESS

Shaftesbury Road, Cambridge CB2 8EA, United Kingdom

One Liberty Plaza, 20th Floor, New York, NY 10006, USA

477 Williamstown Road, Port Melbourne, VIC 3207, Australia

314–321, 3rd Floor, Plot 3, Splendor Forum, Jasola District Centre, New Delhi – 110025, India

103 Penang Road, #05–06/07, Visioncrest Commercial, Singapore 238467

Cambridge University Press is part of Cambridge University Press & Assessment,
a department of the University of Cambridge.

We share the University's mission to contribute to society through the pursuit of
education, learning and research at the highest international levels of excellence.

www.cambridge.org
Information on this title: www.cambridge.org/9781108799171

DOI: 10.1017/9781108872126

© Essaka Joshua 2020

First published 2020
First paperback edition 2022

*A catalogue record for this publication is available from the British Library*

*Library of Congress Cataloging-in-Publication data*
NAMES: Joshua, Essaka, author.
Title: Physical disability in British romantic literature / Essaka Joshua.
DESCRIPTION: Cambridge ; New York : Cambridge University Press, 2020. | Series: Cambridge
studies in romanticism | Includes bibliographical references and index.
IDENTIFIERS: LCCN 2020013778 (print) | LCCN 2020013779 (ebook) | ISBN 9781108836708
(hardback) | ISBN 9781108799171 (paperback) | ISBN 9781108872126 (epub)
SUBJECTS: LCSH: People with disabilities in literature. | English literature–19th century–History and
criticism. | English literature–18th century–History and criticism. | Abnormalities, Human, in
literature. | Romanticism.
CLASSIFICATION: LCC PR468.P35 J67 2020 (print) | LCC PR468.P35 (ebook) |
DDC 820.9/35610907–dc23
LC record available at https://lccn.loc.gov/2020013778
LC ebook record available at https://lccn.loc.gov/2020013779

ISBN    978-1-108-83670-8    Hardback
ISBN    978-1-108-79917-1    Paperback

*For Freddie*

# Contents

# List of Illustrations

## Figure

## Table

# *Acknowledgements*

I am extremely grateful to the provost and fellows of Oriel College, Oxford, for awarding me a Research Fellowship, and also to the Institute for Scholarship in the Liberal Arts and Dean John McGreevy in the College of Arts and Letters at the University of Notre Dame for their generous financial support. I would like to thank Michael Bradshaw for inviting me to co-write the introduction to *Disabling Romanticism: Body, Mind, and Text* (London: Palgrave Macmillan, 2016), and to contribute a chapter. Some of my work from this introduction appears here. Chapter 3 evolved from a talk he invited me to give at the Romanticism Research Forum at Edge Hill University, UK in 2010. Thanks also go to Lilla Maria Crisafulli, Serena Baiesi, and Carlotta Farese for their kind invitation to present my work at their *Frankenstein* conference at the University of Bologna in September 2018, in the year of the *Frankenstein* bicentenary. I am grateful to Sami Schalk and Brittany Schmeir for their research assistance, to Daniel Johnson in the University of Notre Dame library, and to my undergraduate students for allowing me to test some of this material on them. I have been lucky to have engaged with numerous interlocutors, and to have received generous support and encouragement from them over the years. I would like to thank Clare Barker, Kevin Barry, James Chandler, James Collins, Nora Crook, Lennard Davis, John Duffy, Amanda Gulley, Encarnación Juárez-Almendros, Eva Feder Kittay, Daniel Johnson, Alastair MacIntyre, Marc Maurer, Robert McRuer, Stuart Murray, Patrick Rader, Michael Rembis, Carrie Sandhal, Jeremy Schipper, Margrit Shildrick, Tobin Siebers, Michael Waddell, Edward Wheatley, and Jennifer Wistey. My husband, Richard Cross, and my sister, Eleoma Bodammer, have read all of the work presented here. I am extremely grateful to them as always.

Permission has been granted to reprint from my previously published work: 'Introduction', co-authored with Michael Bradshaw, in *Disabling Romanticism: Body, Mind, and Text*, ed. by Michael Bradshaw (London:

Palgrave Macmillan, 2016), 1–17; 'Picturesque Aesthetics: Theorising Deformity in the Romantic Era', in *Disabling Romanticism: Body, Mind, and Text*, ed. by Michael Bradshaw (London: Palgrave Macmillan, 2016), 29–48; 'Disability and Deformity: Function Impairment and Aesthetics in the Long Eighteenth Century', in *The Cambridge Companion to Literature and Disability*, ed. by Clare Barker and Stuart Murray (Cambridge: Cambridge University Press, 2018), 47–61.

# Introduction

We use the word 'disability' in ways that Romantic-era writers do not; and they use the word 'disability' in ways that we do not. So the Romantic era comes *before* our modern understanding of disability. It comes before 'disability' explicitly refers to the bodily and mental causes of an inability to act in certain ways, rather than simply the inability itself; it comes before 'disability' refers both to the aesthetic and functional components of physical and mental impairments; it comes before the dominant idea of disability becomes conceptualized through medicine; it comes before disability is widely used as a state-approved category for administrative purposes; it comes before the collective noun 'the disabled' was used; it comes before the modern *non-alienans* adjectival sense of 'disabled';[1] it comes before 'disability' is regarded as conferring an identity; and it comes before a theorized understanding of 'disability' as the result of the relationship between bodily and mental configurations (impairments) and their contexts.[2] We have lost the senses of 'disability' meaning the prevention (in a human being) of a particular action; we have lost 'disability' as a temporary impairment; we have lost 'disability' as a synonym for 'inability'; and we have lost the sense of 'disabled' as someone who is discharged from military service due to impairments or old age.

The sheer variety of the ways in which the word 'disability' has proliferated in meanings and uses since the Romantic era means that tracing the evolution of disability involves examining a number of concepts that were not associated explicitly with the word. A combination of approaches seems to be the best way to provide a maximally capacious account of pre-disability[3] that avoids circularity or teleological redundancy.[4] An account such as this means exploring specific bodily or mental configurations that are now clustered under the general category of disability; acknowledging generic pre-disability concepts that have no name; seeking out implied concepts of non-impairment; considering the intersections between pre-disability, race, gender, sexuality, money, and rank; and being aware that pre-disability concepts may or may not flow towards modern disability concepts as a *telos*. Imposing the word 'disability' upon the discussion in these instances increases the potential for confusion. 'Disability' will only be used here when it is used by the authors under discussion; and 'pre-disability' will signal a range of concepts that may or may not develop into modern concepts of disability, but that clearly have some family resemblance to the modern concepts.

The writers of the Romantic era follow particular conventions that tend to identify certain bodily configurations as functional and others as aesthetic. Social or personal attributes and contexts, such as gender and rank, often drive these conventions. A mobility impairment may be aesthetic for an aristocratic woman, but functional for a man who uses his limbs to work. Some of the most interesting material from the Romantic period is concerned with the moments where this expected distinction between function and aesthetics is frustrated. Ideas about aesthetics and ideas about function are sharply divergent, and thus what is said about one cannot be assumed about the other. The separateness of function impairment and aesthetics is one of the reasons why we cannot straightforwardly use our modern conventional senses of 'disability' when we discuss disability historically. That is not to say that function and aesthetics are never discussed together; it is to say that when they are discussed together, what is said about one component is not implied about the other, and that the writers of the period maintain this distinction in their use of concepts connected to disability. In contrast to the absence of the modern senses of 'disability', Romantic-era writers have a term for the aesthetic component of numerous bodily configurations relevant to disability: 'deformity'. Not only do they have a term for it, various writers of the period develop very distinctive theories about it. It is for this reason that this book is in two parts. The first part has a greater emphasis on function and the second has a greater emphasis on aesthetics.

Bringing together the two fields of romantic studies and disability studies is not new, but this study is the first to offer a range of alternatives for the term 'disability' – a term that many scholars believe to be anachronistic to the period. Lennard Davis, for example, remarks that 'disability was not an operative category before the eighteenth century'.[5] Iain Hutchison suggests that 'disability', as 'an all-embracing term', did not gain 'currency during the nineteenth century';[6] and Simon Dickie asserts that 'the modern understanding of *disability* as a unified category – at least sufficiently unified to be used by activists and legislators – did not exist' in the eighteenth century.[7] I also set out to challenge, here, the 'first wave' theories or metanarratives of the evolution or history of disability that persist in disability studies.[8] These theories are dependent on the anachronistic term. I demonstrate, throughout the book, how a disability studies approach that does not use the term 'disability' allows us to recover the pre-disability concepts of the period. Unlike prior studies, this book does not offer an explanation of how modern notions of disability emerged. This is simply because they do not emerge in the Romantic period. Instead, this study – which is by no means exhaustive – makes the case for treating the Romantic period as a pre-disability era. The book is about physical disability. This is not because physical disability in any way stands for all disabilities, but because physical disability in the Romantic era has been far less extensively researched than intellectual and emotional disabilities.[9] Furthermore, this book is about group terms for physical disability, rather than about individual disabilities. I have arranged the discussion as a series of case studies (of single authors, groups of writers, and single texts).

### Romantic Disability Studies: A Subfield

This book continues along several trajectories within Romantic studies, most notably the interest in the body.[10] Some of the earliest stirrings of literary disability studies scholarship appeared in writing on the body and at the intersection of body politics and identity politics. Judith Butler influences much of this work. Veronica Kelly and Dorothea von Mücke (1994), for example, explore the ways in which 'corporeality can be thought of in the critique of culture'.[11] Lennard Davis examines ideology about the body in *Enforcing Normalcy* (1995), characterizing disability as a 'social process that intimately involves everyone who has a body and lives in the world of the senses'.[12] David Mitchell and Sharon Snyder (1997) note the widespread exclusion of disability from the discussions of body politics: 'disability has rarely been included in catalogs of marginalized groupings'.[13] According to Alan Richardson, the 'transformative effects' of major interventions, such as feminism, the attention to empire and colonialism, and the breaking down of canonicity in the field of Romantic studies, 'left certain critical tenets in place, at least in relation to the (rapidly imploding) canon of male-authored, poetic texts. In particular, canonical Romanticism continued to be seen as a transcendentalizing, idealist literary movement, implicitly hostile not only to the feminine and to the racially or [ethnic] "other", but to physical nature and to the material body itself'.[14] Richardson's work is an important response to the idea of bodily transcendence or idealism, which he, Jerome McGann, and others recast as a tension between mind and body.[15] Much of this revision has been conducted through the lens of the medical sciences (particularly neuroscience), or ideas connected to 'affect' (such as 'sensibility'), or environmentalism (such as eco-criticism), or cognitive linguistics and philosophy of mind. As Richardson neatly summarizes, 'the new Romantic scholarship on the body gives us, ultimately, a more elaborate and more dynamic sense of the Romantic mind'.[16]

While Richardson gestures towards the mounting attention on 'the abnormal and the "monstrous"', interest has since broadened to consider disabled bodies that fall outside these categories.[17] Disability studies as a subfield within Romantic studies parallels (and occasionally overlaps with) medical and neurobiological approaches to the body and mind. Additionally, it also calls attention to the lived experiences of people with bodily, sensory, and mental differences. This subfield continues the dynamic of inclusion raised by feminist and critical race theory that originates in the civil rights movements that in turn have their origins in Romantic-era thought. Moreover, the ethics of environmentalism, homelessness, imprisonment, war, vegetarianism, animal rights, and human flourishing have been explored through what has come to be known as the 'ethical turn' in literary studies.[18] Christoph Henke observes that the critical refocus towards ethical concerns signals a discontent 'with the orthodoxy of poststructuralist theory ... and its apparent lack of ethical reflection'.[19] The 'ethical turn', according to Laurence Lockridge, includes understanding 'the textually represented world of plot, character, thought, and image, the authorial act of bringing the text into being, and the relatedness of the text to a readership'.[20] Henke views this approach as 'an ethical re-turn, i.e. a return to an idea of art that should combine aesthetics with ethics, albeit in a different way and under very different historical conditions'.[21] For Tobin Siebers, the ethical turn 'involves critics in the process of making decisions and of studying how these choices affect the lives of fellow critics, writers, students, and readers as well as our ways of defining literature and human nature'.[22] The ethical turn did not always embrace women's writing, however, and it has taken longer for disability to be recognized as an important issue for the Romantic engagement with ethics.[23]

Disability, and its cognates and related concepts, raises many questions that bring new understanding of the literature of the period. What place do they have in the development of industrialized economies? What do they tell us about relationships between society and the individual? What role do they have in the emancipation movements? How do they affect changing literary tastes? How do they participate in the key ideas of the period: sentiment, equality, reason, the picturesque, the sublime, the gothic, the fragment, the imagination, childhood, heroism, nostalgia, travel, empire, nature, the outcast, the primitive, the human, the ordinary? Many of these questions will remain unanswered for a long time, though the work has begun in earnest. As Michael Bradshaw and I suggest, in *Disabling Romanticism*, Romantic-era texts 'should be revisited in the light of contemporary disability awareness', because the 'critical practices associated with Romantic studies continue to marginalise and disable the different in body and mind'.[24]

## Theorizing and Historicizing Disability in Disability Studies

Although this book is a revisionist approach to Romantic studies, it is just as much a rethinking of disability studies' approaches to literary history. Theories developed in sociology and cultural studies have dominated much of the debate about literary uses of disability. In the broad-survey scholarship, four distinct claims continue to be made in historically based theoretical work. Firstly, there is the claim that the late eighteenth century is a period of transition from disability being understood as a supernatural sign to disability being regarded as a scientific phenomenon (the *prodigy-to-pathology* thesis). Secondly, there is the claim that the period is not one of transition because multiple views of disability circulate and recirculate at the same time and across time (the *recirculation* thesis). Thirdly, there is the claim that the modern sense of 'disability' emerges during the early nineteenth century as a product of changes in government administration (the *administration* thesis). This claim is linked, in some accounts, with industrialization. Finally, there is the claim that the modern sense of 'disability' emerged out of a number of disciplinary practices, including the development of statistics as a way of measuring norms (the *normalcy* thesis). The first claim is premised on the idea that the concept of disability is straightforwardly present in the Romantic period; the second suggests that multiple concepts of disability are present at all times; and the last two claims suppose that nothing like a modern concept of disability is present before the mid-nineteenth century. The scholars who make these claims discuss disability in a variety of contexts, and so these theses or narratives turn out to be accounts of a range of different phenomena. In particular, the first two claims are not explicitly about disability as such, but relate to a variety of bodily and mental phenomena that are later associated with the concept of disability.[25] The main theses about the evolution of disability proposed by 'first-wave' disability studies scholars have largely focused on the ways attitudes towards disability changed, rather than on understanding the evolution of the term and associated notions. This section will give a fuller account of the emergence of the metanarratives of disability in disability studies scholarship and their relationship to the Romantic period, and will touch on some important concepts in literary and cultural disability studies (e.g. the social model, the medical model, and the impairment/disability distinction).[26]

The first of the major claims about the development of disability is often referred to as the *prodigy-to-pathology* narrative. Proponents of this thesis argue that the Romantic period is in the middle of a transition in which attitudes towards bodily configurations later classified under the concept of disability are characterized as moving from an early modern religious model (where disability is regarded as an omen, a punishment, or a wonder), to, at the beginning of the nineteenth century, a science-based understanding of disability (where disability is seen as a medical condition that is treated or managed).[27] This narrative is directly or indirectly influenced by Auguste Comte's theory that social evolution develops through three stages: the *theological* (or fictitious), the *metaphysical* (or abstract), and the *scientific* (or positive). The theological stage supposes that all 'apparent anomalies of the universe' are explained by supernatural beings; the metaphysical stage replaces these beings with 'abstract forces, real entities or personified abstractions', such as Nature; and the scientific stage gives up the search for origins and turns its focus on the laws that govern phenomena.[28] When adapted for disability history, Comte's transition theory is used to explain both the causes and the symbolic significance of disability. With a few exceptions, the theological stage is presented in the Comtean model as a prejudicial and medically primitive phase in which disability was feared, misunderstood, and explained through a religious worldview, and the Romantic period is seen as on the cusp of the emergence of the modern scientific perspective.

Michael Oliver (1990) is one of the earliest writers on disability to comment on Comte's theory as a framework for understanding the 'changing historical perceptions of disability'.[29] Oliver places disability in the context of the development of attitudes towards deviance. He suggests that we can see patterns in the history of caring for people with disabilities. Care was initially 'based upon a philosophy of compassion linked to religious and philanthropic perspectives; then services were provided based upon the philosophy of protection, both for the disabled individuals and society; and finally care was provided on the basis of optimism, linked to the development of new scientific and pedagogic approaches'.[30] According to Oliver, disability began as a moral problem, became a legal problem, and is now a medical problem. He notes that Comte critiqued his own narrative by suggesting that 'while one perception may dominate at a particular point in history, it does not do so at the expense of the others'.[31] So, while there may be a medical explanation for a disability, 'that does not mean that some ... may not feel that it is a punishment for some previous sin'.[32] Most scholars who draw on the Comtean transition are less troubled by this than Oliver is, however.

The prodigy-to-pathology argument is also employed in the context of unusual disabilities. Rosemarie Garland Thomson uses it in *Freakery* (1996), her study of attitudes towards a group of people with rare and visible impairments. Garland Thomson characterizes the development in attitudes towards people who were called 'freaks' as a movement 'from a narrative of the marvelous to a narrative of the deviant'.[33] Freaks are viewed as 'prodigious monster[s]' and, 'as modernity develops', become 'an index of Nature's fancy', and then 'pathological terata'.[34] So, 'what was once sought after as revelation becomes pursued as entertainment; what aroused awe now inspires horror; what was taken as portent shifts to a site of progress'.[35] For Garland Thomson, 'the exceptional body' in the theological phase 'is most often evidence of God's design, divine wrath, or nature's abundance'.[36] She returns to Comte again in her history of observation, *Staring* (2009), and transfers the argument about freaks to a discussion of disability.[37] There is, she suggests, a movement from viewing disability as connected to the supernatural and expressing wonderment at it, to looking at disability with the observation techniques of science, surveillance, and eventually to a modern way of viewing that holds in tension ennui and enthralment. David T. Mitchell and Sharon L. Snyder (2001) pair the Comtean narrative with Foucault's critique, in *The Birth of the Clinic* (1975), of the increasing power of the dehumanizing diagnostic medical gaze in the early nineteenth century. Using Montaigne, they characterize the transition as a movement *from* the early modern 'cripple' as 'emblematic of creation's "infinity of forms", which God, "in His wisdom", supplies as evidence of his inexhaustible bounty', *to* an 'articulation of bodily difference' in terms of fixed categories that the medical profession deemed appropriate.[38] Whatever we make of the prodigy-to-pathology narrative, it is important to keep in mind that these histories are histories not of disability but of a collection of bodily configurations some of which we now categorize under the heading of 'disability', but which were not then treated as such, or even as a group.[39]

The narrative of evolution from the supernatural to the scientific is challenged by proponents of the *recirculation model* of disability history (the second major claim about the development of disability). These theorists suggest that ideas do not transition in a sequential fashion, that there is no clear development in how disability is conceptualized, and that a range of attitudes towards disability appear and reappear throughout all periods.[40] While there may be a medical explanation for an impairment in the scientific phase, the view that impairment is a punishment for sin may also be present. The argument for the recirculation of ideas is essentially about accommodating anomalous and contradictory examples. Stephen Pender (1996) suggests that the transition narrative 'fails to take account of the complex, often conflictual status of the monstrous in the early modern period', and that 'the reception of the monstrous as portentous did not simply expire', but became more elaborate.[41] Lorraine Daston and Katharine Park suggest in *Wonders and the Orders of Nature* (1998) that while the prodigy-to-pathology narrative made sense 'in the context of the history of science as practiced in the mid-1970s',[42] it should be abandoned in favour of a different set of progressions. In their case study on monsters, Daston and Park discover three 'separate complexes of interpretation and associated emotions – horror, pleasure, and repugnance', each of which have their own rhythms through time.[43] Margrit Shildrick (2005) rejects the prodigy-to-pathology narrative on the grounds that multiple discourses are always at work. She suggests that there is 'a complex mix of interwoven ideas and beliefs [about disability] that belies the notion of periodization'.[44] Shildrick takes issue with the flattening out of history, arguing that there is no shift from early modern ideas about the marvellous or monstrous to a medicalized idea of disability, but rather a 'constant circulation and recirculation of ideas – both articulated and hidden – that are intermeshed with one another'.[45] Shildrick suggests that a genealogy of disability is a messy business, with multiple definitions at work. Disability, she asserts, does not have 'a stable and progressive history', and 'multiple shifts and reversals [have taken place] in how disability is defined and perceived'.[46] The coexistence and polysemy of different discourses of disability, and the variety of senses of disability, makes the idea of a transition from one to another problematic. Working on eighteenth-century France, William Paulson (1987) makes a similar point about the recirculation of ideas about blindness. Paulson aimed to do for blindness what Foucault did for the history of madness – understand the discourses surrounding it – and he grapples with the problems faced by historians of ideas in the wake of Foucault's *The Archaeology of Knowledge* (1972).

Paulson identifies various philosophical, sentimental, and visionary or romantic discourses of blindness. He suggests that they are at times used within the same work, that they are not genre-specific, and that they 'do not so much change their meaning as recombine in changing contexts'.[47] These are, he concludes, 'specific and constraining discursive formations, ways of writing that may have once seemed natural and well-nigh universal, but that from the perspective of our modernity appear definable and strange'.[48]

Some critics argue against the transition narrative from a position of specialism in a particular period.[49] Irina Metzler (2006), for instance, demonstrates that medieval and religious attitudes towards disability are not as straightforwardly prejudicial as Comte's idea of the theological stage suggests. Metzler criticizes the stereotyping of the medieval period as 'barbaric and superstitious', suggesting that the transition narrative does little justice to the complexity of the theology of disability.[50] Geoffrey Hudson (2012) similarly points out the mischaracterization of earlier attitudes towards bodily difference. Working in the early modern period, Hudson notes that disabling injuries sustained by veterans were regarded as 'the work of *other* men and not God (no matter which side he [i.e. the soldier] fought on)'.[51] Hudson draws his evidence from petitions for financial support. David M. Turner (2012) suggests that the idea 'of a wholesale transformation from "religious" to "medical" understandings is too crude to explain attitudes towards impairment in this period'.[52] Turner demonstrates that 'eighteenth-century religious thought provided a rationale for accepting human difference', and that religious and medical understandings were often inseparable.[53] This work builds on Turner's earlier observation (with Kevin Stagg) that 'notions of a wholesale transition in which one set of ideas replaced another' were questionable.[54] Turner states, furthermore, that the grand narratives 'gloss over a complex series of developments with their own histories'.[55] He explores, instead, 'the ways in which meanings of physical disability were formed within different cultural contexts', and allows for more nuanced transitional narratives to be used alongside the recirculation model.[56] Scholarship from the medical humanities likewise offers specialist grounds for challenging the prodigy-to-pathology narrative. For example, Helen Small (1996) demonstrates in her work on female hysteria that the merging of sentimental and medical discourses in the eighteenth century makes the idea of a transition from one to another problematic.[57] Kevis Goodman (2007) challenges the transition narrative through her investigation of nostalgia.[58] She reveals that there is a regressive Comtean narrative: nostalgia began, in the mid-eighteenth century, as a mental illness characterized by home-sickness, and was de-pathologized in the twentieth century and character-ized as a form of sentimentality.[59]

The third claim, that 'disability' transitioned into its modern sense as a consequence of changes in state provision for welfare, is the central thesis of Deborah A. Stone's *The Disabled State* (1984). Stone ties the develop-ment of the disability concept to changes in state provision for welfare, and makes a strong case that, whether the word is present or not, 'disability' refers to a 'socially created category'[60] that 'entitles its members to partic-ular privileges in the form of social aid and exemptions from certain obligations of citizenship'.[61] For Stone, the 'very notion of disability is fundamental to the architecture of the welfare state' because all states inevitably need to resolve the tension between two distributive systems, one based on work and the other on need.[62] In order to determine whether a person should be expected to work, states require a system of rules that incorporate exemptions for people who cannot work (such as children and old people). Stone identifies disability as the most problematic of the *categories* of need', because 'no single condition of "disability" is univer-sally recognized, and because physical and mental incapacity are conditions that can be feigned for secondary gain'.[63] States find disability problematic, furthermore, because the means to certify that someone has a disability are not as straightforward as, for example, determining someone's age. Throughout the nineteenth century there were disagreements over whether government officials or the medical profession should have control over who was identified as being fit for work. For Stone, the clinical idea of disability is merely a validation mechanism for the social category of disability that predated it; and so, for understanding the evolution of the concept of disability, the idea of disability as a category of need (or of exemption from work) is much more important than the issue of medical verification. As Stone puts it, 'disability is a *formal administrative category* that determines the rights and privileges of a large number of people' and that 'represents a politically fashioned compromise at any given time and place about the legitimacy of claims to social aid'.[64]

The Poor Law Amendment Act of 1834 is central to Stone's thesis. According to Stone, the Act identified five categories of pauper who were eligible for outdoor relief (outside the workhouse) and indoor relief (inside the workhouse). These were: 'children, the sick, the insane, "defectives" [i.e. people with sensory impairments], and the "aged and infirm"' (the last of which could be of any age).[65] For Stone, the exemptions defined the mainstream, and the system reflected a policy according to which, 'if a

128      *Quarterly Abstract of the Receipt*

Form

QUARTERLY ABSTRACT, SHOWING THE NUMBER OF
THE AMOUNT OF MONEY

during the Quarter ending the     day of     183

| | NUMBER OF PAUPERS RELIEVED. | | | | | | | | | | | | | | | | | | | | | |
|---|---|---|---|---|---|---|---|---|---|---|---|---|---|---|---|---|---|---|---|---|---|---|

*The table shows columns for:* PARISHES. | Aged and Infirm of both Sexes (Out-door: In-door, Resident, Non-Resident) | Orphan and Foundling Children (In-door, Out-door) | Illegitimate Children (In-door, Out-door) | Insane Persons and Lunatics (In-door, Out-door, In Lunatic Asylums or elsewhere) | Idiots (In-door, Out-door) | Able-bodied: Alleged Insufficiency of Earnings (In-door, Out-door) | Who had lost Work or Place (In-door, Out-door) | on account of Temporary Sickness (In-door, Out-door) | Whose Families were relieved on account of Sickness (In-door, Out-door) | Families Relieved on account of the Number (In-door, Out-door) | Families Destitute on account of Misconduct of Parents (In-door, Out-door) | Names of the other Classes not included in the preceding (In-door, Out-door) | Total Number of Poor receiving Relief. | TOTAL.

Total - -

Increase* -

Diminution*

\* The Increase and Diminution to be stated on a comparison of the corresponding Quarter of last Year.

| Average Weekly Cost per Head of the In-door Paupers. | | | | Workhouses now in Use. | | | | | | | |
|---|---|---|---|---|---|---|---|---|---|---|---|
| | Adults. | Children. | Insane Persons. | Houses where situate. | Classes of Paupers. | Number in each. | Number of In-door Paupers of all Classes at Commencement of the Quarter. | Total Number of all Classes admitted during the Quarter. | Total Number Discharged. | Number of Deaths in the Quarter. | Present Number of In-door Paupers. |
| Food . . | | | | | | | | | | | |
| Clothing . . | | | | | | | | | | | |
| General Charges | | | | | | | | | | | |
| Total . | | | | | | | | | | | |

OFFICERS ON SERVICE IN THE UNION.

| Name. | Office. | Salary |
|---|---|---|
| | | |
| | | |

*First Annual Report of the Poor Law Commissioners for England and Wales* (London: W. Clowes, 1835), 128–9 person didn't fall into one of [the five categories], he was ablebodied by default'.[66] Stone observes that until 1871, there was 'scarcely any mention of a need for a validation device for ... [infirmity]; the infirmities that rendered an adult incapable of working were thought to be obvious'.[67] Setting aside the category of children, Stone regards the remaining groups as components of what became, in social policy, 'a unitary category of "disability"'.[68] She argues that, from the 1840s, disability evolved from an inability to work that was validated by non-clinical means, to an inability to work that was validated by clinical medicine, because clinical medicine 'gave legitimacy to claims for social aid, and it offered a method of validation that would render administration of the category feasible'.[69] Stone concludes that the 'concept of disability is fundamentally the result of political conflict about distributive criteria and the appropriate recipients of social aid', rather than 'a set of objective characteristics that render people needy'.[70] It is fixed neither by the 'objective characteristics of individuals' nor 'by objective requirements of the economy. It is something society creates and constantly redesigns'.[71]

There much about Stone's thesis that is plausible. For example, the evidence for the role of legal and administrative categories in the formation of modern notions of disability is convincing. It is, nevertheless, important to be aware of certain limitations in the details of the evidence. Of the five categories of paupers identified by Stone, the Act itself only specifies 'insane persons'.[72] This group, which had appeared in previous Acts, only appears in the Act to exclude it from the rules concerning detention. The categorization of people into groups of paupers came instead from the Poor Law Commission. This body was set up by the Poor Law Amendment Act to determine who received indoor or outdoor relief. The commission specified twelve categories of pauper, rather than the five that Stone mentions, and it placed six of these categories under the heading 'Able-bodied'.[73] The other five were specified as 'Aged and Infirm of both sexes', 'Orphan and Foundling Children', 'Illegitimate Children', 'Insane Persons and Lunatics', and 'Idiots'.[74] There is also a box that is separate from both of these eleven called 'other Classes not included in the preceding'.[75] Significantly, the five categories that were not identified as 'Able-bodied' are not categorized as 'disabled'.

Stone suggests that the administration did not provide 'a positive definition of "ablebodied"; instead, "able to work" is a residual category whose meaning can be known only after all the "unable to work" categories have been precisely defined'.[76] The Commission's charts, however, give detailed lists of people who counted as able-bodied (e.g. those with merely 'alleged insufficiency of earnings'), and so the exceptions do not define the mainstream to the degree that Stone asserts.[77] Although the Commission does not specify which of the non-able-bodied people were included under the category 'disabled', and so does not have an explicitly delineated group, it does use 'disabled' and 'partially disabled' throughout its first report as an opposite to able-bodied. For instance, part of the job description of the master of a workhouse is to 'keep the partially disabled paupers occupied to the extent of their ability'.[78] There is also a box for signalling 'If Able or Disabled' in an accounts form for outdoor relief.[79] The Board even considered 'that the change from profuse to very limited relief should not be made too suddenly, and this particularly in the cases of infirm or partially disabled people'.[80] These examples suggest that the Commission had some idea of what they meant by 'disabled', even though the report does not explicitly define it. Stone treats 'disabled' as meaning unable to work, but the Commission categorized those with 'temporary sickness' as able-bodied.[81] If sickness prevented people from working but did not place them out of the able-bodied category, then the non-able-bodied designation could mean something along the lines of never able to work. The government was not interested in people it did not need to relieve, and so the administration thesis does not explain how the word 'disabled' came to be used of wealthy people with disabilities or people with disabilities who worked. This is ultimately only a partial definition of 'disability'.

Stone's thesis is the basis for the central claims of Michael Oliver's study, *The Politics of Disablement* (1990) and, with Colin Barnes, *The New Politics of Disablement* (2012), a revision of Oliver's original book. Oliver (and Oliver and Barnes) are concerned with the development of the responsibilities of care (characterized as a movement from family to institution) as a way of understanding how disability emerged as a social category. Oliver makes the case that both disability and impairment are culturally produced, and that the type of economy plays an important role in the production of these categories. Oliver alludes briefly to Victor Finkelstein's (1980) argument that the process of disablement is linked to the process of industrialization in the sense that when work moved away from the home to the factory, people with disabilities were excluded from the workforce and 'came to be regarded as a social and educational problem'.[82] Oliver suggests that the idea that people with disabilities were included in 'some kind of idealised community' is mere speculation, 'largely because history is silent on the experience of disability'.[83] Oliver agrees with Finkelstein that industrialization and capitalism brought important changes, such as the proliferation of institutions that 'facilitated the segregation of disabled people, initially in workhouses and asylums, but gradually in more specialist establishments of one kind or another'.[84] Additionally, Oliver suggests that 'many previously acceptable social roles, such as begging or "village idiot" were disappearing'.[85] Explicitly following Stone's lead, Oliver and Barnes maintain that the Poor Law Amendment Act of 1834 was one of a number of state mechanisms that maintained capitalist social relations by threatening with incarceration anyone who did not conform. According to Oliver, the double impetus of the movement of the workforce away from the countryside, and the increase in institutionalization, caused the 'boundaries of family obligations towards disabled people' to be 're-drawn', and 'the new asylums and workhouses met a need among poor families struggling to cope'.[86]

Oliver argues, furthermore, that disability is as much a product of ideology as it is of economic structures, even though this ideology is in turn partly caused by the economic structures. Essentially, the rise of capitalism brought with it an increase in the ideology of individualism, as the labour market turned people into commodities, so that the workforce became less attached to interdependent communities and families. This new core capitalist ideology, Oliver observes, gave 'rise to the [peripheral] ideological construction of the disabled individual as the antithesis of able-bodiedness and able-mindedness, and the medicalisation of disability as a particular kind of problem'.[87] Disability is, on this reading, a product of 'the rise of capitalism and the development of wage labour', because it is tied to the requirements of the labour market.[88] Prior to the development of this ideology, Oliver suggests, 'differences in individual contributions were noted, and often sanctions applied, [but] individuals did not, in the main, suffer exclusion'.[89] The ideology of individualism, according to Oliver, is invested in keeping people with disabilities in a dependent position, as their 'economic function' is both to 'serve as a warning to those unable or unwilling to work' and to provide labour through the care industries.[90] Disability on this reading disguises the reality that 'we [all] live in a state of mutual interdependence'.[91] Oliver argues that, although individualism is 'central to the breaking down of traditional hierarchies and privileges and in establishing the legal rights of individuals', these social advancements come at the cost of the integration of people with disabilities.[92]

In *The New Politics of Disablement*, Oliver and Barnes acknowledge 'the emergence and role of "sub", "counter", or "oppositional" cultures as sources of resistance to dominant capitalist imagery in culture generally and disability culture in particular'.[93] Oliver mentions, in *The Politics of Disablement*, that literature reflects disability culture and identity, and he laments that scholars have not yet addressed this in sufficient depth: 'There has been little attempt to present the collective experience of disability culturally, and hence the process of identity formation for disabled individuals has usually been constrained by images of superheroes or pathetic victims.'[94] He nevertheless ventures the thesis that disability in literature reflects the ideology of individualism 'in presenting the disabled individual as less than or more than human'.[95] *The New Politics of Disablement* likewise stresses the need for more comprehensive analysis of disability in literature and culture, and cautions that 'without a full analysis of images of disability it is not possible to do other than present examples of these images'.[96] Oliver and Barnes expect that, when this analysis is further along, it will show 'that material factors have a pivotal role in construction of disabling imagery'.[97] Oliver and Barnes see disability in terms of a compromised ability to work in a capitalist economy – a meaning that is certainly recognizable as a concept in the eighteenth and early nineteenth centuries, though it is not tied to the word 'disability'.

Inevitably, a claim as large as the industrialization thesis is at the mercy of details. In particular, the causal relationship between two things as complex as industrialization and disability is difficult to establish. Katherine Gustafson's recent work on William Godwin, for instance, addresses some of the problems in the context of advocacy for child-labour reform in Thomas Percival's *Observations on the State of Population in Manchester* (1789), Thomas Gisborne's *An Enquiry into the Duties of Men* (1794), and Frederick Eden's *State of the Poor* (1797).[98] Gustafson unnecessarily scales up the results of her study, however, by suggesting that 'late eighteenth-century discourses about disability and industrialism were tied up with child labor reform'.[99] Although her essay 'seeks to intervene in the historical study of disability by illustrating the necessity of examining socio-economic status, disability, and age in relation to one another, especially in the Romantic era',[100] Gustafson's dependence on the concept of disability opens the way for potential confusion by supposing that texts that do not contain the word 'disability' self-evidently participate 'in the emerging distinction between disabled and abled bodies'.[101] Additionally, Gustafson makes several problematic and unsubstantiated claims. For example, 'incapacity becomes disability' when 'the enfeebled bodies of the children [discussed in the reform literature] cannot participate economically in a modern society that demands health in its laborers'.[102]

The final metanarrative claims that the modern sense of disability emerged out of a number of disciplinary practices, including the emergence of statistics as a way of measuring norms. Lennard Davis, in *Enforcing Normalcy* (1995), centralizes the role of normalcy in his landmark account of the evolution of the concept of disability and connects Michel Foucault's ideas about power with the idea that industrialization marginalized people with disabilities. Foucault suggests, in *Discipline and Punish* (1975), that during the transition to a modern society at the end of the eighteenth century, the body appears to be controlled through a range of disciplinary practices that make it self-sufficient, productive, and 'normal'. He asserts that, 'like surveillance, and with it, normalization becomes one of the great instruments of power at the end of the classical age'.[103] Building on this thesis, Davis suggests that 'to understand the disabled body, one must return to the concept of the norm, the normal body', because norms 'create the "problem" of the disabled person'.[104] He dates the consciousness of normalcy to 1840–60, aligning its emergence with the development of statistics, an early modern discipline formed to assist with government policy. Normalcy is important for literature, Davis argues, because 'the very structures on which the novel rests tend to be normative, ideologically emphasizing the universal quality of the central character whose normativity encourages us to identify with him or her',[105] and 'if the main character has a major disability', Davis observes, 'then we are encouraged to identify with that character's ability to overcome his or her disability'.[106]

Since *Enforcing Normalcy* was published, the dates of some the earliest uses of the words associated with 'normalcy' have been pushed back. The *OED* (2008) moved the earliest written source for 'normal' from 1840 to 1777. The origin of the word 'norm' moved from 1855 to 1821, and 'normality' moved from 1849 to 1848. Currently, the *OED*'s earliest example of the word 'norm' occurs in a published letter by Samuel Taylor Coleridge. It is worth examining Coleridge's example for a brief moment, because it hints at some of the difficulties that the normalcy thesis raises. In a complex philosophical passage influenced by Plotinus's idea of the projection of light from the One and the Good, Coleridge uses the word 'norm' to describe the way great minds influence people by emanating intellectual light upon them. Here, he celebrates 'those stars of the first magnitude' who shine on the sphere below them which contains 'natures pre-assimilated to their influence, yet call forth likewise, each after its own *norm* or model, whatever is best in whatever is susceptible to each, even in the lowest'.[107] Coleridge's 'norm' is interchangeable with the metaphysical sense of 'ideal'. The 'ideal' has two distinct meanings in this period: it is the perfect instance of a kind, and it is also the archetype in a Platonic sense. Coleridge's use of 'norm' implies the sense of archetype. Significantly, 'norm' is not here being used as a mathematical average (which is how Davis defines it); it is used in the sense of a quality that is shared with others of its kind. Coleridge muses on ideals or norms of different kinds in the same letter series. For instance, he ponders the nature of the ideal contribution to a magazine like *Blackwood's*, suggesting that one method of discovering the qualities of good writing is to 'attempt to construct the most absolute or most perfect form of the object desiderated'.[108] The ideal is, in this instance, unlike the norm, something to which everyone might aspire. While Davis suggests that his argument is not contingent upon accurately dating the lexicographic origins of the word 'normalcy' and its cognates, these revisions in dating and in definition may, nevertheless, point to a different thesis: that the state of conforming to the mathematically typical is one of a number of standardizing concepts, some of which are extremely ancient. There are many theories of the ideal and many standardizing concepts, all of which have a long history in the western tradition.

Davis briefly addresses the idea of pre-normalcy with his suggestion that before the norm there was the 'ideal', the perfect divine and unattainable body. In a culture with only an ideal form of the body, he argues, 'all members of the population are below the ideal' and 'there is in such societies no demand that populations have bodies that conform to the ideal'.[109] Additionally, Davis positions the 'grotesque' as the opposite of the 'ideal', and as a 'signifier of the people, of common life'.[110] He argues that the grotesque is not equivalent to disability because 'the grotesque permeated culture and signified the norm, whereas the disabled body, a later concept, was formulated as by definition excluded from culture, society, the norm'.[111] In effect, the absence of a concept of normalcy places the grotesque in the position of normalcy; and disability is, for Davis, tied to birth of normalcy. Davis contrasts normalcy cultures with cultures that operate with 'the concept of an ideal, in which all people have a non-ideal status' (i.e. non-normalcy cultures).[112] He asserts that in normalcy cultures, 'people with disabilities will be thought of as deviants', and implies that in non-normalcy cultures (such as the eighteenth century) they will not be thought of in this way.[113] Davis invites us to 'try to imagine a world in which the hegemony of normalcy does not exist'.[114] He does not, however, ask us to set aside other normative concepts such as the common, the standard, the natural, the complete, the usual, the average, the proper, the able, the fit, the regular, the sound, the model, and the ordinary. Edmund Burke, for instance, observes that a man with one leg shorter than the other is deformed 'because there is something wanting to *complete* the *whole* idea we form of a man. ... Deformity arises from the want of the *common* proportions; but the necessary result of their existence in any object is not beauty'.[115] Burke's comparator is the complete or whole person. Questions remain as to how these concepts of completeness, wholeness, and commonness contribute to the history of disability.

Others have continued the work on establishing the relationships between disability, discipline, normalcy, and what Rosemarie Garland Thomson calls the 'normate' – that is, the symbolic representation of the social position through which people see themselves or are seen as 'definitive human beings'.[116] Paul Youngquist, for example, in his study of monstrosity, presents the Romantic era as a period in which 'singular bodies become subject to regulatory norms'.[117] Youngquist centralizes 'the proper body' as a pre-norm norm. This, he suggests, 'arises as a performative effect of a multiplicity of discourses and practices that makes such a norm possible without determining it absolutely'.[118] These discourses are 'liberalism, free-market economics, British nationalism, and professionalized medicine'.[119] The monstrous body, Youngquist argues, 'trouble[s] the operation of the proper body, materially diverting forces of normalization away from (stereo)typical ends'.[120] Youngquist identifies the monstrous body as a proto-disability phenomenon. He suggests, for instance, that the 'traditional association between Romanticism and monstrosity (a.k.a. "Romantic Agony") has less to do with psychological trauma or emotional excess than with the social project of proper embodiment in liberal society'.[121] Youngquist elides deformity with function impairment and with some of the modern senses of disability. Taking a different line, Oliver and Barnes regard the pre-normalcy period as a time when 'all human beings were thought to be imperfect', and suggest that 'the construction of the "disabled" individual and group was an inevitable outcome of the displacement of the "ideal" by the "normal/abnormal divide"'.[122] They connect this idea to the prodigy-to-pathology thesis, proposing that this displacement of the ideal also accounts for the fact that 'the dominant discourses around notions of the "grotesque" and the ideal body in the Middle Ages' were 'completely overturned by the "normalizing gaze" of modern science'.[123] They argue, furthermore, that the material basis of normalcy has been under-emphasized, and that 'it was the transition to industrial capitalism and the ensuing inhuman treatment meted out to those unable or unwilling to compete for work in an increasingly alienating political and cultural environment that was a major factor in this discursive separation'.[124] In the light of Davis's work, Oliver and Barnes added eugenics to medicalization and normalcy as peripheral ideologies caused by the core ideology of individualism. More recently, Fuson Wang has recast the normalcy thesis as a Victorian concept. He claims that the Romantic period 'represents a transitional moment between Enlightenment yearning for universal humanism and the Victorian codification of social mores; it sits between two restrictive movements to classify the human against the inhuman and the normal against the abnormal'.[125]

Disability theory proposes several senses of 'disability' that go beyond an assessment of personal functioning (or *medical model*). In the 1990s, early in the evolution of disability studies, the *social-barriers approach* to disability (or *social model*) became an accepted way of circumventing the idea of intrinsic or medicalized disability. This approach suggests that disability is not determined solely by the person's bodily or mental condition. Disability comes from an interaction between a body or mind and its context. Disability is, in this sense, relative. As Colin Barnes and Geof Mercer suggest, the social model of disability explores 'how socially constructed barriers (for example, in the design of buildings, modes of transport and communication, and discriminatory attitudes) have "disabled" people with a perceived impairment'.[126] The social-barriers approach offers us new language, drawn from the disability-activist movement, to differentiate a bodily condition that limits function (an *impairment*) from the disadvantages associated with it (a *disability*). Disability is, according to this definition, the exclusion that arises from a set of social circumstances that interact with a personal function limitation or aesthetic difference. This distinction is useful when talking about the cultural dimensions of disability, because it makes it possible to distinguish impairment from its social context and to demonstrate how the context creates disability. The impairment/disability binary is not unproblematic, however. Michael Schillmeier, for example, argues that in making a distinction between impairment and disability, we make the former wholly individual, and the latter wholly social. Schillmeier suggests that there is no clear-cut division between the individual and the social, and that the situations in which disability or disadvantage arise are complex, dynamic, and heterogeneous. For Schillmeier, the social is not prior to 'bodies, minds, senses, things' that we might call the non-social; it explains them.[127] Acknowledging the conceptual difficulties that Schillmeier raises, 'impairment' is used here both as a convenient substitute for an absent term for bodily conditions, and as a signal for a theorized understanding of functioning that is not restricted to that set out in the social model (with its disability/impairment binary).

The *cultural model* of disability attempts to account for more positive experiences of disability, and for the experience of disability as an identity. This approach distinguishes itself from the *social model* by suggesting that disability is not 'synonymous with the processes of social disablement' but describes a broader experience that includes both the body and the social world and does not solely describe discriminatory encounters.[128] Commenting on the cultural model, Sharon Snyder and David Mitchell suggest 'that impairment is both human variation encountering environmental obstacles *and* socially mediated difference that lends group identity and phenomenological perspective'.[129] This approach connects ideas about disability with feminism, queer theory, critical race theory, and theories concerning class, and examines how cultures manipulate representations of disability in the arts and humanities. Instead of splitting impairment and disability, the cultural model uses 'disability' as a politicized word that incorporates both. Elsewhere, Mitchell and Snyder argue that literary Romanticism positions itself in contrast to the 'burgeoning bodily ideal' that is 'symmetrical, fully functional, independent, racialized, gendered, and economically mobile' and 'increasingly identified as a representative of the "healthy nation" in the eighteenth century'.[130] They argue that the Romantic period is 'an era of literary production where disability came to be more synonymous with – rather than divergent from – conditions indicative of human vulnerability'.[131] For them, the period is 'perhaps one of the richest in Euro-American representational traditions of disability'.[132] It is a time when 'the nonidealized body becomes a vehicle of resistance and social critique'.[133] Mitchell and Snyder suggest that we can see this in the poetry of Wordsworth and Coleridge, where characters with disabilities are guides to sublime experience; in Frankenstein's creature's questioning of his rejection 'on the basis of his nonnormative appearance and functionality'; and in Byron's criticism of normative expectations for the body.[134]

## Literary Disability Studies: An Overview

The first surveys of disability in Romantic-era literature focused on exposing cultural biases against disability through identifying negative image stereotypes. Peter Hays, for instance, interprets limping as a Jungian archetype in the mythology and literature of several countries. He argues that limping represents fertility figures, sterility figures, and 'limited, restricted men'.[135] Hays concludes that 'lameness as a literary device is usually either symbolic of or a euphemism for a genital wound; the wound, in turn, symbolizes a social disability'.[136] Along similar lines, Alan Gartner and Tom Joe address the problem of the disabling stereotype by exposing the literary oversimplification, scapegoating, enfreakment, and demonization of people with disabilities.[137] Lennard Davis, Rosemarie Garland Thomson, and Michael Bérubé all observe, however, that accounts of disability that collect metaphors, stereotypes, tropes, and motifs have their limitations. Davis points out that, 'given the former absence of disability studies in the humanities, there was no real way to talk about disability as disability'.[138] Most readings, he suggests, 'simply metaphorize disability'.[139] Reaction to disability, Davis observes, 'already involves' a combination of looking away or staring, and these processes echo 'metaphorization' or substitution.[140] Approaching disability through metaphor, Davis argues, expresses a need 'to objectivize and stigmatize by an interrelated process of fascination and rejection'.[141] Davis encourages critics to go back to metaphor once a 'firm understanding and foundation in seeing disabilities as they really are in themselves' has been established.[142] Garland Thomson is similarly concerned that metaphorical readings of disability obscure the complexities of the lives of people with disabilities. She suggests that critics need to go 'beyond assailing stereotypes'[143] and offer instead much-needed interrogation of 'the conventions of representation' that produce identity 'within the social narratives of bodily differences'.[144] Her appeal is not an invitation to engage in what Fuson Wang dismisses as ideological dishonesty driven by a 'presentist blame game'[145] or a 'politically predetermined indictment'[146] of ableism; it is a request to critics to value the complexity of the cultural phenomenon of the 'disabled figure', and to separate that figure 'from the subjective experience of disability'.[147] Thomson maps out a disabling literary world in which 'corporeal departures from dominant expectations never go uninterpreted or unpunished, and conformities are almost always rewarded'.[148] Michael Bérubé argues for a different approach, suggesting that comparing stereotypes with lived experiences required critics to practise a kind of literalism that is not usually expected of literary analysis. Bérubé concludes that 'literary representations of people with disabilities often serve to mobilize pity or horror in a moral drama that has nothing to do with the actual experience of disability'.[149] Disability studies, he asserts, is not the 'New Literalism'.[150]

Metaphor is, nevertheless, an important component of the foundational theoretical work in the field. Davis's *Enforcing Normalcy* (1995) broadened the scope of symbolic reading by showing how it could become a valuable theoretical tool when used in a different framework. He examines how disability appears 'in metaphors about the process of knowing, as moments in an epistemological dialectic'.[151] *Narrative Prosthesis* (2000), by David Mitchell and Sharon Snyder, also took this approach to metaphor. That book examines the pervasive use of disability in narrative 'as a stock feature of characterization' and 'as an opportunistic metaphorical device' by positing that disability has a prosthetic role.[152] A literary prosthesis, Mitchell and Snyder argue, attempts 'to accomplish an erasure of difference', but ultimately 'it fails in its primary objective: to return the incomplete body to the invisible status of a normative essence'.[153] Disability has a prosthetic function by providing a narrative with a metaphorical repair that draws attention both to the ambiguous role of portrayals of disability (as highlighting the non-existence of the 'normal' body) and to the failed attempt to conceal the literary function of disability. Characters with disabilities ironically 'expose, rather than conceal, the prosthetic relation'.[154] These new theorized uses of metaphors of disablement led the discipline away from what Garland Thomson calls 'the usual interpretive framework of aesthetics and metaphor', which obscured the complexity of representation, and towards 'the critical arena of cultural studies'.[155] Mitchell and Snyder summarize this approach as understanding 'the impact of the experience of disability upon subjectivity without simultaneously situating the internal and external body within a strict mirroring relationship to one another'.[156]

The earliest critical engagement with disability in literature involved exposing stereotypes and typical metaphorical uses. This developed, in the 1990s, into making a case that disability could be part of the broader project of revisionism on issues of race and gender. Theories developed in sociology, and through the disability activism movement, gave scholars new vocabulary and new concepts for understanding disability (e.g. the disability–impairment distinction). These theories redefined the relationship between bodily and mental particularities and the social and physical context surrounding them. They raised the question of the instability of the concept of disability; and they developed the concept of ableism.[157] Literary disability studies began with recovering the cultural and literary history of people with disabilities, and their contexts, and moved on to exploring the ways in which understanding disability differently can change the methodologies and tools we use in literary study. As Rebecca Sanchez observes in her consideration of deafness and modernism, 'we have been deafened by the incredibly powerful and institutionalized accounts of the period that have tended to exclude the deaf'.[158] Her choice to 'concentrate on modernist works that are neither by nor about individuals who are deaf' is an important one, as it enables her to demonstrate how 'Deaf studies illuminates texts with not obvious or literal connection to deafness'.[159] Her project is part of a more recent turn in the field towards convincing the academy not to 'ghettoize disability'.[160]

## Romantic Studies and Disability

Andrew Elfenbein's 2001 special issue of *European Romantic Review* on Byron stands out as the first call to Romanticists to explore disability as a topic. Elfenbein's collection focuses on how 'disability might be voiced' in the work of 'the most famous disabled man of his day',[161] and aimed to 'start a dialogue about disability in romanticism more generally'.[162] Writing in this collection, Rosemarie Garland Thomson promotes Byron as a significant voice in this revisionism because he works outside 'an almost overwhelming tradition of representing disability as deviance', and reimagines 'disability's radical potential to disrupt the norm'.[163] Paul Youngquist reads Byron this way too, arguing that Byron's unfinished play, *The Deformed Transformed* (1824), is a 'sustained protest against the norm of the proper body and its patriotic force'.[164] He contrasts Byron with Coleridge, whose addiction to opium 'enhances the transformatory effect' of his poetry, but who nevertheless reaffirms regulatory social norms in his philosophy. For Youngquist, 'monstrosities of various kinds become occasions for advancing, resisting, or transforming' the standards of the period.[165] Michael Bradshaw's *Disabling Romanticism* (2016) stands out as the first collection of essays on disability in the period written from a disability studies perspective. The book is aligned with 'the more general project of historicist scholarship, which rereads cultural texts in order to challenge assenting and complicit interpretations'.[166] It also 'attends to suppressed or marginalised voices, and identifies agency in the way they dissent from hegemonic narratives'.[167] The collection focuses on Wordsworth, Coleridge, Blake, Southey, Byron, Mary Shelley, Mary Robinson, George Darley, and the picturesque theorists.[168]

Between these two landmarks, there are other significant considerations of Romantic disability. These largely centre on identity and body politics and on writers with disabilities. In the work on body politics, the intersection of gender and disability has received the most attention. Barbara Benedict (2000) examines disability, monstrosity, and gender during the panic about the London slasher known popularly as the 'Monster'.[169] She investigates the metaphorical uses of monstrosity in the context of hate crimes against women as a way to understand the normative values reinforced by the public outcry against the perpetrator. Disability and motherhood are examined in two important studies. Philip Wilson (2002) traces the literary uses of the idea that deformities are caused *in utero* by maternal imagination, reading 'the skin as the corporeal text upon which monstrosity or freakishness was inscribed'; and Youngquist (2003) investigates the politicization of the maternal body and the significance of bodily agency in the thought of Mary Wollstonecraft.[170] Felicity Nussbaum's *The Limits of the Human* (2003) links disability with the body politics of race, gender, and national identity, and considers the categories of human in a time before modern notions of sexual and racial differences emerged within ideas of national identity. For Nussbaum, 'various kinds of difference interrelate to complicate prevailing ideas about the cultural meanings of normalcy and of humankind'.[171] She argues that the disabled body becomes a locus for 'intense national fears about encroaching degeneracy in the population', particularly in the discussions of the rights of women in the 1790s.[172] Mark Mossman (2009) makes connections between representations of disability and the Irish body in the nineteenth century, and suggests that both identities trouble the norm. Irish bodies, he argues, are 'colonized bodies, bodies with impairments and differences that are constructed often negatively as "disability" – by medical and scientific discourses'.[173] Finally, Jason Farr (2014) explores the relationship between the educated mind and the disabled body in the case of Frances Burney's *Camilla* (1796), suggesting that there is a tension in the novel resulting from its 'efforts to privilege Eugenia's brilliant mind over her crippled body'.[174]

David Mitchell and Sharon Snyder stress the importance of biographical work for discerning how 'disabled and chronically ill' writers such as Byron and Keats were affected by their conditions. Mitchell and Snyder suggest that 'revisiting texts from this orientation will yield important insights into the influence of disability identities upon creative efforts'.[175] David Turner (2012) includes the voices of disabled memoirists in historical study of disability, in order to trace 'how disabled men and women used, appropriated, or rejected these representations in making sense of their own experiences'.[176] Work on Harriet Martineau has also been important, and a great deal of scholarship has explored her deafness and chronic illnesses.[177] William Wordsworth's illnesses have likewise attracted some attention. Heather Tilley (2010) argues for a 'biographically grounded' reading of Wordsworth's blind figures as a challenge to readings that 'uphold an idealist model of the mind and imagination, which privileges the sovereignty of the mind of above the senses'.[178] Tilley suggests that

> Wordsworth seems to have first experienced symptoms of ... trachoma in 1804, shortly after his sister Dorothy noted she had caught an eye infection. Endemic at the time, trachoma caused the formation of pustules along the eyelashes and eyelid margins and could lead to permanent loss of vision if it spread to the eyeball. This chronic inflammation is likely to have been a case of Egyptian ophthalmia, brought over by soldiers from the Napoleonic wars ... By the early nineteenth century, along with smallpox, ophthalmia was one of the most common causes of blindness.[179]

According to Tilley, the blind beggar figure in the *Prelude* 'calls into question the nature of both sight and visual representation: what it means to see and also to interpret visual signs'.[180] For her, 'Wordsworth's "alienated relation" to vision opens up a range of questions and implications for our understanding of blindness in both his own writing and the writing of the Romantic period more generally'.[181] Youngquist (1999) finds 'a physiological aesthetics' in Wordsworth's poetry, 'one that puts bodily health among its main concerns', and which places Wordsworth in the role of physician.[182] He reminds us that *Lyrical Ballads* is 'full of sick people: mad mothers, deranged vagrants, decrepit old men'.[183] Dwight Codr (2009) reads the 'struggles with the body' in the novels of Elizabeth Inchbald as informed by the writer's 'lifelong struggles with stuttering'.[184] Even though, as Codr admits, Inchbald would not have considered 'herself to be in the same category as individuals with other disabilities', he argues that the sentimental and affective responses to the spectacle of the suffering body in her novels offer an opportunity to understand the culture of sensibility differently.[185] Codr understands 'the inability to speak, the irruptive power of tears, and the uncontrollable and often painful resistance of the body to the will' to be 'collectively absorbed by the tractable multiform discourse of sensibility that makes disability all but invisible'.[186] Deborah Needleman Armintor (2011) connects disability with the self-fashioning of an image appropriate for publication in Josef Boruwlaski's autobiography, *Memoirs of the Celebrated Dwarf* (1788).[187] Kerry Duff (2005) and Barbara Benedict (2006) explore what Armintor calls 'the paradox inherent in Boruwlaski's attempt to assimilate and establish a sentimental middle-class identity as a self-made man by selling himself as an aristocratic object of curiosity'.[188] Duff observes that the memoir obscures 'not the fact of difference, but the conditions of its production: the midget as a commodity (whether of a corporeal or textual form) sold as an object of curiosity specifically because of difference from the norm'.[189]

According to Armintor, the memoir encompasses 'the century's wide and shifting range of little-men-oriented themes', as Boruwlaski's identities move from that of court dwarf to man of feeling in a companionate marriage.[190]

A great deal of work informed by biography is emerging at the intersection of disability studies, the medical humanities, and cognitive science.[191] Scholars are, for instance, beginning to investigate people with disabilities who worked within the medical professions. Emily Stanback (2011) suggests that John Thelwall's experience of stuttering enabled him to establish 'his professional services and techniques' as a speech therapist in ways that did 'not promote normative assumptions or adhere to standard social hierarchies'.[192] The establishment of a productive conversation with scientific and medical scholarship has in the past proved difficult, since disability studies has been wary of combining the cultural dimensions of disability with the history of medical science and medical cultures. This has been for good reasons. For example, not all disabilities require medical attention, and, although medicine has for some time dominated how disability has been defined, this has not always been the case.

Importantly, some biographical work has been wary of claiming disability as an identity category in the eighteenth and early nineteenth centuries. This has been in part due to the fact that it is properly characterized as a pre-disability period. Davis offers the example of Dr Johnson, who 'to his contemporaries' was 'a brilliant man who had some oddities rather than . . . a seriously disabled person'.[193] There is, however, much more evidence of 'deformity' as an identity category in the biographical and autobiographical work of the eighteenth century and there are strong examples of this in the period, such as William Hay. Davis was one of the earliest scholars to rediscover Hay.[194] Hay offers one of the fullest and most remarkable accounts of deformity identity in his autobiographical reflection, 'Deformity: An Essay' (1754).[195] He claims an affinity with other deformed people, calling them 'brother[s] in blood', and suggests that deformity is 'visible to every eye; but the effects of it are known to very few'.[196] Hay also challenges a number of assumptions about deformity. For instance, he observes that some deformities are treated more cruelly than others, and that the mob finds more to mock in 'a crooked man, than one that is deaf, lame, squinting, or purblind'.[197] He understands deformity as something more than a personal attribute; it is as an aesthetic difference which provokes an unreasonably hostile response, and which prompts experiences that are distinctive for people who also appear to be of this group.[198]

There have been, to date, few overviews of the subfield. Dwight Christopher Gabbard's 'Disability Studies in the British Long Eighteenth Century' (2011) is the first account that traces the continuities between eighteenth-century and Romantic-era studies. Gabbard centralizes the prodigy-to-pathology metanarrative, suggesting that 'disability studies approaches the British eighteenth century as a period in transition, with the conception of disability as spiritual sign of wonder or warning giving way to an understanding of it as pathology and abnormality'.[199] Fuson Wang (2017) characterizes the field as moving from 'abstractly polemical origins to its current historicist orientation',[200] and, following *Disabling Romanticism* (2016), Michael Bradshaw (2019) emphasizes the variety of the accounts.[201]

Disability studies has, since its inception, sought among other things to understand how and when the term 'disability' came to be applied to such a diverse group of people. In spite of the wealth of critical engagement demonstrating a wide variety of approaches, the disability concept has not been sufficiently challenged. Pre-twentieth-century fields have clung on to the term even whilst acknowledging that it was not present in its modern senses, and many critics and historians use 'disability' without acknowledging the absence of the word in the material they are discussing. My account aims to refocus the field on alternative group terms that are appropriate for their time. More attention needs to be given to 'deformity' than hitherto in the discussions of the period. Furthermore, scholars keep returning to the metanarratives of disability without fully engaging with their limitations. *Physical Disability in British Romantic Literature* calls for pre-twentieth-century literary disability studies to dissociate itself from modern notions of disability. It calls for critics of all kinds to understand that disability theory is not relevant solely to disabled people or disabled characters, but allows us to read all texts anew.[202]

## Chapter Overview

Part I of this study focuses on the politics of ability. Political philosophers and literary critics have scrutinized William Godwin's work for what it can tell us about rank, equity, education, duty, and social goods. They have not realized, however, how central the idea of 'capacity' is to Godwin's ideas, and have not examined the implications of Godwin's philosophy for people whose capacities he regards as socially devalued (Chapter 1). In spite of his assurance that equality is unrelated to physical or intellectual ability, Godwin makes individual and social liberty contingent upon the types of contributions one's capacities allow. His political system inevitably produces exceptions (those who do not or cannot contribute to the general good) for which he needs to devise additional measures. People who lack the right kinds of capacity nevertheless prove to be an intractable problem. Godwin's political preoccupation with capacity is also prominent in his fiction. We see it in his repeated use of automata, dolls, and characters who disengage from their bodies in various ways; and we see it in his fictional use of rejuvenation and cure. Godwin speculates that when reason governs society, illness and incapacity will no longer be present. Godwin's attitude towards deformity is quite separate from his views on capacity. He tends to treat deformity in a moral sense, but not in a religious sense. Deformity, in Godwin's fiction, is usually a visual sign of an evil character (though there are some important exceptions), and he does not articulate the *prodigious* phase of disability.

Godwin's place in the period is central, and we see similar arguments in the work of his contemporaries. Mary Wollstonecraft takes the discussion of capacity more explicitly into the realm of gender (Chapter 2). In her emancipation arguments, Wollstonecraft challenges the social disablement of women by promoting a vigorous and curative feminism that establishes their qualification for equality by virtue of their capacities. She associates female weakness with inutility and social degradation, and promotes bodily and physical independence as ideals. Misogynistic cultures weaken the bodies and minds of women, Wollstonecraft asserts, and she petitions for women to develop (and be permitted to develop) their physical and intellectual abilities rather than to perpetuate a culture that is focused on the aesthetics of their bodies. Significantly, she suggests that it is absurd that weakness (i.e. physical delicacy, sickliness, inability to work, lack of bodily strength, and intellectual underdevelopment) is treated as an aes- thetic issue – as something aesthetically desirable in women. This debate connects with debates about sincerity that we see in the work of Eliza Fenwick and Mary Hays. Wollstonecraft concludes that society cannot maintain social inutility as an aesthetic, as it is detrimental to social progress. The curative approach to capacity in Godwin and Wollstonecraft belongs to a social reformism that prefers to remove the problem of incapacity as a way to address prejudice: an approach which is lampooned by Elizabeth Hamilton, who satirizes the radical interest in vigour and energy.

Whereas the first two chapters explore the politicization of capacities across the range of the writers' works, Chapter 3 explores the issue in one poem, William Wordsworth's 'The Discharged Soldier' (1798). This chapter centres on the military body and, in particular, the stories about the acquisition of impairments (origin stories) that fictional disabled soldiers are required to tell. Disabled soldiers' stories often make persuasive cases for desert (in that soldiers are deemed worthy of *charity* or reward) using particular narrative conventions. This chapter offers a close reading, addressing some significant difficulties in the critical reception of Wordsworth's poem. The abrupt opening, the soldier's lack of interest in telling his story in a genre that requires it, and the speaker's lack of effusive sympathy, have left critics puzzled. Concentration on Wordsworth's theory of desert rather than on sentiment provides a new way to understand the poem, and the key to this is the poem's interplay between capacity and aesthetics.

The second part of the book focuses on deformity. In order to establish something of the importance of this aesthetic concept, the first two chapters of this part will flesh out the term. Chapter 4 examines how deformed bodies were held to an aesthetic standard, and centres on the controversy over whether the picturesque deformity that was appreciated in buildings and landscapes could also be appreciated in people with deformities, be these people real or represented. William Gilpin writes about ruins and people in ways that suggest that they possess the same aesthetic value. Fitness for representation is Gilpin's criterion for a certain type of aesthetic appreciation, and, using this criterion, he regards picturesque deformity in a positive light. Uvedale Price, however, offers the idea that beauty, the picturesque, and deformity exist on a continuum. He makes deformity a question of degree, and uses some of the characteristics of deformity to define picturesqueness. Price also defines the picturesque as a 'striking' form of deformity. The quality of being striking enables Price to think of people and things as giving aesthetic pleasure in the same way, and on the same continuum. Drawing on Addison's aesthetics, Richard Payne Knight makes a distinction between real and represented deformity. Knight argues, like Percy Shelley, that art has a transformative power that makes deformity aesthetically pleasing. The picturesque theorists are concerned with reconciling deformity (as a quality of the picturesque) with the aesthetic pleasure that derives from it. By valuing non-normative and non-ideal aesthetics, the picturesque theorists complicate the *normalcy* thesis. These writers engage with elements of deformity in their challenges to the neoclassical ideals of harmony, proportion, and order, and find aesthetic pleasure in the version of deformity that they call picturesque.

Chapter 5 centres on Frances Burney's *Camilla* (1796), a novel in which a major character, Eugenia Tyrold, is not told that her physical appearance is perceived socially as deformity. Burney considers the possibility that deformity is separable from its conventional social meanings. *Camilla* criticizes the inflated social currency of physical beauty and promotes moral beauty as deserving of higher value, while demonstrating that concepts of impairment, whether aesthetic or functional, shift in different contexts. The sophisticated deformity aesthetics in Burney's novel antici-pates the theoretical work concerning the relational aspects of disability that occurs in disability theory in the twentieth century (the *disability/ impairment* distinction). Burney explores the ways in which deformities are aesthetic in certain social contexts and are functional in others. Her work demonstrates the importance of understanding how the other attributes of a person, for example, their gender and social class, affect whether bodily particularities are perceived as aesthetic or functional. The novel troubles the *normalcy* thesis (which ties disability to normalcy as its definitional opposite). Beauty, rather than normalcy, creates the problem of the deformed body; but neither beauty nor deformity are fixed ideas.

Chapter 6 continues the discussion of deformity in the context of Mary Shelley's *Frankenstein*, where the concept is interchangeable with monstrosity. This chapter situates the central tragedy of the novel (that the creature is unable to transform the other characters' ways of looking at monstrosity/deformity) in the context of a theorized understanding of looking. The novel gives us many examples of why and how people can change the way they view things. The creature's meeting with a blind character offers an opportunity for transformative listening, but the acci-dental failure of this encounter allows Shelley to maintain a sense that visual prejudice is relentless. The chapter also considers the relationship between moral and physical deformity, and the critical reception of defor-mity and monstrosity in relation to the novel.

The two parts of this book share central ideas, though they are about different concepts. The Romantics and their contemporaries are keenly aware of the social cost of limited capacity and aesthetic difference, and while they do not always express sympathy for the social exclusion that these led to, they are sometimes interested in ways of limiting it. Both parts of this book address writers who are keen to explore (and sometimes perpetuate) the exclusionary practices of their society, and writers who explore ability and aesthetic differ-ence in social and cultural spaces that are more inclusive. These are not neat divisions, however, and we see both approaches within individual works. Throughout the book, I will be more focused on latent or explicit group terms that describe people with physical impairments than on individual conditions, though the division between a group term and a condition is about as precise as the medical opinion of the time.

# PART I

# Politics of Ability

## CHAPTER I

# William Godwin and Capacity

I dwelt upon the *capacities* of our nature, the researches of a Newton, the elevation of a Milton, and the virtues of an Alfred; and, having filled my mind with these, I contemplated even with horror, the ignorance, the brutality, the stupidity, the selfishness, and, as it appeared to me, the venality and profligacy, in which millions and millions of my fellow-creatures are involved. I estimated mankind, with an eye to the goal which it is ardently to be desired they might reach.[1]

In *Enquiry Concerning Political Justice* (1793), William Godwin proposes that a rescuer faced with the prospect of saving either Archbishop Fénelon or the archbishop's chambermaid from a burning palace should, if acting rationally and justly, save the archbishop. The archbishop's life is preferred because his scholarship 'will be most conducive to the general good'.[2] Moreover, the decision should be the same, Godwin suggests, even if the servant is the mother of the rescuer.[3] The example is 'notorious'.[4] Evan Radcliffe calls it an 'inhuman calculation', and 'the moment that defined Godwin's politics and philosophy'.[5] Godwin concedes that the nearness of the familial relationship, and the sense of obligation the rescuer has to their parent, makes this a difficult decision; but it is, nevertheless, one that ought to be made in favour of the archbishop. At best, critics and philosophers treat the Fénelon case as an illustration of Godwin's idea that 'reason should decide the issue in human affairs and human government, not power based on money, age, rank, sex, or physical strength'.[6] At worst, it is regarded as an instance of his failure to include emotions in his account of moral duty, or as misguided impartialism.[7] Don Locke calls Godwin's 'a morality of remote cold-blooded intellect in which normal human feelings are allowed no place'.[8] Literary critics and philosophers have scrutinized the Fénelon case for what it can tell us about Godwin's views on rank, education, and duty; but they have not realized how central capacity is to the case, and to Godwin's philosophy more broadly; and they

have not examined the implications of Godwin's ideas for people whose
capacities he regards as limited or socially devalued.⁹ In the critical
responses, Godwin's example is sometimes seen to involve the rescuer
rejecting someone for whom one has affection and obligation; sometimes
concern is expressed about issues of class and gender; sometimes it is noted
that the dilemma rests on the social benefits of the archbishop's scholarship. But there is little acknowledgement that the difference in intellectual
*capacity* between Fénelon and his chambermaid is the ultimate driver
behind the choice between them.

This study begins with Godwin for two reasons. Firstly, Godwin's
influence on political philosophy and on literature in the aftermath of
the French Revolution is extensive and important. Although Godwin is
now regarded as a central figure, he was, as Don Locke notes, more
obscure in the 1980s, when it was necessary to make the case that 'there
was a time when [*Political Justice*] was a popular sensation, a veritable
prodigy of imagination and intellect, and William Godwin the most
famous, certainly the most notorious, writer in the land'.¹⁰ Adam Rounce
comments further that 'not the least of the reasons for Godwin's enormous
impact in the tremendously politically-charged atmosphere of the 1790s
was his accessibility as a writer and thinker'.¹¹ Nancy Johnson comments
that 'Godwin's views reverberate through the prefaces of other English
Jacobin authors when they write of their motivations and intentions for
using the novel as a vehicle to illustrate reality and vision, the way things
are and the way things ought to be'.¹² There is much evidence for Godwin's significance in the period. William Hazlitt, in *The Spirit of the Age*
(1825), writes of Godwin that 'no one was more talked of, more looked up
to, more sought after, and wherever liberty, truth, justice was the theme,
his name was not far off'.¹³ Godwin inspired the work of William
Wordsworth,¹⁴ Samuel Taylor Coleridge,¹⁵ Mary Wollstonecraft,¹⁶ Amelia Opie, Charlotte Smith, Thomas Holcroft, Percy Shelley, Mary Shelley,
Charles Brockden Brown, and many others. As Pamela Clemit suggests,
Godwin established a 'distinctive type' of intellectual novel that was an
'innovative blend of philosophy and fiction', and that was influential on a
number of authors.¹⁷ Secondly, Godwin's philosophical writings provide
us with a definitional framework for his literary work, so he is a useful
starting place for systematically unpacking some of the pre-disability
concepts of the period.

According to Godwin's margin summaries, the Fénelon case is about
the 'distribution measure [of justice] by the *capacity* of the subject'.¹⁸ As
Godwin's note signals, the Fénelon scenario makes the nature of one's

contribution to society central to determining one's worth, and, in particular, singles out capacity as fundamental to determining the level of
contribution. The degree to which one possesses capacities (and the nature
of their use) underpins a number of further features of Godwin's thought:
his understanding of agency and freedom, of duty and virtue, of social
value, and of what it means to be treated justly. Godwin makes physical
and intellectual independence a prerequisite for the kind of political
independence he would like to prevail. Archbishop Fénelon is a 'man of
more worth' than a chambermaid because he is, Godwin explains, 'possessed of higher *faculties*, [and] he is *capable* of more refined and genuine
happiness'.[19] Fénelon is therefore likely, according to Godwin, to contribute more to the general good. The centrality of capacity to Godwin's
thinking is sometimes implied in the critical literature, but it is rarely
discussed explicitly. One rare instance is in Peter Singer's account of
Godwin's impartialism, and even this is tangential to a more central point
on Samuel Parr. Singer and his co-authors consider the counter-arguments
to impartialist ethics put forward by Samuel Parr in *A Spital Sermon*
(1801). They comment that Parr 'argues against impartialism in ethics
[and against Godwin] on the grounds that it takes an unrealistic view of
human nature, and hence demands something that human beings cannot,
in general and most of the time, give: "the moral obligations of men", Parr
writes, "cannot be stretched beyond their physical powers"'.[20] Significantly, Singer and his co-authors focus on capacity only in relation to
the agent and not the object. The point of the Fénelon example, however,
is that Godwin thinks that a greater capacity in the object of an action (the
rescuable archbishop) generates a greater obligation on the part of the
agent (the rescuer).

Godwin takes an interest in capacity in the wake of an important
publication on mental powers: Thomas Reid's *Essays on the Intellectual
Powers of Man*.[21] In 1785, Godwin's publishers, the Robinsons, collaborated with John Bell in Edinburgh to print Reid's book.[22] Here Reid
considers how commonly used words, such as 'power', 'faculty', 'capacity',
and 'habit', can be used to delineate the different ways in which we can
talk about mental and bodily functioning. Reid defines a *power* as an
ability that may or may not be in use: 'I may have power to walk, when
I sit; or to speak, when I am silent.'[23] '*Faculty* is most properly applied to
those powers of the mind which are original and natural, and which make
a part of the constitution of the mind.'[24] So 'power' is the general term;
'faculty' picks out specifically mental powers. Reid reserves *habits* for
'powers which are acquired by use, exercise or study', and he defines

*capacity* as 'something in the constitution of the mind necessary to our being able to acquire habits'.[25] Faculties are constitutive mental powers; capacities are that subset of faculties that enable us to acquire habits; and habits are acquired powers. Capacities, according to Reid, can vary 'in very different degrees' in different people.[26]

'Capacity', unlike 'power', picks out a particular feature of an individual and not a political system or agents considered in virtue of their place or role in a political system. 'Power' has a wider extension, and can include things to which capacity would not usually refer – for example, the government's power. Godwin writes that 'capacity' indicates 'the assemblage of properties in any substance' (that is, of those properties relevant to activity), and he occasionally uses 'power' in the sense of capacity.[27] For example, 'Man is an intellectual being. There is no way to make him virtuous, but in calling forth his intellectual powers.'[28] Godwin uses 'habit' interchangeably with 'custom' and hints at concern over the sway habits hold over independent reasoning: 'habit has a resistless empire over the human mind'.[29] He uses 'capacity' in two senses: the *universal* sense – that which it is possible for humankind as such to do; and the *particular* sense – that which it is possible for an individual person to do.[30] Godwin only rarely uses the word 'incapacity', and it is an equivalent to 'inability'.[31]

Godwin suggests that 'there are two considerations relative to any particular being, that excite our approbation, and this is whether the being be possessed of consciousness or no. These considerations are *capacity* and the application of that *capacity*'.[32] For example, a capacity, Godwin writes, may be present in a knife, or a person, even when it is not currently being used.[33] Thus a knife has 'the capacity of cutting', and in the 'same manner a human being has a capacity of walking: though it may be no more true of him than of the inanimate substance, that he has the power of exercising or not exercising that capacity'.[34] This sense of 'capacity' is close to that of Reid's word 'power'. Furthermore, there are 'different *degrees* as well as different *classes* of capacity',[35] where difference in class is defined in terms of difference in types of activity. For example, 'a candlestick has the power or capacity of retaining a candle in a perpendicular direction. A knife has a capacity of cutting'.[36] By difference in degree, Godwin means that 'one knife is better adapted for the purposes of cutting than another', or that an archbishop has a greater capacity for scholarship than a chambermaid. Godwin claims that the difference in the *degree* of capacities and the difference in the *application* of capacities makes a person more or less socially valuable. So, both capacities and their application are open to moral evaluation. A knife is capable of being used for good or ill; and 'in the same manner . . . as the knife may be applied to various purposes at the pleasure of its possessor, so an individual endowed with certain qualifications, may engage in various pursuits, according to the views that are presented to him, and the motives that actuate his mind'.[37]

Unlike Reid, whose focus is mainly on distinguishing the intellectual powers, Godwin is also interested in the social implications of capacities. The Fénelon case supposes that some people are more capable than others, and that those with higher capacities (that are applied well) have more social value than those with lower capacities (and those who do not apply their capacities well). Throughout his work, Godwin promotes the social value of certain kinds of human capacities, and the consequent application of those capacities. Certain kinds of capacities, for instance, are required for promoting the general good.[38] 'Good is a general name, including pleasure, and the means by which pleasure is procured.'[39] Godwin identifies these goods as the production and equitable distribution of the means to sustain life;[40] social and political equality;[41] the development of the full use of the human capacities;[42] and the establishment of the conditions needed for independent and rational decision-making.[43] As promoting these general goods requires certain capacities, Godwin emphasizes the social importance of 'the strength of the body or the faculties of the mind'.[44] He writes that 'it is just that I should be careful to maintain my body and mind in the utmost vigour, and in the best condition for service',[45] as the body and mind of the individual citizen are in the service of the whole of mankind. For instance, a person who chose to self-amputate would be committing a crime against society, because, as Godwin puts it, 'no man, if he were alone in the world, would have a right to make himself impotent'.[46] He also imagines that the wealth generated to provide the necessities for society would come from the exercise of individual capacities. Each person would do half an hour of manual labour and devote the remainder of their time to intellectual improvement.[47] The value of one's life, Godwin asserts, would be measured according to how much one's capacities can contribute to the general good: 'If the extraordinary case should occur in which I can promote the general good by my death, more than by my life, justice requires that I should be content to die.'[48] A person 'has no right to his life, when his duty calls him to resign it'.[49]

The use of one's capacities must also be consonant with disinterested benevolence. Godwin regards capacities that are used without 'disinterested benevolence' as unworthy of 'enlightened admiration'.[50] While strength and intellectual agility are important capacities in Godwin's work, they must be applied appropriately. Squire Tyrrel in *Caleb Williams*, for example, 'might have been selected by a painter as a model for that hero of antiquity, whose prowess consisted in felling an ox with his fist, and devouring him at a meal'.[51] Nevertheless, his 'muscular form, [and] the well-known eminence of his intellectual powers',[52] contribute to making him 'insupportably arrogant, tyrannical to his inferiors, and insolent to his equals'.[53] Additionally, the devious and physically strong 'Amazonian'[54] old woman who keeps a safe house for the highwaymen with whom Caleb hides also has misdirected energy. Female vigour coupled with intellectual prowess may be socially liberating, but it adds menace to an evil character who misapplies these capacities. The band of robbers in *Caleb Williams* also misuse their capacities as they are 'unassisted by liberal and enlightened views, and directed only to the most narrow and contemptible purposes'.[55] Caleb finds it difficult to contemplate the social waste: 'The uncommon vigour of their minds, and acuteness of their invention in the business they pursued, compared with the odiousness of that business and their habitual depravity awakened in me sensations too painful to be endured.'[56]

According to Godwin, the moral assessment of their actions depends upon a comparison being made between their capacities and the use of these capacities: 'It is only after having formed the most accurate notions we are able respecting the capacity of a man, and compared this capacity with his performance, that we can decide with any degree of satisfaction, whether he is entitled to the appellation of virtuous.'[57] Duties are tied to one's capacities in the sense that one is obliged to use one's capacities for the general good. Duty is the best possible application of a capacity, and one's duty cannot exceed one's capacity.[58] For example, if someone is unaware of a particular set of events that they could have prevented if they had known about them, they are not to be held accountable for lack of action. One's duty is limited to that of which one is capable.[59] Just as one is not accountable for a lack of awareness of particular events, one is not accountable for not using capacities that are not possessed.

Significantly, Godwin makes an explicit distinction between two types of equality: 'physical or moral'.[60] A person's 'physical equality [with other persons] may be considered either as it relates to the strength of the body or the faculties of the mind'.[61] Moral equality, for Godwin, is 'the propriety of applying one unalterable rule of justice to every case that might arise'.[62] In belonging to the category of human, with the same pleasures and pains, Godwin claims, we are *all* entitled to moral equality, other things being equal. He reasons that 'we are partakers of a common

nature, and the same causes that contribute to the benefit of one contribute to the benefit of another', because 'our senses and faculties are of the
same denomination'.[63] Godwin makes a crucial qualification, however:
'The treatment to which men are entitled is to be measured by their merits
and their virtues.'[64] On the face of it, moral equality is separate from
physical and intellectual capacity, and Godwin makes the argument that
differences in capacity should not lead to moral inequality. As he puts it,
'in every state of human society, there will be men of an intellectual
capacity much superior to their neighbours'; and these physical and
intellectual differences, in his estimation, do not affect moral equality,
even if they are the source of physical inequality.[65] Godwin even defends
this view in his attack on L'Abbé Raynal's *Révolution de l'Amérique* (1781),
which states that equality 'will always be an unintelligible fiction, so long as
the *capacities* of men shall be unequal'; and he defends the view against one
according to which moral inequality derives from physical and mental
inequality.[66] Godwin's assertion that 'pure, unadulterated justice' favours
the person who is 'most valuable' is in conflict with these ideals, however.[67] The latter view makes it impossible to defend the fairness of the
application of the rule of justice in the case of those with capacities that are
less valued. If Godwin's negative assessment of a person's contribution to
the general good leaves that person in the burning building, it is not
difficult to see that their entitlement to moral equality irrespective of
capacity has not been protected. The capacities-based assessment of how
we contribute to the general good has lessened the value of that person's
life. Godwin could mitigate this consequence by considering as salient not
the absolute ability of a person to contribute to society but the capacity of
that person to maximize their contribution relative to their abilities, but no
such consideration enters into Godwin's treatment of the archbishop's
chambermaid. Godwin comes close to making a claim like this in his brief
comment that expectations about one's duty are limited 'by the extent of
the capacity of that being', but this hint is contradicted by many of his
other statements on the issue.[68]

Godwin introduces an additional complication. Capacity in humans is,
he argues, 'in a state of flux'.[69] This is meant not merely in the sense of
capacity development, such as when a child grows into an adult, 'a raw and
inexperienced boy, *capable* of being moulded to any form you pleased'.[70]
Godwin supports a dynamic account of capacity according to which a
person's potential ability cannot entirely be known. Desire, for instance,
can generate a capacity in the sense that one can gain an unexpected ability
when under extreme pressure. Godwin's fiction provides many examples of

the fluid nature of human capacity. Several of his characters discover
mental and physical strength when faced with extreme circumstances.
Additionally, time and ageing can affect capacity. Godwin observes that,
'[t]hat of which I am capable ... as to my conduct to-day, falls extremely
short of that of which I am capable, as to my conduct in the two or three
next ensuing years'.[71] In principle, this statement could be developed into
the idea that capacity is context-dependent (an important aspect of the
social barriers model), but Godwin does not take this route. Since his
theory of virtue is based on the extent to which one's *known* capacities are
used to the full, his view that these capacities exist in a state of flux presents
a significant problem, one to which he has no answer. The best he can
offer is an acknowledgement of the necessity of ambiguity and indetermi-
nacy in the assessment of capacity. He concludes that 'we are obliged
however in the decisions of morality to submit to these uncertainties'.[72] In
a brief aside in the later editions of *Political Justice*, Godwin appears to offer
a possible exemption from social contribution for people with capacities
that he does not value highly. He suggests that people should strive for
'every perfection or excellence that human beings are competent to
conceive ... unless in cases that are palpably and unequivocally excluded
by the structure of their frame'.[73] To the extent that this provides a check
to the moral assessment of people in terms of their ability to contribute, it
is merely an ad hoc one that remains inconsistent with the requirements of
justice in the Fénelon case. Furthermore, it is also unlikely to imply more
than an exemption from the need to strive; and, if so, it is not something
that would allow people with devalued capacities to avoid being seen as
socially problematic.

Identifying general goods that are not disadvantageous to people with
disabilities has proven notoriously difficult for political scientists. As Nancy
Hirschmann has shown in her work on Hobbes and Locke, theories about
rights, duties, and obligations often depend on 'a particular body with
particular physical and mental capacities and orientations, a particular set
of assumptions about what constitutes a human being, and a particular set
of social relations that exclude disabled individuals from the role of
political citizen'.[74] Martha Nussbaum likewise suggests that political theorists do not start in the right place. Classical social contract theory,[75] for
instance, 'specifies certain abilities (rationality, language, roughly equal
physical and mental capacity) as prerequisites for participation' in society,
and for inclusion as a citizen who has dignity and equality.[76] Nussbaum
observes that social contract theory excludes people with disabilities
because it builds a procedure for justice that treats function impairment

as an exception that need not be accounted for in the foundational principles of a society. Godwin's work demonstrates that the exclusionary tactics identified by Nussbaum can also be found in political theorists who are not contractarians. Eva Kittay comments that 'in most dominant theories of justice, dignity is coupled with the capacity for autonomy'.[77] Kittay draws attention to what she calls the 'fiction' and 'idealization' of independence.[78] Her work is indebted to that of Alasdair MacIntyre, and, in particular, his concern that it is morally important to acknowledge vulnerability and dependence, even though moral philosophy has placed great emphasis on 'individual autonomy' and 'upon the capacity for making independent choices'.[79] Godwin, however, ties his concept of capacity to ideas about independence, virtue, and social value; vulnerability and dependence, in his work, are not in any sense virtuous, and certainly not human goods.

## Capacity, Social Devaluation, and Rhetorical Intermixing in Godwin's Fiction

Godwin explicitly identifies as socially and morally problematic those who are either unwilling or unable to contribute to the general good. These people, in Godwin's system, fall broadly into two groups: the *powerless* and the *powerful*.[80] The *powerless* are poor people, factory workers, peasants, servants, slaves, women, children, the uneducated, prisoners, and soldiers. According to Godwin, the powerless are prevented from contributing to the general good because they are not permitted to reach their intellectual and physical potential to develop and apply capacities well, and because their freedom to act has been curtailed by their social situation, beliefs, education, or the kind of work they are constrained to do. In his fiction, this group is usually dehumanized and reduced to the status of objects and possessions. The *powerful* are monarchs, aristocrats, wealthy people, and those with political authority. These people are problematic owing to their misuse of capacities. Additionally, their social entitlements mean they impose upon their subordinates. For Godwin, aristocratic cultures of luxury and leisure do not stress utility, and this arrangement of government impedes rational decision-making. Godwin characterizes the powerful as tyrannical, hierarchical, devious, self-centred, self-serving, and steeped in arcane and irrational honour codes. In theory, however, both the powerless and the powerful have the potential to become socially valuable because they have intellectual and physical capacities that could be developed or could be put to good use. The social and individual imperative, Godwin asserts, should be that people become socially and morally valuable, develop their capacities, and apply them correctly.

Those who do not have the potential to develop and apply their capacities and become contributors to the general good, however, are in a different position. They cannot become socially valuable, given Godwin's account of contribution. Godwin attempts to solve the problem of enabling people who cannot develop the relevant capacities for becoming socially valuable by drawing on two theories. Firstly, human ability is an unknown that can change in extreme circumstances (Godwin's dynamic account of human capacity); and, secondly, the capacities of the human race are in any case improving over time – his theory of perfectibility. The former is a theory of capacity in the particular sense and the latter a theory of capacity in a universal sense. According to the first theory, physical weakness can be eliminated by intellectual exertion, and people are not so physically weak that, for example, they cannot *in extremis* rebel against subjection by someone who is physically stronger. In Godwin's estimation, rational thought can enable people to bring about their own independence by affecting capacity. He goes so far as to propose that 'true independence of mind' will bring about the goal of general happiness because thought, and not physical weakness, holds people in subjection.[81] This view on curing incapacity is rooted in Godwin's idea that reason will one day improve the physical health of the human race and that we will be able to heal ourselves by means of thought, in the same way that we can use thought to move our bodies or affect our bodies psychosomatically. This makes the unity of body and mind a vital attribute of people who are socially valued, and explains why disembodiment, physical constraint, and mental absence so frequently distinguish socially devalued characters in Godwin's fiction.

Godwin's theory of perfectibility suggests that capacities in the universal sense are always in a state of amelioration. He observes that 'man is perfectible, or in other words susceptible of perpetual improvement'.[82] He explains that 'by perfectible, it is not meant that he [i.e. humankind] is capable of being brought to perfection. But the word seems sufficiently adapted to express the faculty of being continually made better and receiving perpetual improvement; and in this sense it is here to be understood'.[83] Although there is no professed goal for perfection, Godwin commits himself to an ideal direction in which humanity is to develop, and this ideal entails an appeal to a set of capacities (even though it 'does not imply the *capacity* of being brought to perfection').[84] Godwin concludes that 'the perfection of the human character consists in approaching as nearly as possible to the perfectly voluntary state'.[85] He draws on

Benjamin Franklin's statement, 'that "mind would one day become omnipotent over matter"', to support his case.[86] Godwin notes that while Franklin meant that one day machines would be improved by intellectual endeavour, Godwin himself understands the aphorism to suggest that intellectual advances might one day lead to the dominance of the mind 'over the matter of our own bodies'.[87] Godwin's conjecture is more forceful in 1793, where he includes the question 'why may not man be one day immortal?'[88] His theory is not solely about the potential for immortality, however; it is also about eradicating incapacities.[89]

Godwin employs in his fiction a form of *rhetorical intermixing* whereby he describes various types of socially devalued characters using the attributes of other types, and by doing so makes close links between them. The bodies of old people, for instance, are akin to prisons; prisoners are physically or mentally incapacitated; objectified women are despotic; noblemen are slaves; and servants are noble. In connecting these groups rhetorically, Godwin affirms that the powerless and the powerful have a great deal in common in terms of their social accountability.[90] In blending the many attributes of socially devalued characters, Godwin points to the characters' shared status across different groups. This rhetorical interchangeability, however, masks a fundamental distinction between those who cannot possess the valued capacities, and those who could in the right circumstances come to possess them (or to apply them appropriately). Only some people have the potential to leave the socially devalued group. This is because Godwin understands emancipation to require certain capacities (e.g. physical and mental strength). If those capacities cannot be acquired, then it is impossible to remove one's devalued status. Godwin values the potential for the development of capacities, and sometimes ties this to his theory of virtue. For example, in *St. Leon* (1799), Hector, the black servant who works as a turnkey in the prison in Constance, is shown to have 'a sound understanding and an excellent heart' irrespective of the neglect of his education, 'the meanness of his rank and his apparent poverty'.[91] Hector's disinterested benevolence allows Reginald St Leon to overlook his lack of education in favour of celebrating what Hector could have become given the right circumstances. Hector's 'sublime'[92] integrity impresses Reginald because it is present in spite of his appearing to be 'destitute of knowledge, of intellectual cultivation, and all those exquisite sensations that most distinguish the man from the brute'.[93] Godwin's novels consistently show approval of people who have a benevolent nature but lack abilities, and he treats them more sympathetically than he does people who have abilities but lack benevolence.

Godwin emphatically links social deficit with physical and intellectual incapacity. In his view, the social deficits that lead to social devaluation also cause incapacities, and these incapacities contribute to the relevant social deficits. For example, Godwin asserts that factory work causes mental and physical incapacities, and that these incapacities prevent people from contributing to the general good. Manual labourers, he suggests in *Political Justice*, work 'till their understandings are benumbed with toil, their sinews contracted and made callous by being forever on the stretch, and their bodies invaded with infirmities, and surrendered to an untimely grave'.[94] He takes up this idea in *Fleetwood* (1805), where Casimir Fleetwood's patron, Monsieur Ruffigny, tells of being forced, as a boy of eight, to work in the silk mills of Lyons.[95] Ruffigny comments that 'numbness and vacancy of mind are the fruits of such an employment. It ultimately transforms the being who is subjected to it, into quite a different class or species of animal'.[96] The factory worker becomes 'a sort of machine; his limbs and articulations are converted, as it were, into wood and wires'.[97] Mindless and excessive work, Ruffigny asserts, produces 'weariness, *ennui*, imbecility, and idiotism' in the workers.[98] Such workers are, he laments, 'the lowest class of mechanics, paupers, brutified in intellect, and squalid in attire'.[99] The other factory children show no 'signs of vigour and robust health'; they are 'all sallow; their muscles flaccid, and their form emaciated'.[100] The only thing that prevents Ruffigny from becoming an 'automaton' is his day of rest on Sundays.[101] He concludes that 'liberty is the parent of strength. Nature teaches the child, by the play of the muscles, and pushing out his limbs in every direction, to give them scope to develope [sic] themselves'.[102] In Godwinian fashion, imprisonment leads to physical and mental incapacities, but the mind can free the body in the case of those with nascent capacities. Casimir learns from this experience that 'the merits of the poor man were always clouded, undervalued, and baffled of their utility; while those of the rich were illuminated by the beams of applause, and enabled to appear with tenfold effect upon the theatre of society'.[103]

Godwin views aristocrats and wealthy people (the powerful) as socially problematic for several reasons. His fiction depicts this group as misusing their capacities, their wealth and authority, as well as pursuing personal goals rather than general goods. They are also often physically and intellectually impaired. Even though Godwin argues that the high born and the low born are likely to have the same capacities, and he is adamant that there is no difference between a baby born into the aristocracy and a baby born amongst working people, he refutes the principle of hereditary power on the grounds of the inherited physical and intellectual unfitness of the aristocracy. His statement, in *Thoughts on Man* (1831), that 'Nature distributes her gifts without reference to the distinctions of artificial society' is incompatible with his assertion, in *Political Justice*, that 'it is not satire, but a simple statement of fact . . . that it is not easy to find a set of men in society, sunk more below the ordinary *standard* of man in his constituent characteristics, than the body of the English, or any other, peerage'.[104]

Godwin reinforces the aristocrat's socially problematic status by associating it with physical and intellectual incapacities and spends a great deal of time outlining ways in which aristocratic cultures of luxury impair physical and intellectual function. Indeed, much of Godwin's opposition to the concentration of power in the aristocracy relates to his perception of aristocratic incapacities. He claims, for instance, that prosperity invites 'our bodies to indolence, and our minds to lethargy', and that a 'superfluity of wealth . . . deprives us of all intercourse with our fellow men upon equal terms, and makes us prisoners of state . . . shut out from the real benefits of society and the perception of truth'.[105] His ideas are similar to those of Edmund Burke. Burke asserts, in *A Vindication of Natural Society*, that devotion to leisure produces in the aristocracy 'a weak valetudinary State of Body, attended by all those horrid Disorders . . . The Mind has its share of the Misfortune; it grows lazy and enervate, unwilling and unable to search for Truth, and utterly uncapable of knowing, much less relishing real Happiness'.[106] Godwin similarly reinforces the idea of aristocratic incapacity when he recalls Madame de Genlis's description of the children of the Duke of Orleans in *Leçons d'une Gouvernante à Ses Eleves* (1791). Godwin summarizes de Genlis as calling the children 'effeminate' – a word he often uses to indicate incapacity in men.[107] Godwin writes that de Genlis observes disparagingly that the Duke's children were

> unable to run or to leap, or even so much as to walk at a round pace, or for more than half an hour together . . . The eldest, who was eight years of age, never came down stairs without being supported by the arm of one or two persons; the domestics were obliged to render them the meanest services, and, for a cold or any slight indisposition, sat up with them for nights together.[108]

Having unvalued capacities, or appearing to have them, is here the mark of high birth and privilege; and such people, Godwin argues, cannot contribute to the general good of society.

Godwin links wealth and incapacity in all of his novels. Lionel Clifford observes, in *Mandeville* (1817), for instance, that the rich are unable to 'move without scores of menials to attend' them.[109] The poor man is free, however, because 'his legs are his footmen; and his arms are ever ready and prompt to perform all he wishes'.[110] Lionel conjectures that if he were to spend his life focused on making money, by the end of it 'all the finer sensibilities' of his 'nature' would have 'evaporated', with 'nothing left of heart within me, but what is as dry and impenetrable as an Egyptian mummy'.[111] In effect, he would acquire incapacities and thereby become socially devalued – of less or no use for the common good. Furthermore, the Civil War context in *Mandeville* (1817) enables Godwin to link monarchy and incapacity. Charles I is briefly described, in a politically dangerous book, as a child 'urchin' with 'crooked legs', crying because his elder brother Henry has told him that he need not worry about his deformity as he will eventually make him '"a bishop, and thy petticoats shall hide them"'.[112]

Aristocratic rank also distracts from incapacities and deformities. *Fleetwood* provides several instances of unattractive characters whose social status nevertheless allows them to be viewed by others as appealing. Casimir spends time in Paris with Sir Charles Gleed, whom he remembers being a 'slow and indocile' student at Oxford, incapable of being taught.[113] Casimir marvels that this does not prevent Gleed from entertaining aristocratic mistresses. Gleed contrasts physically and intellectually with the self-made man, Mr. Scarborough, who is 'tall, and of a carriage bold and graceful', and who 'seemed born to command'.[114] Scarborough abandons arranging a marriage between his daughter, Miss Scarborough, and the son of Lord Lindsey, realizing that he has been erroneously concerned with the man's status and not with his abilities and physical appeal. Scarborough says: 'I will now confess, that his most striking characteristics are ugliness, imbecility, and effeminacy. But, infatuated with the grandeur of his alliance, I did not at that time notice these disadvantages.'[115] He says that Miss Scarborough 'could never, without a certain kind of prostitution, have become his [Lord Lindsey's son's] wife' as her affections were engaged elsewhere.[116] Godwin's play on social rank as a disguise for incapacity is part of his exploration of psychosomatic disunity and inauthentic bodies. He is explicit throughout his fiction that physical incapacity is a general expectation in members of the aristocracy, and that those who do not fit this type, such as Reginald St Leon, are unusual. Reginald says of himself that, although he was brought up to believe in feudal privileges, he 'was not pampered into corporeal imbecility, or suffered to rust in inactivity of mind'.[117] The term 'corporeal imbecility' rhetorically mixes physical and mental incapacity. Reginald's exceptional physical and intellectual development is due to an incomparable mother, the descriptions of whom also exhibit rhetorical mixing. She has 'rather a masculine understanding', is 'full of the prejudices of nobility and magnificence', and her abilities enable her to disregard her social conditioning and develop her son's capacities.[118]

Throughout his fiction, Godwin endorses a hierarchy of capacity that informs social value. *Mandeville* is perhaps his most extensive investigation of the connections between health, physical capacity, and degrees of social worth. Much of the exploration of capacity-related concepts occurs in relation to the 'deformed' character, Audley Mandeville, who is the protagonist Charles Mandeville's reclusive uncle. Audley's father (the Commodore) and his Aunt Dorothy arrange for Amelia Montfort, who is their dependant and niece, to marry one of two riotous disabled seamen who lodge in the male part of the house. Having observed Audley and Amelia falling in love, they deem their match to be unsuitable because of Audley's incapacities and deformities and Amelia's lack of social status and wealth. Their deficits disqualify them from each other. Audley's father has no plan for him to marry because he is concerned that his 'children, I dare swear, would be all such poor helpless creatures as himself'.[119] The seamen, however, are eligible for Amelia's hand, because their incapacities are acquired rather than appear to be congenital. Aunt Dorothy and the Commodore make a comparative assessment of suitability that takes into account one sailor's having one arm and the other's having a fracture of the knee-pan. Charles recounts that 'it was canvassed with all due formality, whether the cripple, or he that was maimed of an arm only, was the most eligible for the purpose'.[120] They decide upon 'Thomson, the cripple' on the grounds that 'he was completely a man in every dimension; when he sat, or when he stood, there was nothing to object to in his figure; it was only when he moved that he was deficient'.[121] They deem the supposed completeness of Thomson's body, and his ability to pass, to be more important than the extent of his functionality, thus making the decision on the basis of aesthetics rather than capacity. It is likely that we are meant to find this assessment absurd, as function in this case would usually be more important than appearance.

*Mandeville* also includes another disabled sailor, Mr. Willis. Willis left the 'sea-service, but having sustained considerable injury from an accident, became a cripple for life, and had retired on a small pension'.[122] He becomes a man of feeling, through the intervention of his wife who is an 'exemplary matron', and of whom 'he was in some sense a copy ... with inferior intellects'.[123] The Willises live in what Charles Mandeville calls a small 'society of "just men made perfect"', where all sought the good of all, and no one lived for himself, or studied for himself'.[124] Charles's quotation, from Hebrews 12:23, may have appealed to Godwin because of the reference to self-cure. The chapter exhorts the righteous to 'lift up your drooping hands and strengthen your weak knees and make straight paths for your feet, so that what is lame may not be put out of joint but rather be healed'.[125] Significantly, Charles gives a sentimental account of Willis's incapacity that does not seem to accord with Godwin's wider views. Thus, he signals that Willis's body heightens his virtue because it prevents him from having the capacity to do harm.

> His very lameness seemed to give him additional interest with the spectator: the goodness of his heart blended, in a way I am not able to describe, with his infirmity; and you loved him the more, because he was feeble and helpless, and joined the sentiment of a true philanthropy, with an apparent want of power, as well as of will, to do you harm.[126]

Although sentimental, this use of incapacity goes beyond the usual portraits of disabled servicemen of the period. Willis has a particular kind of virtue, is noted for his benevolence, and has an integrated place within an egalitarian family community. He loses some agency by being considered a 'copy' of his wife; but it is his 'adoration' of her, rather than his incapacity, that makes his personality less dominant than hers.[127]

Godwin uses the ideological force of limited, misused, or devalued capacities to signal that the deficits of the powerless or powerful are incontrovertible. Moreover, he associates the path to social value with the development or reapplication of capacities. Importantly, this leads to a repeated association in his work between emancipation from social devaluation and the cure of physical or mental illness. Godwin's political goals are repeatedly shown as achievable by enabling socially disadvantaged people to develop and apply capacities that allow them to contribute to the general good. He suggests, for example, that society can remove the social cost of being poor by distributing resources equally and enabling poor people to develop their capacities. One can remove the social cost of being a woman by educating women to become intellectually and physically independent, and by introducing a merit-based system that does not reward rich, powerful, and well-connected men whose abilities and decisions do not make them useful. A chambermaid who wishes to be rescued from the Archbishop's palace must write a better book than he can. Godwin's fiction confirms that he conceptualizes many forms of social devaluation in terms of limited capacity, and his theory of political justice is determined by able-bodied and able-minded general goods. With the exception of Willis, whose incapacity draws on the honorific connotations of wounded soldiers, there is no social place for those without the required capacities, even to the extent that Godwin disallows philanthropic or other kinds of support. All this indicates a major inconsistency in Godwin's work, one that demonstrates his lack of commitment to moral equality (equality that is due regardless of capacity).

## 'Curing' Social Devaluation

In his fiction, Godwin depicts the enablement of contribution to the general good as the removal of temporary and even apparently permanent incapacities, and he uses these moments to connect emancipation and cure. Much of his negative assessment of incapacity centres on his assumption that the impaired body curtails personal freedom. Reginald St Leon suggests, for example, that physical incapacities acquired due to age are a form of imprisonment that alienates a person from rights: 'Yesterday I was a prisoner, crippled in every articulation; to-day I was a citizen of the world, capable of all its delights.'[128] When Reginald is weak after an illness, he feels 'so much ashamed of the debilitated state in which my fever had left me, as I could have done of the most inglorious effeminacy and cowardice of soul'.[129] As he endeavours to get well, he puts into practice Godwin's observation that mental strength can improve bodily strength, commenting that 'in many cases it is reasonable to bid a valetudinarian take care of himself'.[130] Reginald realizes that 'extraordinary circumstances often bring along with them extraordinary strength. No man knows, till the experiment, what he is capable of effecting ... I doubt not that the despair of my mind will give redoubled energy to my efforts'.[131] *St. Leon* affords many examples of cure associated with social emancipation. For example, when Reginald's family falls into poverty, his wife, Marguerite, sees this change in circumstance as a revelation that affords them the opportunity both to improve their health and to become socially valuable. She believes that her children will become more virtuous as they become independent, and that the family will become healthier through the physical exercise involved in farming and food preparation. Reginald takes a different path, however. He heals himself with the elixir of life – a magical version of Godwin's utopian hope for the power of reason – that gives him a body that can heal and rejuvenate at will. Reginald also relieves his poverty with the philosopher's stone. Unexplained wealth and inexplicable youth leads to exile, however, as Reginald is unable to be socially useful without arousing suspicion.

Similarly, the reclusive and wealthy Audley Mandeville is potentially capable, in spite of being 'a poor unfortunate being, deformed, and that never had a day's health ... and knows no more of the world than a child'.[132] Although his body is deemed 'scarcely equal to the most ordinary corporeal exertions; and the temper of his mind corresponded to the frame of his body, tender as a flower ... and sinking, as without power of resistance, under any thing that presented itself in the form of hostility', he finds strength in an important moment.[133] When called upon by his family to renounce his love for Amelia, Audley shakes 'off his infirmities, and appeared altogether another creature from what he had been from his birth up to the present moment'.[134] Standing up to his father, he finds the strength to deliver a 'harangue' of an 'oriental and unsparing sort', so forceful that one would have thought that it 'would have sunk him into earth, or shivered his delicate frame into a thousand atoms. It proved otherwise. What cannot the powers of almighty love effect?'[135] Audley temporarily self-cures in the face of adversity, having lived in fear of a father whom he has dreaded to approach more 'than the vilest slave to the most cruel eastern tyrant'.[136] Godwin implies that, because of this unknown capacity, Audley acquires duties as someone who could strive to become socially valuable. His nephew, Charles, nevertheless, observes that Audley was 'certainly not the most useful of mankind. He was engaged in no illustrious acts, either of intellect or philanthropy', and sees him as having had no history; his life was a 'blank'.[137] He is, in his nephew's estimation, not socially valuable.

Charles similarly connects recovery from physical incapacity with his own perception of freedom. Reconsidering the value of his lost capacities after he breaks his leg in a riding accident, Charles judges his recovery to be tedious and unheroic. The injury makes him brood, and he wonders whether the leg fracture reduces him 'below the genuine attitude of man' or whether it 'merely brought me down to the true level and standard of my species'.[138] Charles contemplates the mental power required for recovery and describes regaining his capacities as akin to experiencing the world as a new Adam, or levitating. Sickness is, for him, 'like a gap in existence'.[139] Temporary incapacity teaches Charles that he uses the distraction of 'bodily exertions' to 'overcome ... the sufferings' of his 'soul'.[140] Regaining his physical abilities frees him to 'form a new system of life'.[141] He puts into practice two of Godwin's propositions from *Political Justice*: the idea that 'a man must have experienced or imagined the inconveniences of sickness, before he can derive positive pleasure from the enjoyment of health', and the idea that 'health is undoubtedly in most cases the prerequisite of the best exertions of mind'.[142]

Caleb Williams makes the Godwinian suggestion that there is an important link between intellect and freedom, and that the body might one day be capable of being empowered by the mind and overcome whatever hindrances it faces. Caleb observes that '"the mind is master of itself; and is endowed with powers that might enable it to laugh at the tyrant's vigilance"'.[143] When, during his first prison break, a large stone nearly dislocates his ankle, and he is captured, he describes his pain as 'so intense that I was scarcely able to stand, and, after having limped a few paces, I twisted my foot under me, and fell down again'.[144] During his second jailbreak, however, he demonstrates Godwin's dynamic theory of capacity: having 'lost the command of [his] limbs' and walking with 'weak and tottering steps', Caleb is 'determined to steer as far as possible from the hateful scene where I had been so long confined'.[145] Inspired by the hope of liberty, Caleb's mind 'suddenly became glowing, animated and cheerful', and he recalls that he thought 'never did man more strenuously prefer poverty with independence, to the artificial allurements of a life of slavery'.[146] He runs 'fleet as a greyhound', leaps 'like a young roe upon the mountains', and 'regains his rights' of freedom and of freedom of movement at the same time.[147] This emancipatory suspension of pain is so revolutionary that Caleb exclaims, 'how enviable was the enthusiasm which could thus furnish me with energy, in the midst of hunger, poverty, and universal desertion!'[148]

Characters in Godwin's novels who demonstrate the will to become socially valuable through the development and application of their capacities often appeal to their able-bodiedness and able-mindedness as a qualification for emancipation. Caleb, who is 'uncommonly vigorous and active', reproaches Falkland for underestimating his capacities.[149] He cries out, 'didst thou believe me impotent, imbecile, and idiot-like, with no understanding to contrive thy ruin, and no energy to perpetrate it?'[150] Hawkins, who is wrongly convicted of Falkland's crime, likewise appeals to his capacities during his persecution by Falkland. Hawkins expresses hope that his independent spirit will release him from persecution: 'Have not I, thinks I, arms and legs as well as other people? ... Sure I aren't a cabbage, that if you pull it out of the ground it must die. I am pennyless. ... [I]f we little folks had but the wit to do for ourselves, the great folks would not be such maggoty changelings as they are.'[151] These appeals to able-bodiedness and able-mindedness are consonant with the similar justifications we see in Wollstonecraft's polemical work, and are part of the broader cultural practice of maintaining capacity-based hierarchies.

## Psychosomatic Disunity: Mind–Body Problems
## in Godwin's Fiction

Godwin's political emphasis on capacity, and on psychosomatic unity (in particular, the capacity of the mind to control the body), explains the regularity of incidents in which socially problematic characters in his novels in some sense disengage from their bodies or minds and from the voluntary state that Godwin values. Gary Handwerk remarks that Godwin is particularly insightful 'about the patterns and processes that entrap' his protagonists as they navigate the recursive tides of history and find themselves reading the present in terms of the past.[152] These characters find their 'capacities for acting in and upon the present' circumscribed by plots that are 'almost obsessively repetitive in structure'.[153] They are 'compulsively resistant to change' and caught in an 'intricate interweaving of personal and ideological affect'.[154] Handwerk reads this rhythm as indicative of Godwin's interest in historical stasis (or recursion) and trauma. The past disrupts the present because 'history has its origins in traumas that seem to lie beyond what the liberal imagination can conceive or alter'.[155] As Handwerk acknowledges, this trauma frequently takes the form of the circumscription of the protagonist's 'power as an agent of change'.[156] I would add that Godwin presents this trauma through psychosomatic disunities that affect capacities (and their application), and that these disunities restrict the voluntary state and contribution to the general good.

Godwin investigates absent minds through characters whose mental states make them appear to be mesmerized, mechanistic, doll-like automata, or who have periods of temporary insanity, or are consumed by love, grief, or overwork. Some of his characters figuratively or literally have absent bodies. They seem to be ghostly, cannot use their bodies as tools, or are alienated from their bodies by disguise or hidden identities. Godwin also explores the experience of discarding the body through incarceration, illness, and temporary physical incapacity. There are also striking instances in which uncanny bodies appear during moments of emotional intensity. These often serve as warnings about bodily and mental integrity. When Reginald St Leon is caught alone in a storm that devastates his farm, and fears for the safety of his family, he comes across the 'body of a woman ... who appeared to be dead, destroyed by the storm. Near her lay a female infant, apparently about six years of age'.[157] He initially imagines the bodies belong to his wife and daughter, but when he examines them closely, he realizes they are strangers. Godwin is fascinated, too, by moments when bodies and minds that have become uncoupled are reunited. For example, a character that undergoes an incapacitating separation of mind and body may become capable again; or a disguised body that has disconnected from its true sense of self may be re-identified and once again able to live authentically and function in a useful manner. Absent minds and bodies appear as part of Godwin's discussion of capacity in his fiction because the mind's capacity for controlling the body (the voluntary state) is, according to his system, necessary for social value.

There are many incidents in Godwin's fiction where socially devalued characters experience periods of incapacity as a disconnection of mind and body. Reginald, weak from his interrogation by the Spanish and the trauma of escaping an *auto da fé*, finds that his 'limbs felt palsied, and absolutely lifeless. ... I was incapable of rising from the bed. I found myself in the extremest [sic] degree feeble and languid'.[158] His imprisonment has a mental effect, too: 'my mind had been as much cribbed and immured as my body' and his body becomes insubstantial and shadowy.[159] He says, 'I was the mere shadow of a man, of no more power and worth than that which a magic lantern produces upon a wall.'[160] Imprisonment leads to a separation of his mind and body. Although Reginald's 'body was restrained, his mind occasionally soared to the furthest regions of the empyrean, or plunged into the deepest of the recesses in which nature conceals her operations'.[161] During his recovery from a broken leg, Charles Mandeville has a similar out-of-body experience that he perceives to be liberating. He says that he 'felt, as if the power of gravitation that binds material substances to the earth on which they are placed, was removed, that my limbs and my whole frame had lost their cumbrousness, that I was in danger of mounting up in the air, and could sail as I pleased, sustained and cushioned upon the clouds of heaven'.[162] At Winchester, Charles becomes a solitary character given to bouts of melancholy that disengage his mind and body. He comments that he 'had no respect for the limbs and members of my body, and viewed them as an incumbrance upon the activity of my spirit. They were mine, not me'.[163] On occasion, he experiences his bodily disengagement as akin to the use of prostheses: 'My arm was but an implement and a tool, of the same nature as a hooked stick, and of no value but for the commission in which it was employed.'[164] As his melancholy turns to madness, he considers himself as 'one who could never become useful to society, and whose existence would be a burden to his fellow-creatures'.[165] Prison generates mind–body separations in several of Godwin's characters. Godwin views imprisonment as preventing people from being socially valuable, and denounces it as inhumane and ineffective. In solitary confinement, Caleb becomes a mind with no body, passing the time, as he puts it, losing his physical state in 'imaginary adventures'.[166] Emily Tyrrel has a similar experience of imprisonment. She cries out against her persecution by her cousin, with the words 'you may imprison my body, but you cannot conquer my mind'.[167] The mind–body separation leads Caleb to speculate that the body is nothing more than an inconvenient burden. Caleb observes of himself that 'these limbs and this trunk are a cumbrous and unfortunate load for the power of thinking to drag along with it; but why should not the power of thinking be able to lighten the load, till it shall be no longer felt?'[168]

Many of Godwin's characters experience madness or melancholy as mind–body separation. All of Godwin's protagonists experience some form of insanity, as do many of the minor characters. Madness, the most common incapacity in Godwin's work, is often described as mental or spiritual absence. Reginald comments that he 'cannot speak of every species of madness; but I also have been mad! This I know, that there is a vacancy of soul, where all appears buried in stupidity, and scarcely deserves the name of thought ... there is an incoherence, in which the mind seems to wander without rudder and pilot'.[169] He recovers, but his grief causes intermittent physical incapacity: 'I seemed like a man in that species of distemper, in which the patient suffers a wasting of the bones, and at length presents to us the shadow, without the powers, of a human body.'[170] When Hector goes insane, in *St. Leon*, he becomes 'obstinate, self-willed, and ungovernable', and throws 'off the character of a servant' in order to rebel against his captors.[171] Similarly, Caleb's impulsive and disobedient opening of Falkland's trunk – which leads to years of persecution – is described as 'act of insanity ... a short-lived and passing alienation of mind'.[172] Casimir Fleetwood is 'turbulent and ungovernable' in his madness,[173] and Deloraine's insanity is animal-like: 'I stamped with my feet, I spread my arms with wildness and ferocity, and roared like a savage beast, who has just escaped from the toils that controled [sic] him.'[174] In Godwin's work, madness is both a trope for an uncontrollable mind that frees itself from restraints, and a futile alienation from social utility.

We see this double usage in Godwin's investigation of disguise. Disguise sometimes restricts characters from using their body to express their thoughts directly, and disrupts the mind's use of the body as a tool. It is, like madness, also used to evade oppression. In order to escape scrutiny, Godwin's heroes often disguise themselves as someone from a socially disadvantaged group. Godwin's disguised characters regularly include incapacities as part of their concealment. Caleb's first disguise is that of a one-eyed Irish beggar with 'a peculiar slouching and clownish gait'.[175] In spite of the effectiveness of being incognito, Caleb, like Godwin's other disguised characters, finds it degrading to hide the true nature of the mind. He comments: 'such are the miserable expedients and so great the studied artifice which man, who never deserves the name of manhood but in proportion as he is erect and independent, may find it necessary to employ for the purpose of eluding the inexorable animosity and unfeeling tyranny of his fellow man!'[176] Here Godwin contrasts the uprightness of the undisguised and supposedly independent body with the body of the impaired beggar. He conceptualizes social powerlessness as physical and sensory incapacity. On another occasion, Caleb takes on the characteristics of a 'twisted and deformed' man with poor health and a lisp.[177] In a theatrical scene, the henchman Gines challenges Caleb to 'pull off your face; or, if you cannot do that, at least you can pull off your clothes, and let us see what your hump is made of'.[178] Caleb stands upright, 'tired with this scene of mummery, and disgusted beyond measure with the base and hypocritical figure I seemed to exhibit', and gives himself up for capture.[179] While disguise helps Caleb to evade Falkland, it has an emotional cost as he is 'seized at intervals with temporary frenzy', and is twice driven to contemplate suicide.[180]

Disembodiment as disguise is used to great effect in *Deloraine*, where dissimulation results in a puppet-like and restrictive existence. Having murdered William, his wife's former lover, Deloraine attempts to evade justice by adopting a new identity. He says that in private he can 'spread out my arms, use the gestures which my constitution of mind and habits prompted, and employ the faculty of speech with unstudied phraseology and intonations', but in public he is as if 'bound hand and foot' and unable to 'move an articulation of my body but in correspondence to a preconcerted system. I was like a puppet, all of whose motions are regulated by the wires, the string of which is held by the conductor of the shew'.[181] He complains that disguise impairs him because 'the essence of the nature of man lives in the spontaneous obedience of his limbs and his organs to the genuine impulse of his mind'.[182] Godwin implies here, as in *Political Justice*, the importance of approaching as near as possible to the voluntary state. Bodily and mental restriction of any kind, Deloraine concludes, are 'the worst of slaveries'.[183]

Godwin connects disguise with self-alienation in *Cloudesley* (1830). When Lord Danvers's baby nephew is orphaned abroad, Danvers steals his title and wealth and arranges for a servant to adopt the boy. Both nephew and uncle are thus alienated from their true identities. This usurpation of his nephew's entitlements takes a physical and mental toll on Danvers, who opines during his confession, 'what a relief it is to me to speak of myself without reserve! I am placed every day upon a stage. I appear for ever in an assumed character'.[184] Danvers's self-vindication includes Godwin's arguments, from *Political Justice*, that titles, wealth, and nobility are worthless snares that add nothing to one's happiness. He repeatedly describes his guilt as an incapacity and as causing incapacity. His crime is 'a foul mass of loathsomeness and moral putrefaction' that 'had been fastened on my heart, which no operation, and no incision-knife, though guided by the most skilful hand, could ever extirpate'.[185] Danvers describes himself as like 'a soldier who has received his death's wound in the field of battle, whose limbs are shattered, and his bosom trenched, while every step in the progress of the vehicle that removes him, tears him to pieces with insufferable agonies'.[186] The crime, he says, 'gnawed at my heart, blanched my cheeks, and reduced this human figure of mine to an assemblage of skin only and bones'.[187] This description of a barely alive body echoes that of Falkland at the end of *Caleb Williams*, whose 'whole figure was thin, to a degree that suggested the idea rather of a skeleton than a person actually alive. Life seemed hardly to be the capable inhabitant of so woe-begone and ghost-like a figure'.[188] Falkland is steeped in honour codes and crimes that devalue him socially in Godwin's system.

Godwin occasionally makes marriage a cause of psychosomatic disunity. In *Political Justice* he calls marriage a 'system of fraud' that is at odds with disinterested benevolence.[189] He thinks that marriage tends to force the partners to monopolize each other's attention at the expense of social engagement. He also argues that it is difficult to dissolve, and that it thus causes powerlessness for both partners. Married people can make decisions neither according to disinterested benevolence nor according to their own preferences. Casimir Fleetwood, who marries late, mourns the loss of his single life. Godwin intermixes images of imprisonment, sickness, and mesmerism in his descriptions of what he sees as the social ineffectiveness of marriage. Casimir feels 'like the persons I have somewhere read of, acted upon by a magnetic influence, who wore no chains or fetters, and yet were prisoners, struggling, perhaps, to advance in an opposite direction, but always compelled to follow the steps of him who exerted this ascendance over them'.[190] Gradually, he becomes 'jaundiced, [in] body and soul', his 'blood loiteringly crept through palsied veins', and he 'appeared, to the eye of the bystander, bereft of all sensation, and was wholly without motion or notice to indicate that there was a soul shut up in my corporeal bulk'.[191] Casimir perceives this state as psychosomatic disunity, commenting that 'love is a passion in which soul and body hold divided empire'.[192] He sees himself as effeminized and enslaved as his marriage renders him incapable of being socially useful.

Many female characters in Godwin's fiction demonstrate mind–body disengagement because of marriage, or in response to the prospect of marriage. Marriage renders their capacities ineffectual, and they often appear as automata. Casimir objectifies his wife, saying, 'I could not avoid sometimes viewing her under the notion of a beautiful toy, a plume of costly feathers, or a copious train of thinnest gauze, which nods gracefully, or floats in a thousand pleasing folds, but which is destitute of substance, firmness, or utility.'[193] We see further separations of mind and body in Mary's sleepwalking and in her mental illness ('alienation of the understanding').[194] The most striking example of marriage prompting disembodiment is that of Margaret Borradale in *Deloraine*, however. Margaret is persistently described as statue-like and ghostly in her mourning, and she marries Deloraine when her 'thoughts were not in the places where she was corporeally present'.[195] Of all of Godwin's female characters, she is the one most often compared with mindless or involuntary bodies. She is 'the unperishing remains of the mighty dead of Ancient Egypt'; a 'corpse' without the unappealing aspects of death; a sick person without the aspects which convey 'to us the idea of disorganization, [such as] an unhealthful and ruined frame'; and she is 'like one of those simulacra, those insubstantial effigies, spoken of by Lucretius, that "mock our eyes with air", and seem to be with us, when the actual persons are far absent, and are wholly unconscious of where their representatives are, and what they appear to be doing'.[196] Female characters in Godwin's work often assume this automaton-like quality in marriage, even in moments of empowerment. Margaret's mother, for example, finds herself ventriloquizing an empowered voice that is not her own: 'her organs seemed as if they were usurped and taken possession of by a power above herself, as if her unconscious tongue was made a vehicle to declare the secrets of the world unknown'.[197] Like Audley Mandeville, she finds unexpected strength. Godwin's depiction of women as psychosomatically disengaged is a way to emphasize the social deficit incurred by their marriage and gender, and their consequent inability to develop their capacities and use them to contribute to the general good.

*Fleetwood* demonstrates that even those who are aware of the compromises that marriage might entail find it difficult to resist mind–body separation.[198] Casimir's wife, Mary, comments before her marriage that she is 'not idle and thoughtless enough, to promise to sink my being and individuality in yours. I shall have my distinct propensities and preferences. . . . In me you will have a wife, and not a passive machine'.[199] Nevertheless, Mary's loss of fortune, shortly before she marries Casimir, deprives her of her utility, and she eventually goes mad. With her money, Casimir observes, she might 'relieve the wants of multitudes, might unfold talent, encourage industry, and multiply around her the class of sober and honourable citizens in the state'.[200] His unfounded suspicion of his wife's infidelity reaches a pitch when he makes uncanny life-sized dolls of her, their unborn child, and Lt. Edward Kenrick, the cousin whom he mistakenly believes is the father of the child.[201] Steven Bruhm reads Casimir's treatment of Mary as his 'imaginative projection of what [he] wants Mary to be',[202] which is an 'object incapable of sentience'.[203] For Bruhm, a series of bodily displacements occurs as Casimir inflicts trauma upon himself. The 'effigy first replaces Mary's body, but *it is then replaced by Fleetwood's*. He becomes the victim in the torture he has executed'.[204] According to Bruhm, Casimir 'projects himself into the body in pain' by moving from a sentimental standpoint of empathy to locating 'pain solely in himself' and thus obliterating 'the object with which he had claimed to identify'.[205] Mona Scheuermann sees Casimir as 'a man whose sense of self simply, [and] with increasingly dire consequences, gets in the way of his ability to function'.[206] I see these dolls as symbolic of an inability to function in a voluntary and socially useful manner. Casimir's engagement with them reveals he is unable to 'distinguish fiction from reality'.[207] They echo his mind–body separation and his inability to use his capacities in socially productive ways.

## Deformity, Capacities, and Moral Impulses

Although Godwin does not have a fully worked out aesthetic theory, his views on the aesthetics of deformity are sometimes evident in his political philosophy and philosophy of mind. Broadly, Godwin thinks that ethical behaviour is unrelated to physical or aesthetic appearance. People of all appearances are as likely to be receptive to moral impulses as each other: 'those moral causes that awaken the mind, that inspire sensibility, imagination and perseverance, are distributed without distinction to the tall or the dwarfish, the graceful or the deformed, the lynx-eyed or the blind'.[208] Godwin's opinion develops in a different direction in the later editions of *Political Justice*, however. Here he is drawn to the pseudo-science of physiognomy, and promotes the idea that intellect can be perceived visually.[209] While the capacity for ethical behaviour may be initially unrelated to one's body type, Godwin suggests that a person's character *becomes* visible on their body over time. There are, in effect, visible manifestations of intellectual states, and there is 'a correspondence between the physiognomy and the intellectual and moral qualities of the mind'.[210] This happens, Godwin supposes, 'by the continual propensity of the mind to modify its material engine in a particular way'.[211]

For Godwin, a person's character is made up of their many and varied experiences, and it is 'determined in all their most essential circumstances by education' in the broadest sense of the word.[212] A person is 'born into the world' as 'an unfinished sketch, without character or decisive feature impressed upon it'.[213] If the correct education has not taken place, however, Godwin claims we will find in the face of that person 'traces of stupidity, of low cunning, of rooted insolence, of withered hope, and narrow selfishness, where the characters of wisdom and independence and disinterestedness, might have been inscribed'.[214] While there are hints of aesthetic terminology in Godwin's discussions of physiognomy, his theory of the development of physical indicators of intellectual states avoids the kinds of aesthetic engagement that we see, for example, in the work of Johann Caspar Lavater. Lavater asserts, for instance, that there is a 'harmony between moral and physical beauty' and that 'every shade of virtue and vice has its expression in the human exterior'.[215] Godwin is not interested, in his theoretical work, in making an aesthetic judgement on moral qualities. He occasionally nods to the prevalent concept that virtue is in some sense beautiful, but this seems more a convention than a genuine theory. He observes, for instance, that 'no man can so much as love virtue sufficiently, who has not an acute and lively perception of its beauty, and its tendency to produce the most solid and permanent happiness'.[216]

For the most part, Godwin avoids connecting physiognomy and ethics in his fiction too.[217] *Caleb Williams* and *Cloudesley*, however, explore the discernibility of crime on the body. Falkland and Danvers both become chronically ill in consequence of their guilt. But despite this, they are nevertheless described in terms of capacity rather than aesthetics. Falkland is 'unable to stand, fatigued ... his limbs destitute of motion, almost of life'.[218] There are brief occasions, however, when Godwin associates evil with an aesthetic discourse. The Turks in *St. Leon*, for example, have racialized deformities. When the malevolent nature of Bethlem Gabor is revealed, it increases his deformity. Reginald remarks that he 'had never beheld him [Gabor] so deformed or so tremendous'.[219] Godwin is fond of

alluding to moral evil in terms that evoke physical monstrosity, suggesting
links between the moral and aesthetic categories. Danvers is terrified that
fate could one day 'tear away the cloak that covered me, and the mask
behind which my true features were hid, and shew me to all the world an
unheard-of monster, from the sight of whom every human creature would
instinctively shrink'.[220] When Reginald feels alienated from humanity, he
looks upon himself 'as a monster that did not deserve to exist'.[221] Godwin
also depicts deformity and monstrosity as deserving of ill-treatment.[222]
The guilt that Reginald feels at having brought his family to financial ruin
is exacerbated, he suggests, by the beauty of his children.

> It would have been a relief to me if my children had been covered with the
> most loathsome disease, deformed and monstrous.[223] It would have been a
> relief to me if they had been abortive in understanding, and odious in
> propensities, if their hearts had teemed with every vice, and every day had
> marked them the predestined victims of infamy. The guilt of having
> stripped them of every external faculty would then have sat light upon
> me.[224]

Conversely, Godwin gives beauty a prized place. Reginald's daughter-in-
law, Pandora, for instance is transcendentally beautiful. Her perfections are
'of a nature that' Reginald 'had not observed in any other woman. Her
symmetry was so perfect, the pearly lustre of her skin so admirable, and her
form and carriage so light and ethereal, that at first view it was difficult to
persuade one's self that she was framed of the same gross materials as the
rest of the species'.[225] Beauty is persistently associated with goodness in
Godwin's work.[226] Godwin even suggests that Audley Mandeville's virtues
have an effect on the perception of his deformities: 'though deformed in
his person, his eyes were remarkably beautiful, and his countenance had an
expression of sweetness, modesty and diffidence, that seemed irresistible'.[227] Audley is an unusual character in this respect, as Godwin, like
many writers of his time, usually associates deformity with negative
characteristics.

Outside of its physiological usage, deformity as a concept does not
usually reference or imply functions or capacities. Godwin generally follows this convention, but occasionally includes characters who have both
deformities and incapacities. Audley, for instance, is 'deformed in his
person', meaning that he does not meet the aesthetic requirements for
beauty.[228] He is also described as 'scarcely equal to the most ordinary
corporeal exertions; and the temper of his mind corresponded to the frame
of his body, tender as a flower'.[229] Godwin appropriately turns to Pope's

description of 'a puny insect, trembling at a breeze' to reinforce the sense of Audley's delicacy.[230] Surprisingly, Godwin sometimes implies capacity when he talks about deformity; and this may be because he is using it in its physiological sense. He writes in *Political Justice*, for instance, that 'what I am capable of, if you consider me merely as a man, is one thing; what I am capable of as a man of a deformed figure, of weak understanding, of superstitious prejudices, or as the case may happen, is another'.[231] Although this is a passing comment, Godwin may hint at the beginnings of the conflation of the aesthetic and capacity concepts that we see in modern disability.

Godwin gives the issue more attention in his essay 'Of the Distribution of Talents' (1831), where he uses deformity and monstrosity to identify a group that has limited capacities. Godwin's main argument is that education should be tailored to the individual's capacities rather than to the individual's social class. As he succinctly puts it, 'a child is not designed by his original formation to be a manufacturer of shoes'.[232] Godwin begins with the idea that there are physical and intellectual expectations for the human species, and proceeds to make the case that, in order to establish an idea of what these human capacities are, one should set aside atypical bodies: 'all men, the monster and the *lusus naturae* excepted, have a certain form, a certain compliment of limbs, a certain internal structure, and organs of sense – may we not add further, certain powers of intellect?'[233] Additionally, 'idiots and extraordinary cases' are also part of the atypical group.[234] Godwin is concerned that people who do not believe in social equality will not admit of a common set of human capacities; and he proposes that, if we remove exceptions from consideration, people's capacities will be deemed equal. With these provisos, 'it seems to follow, that man is more like and equal to man, deformities of body and abortions of intellect excepted, than the disdainful and fastidious censors of our common nature are willing to admit'.[235] Godwin appears to be using deformity as (a physiological concept) alongside intellectual impairment as a way to delineate a common concept of capacity. In this, and in Godwin's discussion of capacity more broadly, we may be seeing the beginnings of the grouping together of intellectual and physical impairments that are present in the modern idea of disability.

## Conclusion

For Godwin, those with physical and intellectual incapacities are a subset of an unnamed larger group that he sees as in need of enablement in order to contribute to the general good. His definition of a beneficial social contribution prescribes a set of abilities that adversely affect the inclusion of people with physical and cognitive incapacities in his proposed political system. Godwin attaches benefits to capacities, and creates both a hierarchy and a rhetoric of capacity. These inform social value and make incapacity a social problem. Godwin's measures are not norms or ideals, but his own set of general goods. He bases his emancipatory arguments concerning social deficits on his presumption that there is an indisputable wish to repair intellectual and physical incapacity. His solution to all types of social devaluation is for people to be enabled to become valuable. Lack of capacity constitutes an intractable problem in Godwin's system. His promotion of a dynamic understanding of human capacity, in which capacities are variable according to context and will, and his frequent use of automata and disembodied consciousness, are tactics that reinforce the impression that psychosomatic wholeness is essential for social value. This understanding of capacity possibly motivates Godwin's conjecture that one day, when reason is in the ascendancy, mankind will become immortal and people will be able to heal themselves with the power of thought. In the context of Godwin's attitude towards capacity, this aspiration is less an eccentric and idle speculation (as has traditionally been thought), and more in line with a system of political justice that defines utility in terms of a particular range of physical and intellectual capacities.

Reading Godwin with attention to capacity reveals a man impatient with physical and intellectual limitation. As Scott Jeungel points out, 'Godwin's political program necessarily and systematically attempts to attenuate the role of corporeality in human behaviour' to the extent that the human body 'would seem to be an encumbrance in the rational progress of man, a monstrous freight given to appetite, susceptible to disease, gravitating towards decay'.[236] Furthermore, Godwin's interest in capacity was not lost on those who satirized his work. Elizabeth Hamilton, for instance, gives the following Godwinian speech to Vallaton:

> When our minds, purified from every narrow and illiberal prejudice, are enabled to take this large and comprehensive view, our regards will no longer be influenced by the mean consideration of friendship or affection; we shall no longer admire any casual virtue; but in exact and just proportion to the talents, the powers, and *capacity* of the object, will be our reverence and esteem.[237]

Godwin's views on the role of capacity in questions that concern social justice contrast sharply with those of Martha Nussbaum. Nussbaum's capabilities approach identifies central requirements or 'core social entitlements' for life with dignity, suggesting that these outcomes are the minimum for social justice.[238] Capabilities are not the means by which a society improves, but the 'general goals' in themselves, with each person being 'treated as an end' in themselves.[239] In contrast, Godwin treats individuals as a means to an end. For Nussbaum, the political goal is capability (in the sense of having the opportunity) and not functioning (in the sense of capacity). The capabilities approach is 'not intended to provide a complete account of social justice', however, and Nussbaum leaves open the question of how to handle 'issues of justice and distribution'.[240] Nussbaum, like Godwin, is not a contractarian; she dismisses this theory as creating fundamental problems through its metaphor of exchange. Unlike Godwin, however, she finds utility problematic in that it sets aside personal preferences and aims for contentment without realizing that active striving is an important part of human flourishing.[241]

Godwin's views on deformity as an aesthetic are quite distinct from his views on deformity in its physiological sense (which accord with his views on capacity). While he does not explicitly design his political goals around aesthetic concepts, he follows convention in regarding certain ideas as attractive (such as the beauty of equality) and others as 'disfigured and distorted' (such as the inconsistencies in the customary attribution of some actions as virtuous and others as not).[242] Godwin thinks that vice is, over time, impressed upon faces,[243] although he distances himself from the aesthetic interests that more popularly characterize the science of physiognomy.

It is striking that a figure who is so devoted to liberty and justice should include so much implicit and explicit ableism (and what we might call 'deformism'[244]) in his work. These perspectives are typical of the time, but Godwin often shows intentionality in his ableism, and, on occasion, chooses not to accept the inclusive implications of some of his arguments.[245] Although he is explicit that one's capacities do not affect moral equality, Godwin allows himself to contradict this position in several important ways: in the hierarchy of capacity exemplified in the Fénelon case, in his requirement that people should be physically and intellectually independent, and in his commitment to able-bodied and able-minded general goods. Many of his ideas on the subject of capacity are inconsistent. For example, he rejects the common idea that strength relates to intelligence, but argues, nonetheless, that strong bodies and minds are necessary for rational autonomy.[246] Godwin suggests that class does not determine capacity, but argues that aristocrats as a group are born with physical and intellectual limitations. Godwin's work as a whole provides evidence that late eighteenth-century writing on social equality shows a deep interest in capacity, and, as we shall explore in the next chapter, he is not alone in promoting gender, class, and race equality in ways that are disadvantageous to groups he deems to have limited capacities.

## CHAPTER 2

# Invigorating Women
## Female Weakness in the Work of Mary Wollstonecraft

Who can recount the misery, which many unfortunate beings, whose minds and bodies are equally weak, suffer in such situations – unable to work, and ashamed to beg?[1]

Mary Wollstonecraft's question is not about an impoverished non-able-minded and non-able-bodied person, but about an able-minded and able-bodied financially dependent woman whose brother has just married. In this scenario, set out in *A Vindication of the Rights of Woman* (1792), the brother's wife, whose education has not equipped her to think or feel that the two women are in a similar position, 'is displeased at seeing the property of *her* children lavished on an helpless sister'.[2] If the two had been 'differently educated', Wollstonecraft supposes, the wife would have demonstrated more sympathy, and the sister 'might have been able to struggle for herself instead of eating the bitter bread of dependence'.[3] In Wollstonecraft's view, the sister and the wife both perform the dominant social roles of being female, or what I shall, for convenience, term 'the culturally feminine woman'.[4] Neither woman can support herself financially, Wollstonecraft argues, because each is intellectually and physically weakened by her cultural context. The case of the dependent sister raises important questions about the use of weakness in emancipation arguments. In what ways is the culturally feminine woman 'weak'? Is culturally derived weakness the same as other kinds of impairment? Do Wollstonecraft's emancipation arguments for men and women include people whose weaknesses are not culturally derived? To what extent is the stance that Wollstonecraft takes shared with the contemporaries she influenced, such as Eliza Fenwick and Mary Hays?

Douglas Baynton points out, in his discussion of nineteenth-century American suffragist literature, that historians of women's rights 'have given their attention entirely to gender inequality and not at all to the construction and maintenance of cultural hierarchies based on disability' that are prevalent in the arguments for rights.[5] Baynton suggests that 'disability figured not just in arguments *for* the inequality of women and minorities but also in the arguments *against* those inequalities', and that the ableist assumptions in these debates were 'rarely challenged'.[6] According to Baynton, the suffragists used three main arguments that relate to disability: 'one, women were not disabled and therefore deserved the vote; two, women were being erroneously and slanderously classed with disabled people, with those who were legitimately denied suffrage; and three, women were not naturally or inherently disabled but were *made* disabled by inequality – suffrage would ameliorate or cure these disabilities'.[7] Something similar is true in the case of the eighteenth and early nineteenth centuries, though 'disability' is not the operative category. While Wollstonecraft has been lauded for the arguments she makes about women's capacities, she has, conversely, been criticized for her characterization of fashionable women as weak and fashionable men as effeminized. Critics see this as misogyny[8] and homophobia.[9] These assessments of Wollstonecraft leave unquestioned and unexamined her negative assumptions about capacity, however, and miss the opportunity for understanding eighteenth-century concepts of pre-disability and what Baynton sees as 'the construction and maintenance of cultural hierarchies based on' them.[10] Although Wollstonecraft does not directly push for women's enfranchisement, and does not use 'disability' as a category, she makes claims for women's capacities as qualifiers for equality, and denounces corporeal, intellectual, and emotional weakness as a culturally derived imposition.

The following discussion of her work will examine the ways in which Wollstonecraft depicts the culturally feminine woman as physically, intellectually, and emotionally weak; and will show that Wollstonecraft makes negative presuppositions about weakness and its personal and social effects, and about what she regards as its inauthenticity. Additionally, Wollstonecraft criticizes misogynistic cultures that produce women's weakness on the grounds that the celebration of weakness is incongruous in a culture that does not tend to view weakness positively. Wollstonecraft comes to the conclusion that female weakness is either feigned or avoidable, that it is unnatural, and that people who are weak live unhappy and non-useful lives. Furthermore, she defines freedom in terms of economic, intellectual, physical, political, and domestic independence, and uses physical vigour as a shorthand for this. Wollstonecraft promotes physical and mental strength as justifying equality, and as central to her concept of freedom, in order to reinforce her point that culturally enforced weakness has detrimental personal and social effects. She recognizes some positive personal and social consequences of authentic illness, however, and these accounts of illness are developed in the context of non-hierarchical and mutually sustaining partnerships that seem to be unavailable in other circumstances. For Wollstonecraft, illness is a unique state in which social interdependence is privileged over independence. On the few occasions when Wollstonecraft offers an idea of authentic weakness that is not related to illness, she does not use women in her examples. Nevertheless, these examples signal the possibility that Wollstonecraft regards men with authentic physical impairments as socially valuable. In the course of her discussions, Wollstonecraft often articulates a combined moral and aesthetic theory that perpetuates culturally dominant ideas in which deformity is associated with vice, and beauty with virtue; and she maintains the conventional idea that beauty and deformity are opposites. Her more developed account of the moral aspects of beauty, however, leaves her with a version of deformity (inferred through its position as an opposite) that is at odds with some of the sensitivities that she expresses towards people with deformities.

## Cultural Femininity and Weakness

> I once knew a weak woman of fashion who was more than commonly proud of her delicacy and sensibility. She thought a distinguishing taste and puny appetite the height of all human perfection, and acted accordingly. – I have seen this weak sophisticated being neglect all the duties of life, yet recline with self-complacency on a sofa, and boast of her want of appetite as proof of delicacy that extended to, or, perhaps, arose from, her exquisite sensibility: for it is difficult to render intelligible such ridiculous jargon.[11]

The weakness of the culturally feminine woman is, for Wollstonecraft, not merely metaphorical or figurative, although she sometimes uses weakness in this way. Wollstonecraft suggests that the culturally feminine woman *is* physically and intellectually weak, and that this weakness has negative personal and social consequences. The terms she uses to describe the attributes of these women include 'feeble', 'fragile', 'helpless', 'delicate', 'indolent', 'enervated', 'defective', 'irrational', 'imbecilic', and their cognates. Some of these terms are staples of the discourse of sensibility and often feature in the gothic novel of the period.[12] Wollstonecraft argues that these incapacities are not intrinsic to women, but are the result of a coercive culture. The terms she uses to describe the effects of these impairments include 'dependent', 'subordinate', 'helpless', 'passive', 'useless', 'infantine', 'degraded', 'fettered', 'enslaved', 'undignified', and their cognates.

Wollstonecraft models her idea of the culturally feminine woman on the ideals of womanhood outlined in Milton, Rousseau, the conduct-book writer Dr John Gregory, and from her own observations of the women around her. Rousseau and Gregory, along with many other writers, she protests, have celebrated the weakness of women, and in so doing have 'contributed to render women more artificial, weak characters, than they would otherwise have been; and, consequently, more useless members of society'.[13] She focuses her attack, in *A Vindication of the Rights of Woman*, on five arguments that are commonly made against developing women's capacities: (1) that women are naturally weak, physically and intellectually; (2) that they have inherited their subordinate social position from Eve; (3) that underdeveloped capacities make women attractive to men; (4) that women have sufficient influence without developing their capacities; and (5) that the development of these capacities runs counter to the female virtues of innocence, modesty, chastity, patience, good humour, docility, and obedience.

Wollstonecraft addresses these arguments point for point, but the central principle guiding her refutations is that the underdevelopment of the capacities of women, along with extrinsic cultural factors that cause dependence, means that culturally feminine women are not free. These capacities are the same capacities that she suggests should be shared by all human beings who are free: the 'bodily and mental powers' or, in other words, the capacity for rational thought and the ability for consequent physical activity.[14] Wollstonecraft follows Locke in her assumption that liberty is a matter of both intrinsic and extrinsic capacity. In his discussion of action theory, in *Essay Concerning Human Understanding*, Locke makes the case that physical incapacity is an impediment to freedom.[15] He argues that the inability to move due to a palsy is the same as the inability to move due to being in the stocks. For Locke, 'there is want of *Freedom*' in both scenarios.[16] Locke's action theory informs his political theory.[17] The physical component of independence (that is, having no bodily impediments to action) is also an important part of Wollstonecraft's understanding of freedom. Wollstonecraft implies that someone cannot be free if they have the capacity to act but coercion prevents them from acting; and they cannot be free if they do not have the capacity. Her idea of freedom, then, is tied to her understanding of capacity: freedom is the ability to act with independence in three senses: social, intellectual, and physical.[18]

Wollstonecraft counters argument (1), that women are naturally weak in body and mind, with the claim that nature proves that their intellectual and physical underdevelopment is artificially imposed (Baynton's third argument). So, women are, in general, physically weaker than men, but 'men have increased that inferiority till women are almost sunk below the standard of rational creatures'.[19] She offers as evidence 'the woman who strengthens her body and exercises her mind', and who will, 'by managing her family and practising various virtues, become the friend, and not the humble dependent of her husband'.[20] Having established that women's natural weakness can be surmounted, Wollstonecraft concentrates on the personal and social gains of physical and mental strength and makes them requirements for equality and virtue. Significantly, physical and mental strength have a number of important consequences here: they enable a woman to become virtuous, to develop a married relationship that is mutual, and to become equal with men. Rousseau's Sophie, for instance, is dismissed as a 'grossly unnatural'[21] reminder of the reasons why women 'must return to nature and equality'.[22] Wollstonecraft regards Rousseau's 'arguments, which he pretends to draw from the indications of nature', as in reality deriving from 'pride and sensuality', and she claims the natural argument for herself.[23] She also attacks the natural weakness argument on the grounds that the incapacities of the culturally feminine woman are inauthentic. She believes them to be so for two reasons. Firstly, because these incapacities are avoidable. Therefore, when sedentary pursuits such as sewing 'render the majority of women sickly', Wollstonecraft regards this sickliness as inauthentic because it is caused by a culturally imposed and false notion of femininity.[24] Secondly, the capacities of the culturally feminine woman are inauthentic because they are feigned: women '*affect* weakness under the name of delicacy', and their inappropriate education gives the '*appearance* of weakness'.[25]

Wollstonecraft's interest in authenticity is part of a wider appreciation for sincerity that is a major feature of 1790s radical literature, though it is not exclusive to it. She comments, for example, on the lack of authenticity involved in following fashions. The contemporary fashion for appreciating rural scenes, Wollstonecraft suggests, appears to be little more than 'artificial sentiment, rather inspired by poetry and romances, than a real perception of the beauties of nature'.[26] Natural beauty, she argues, is no longer 'forcibly felt, when civilization and its canker-worm, luxury, have made considerable advances'.[27] Elsewhere we see this distaste for insincerity in Eliza Fenwick's *Secresy* (1795). This novel centres on authenticity, and, particularly, on authentic feelings as well as authentic capacities. Fenwick draws on Wollstonecraft's ideas to explore multiple ways in which inauthenticity is destructive, and creates the narrative circumstances that enable her heroine, Sibella Valmont, to be at once an example of a

dependent woman and of a liberated woman. Sibella's early education
emphasizes naturalness, openness, freedom, and equality, and this is
closely followed by a period of dependence in which she demonstrates
her ability to think beyond the limitations of her situation. Although
Sibella is 'born to the exercise of no will; and to the exercise of no duties
but submission', she is educated for a brief period by Mr Bonneville, who
teaches her that she is rational, and that she is 'an unimpaired *one* of the
vast brotherhood of human kind'.[28] Sibella is vigorous, healthy, and
independently minded; and, as such she is regarded as an eccentric
exception by the few people who meet her. Her friend, Caroline Ash-
burn, describes her as receiving 'some singular lessons on the value of
sincerity, independence, courage, and capacity' that result in her 'rather
think[ing] herself born to navigate ships and build edifices, than to come
into a world for no other purpose, than to twist her hair into ringlets,
learn to be feeble, and to find her feet too hallowed to tread on the
ground beneath her'.[29] Sibella's uncle, Mr Valmont, 'with his wire-
drawn principles about female weakness and female obedience', and
her aunt, a 'coquettish' woman whom we are told 'droops into an
hypochondriac', hide her fortune from her, and she believes herself to
be financially dependent on them.[30] Valmont imagines that this feigned
financial dependence will make her comply with their marriage plans
for her.

   Sibella's authenticity, and her rejection of cultural norms for women,
are prized by the novel's man of feeling, Arthur Murden. He instructs her
to 'go not into the world, where artifice might assail and example corrupt
that noble sincerity'.[31] Arthur, who is disguised as a ghost when he says
this, does not seem to live by this code himself. Sibella dismisses him as
using 'pretences of falsehood and guile' to gain access to her.[32] Fenwick,
like Wollstonecraft, skilfully repurposes eighteenth-century stock characters in order to emphasize the social benefits of authenticity. Her vignettes
of fashionable and wealthy women repeatedly employ the coquette as a
critique of weak women. Lady Laura Bowden, for instance, has 'a delicate
languor [that] pervades her manners and this is generally honoured with
the name of sensibility. I am apt to call it affectation; for the sensibility that
I understand and admire, is extreme only in proportion to the greatness of
the occasion; it does not waste itself in vapours, nor is it ever on the watch
for wasps and spiders'.[33] The fashion for authenticity and sincerity is a
central concern for Romanticism more broadly, and the inauthenticity of
female weakness is frequently alluded to in the radical novel throughout
the 1790s.[34]

Wollstonecraft, like other radical writers of the period (such as Robert Bage and William Godwin) also uses inauthenticity and weakness to attack the wealthy. She distinguishes between inherited wealth and wealth gained by commercial means, but invokes incapacity in her condemnation of both. For example, she observes that people who inherit their wealth 'seldom exert the locomotive faculty of body or mind'.[35] Wollstonecraft characterizes the 'victim' of hereditary wealth as someone who 'stalk[s] in masquerade, dragging from one scene of dissipation to another the nerveless limbs that hang with stupid listlessness', and who rolls 'around the vacant eye which plainly tells us that there is no mind at home'.[36] She suggests, like Godwin, that unhealthy and luxurious lifestyles cause weakness, and that this weakness is comparable to that seen in the culturally feminine woman: 'Women are, in common with men, rendered weak and luxurious by the relaxing pleasures which wealth procures.'[37] Furthermore, Wollstonecraft argues that money and commercial business weakens and effeminizes men: 'wealth enervates men' and 'wealth and female softness equally tend to debase mankind, and are produced by the same cause'.[38] She comments on the moral consequences of chasing after wealth, in *Letters Written during a Short Residence in Sweden, Norway, and Denmark* (1796). Here, Wollstonecraft recalls a story told to her by John Dickinson about the 'characteristics of the Hamburgers'.[39] She quotes Dickinson as saying '"you will not meet with a man who has any calf to his leg; body and soul, muscles and heart, are equally shriveled up by a thirst of gain"'.[40] Concentrating on acquiring wealth, through obsessive dedication to business, causes bodily and emotional weakness. Devotion to commerce is so unnatural that 'whole knots of men [are] turned into machines' by it.[41] She wonders 'whether a nation can go back to the purity of manners ... when, emasculated by pleasure, the luxuries of prosperity are become the wants of nature?'[42] Wollstonecraft views weakness caused by wealth as 'false', unnatural, and as generating a 'negative supineness'.[43]

Wollstonecraft spends a surprising amount of time linking wealth to overeating. As Eva Badowska observes, 'the image of an appetitive body ... its hungers, its tastes, as well as its (uncertain) boundaries' pervades *A Vindication of the Rights of Woman*.[44] Wollstonecraft regards overeating as immoral, and as the cause of physical and intellectual impairments. For example, she asserts that, in people who overeat, 'the constitution is insensibly destroyed, and old age comes on, loaded with infirmities', and the mind becomes 'oppressed, and becomes a slave of the body, or both are listless and inactive'.[45] Badowska observes that 'Wollstonecraft's critique of excessive (and thus "unnatural") appetitiveness, and her concomitant attempt to reinvent bourgeois femininity as a negation of gluttony and a new refinement of the body' has a wider enlightenment purpose.[46] She argues that Wollstonecraft's political aim is to reject 'aristocratic anorexia' and accept 'renunciation as a natural, non-performative condition' that has an aesthetic and an ethical purpose for the 'rational middle-class' woman.[47] Badowska argues that

> it is not the argumentative dimension of *A Vindication of the Rights of Woman* that produces the figural specter of bodies and appetites, rather, the drift of Wollstonecraft's metaphors and narrative digressions, their seemingly compulsive character, gives rise to this appetitive undercurrent: in Wollstonecraft's writing, women 'eat the bitter bread of dependence' and become 'standing dishes to which every glutton may have access'.[48]

I argue, instead, that appetite is part of Wollstonecraft's argument *and* part of her figurative language. The blurred boundaries between figural and non-figural descriptions in Wollstonecraft's work signal her interest in the blurred distinction between women's weakness being both figural (cultural) and non-figural (literal). Badowska concludes, somewhat differently from me, that *A Vindication of the Rights of Woman* 'associates the anorexic syndrome with a repudiation of figurative language'.[49]

Wollstonecraft uses weakness and obesity to challenge what she perceives to be the oppression of monarchical government. The obesity of Louis XVI, she observes, made him 'sluggish' and indolent.[50] His person is, she remarks, 'in itself very disgusting' and is 'rendered more so by gluttony, and a total disregard of delicacy, and even decency in his apartments'.[51] Obesity, as an inauthentic impairment, signals the moral degeneracy of the monarch. Wollstonecraft describes Marie-Antoinette as a woman at the mercy of the King's 'devouring passion', an image in which appetite and sexual desire become one.[52] Furthermore, intellectual weakness assists Wollstonecraft in her denouncement of the French monarchy. She suggests that the French system of government 'produces idiotism into the noble stem' of the generations of a population, because hereditary power is at odds with 'the mental superiority that naturally raises a man above his fellows'.[53] Just as Wollstonecraft argues that misogynistic cultures are responsible for 'weakening the mind' in women, and forcing them into 'imbecility', so the effects of monarchical oppression are indistinguishable from mental weakness. She writes of Christian VII, the Danish king, that he is 'a notorious debauchee, and an idiot into the bargain'.[54] Wollstonecraft describes him as a 'puppet of a monarch' manipulated by his foreign minister.[55] King Christian sits 'with vacant eye, erect, receiving the homage of courtiers, who mock him with a shew of respect'.[56] Moreover, she links overeating to political oppression and sexual excess often in circuitous ways. For example, she suggests that boys who are sent away to school replace the loss of their families with eating, and 'very early rush into libertinism which destroys the constitution before it is formed; hardening the heart as it weakens the understanding'.[57] Wollstonecraft reinforces this view with an appeal to nature: 'Nature must ever be the standard of taste, the gauge of appetite – yet how grossly is nature insulted by the voluptuary.'[58]

Wollstonecraft addresses the argument that women have inherited their subordinate position from Eve (argument 2) in her discussion of Milton. Milton, she suggests, offers contradictory accounts of the relative power of Adam and Eve.[59] Eve is both the person to be obeyed and the person who must be obedient. Milton's description of Eve as a 'fair defect/Of nature' signals to Wollstonecraft that beauty tempts women to gain power on a false basis.[60] Milton's phrase 'fair defect' implies that woman is by nature both physically beautiful and morally dangerous; that she is a defective man in the Aristotelian sense; and that she is, as Robert Jungman supposes, a rebel or defector 'from the party of God and Adam'.[61] Wollstonecraft does not concede, however, that moral defect is inherent in women, but argues that it is a consequence of the misuse of female beauty. She uses an aesthetic argument to reinforce this position. Milton's 'fair defect', she suggests, implies that the underdevelopment of a capacity is itself beautiful. When women are talked about in this way, Wollstonecraft observes, they are 'exalted by their inferiority', and men 'are most inclined to tyrannize over, and despise, the very weakness they cherish'.[62] Weakness and oxymoronic defect are at the heart of Wollstonecraft's emancipation argument. Men, she observes, 'soften their insults' with such 'heterogeneous associations, as fair *defects*, amiable *weaknesses*, etc.'[63] Men may argue that the lack of women's rights is a direct consequence of 'inheriting, in a lineal descent from the first fair defect in nature, the sovereignty of beauty', but in submitting to this argument, women resign 'the natural rights' that have been given to them by virtue of being rational beings.[64]

Wollstonecraft counters the contention that underdeveloped capacities make women attractive to men (argument 3) by suggesting that physical and intellectual weakness, deformity, and illness are unattractive. For Wollstonecraft, the fashion for weak women is at odds with the cultural urge towards perfectibility. Femininity, she argues, prevents the body 'from attaining that grace and beauty which relaxed half-formed limbs never exhibit'.[65] According to Wollstonecraft, culturally feminine women are 'so infatuated as to be proud of a defect', and are so deluded by 'a romantic species of modesty' that they 'sometimes boast of their weakness, cunningly obtaining power by playing on the *weakness* of men'.[66] In this way, women sacrifice their virtue for 'temporary gratifications'.[67] Women are, she asserts, prevented from developing their physical capacities by fear of being thought to be unattractive. They are afraid that bodily strength will take away 'from their feminine graces; and from that lovely weakness the source of their undue power'.[68] They destroy their bodies with 'mistaken notions of beauty and female excellence' in order to pursue incapacity as an aesthetic goal.[69] The widespread misperception of the aesthetics of the body, Wollstonecraft asserts, has a detrimental effect on the body's functioning. She counsels that girls should never 'be allowed to imbibe the pernicious notion that a defect can, by any chemical process of reasoning, become an excellence'.[70] Women's adherence to these aesthetic preferences for weakness, she argues, has a direct effect on their intellectual development, and, consequently, in turn, on their bodies: 'False notions of beauty and delicacy stop the growth of their limbs', such that women cannot 'attain the vigour necessary to enable them to throw off that factitious character'.[71] Wollstonecraft maintains that weakness is incongruously understood as beautiful, arguing that beauty requires health and strength (as I shall explore in the section on deformity below).

In making her case, Wollstonecraft reiterates the arguments that Burke rejects in *A Philosophical Enquiry*. Burke suggests that beauty in the female sex 'always carries with it an idea of weakness and imperfection'.[72] Using the argument from nature, Burke asserts that women instinctively feign illness in order to make themselves seem more beautiful. They 'learn to lisp, to totter in their walk, to counterfeit weakness, and even sickness. In all this they are guided by nature'.[73] Burke argues, moreover, that 'an air of robustness and strength is very prejudicial to beauty. An appearance of *delicacy*, and even of fragility, is almost essential to it'.[74] He is keen to stress, however, that this kind of fragility is unrelated to poor health.

> The beauty of women is considerably owing to their weakness, or delicacy, and is even enhanced by their timidity, a quality of mind analogous to it. I would not here be understood to say, that weakness betraying very bad health has any share in beauty; but the ill effect of this is not because it is weakness, but because the ill state of health which produces such weakness alters the other conditions of beauty; the parts in such a case collapse; the bright colour, the *lumen purpureum juevente* ['glowing light of youth'] is gone; and the fine variation is lost in wrinkles, sudden breaks, and right lines.[75]

The points about weakness as delicacy that Burke makes with approval, Wollstonecraft makes with disapproval. In her direct response to this passage in Burke, Wollstonecraft asks, 'where is the dignity, the infallibility of sensibility, in the fair ladies' who witness the torture of enslaved people?[76] The fact that white women can view these experiences shows that their sensibility is merely counterfeit. Addressing Burke directly, Wollstonecraft writes:

> you may have convinced them that *littleness* and *weakness* are the very essence of beauty; and that the Supreme Being, in giving women beauty in the most supereminent degree, seemed to command them, by the powerful voice of Nature, not to cultivate the moral virtues that might change to excite respect, and interfere with the pleasing sensations they were created to inspire.[77]

The weakness and timidity associated with culturally feminine women are, however, antipathetic to the cultivation of virtue, Wollstonecraft concludes.

Wollstonecraft dismisses the argument that women can use their influence without developing their capacities (argument 4) on the grounds that influence without reasoning is an 'illegitimate power, which women obtain, by degrading themselves'.[78] This form of power derives from the display of weakness and from 'the arbitrary power of beauty'.[79] The power of beauty is not truly power, because it has no firm basis. Furthermore, power of this kind does not allow for freedom, which requires independent thought. Wollstonecraft acknowledges that, in the contemporary cultural climate, a 'woman of talents, if she be not absolutely ugly, will always obtain great power' through her influence; but she laments that even this type of woman is 'raised by the weakness of her sex' and not 'by the exercise of reason' or 'the cultivation of the understanding'.[80] This non-rational means for negotiating power takes multiple forms, and Wollstonecraft gives many examples to indicate that women are weak and non-human when they do this. For example, 'the sexual weakness that makes woman depend on man for a subsistence produces a kind of cattish affection which leads a wife to purr about her husband as she would about any man who fed and caressed her'.[81] This 'winning softness' is paradoxical in its effect, since it 'governs by obeying'.[82] These women are like queens, and 'the regal homage which they receive is so intoxicating' that it is difficult to relinquish.[83] Wollstonecraft concludes that culturally feminine women govern using 'sinister methods'.[84] Furthermore, the duplicitousness and cunning required to do this, she argues, does not allow women to be virtuous. The regal allusion is an important one.

It allows Wollstonecraft to link the call for women's emancipation to the revolutionary changes in France. Men are the tyrannical monarchs who seek 'blind obedience' from weak women who are the oppressed masses.[85] Women are also like the tyrannical sovereigns themselves, however. Wollstonecraft suggests that they have been 'duped by their lovers, as princes by their ministers, whilst dreaming that they reigned over them', and do not realize that their power is illusory and can end abruptly.[86]

The final argument about impairment and cultural femininity that Wollstonecraft addresses (argument 5) centres on the claim that female virtues (innocence, modesty, chastity, patience, good humour, docility, and obedience) are dependent on weakness. In order to counter this, Wollstonecraft proposes (1) that liberty is a requirement for virtue ('Liberty is the mother of virtue'[87]); (2) that liberty requires certain intrinsic and extrinsic capacities; and (3) that the kinds of virtues that are deemed appropriate for women in a state of inequality are not in a strict sense virtues at all. Wollstonecraft is determined 'especially to prove, that the weakness of mind and body [in women], which men have endeavoured, impelled by various motives, to perpetuate, prevents their discharging the peculiar duty of their sex: for when weakness of body will not permit them to suckle their children, and weakness of mind makes them spoil their tempers – is woman in a natural state?'[88] Women can become virtuous through performing maternal duties, and weakness, Wollstonecraft argues, prevents this obligation.

Wollstonecraft spends a great deal of time establishing the interrelationships between liberty, independence, nature, intellect, and physical strength, such that all are necessary before it is possible to act virtuously. For example, alert to the contradictions surrounding chaste behaviour, one of the traditional female virtues, Wollstonecraft recasts feminine languor (that is widely read as a sign of modesty) as a sign of a sexual appetite. When men prevent women from developing their capacities, she argues, they produce 'weak and enervated women who particularly catch the attention of libertines'.[89] She observes that 'libertines will . . . exclaim, that women would be unsexed by acquiring strength of body and mind, and that beauty, soft bewitching beauty! would no longer adorn the daughters of men'.[90] Drawing on the idea of the harem to reinforce her point, Wollstonecraft asks, 'can they supinely dream life away in the lap of pleasure, or the languor of weariness, rather than assert their claim to pursue reasonable pleasures and render themselves conspicuous by practising the virtues which dignify mankind?'[91] Such women are, Wollstonecraft asserts, fit only for the seraglio, and she advises that they should set aside these supposed 'graces of helplessness' and 'make us respect the human body as a majestic pile fit to receive a noble inhabitant'.[92] Moreover, Wollstonecraft finds it absurd that dancing vigorously is held to be a sign of sexual appetite, when languor and idleness more properly characterize the woman who is sexually persuadable. It makes no sense, she asserts, to curtail a woman's physical capacities on the grounds that libertines may draw inferences about one's interest in sexual matters: 'Dr Gregory ... recommends dissimulation, and advises an innocent girl to give the lie to her feelings, and not dance with spirit, when gaiety of heart would make her feet eloquent without making her gestures immodest.'[93] Languid women cannot be chaste, Wollstonecraft suggests, because a state of dependence makes them sell their bodies in marriage, which she famously sees as a form 'legal prostitution'.[94] Women's weakness, Wollstonecraft concludes, is partially caused by a misunderstanding of modesty.

Wollstonecraft explores the social effects of female weakness, and the potential for women to transcend their cultural position and develop strength, in her first novel, *Mary: A Fiction* (1788). As the advertisement to the novel puts it: 'In an artless tale, without episodes, the mind of a woman [Mary], who has thinking powers is displayed. The female organs have been thought too weak for this arduous employment; and experience seems to justify the assertion. Without arguing physically about *possibilities* – in a fiction, such a being may be allowed to exist.'[95] Mary's mother Eliza, who is a 'gentle, fashionable girl, with a kind of indolence in her temper', contrasts with her daughter, who has eschewed 'female acquirements', spending her time trying 'to discern what end her various faculties were destined to pursue'.[96] Eliza's 'sickly, die-away languor' signals her dependence.[97] Her voice is but 'the shadow of a sound, and she had, to complete her delicacy, so relaxed her nerves, that she became a mere nothing'.[98] The narrator intends Eliza to stand as a paradigm case of the culturally feminine woman, and remarks that '[m]any such noughts are there in the female world'.[99] Eliza's education has impaired her faculties to the extent that she is regarded by the narrator as incapable of virtue. She is unable to care for herself or for others, she is socially dependent, she reads without thinking, and is so indolent that she becomes ill. The only concern Eliza is able to show is for her dogs, and even this is motivated by vanity. The dogs give her 'an opportunity of lisping out the prettiest French expressions of ecstatic fondness, in accents that had never been attuned by tenderness'.[100] Eliza's underdeveloped capacities, Wollstonecraft suggests, are the product of her education and of the misogynistic cultures surrounding her.

Although brief, the portrait of Eliza is significant because it draws on several of Wollstonecraft's arguments in favour of developing women's strength. Eliza's weakness is initially feigned; and her imitation of weakness causes her illness. She becomes consumptive after her son and daughter are born. Wollstonecraft would deem her weakness to be inauthentic in two senses: it is feigned and avoidable. Wollstonecraft switches seamlessly between the two types of inauthenticity, attributing Eliza's neglect of her children to her feminine indolence *and* to her illness. The narrator imputes Eliza's not 'recovering strength' after her pregnancies to her '[w]ant of exercise', and her inactivity ('vegetating')[101] is caused by her femininity.[102] This overlap of weakness, illness, and femininity is also evident in the response of Eliza's husband. He cannot tell the difference between 'a lingering complaint' and feminine charms.[103] Consequently, he 'visibly harassed' Eliza when her illness interfered with his pleasure seeking.[104] Furthermore, Eliza's husband is at fault because does not advise her to 'exert herself' in order to restore her health. He imagines, instead, that she 'was only grown still more whimsical', and that the illness was not authentic.[105] Eliza's illness has two ironic consequences. Firstly, it enables and prompts her husband's infidelity, and so serves as an example of why feminine indolence is not a source of power. He prefers the 'ruddy glow of health' on the faces of his 'pretty tenants' to 'his wife's countenance'.[106] Secondly, Eliza's illness occasions her daughter's freedom of thought, as she is unable to condition her daughter into becoming a culturally feminine woman.

## Weakness Rhetoric and Wollstonecraft's Critics

Wollstonecraft's recent critics read her account of female weakness in different ways. One group suggests that Wollstonecraft uses weakness to undermine other binaries (such as male/female and mind/body).[107] Mary Poovey, the earliest of this group to comment, understands weakness as an 'ideology at work' in Wollstonecraft's 'society and in herself', and argues that Wollstonecraft 'rejects the female experience of helplessness and frustration for the defiant bourgeois assertion that one can, in fact, be anything one wants'.[108] Poovey observes that one of Wollstonecraft's important contributions to feminist thought is her 'important realization in *The Rights of Woman* ... that the attitudes and expectations that perpetuate female weakness are institutionalized in the very texts that purport to be "authorities" and even by the values encoded in the language'.[109] To follow feminine propriety is to 'court an absolute loss of control'.[110]

Adriana Craciun characterizes *A Vindication of the Rights of Woman* as primarily a 'debate on the nature of strength and weakness'.[111] Craciun takes her reading in a different direction from Poovey's, concluding that Wollstonecraft views weakness and strength as social constructs. Craciun observes that for Wollstonecraft '*strength*, was in fact a construction', and she saw it 'as a quality that both established and destabilized boundaries between sex and class, making it both dangerous and potentially revolutionary, and thus absolutely central to her project'.[112] Craciun reads Wollstonecraft's attack on women's weakness, and her association of strength with masculine force, as placing strong women in an ambiguously gendered space. Strength is, in Wollstonecraft's work, both masculine force *and* feminine forbearance; and so a call to strengthen is not straightforwardly a call to masculinize. Wollstonecraft, Craciun reminds us, appeals for 'increased female strength while conceding a natural (and conditional) male superiority'.[113] This appeal gives Craciun some unease as she outlines the potential feminist objections. For example, a call to strengthen can be 'dismissed by some as an end to femaleness and an absorption of the female body by the male universal, sometimes disguised as the androgynous body'.[114] Wollstonecraft's occasional lack of clarity (over whether she is engaging with masculine or feminine ideas of strength) is, Craciun observes, a deliberate attempt to undermine the gendering of strength as male (the male/female binary).[115] Wollstonecraft, Craciun acknowledges, is actively engaged in a campaign for 'corporeal reform' that 'suggests a possibility for physical equality as an additional means for gaining political equality, while grounding political and philosophical critique of female oppression in the body'.[116]

Laurie Finke offers a different binary (reason/emotion), and argues that weakness rhetoric critiques a 'patriarchal culture' that is beholden to the 'dialectics of eighteenth-century philosophy'.[117] Developing Poovey's arguments on the importance of Wollstonecraft's distinctive rhetorical style (which mixes traditional binaries), Finke proposes that Wollstonecraft legitimately employs weakness rhetoric as a 'strategy . . . [that] exposes the neat dialectics of patriarchy as a tool of oppression'.[118] Finke suggests that there are tensions between masculine (objective, ambitious, orderly, and abstract) and feminine (emotional, cautious, weak, and dependent) rhetoric in *A Vindication of the Rights of Woman*. As Wendy Gunther-Canada puts it, 'Wollstonecraft's intellectual cross-dressing disrupts political discourse, and enables her to create and champion a new understanding of political rights and citizenship.'[119] Poovey and Finke read Wollstonecraft's rhetorical incongruities as powerfully combining the tools of the oppressor with the language of the oppressed. In other words, Wollstonecraft appropriates rhetoric to signal positions she intends to dismantle. Wollstonecraft, however, does not dismantle the strength/weakness binary, and neither critic is concerned about this. She leaves this binary intact in order to make the case that women are not naturally helpless, that celebrating their weakness is oppressive to them, and that women's weakness is detrimental to society as a whole. As Rosemarie Garland Thomson explains, 'such representations ultimately portray subjugated bodies not only as inadequate or unrestrained but at the same time as redundant and expendable'.[120]

Catherine Packham's study is principally concerned with the mind/body binary. She sees 'vitalism' ('the theory that life is generated and sustained through some form of non-mechanical force or power specific to it and located in living bodies')[121] as contributing to a debate that reoriented 'the account of the relationship between mind and body which was central to understandings of the human person at this time'.[122] Packham observes that 'sensibility shares with (or borrows from vitalist physiology a body narrative which emphasizes the same forms of automatic, unconscious physical response and independent somatic organization as are foregrounded in, and essential to, sensibility'.[123] She argues that Wollstonecraft's 'mutual association of material and moral weakness' almost suggests that 'virtue has a material being, or physical embodiment'.[124] Packham argues that Wollstonecraft understands sensibility as a bodily response inseparable from 'social and moral impulses'.[125] Sensibility manifests through '"nervous" responses [that] demonstrate and articulate its subject's sympathy and humanity'.[126] She reads Eliza as a character whose 'material delicacy ... does not extend to her mind'.[127] This kind of weakness is, Packham argues, entirely 'limited' to the body and 'confined ... to the corporeal'.[128] Her interpretation, however, leaves aside Wollstonecraft's suggestion that there is a causal relationship between feigning weakness and becoming weak, and does not recognize the exclusionary nature of Wollstonecraft's claims.

Several critics read the motivation for Wollstonecraft's arguments for female vigour as an absorption of bourgeois ideology[129] with its emphasis on individualism.[130] Poovey suggests, for instance, that Wollstonecraft 'is allying herself with the individualistic values of middle-class men and heaping scorn on the posture of helplessness, which she can see only as weakness and personal failure'.[131] She reads *A Vindication of the Rights of Woman* as 'pre-eminently' a 'bourgeois assault ... on self-indulgence and submission ... in the name of individual effort and proven merit, against aristocratic privilege and passivity'.[132] Moreover, Poovey criticizes Wollstonecraft for not realizing the extent to which 'the individual's situation – his or her own position within class, gender, economics, and history – really delimits freedom and virtually defines the "self"'.[133] This line of argument is not far from Michael Oliver's account of disability as a product of the ideology of individualism, though Oliver acknowledges that the political advancements gained by individualism come at the expense of people with disabilities. Poovey does not herself make the case that Wollstonecraft limits the notion of freedom by tying it to capacities. We see a similar argument about individualism in G. J. Barker-Benfield's interpretation of Wollstonecraft's stance on women's weakness. Barker-Benfield parallels the rise of prosperity in the eighteenth century with an 'embourgeoisement' that 'would give rise to a persistent, two hundred years lamentation over the declension in the activity and health of women'.[134] 'There is', he writes, 'a connection between embourgeoisement and sickness – real and feigned – in women.[135] Sickness was in some sense simply a development of invalidation, of weakness, and of incapacity, an exaggeration of that "set of immediately recognizable external behaviour traits" which distinguished ladyhood, a further "refinement" from the dross of work.'[136] Elsewhere Barker-Benfield expands his degenerative theory of Wollstonecraft's embourgeoisement to include the commonwealth and dissenting traditions, finding parallels to her weakness rhetoric in the work of Adam Ferguson and James Burgh.[137]

Reading Wollstonecraft through the framework of Foucault, Angela Keane understands her as an early critic of modern biopolitics. In Keane's view, Wollstonecraft recognized that capitalism was driving gender politics, and the central issue for her was the mind–body problem: 'women's minds [were alienated] from their bodies' and men were alienated from women.[138] For Keane, maternity is Wollstonecraft's key issue, and she comments on Wollstonecraft's observation about Danish bourgeois women, that 'they are rendered by maternity the "slaves of infants, enfeebling both body and mind"'.[139] Capitalism, Keane suggests, valued women's bodies as 'machines or as property, reproducer or commodity'.[140] Keane views the mind–body problem as part of the political landscape. Godwin's 'rational schemes for social improvement', Keane suggests, envisaged 'the triumph of the will over the body; a triumph which would, in a utopian future, make humanity's desires commensurate with their rational needs, and eradicate the present causes of human suffering, including the most recalcitrant reminders of the body's presence: disease and death'.[141] Keane argues, instead, that Wollstonecraft, because of her 'liberal philosophical inheritance',[142] could only conceive of the mind–body problem through the system she sought to challenge; and so Wollstonecraft could only ask for women to be valued as rational beings for their role as reproducers (or mothers). Keane understands that Wollstonecraft seeks a fantasy 'of independence from her body and from other bodies', and wishes for an 'imaginative transcendence ... which not only negates the need for other people (minds and bodies) but demands their elimination from the imagined scene, until matter becomes a figment of the mind's eye'.[143] Additionally, Keane reads Wollstonecraft's inability to get beyond the body as owing to her grounding in eighteenth-century sentimentalism – a form of experience in which 'the imagination functions as an extension of the body'.[144]

The final group of critics I shall discuss here are those who find Wollstonecraft's weakness rhetoric problematic on the grounds that her characterization of women as weak disparages them (Baynton's second argument).[145] Sandra Gubar addresses what she sees as the 'feminist misogyny' implied in Wollstonecraft's work, identifying her as the originator of a tenacious strand in feminism that, 'repeatedly and disconcertedly, associates the feminine with', amongst other traits, 'weakness, childishness ... [and] irrationality'.[146] Gubar takes Wollstonecraft to task for insinuating that femininity is 'a virus spreading corruption', 'an illness condemning its victim to madness', and 'like gangrene contaminating the healthy'.[147] Gubar's response to Wollstonecraft's sense of her own weakness is that it is part of a 'dialogue between self and soul', as well as a 'derogation of the feminine'.[148] Gubar dismisses what she sees as sexism in Wollstonecraft's account of 'debased ... femininity', and views it as 'the culturally induced schizophrenia of an anti-narcissist'.[149] Barbara Taylor similarly finds Wollstonecraft's characterization of women as weak to be misogynistic:

> The savagery of the denunciation is shocking. And while the feminist point behind it – the point to which the whole book tends – is that women are coerced into this debilitated condition by a male-dominated society, the rhetorical weight of Wollstonecraft's attack falls so heavily on her own sex as to make a reader begin to wonder whether the aim is less to free women than to abolish them.[150]

For Poovey, Craciun, and Finke, weakness is part of the array of bodily characteristics socially expected from women in the late eighteenth century, and Wollstonecraft is a pioneer in seeking to position vigour and strength as the signifier of a free mind and body. For Craciun, the feminist objection centres on the identification of women as deviating from a 'male universal'.[151] For Gubar and Taylor, the problem lies with the disparagement of women as weak. Claudia Johnson finds that Wollstonecraft's women 'are relentlessly degraded'.[152] Johnson adds to this her concern about Wollstonecraft's disparagement of men as weak, suggesting that 'a revulsion at degraded bodiliness animates virtually all of *Rights of Woman*'.[153] For disability studies scholars, though, the lack of acknowledgement of an implied able-bodied and able-minded universal, and of the negative cultural effects of the disparagement of weakness as a physical and moral category, are problematic. Wollstonecraft's call for the transformation of female weakness into liberated strength is not liberating for the genuinely weak.

The lack of awareness of ableist argumentation is not the whole picture, however. Critics have found it difficult to read Wollstonecraft without reproducing her ableist rhetoric. In particular, critics often evoke the idea of 'crippling' in their descriptions of Wollstonecraft's stance on women's weakness. Poovey opens her first chapter on the author with praise for Wollstonecraft as a pioneer in taking 'the first step toward liberating herself from the *crippling* strictures of feminine propriety'.[154] Wollstonecraft herself, we learn later in the study, was repeatedly '*crippled*' by the 'collusion of sexuality and sentimentality', because sensibility 'was the only form in which her society allowed her to express either her sexuality or her craving for transcendent meaning'.[155] Poovey suggests, furthermore, that her 'narrator falls victim to the same sentimental idealism that *cripples* Maria*'.[156] Barker-Benfield refers to the women Wollstonecraft critiques as having 'sensibilities developed at the expense of reason, their ambitions confined to love and marriage, making them *physical and psychological cripples*', adding the endorsement that 'this she said with brilliant passion in *Vindication*'.[157] Claudia Johnson writes of Wollstonecraft's account of 'men's deforming taste in loveliness' as having the 'primary objective' of exposing 'how Burke has *crippled* rather than enhanced male virtue itself by feminizing the state'.[158] Badowska is strikingly graphic in finding the '"weak woman of fashion" ... a paradigmatic sap'.[159] Wollstonecraft's characterization of the feminine language of affectation 'dropping glibly from the tongue'[160] brings to Badowska's 'mind small quantities of liquid, such as saliva' that 'impairs the sense of taste and creates a nauseating effect'.[161] Additionally, the early reception of Wollstonecraft's work (in personal attacks and celebrations), employs the weakness–vigour discourse that the author herself uses. The conservative periodical *The Critical Review* describes Wollstonecraft's style as 'weak, desultory, and trifling', and a few lines later as 'weak, diffuse, and confused'.[162] More positive,

*The New Annual Register* found her to be 'a writer who possesses a vigorous and well informed mind', and *The Monthly Review* regarded her as having 'a mind naturally vigorous'.[163] It also comments on 'the vigour of her imagination'.[164] Hannah Mather Crocker, an early American reader of Wollstonecraft's work, describes Wollstonecraft as 'a woman of great energy and a very independent mind'.[165] Some of this language appears in work on Godwin, too. Chris Pierson observes that 'it is clear from Godwin's critique of a society *crippled* by great inequality that it is as much the spirit of *dependence* – "the pauper fawning with abject vileness upon his rich benefactor" – as the existence of absolute destitution that is to be condemned'.[166]

## Vigour as Cultural Liberation

Throughout *A Vindication of the Rights of Woman*, as Adriana Craciun observes, 'Wollstonecraft links physical strength with mental strength, and repeatedly urges women to pursue both'.[167] Wollstonecraft promotes the cultivation of 'strength, both of mind and body' as a virtuous way to overcome 'slavish dependence'.[168] For her, freedom is a form of personal independence within a non-coercive political or domestic situation. A woman is not free, for example, when she is subject to legal insecurity, lacks the opportunity to provide for herself financially, or to develop her capacities, and when she lives under any kind of arbitrary or coercive power.[169] Alan Coffee (2014) and Lena Halldenius (2015) have recently explored the concept of independence in Wollstonecraft. Coffee remarks that independence 'is a central and recurring theme' in Wollstonecraft that has been largely ignored.[170] Coffee defines Wollstonecraft's concept of independence slightly differently from me, though he suggests that there are three aspects to it. It is 'an egalitarian ideal according to which men and women must be protected to the same extent in all areas of their lives';[171] it is 'a flexible ideal that allows for both sexes to interact and participate socially on differentiated terms that reflect their respective outlooks and interests';[172] and it 'is a collaborative ideal according to which the social and political terms of freedom ... must be established collectively by both men and women together'.[173] The latter two definitions are part of what I call 'social independence'. Coffee recognizes Wollstonecraft's uses of independence of mind and civil independence, but he does not express a view on Wollstonecraft's attention to physical independence.

Halldenius identifies independence as the 'core concept' of Wollstone-craft's 'politics and morality'.[174] She suggests that Wollstonecraft connects two aspects of independence: 'the person's independence or dependence in relation to others, and the person's independence or dependence of mind'.[175] Social independence and intellectual independence are, Halldenius states, 'analytically distinct, yet heavily, though asymmetrically, dependent on each other', and they are a requirement for Wollstonecraft's idea of freedom.[176] There is a third type of independence in Wollstonecraft's work, however, that neither Halldenius nor Coffee identify: physical independence. For Wollstonecraft independence is threefold: intellectual, social, and physical. *Intellectual* independence is the ability to use reason to make decisions; *social* independence is the possession of a non-coercive social context (such as having sufficient wealth to allow for independent decision-making, the ability to conduct appropriate domestic relationships,[177] and the enjoyment of legally protected rights); and *physical* independence is bodily self-reliance, strength, and health. For Wollstonecraft, to be free is to have all three of these forms of independence in place. It is not clear which form of independence Wollstonecraft thinks is a necessary condition for the others, however. The following two statements are the clearest Wollstonecraft offers: physical independence makes intellectual independence possible, as 'dependence of body naturally produces dependence of mind';[178] and social independence is necessary for the exercise of physical and intellectual independence. So, a woman 'must not be dependent on her husband's bounty for her subsistence during his life' if she is to be virtuous; and if she is 'only the wanton solace of men' she becomes 'weak in mind and body'.[179] Wollstonecraft calls for the removal of barriers that prevent what she sees as intellectual, social, and physical independence, in order to qualify the 'strong' for equality.

Wollstonecraft connects vigour to virtue to the extent that vigour is necessary for virtue.[180] She establishes this through her comparisons of female and male virtues, and through her discussion of the fitness of the aristocracy and the wealthy to govern. Wollstonecraft observes that 'women, commonly called Ladies, are not allowed to exert any manual strength; and from them the negative virtues only are expected . . . virtues incompatible with any vigorous exertion of intellect'.[181] Physical strength, however, gives men greater opportunities for virtue than culturally feminine women have: men are 'from the constitution of their bodies . . . designed by Providence to attain a greater degree of virtue; their strength enables them to demonstrate virtue'.[182] Wollstonecraft grants vigour a moral status in her description of a woman who has a 'constitution strengthened by exercise, has allowed her body to acquire its full vigour; her mind, at the same time, gradually expanding itself to comprehend the moral duties of life'.[183] We see these connections between vigour and virtue again in Wollstonecraft's description of the ideal education for men and women. The 'most perfect education', Wollstonecraft suggests, 'is such an exercise of the understanding as is best calculated to strengthen the body and form the heart. Or, in other words, to enable the individual to attain such habits of virtue as will render it independent'.[184] She compares culturally feminine women with men of the higher ranks who 'are not allowed to exert any manual strength', and concludes that the virtues displayed by both groups are 'incompatible with any vigorous exertion of intellect'.[185] Thus, like men of rank, women in this situation maintain their false positions of entitlement and their dignity on specious grounds.[186] Bodily and intellectual strength, in Wollstonecraft's opinion, have an important role in making virtue and freedom possible, and 'the care necessary to support and guard the body is the first step to unfold the mind, and inspire a manly spirit of independence'.[187] The acquisition and exercise of virtues derives from rational and equitable participation in social relationships (such as friendship, companionship, and the rearing of children), and independence must be preserved in these relationships.[188]

Vigour is central to Wollstonecraft's understanding of virtue in *Mary*, for instance. The epigraph to the novel is taken from *Julie* (1761), where Rousseau writes, 'L'exercice des plus sublimes virtus élève et nourrit le genie.'[189] With these words, Julie reproaches Saint-Preux for having got into bad company in Paris. Saint-Preux spends time drinking and in brothels instead of talking with men of intellect and investigating how he might relieve the wants of the poor. Julie warns him that the vices of the rich are contagious, and that his mind will shrink as his soul becomes corrupt. But, she maintains, he will soon become aware 'how much *the practice of sublime virtues elevates and sustains one's genius*; how much a tender interest in others' misfortunes serves better to discover their source, and to keep us far in every way from the vices that have produced them'.[190] Wollstonecraft echoes and modifies this sentiment later in her novel, adding of Mary that 'the exercise of her various virtues gave vigor [sic] to her genius, and dignity to her mind'.[191] Rousseau's idea is that virtue provides sublime elevation and sustains character. Wollstonecraft, significantly, recasts virtue as giving vigour and dignity. The connections between virtue and intellectual independence are Rousseau's, but the further connection to vigour is Wollstonecraft's.

Wollstonecraft links virtue, intellectual independence, and vigour throughout *Mary*. Mary, for instance, reads books that 'were addressed to the understanding',[192] and she delights in the 'society of men of genius' who have 'improved her faculties'.[193] This independence of mind enables Mary to develop a forceful character. For example, she expresses 'contempt with such energy, that few could stand the flash of her eyes'.[194] Mary's physical vigour is signalled by her rambling about the countryside, by her ability to care for herself and for others, by the intensity of her emotions, and by her self-control. She has 'such power over her appetites and whims, that without any great effort she conquered them so entirely, that when her understanding or affections had an object, she almost forgot she had a body which required nourishment'.[195] Mary, we are told, could 'endure the greatest fatigue without appearing sensible of it'.[196] Social independence is more difficult for her, however. She anticipates that her arranged marriage will reduce her limited freedom, and she resorts to manipulation in order to spend time away from her husband. The novel, nevertheless, presents the case that the heroine's unwillingness to submit to social dependence makes her virtuous.

The physically and intellectually vigorous heroine becomes an important symbol of the culturally liberated woman in the radical novel of the 1790s. Mary Raymond, the heroine of Mary Hays's *The Victim of Prejudice* (1799), for instance, recalls that 'at ten years of age, I could ride the forest-horses without bridle or saddle; could leap a fence or surmount a gate with admirable dexterity; could climb the highest trees, wrestle with the children of the village, or mingle in the dance with grace and activity'.[197] In portraying her heroine in this way, Hays uses Wollstonecraft's idea that women have naturally vigorous bodies. Tutored alongside William and Edward Pelham, Mary physically and intellectually outstrips both of her male companions 'with an active mind and an ardent curiosity',[198] and has 'an enthusiastic love of science and literature'.[199] She develops her physical and intellectual capacities because of her tutor's contempt for female accomplishments. Mary comments that it was 'to the wisdom and kindness of my benefactor, who with a contempt of vulgar prejudices, cherished notions somewhat singular respecting female accomplishments, I was indebted for a robust constitution, a cultivated understanding, and a vigorous intellect'.[200] Hays is quick to associate herself further with Wollstonecraft's weakness arguments. Mary's first significant experience involves her association with Eve's defect (Wollstonecraft's argument 2). She is persuaded by William to steal some fruit from Sir Peter Osborne's greenhouse, is caught by Sir Peter, and runs away before he can steal a kiss from her. Attracted by her beauty, Sir Peter calls Mary 'a true daughter of Eve!' and plans to seduce or rape her.[201] The narrative later reveals that

Mary is the daughter of a seduced woman. This context assists in removing her potential for social independence, as the inheritance of her mother's shame prevents her from attempting a companionate marriage with William. She also cannot gain social independence, both because of her lack of wealth, and because of Sir Peter's relentless pursuit of her. Eventually, Mary loses her strength: 'it seemed as if a premature old age had withered my bloom and blasted the *vigour* of my youth: no longer *robust*, sanguine, active, broken spirits and a shattered constitution sunk me to the *weakness of infancy*, imaginary terrors haunted my mind, and a complication of nameless depressing pangs racked my frame'.[202] Moreover, Hays reinforces the importance of vigour in her tract 'Improvements Suggested in Female Education' (1797), where she comments that 'a woman enabled to support herself, and to acquire property by her industry, would gain by regular occupation, and the healthful exertion of her faculties, more firmness of mind and greater *vigour* of body'.[203]

Vigorous virtue goes beyond the proto-feminist writing in the period. Thomas Holcroft, for instance, uses the phrase 'the energies of virtue' to describe the vigour and strength needed for virtue.[204] 'Energy' features extensively in his novel *Anna St. Ives* (1792). Frank Henley, the freethinking son of Sir Arthur St Ives's gardener, is wedded to 'duty, virtue and energy', and sees it as his responsibility to protect the St Ives family from the greed of his father.[205] Anna, Sir Arthur's daughter, similarly expresses virtue in conjunction with energy. She is described as being so pure that 'even mistake itself is lovely in her; and assumes all the energy, all the dignity of virtue'.[206] Furthermore, Elizabeth Hamilton satirizes the radical interest in strength, vigour, and energy in her novel *Memoirs of Modern Philosophers* (1800). Hamilton mocks the intellect and deformities of the egalitarian Bridgetina Botherim, whom she sees as parroting poorly understood ideas. Bridgetina, a middle-ranking woman of independent means who has 'a little cast in my eyes, and a little twist in my left shoulder',[207] describes herself as having made more progress in philosophical study than the conventionally beautiful Miss Julia Delmond, and thus regards herself as more apt to inspire a young man to love. 'Nothing but the unjust prejudices of an unnatural state of civilization, could make Julia loved in preference to me', Bridgetina opines.[208] Like Godwin, Bridgetina believes in the power of the mind over the body. When Mr Vallaton breaks his arm, she congratulates him on

> the glorious opportunity you now enjoy of proving the omnipotence of mind over matter ... Physical causes sink into nothing, when compared

with those that are moral. Happy had it been for the world, if not only your arm, but every bone in your body had been broken, so that it had been the means of furnishing mankind with a proof of the perfectibility of philosophical energy.[209]

Hamilton recognizes the important role of strength-related rhetoric in the emancipation debates, and, through Bridgetina's comparison of female beauty and intellectual vigour, attempts to bring out the absurdity of the radical understanding of energy. Additionally, Hamilton illustrates how vigour might be seen to be at odds with sensibility, benevolence, and familial love. Through the story of Mrs Biggs, a widow who has broken her back, and her daughters, who work to support her and their intellectually impaired brother, Hamilton reminds the reader that familial duty and charity have no place in Godwin's vision of political justice. Bridgetina characterizes their efforts as misplaced energy, suggesting that the women could do more for 'general utility'.[210]

## Authenticity and Interdependence

Inauthentic (i.e. avoidable or feigned) illness and general female weaknesses are clearly different from the unavoidable and unfeigned illnesses that Wollstonecraft regards as authentic; but it is not clear that they are different in any respect other than their supposed authenticity.[211] False delicacy, in Wollstonecraft's work, causes physical illness. She writes in *A Vindication of the Rights of Woman*, for example, that

> False notions of beauty and delicacy stop the growth of their [women's] limbs and produce a sickly soreness, rather than delicacy of organs; and thus weakened by being employed in unfolding instead of examining the first associations, forced on them by every surrounding object, how can they attain that *vigour* necessary to enable them to throw off that factitious character?[212]

Wollstonecraft is clear, however, that authentic illnesses have some positive social consequences that inauthentic ones do not have. For instance, in *Mary*, Wollstonecraft presents positive relationships of interdependence that involve ill people. Henry, for example, wishes to have Mary's portrait painted 'with the expression I have seen in your face, when you have been supporting your friend'.[213] Additionally, caring for an ill person can bring the ill person an esteem that is akin to social elevation. The care with which Mary attends her friend Ann is recast by three unnamed fashionable ladies (a mother and her daughters) as strange or 'romantic',[214] because Mary is a woman of fortune, and her care gives more consequence to Ann than they think Ann's rank deserves. The mother comments that Mary inexplicably 'pays as much attention to [Ann] as if she [Ann] was a lady of quality'.[215] The narrator dismisses the sneering women as 'weak people' who are merely 'satellites' who dance around the 'fine planet' of a remote family connection, a Countess.[216] Wollstonecraft also implies, in *Mary*, that illness brings intellectual gains, even though this is at odds with her theory that physical vigour is necessary for intellectual power. Henry recalls that his childhood illnesses have given him scholarly interests. He remembers that 'two or three lingering disorders' in his youth gave him 'a habit of reflecting' and enabled him 'to obtain some dominion over' his passions.[217] Henry's 'naturally weak'[218] constitution makes it difficult for him to become a priest, but it allows him to enter into literary pursuits 'with warmth' and 'eagerness'.[219]

Authentic illness offers Wollstonecraft the scope to explore interdependence as a companionate way of living.[220] Nearly all of the characters in *Mary* are ill, and while not all these illnesses are referred to as authentic, the relationships between authentically ill people and their friends are generally mutually sustaining. Early in their friendship, Mary imagines that her friend Ann 'looked sickly or unhappy' in order to remove her disappointment at Ann's lack of romantic attachment to her.[221] Imagining that Ann's illness has worsened enables Mary to circumvent her sense of being rejected by Ann. Illness provides a way for Mary to demand less emotion from her friend, as it does in the case of Mary's relationship with her own mother. Mary's relationship with her mother, however, is less mutual, and it threatens to overwhelm Mary's own need to care for herself: 'her [mother's] sickness called forth all Mary's tenderness, and exercised her compassion so continually, that it became more than a match for self-love'.[222] Later in her relationship with Ann, Mary comments that 'continual attention to health, and to the tender office of a nurse, have created an affection very like a maternal one – I am her only support, she leans on me'.[223] Mary becomes the caring mother, supporting her friend; but Ann is also Mary's support, a role Mary recognizes more fully when Ann dies. After Ann's death, Henry, although fragile, becomes Mary's support, and 'without this dear prop she had sunk into the grave of her lost – long-loved friend'.[224]

Authentic illness has further emancipatory social effects. Ann's illness justifies Mary's cohabitation with her, and it prompts Mary to study medicine – knowledge that she uses to help another sick person later in the narrative. Henry's illness also enables Mary both to express and to cloak her desire for him. It allows her a greater degree of social freedom, allows their relationship to progress quickly, and provides her with access to him: 'Henry's illness was not alarming, it was rather pleasing, as it gave Mary an excuse to herself for shewing him how much she was interested about him.'[225] When Henry's illness does become worrying, Mary still enjoys 'the melancholy pleasure of nursing him'.[226] Additionally, Henry's illness allows him to express his love for Mary. He hides his affection with 'a sigh that was coughed away'.[227] Because of their authenticity, the illnesses of Ann and Henry have none of the moral culpability that we see in the case of Eliza. Ann is the impoverished daughter of a clergyman, and for this reason has not acquired the artificial illnesses associated with middle- and high-ranking women. Henry, though from a wealthy family, is a younger son who was left to ramble 'about the world' to see 'mankind in every rank of life' and to learn from his experiences to become independent.[228] While his illnesses are not those of the wealthy and leisured class, the novel hints that they are nevertheless the product of his social role. Henry's mother confesses to Mary that her 'neglect, perhaps, first injured his constitution', and that she is being punished for this by Henry's illness.[229] As he nears death, Henry reveals that his 'ill-fated love', while it may have 'added strength to my disease', has made it easier for him to die.[230]

Wollstonecraft does not describe an authentically weak woman outside the category of chronic illness, but she does suggest, in *Original Stories from Real Life* (1788), that a man with an authentic impairment can live a happy and socially valuable life. *Original Stories* is a succession of narratives intended as a conduct manual for young women. The protagonists are Mary, who is fourteen and has a 'turn for ridicule', and Caroline, who is twelve and is 'vain of her person'.[231] The girls are given moral lessons by their governess, Mrs Mason.[232] They learn to be kind to animals, treat servants with dignity, curb their anger, observe personal hygiene, tell the truth, ignore minor injuries, prize virtue and inner beauty over physical beauty, not to eat too much, not to procrastinate or be lazy, not to laugh at deformed people, and neither to waste money on trinkets nor run up debts. Some of the lessons come from stories told to the children; others derive from their experiences. On one occasion, the children and Mrs Mason shelter in a cottage during a storm. It is the home of Honest Jack, a partially sighted amputee and former sailor. As is conventional, the sailor tells the story of how he came by his impairments. He 'lost the use of [his] limbs' in a shipwreck by rescuing a woman from drowning, and he lost the sight in one eye and has reduced vision in the other eye because of a flash of lightning caused by the same storm.[233] The woman he saved employs Jack as a fisherman, and he is grateful to her because, as he puts it, 'I might now have been begging about the streets but for her, God bless her!'[234] The tale is a sentimental vehicle for Mrs Mason to demonstrate her compassion and sensibility; but it is also a story of social integration that demonstrates that Jack can live a fulfilling life.[235] He lives with his wife and family in a cottage, and, although he does not have much money, the family is able to be hospitable to unexpected guests. Jack hopes to repay his good fortune, and is rewarded for the authenticity of his impairment with employment. He watches for storms so that he can 'be as kind to a poor perishing soul as she [his benefactor] has been to me'.[236]

## Deformity

Wollstonecraft's writing on deformity is not extensive, but from the little comment she makes it is possible to determine a few principles. As is standard in the period, Wollstonecraft treats deformity and beauty as opposites, and sees them as connected to vice and virtue respectively. Deformity and beauty in her work often involve both aesthetic and moral components. Like Godwin, Wollstonecraft is convinced of the moral expressivity of the body, in the sense that the body bears visible signs of vice or virtue. This can be as simple as the comment on ugliness in *Thoughts on the Education of Daughters* (1787), where Wollstonecraft suggests that she 'never knew a person really ugly, who was not foolish or vicious'.[237] Wollstonecraft makes more observations on beauty than on deformity. Beauty signals good character in several different ways. For instance, she observes that 'the soul of beauty ... consists in the body gracefully exhibiting the emotions and variations of the informing mind'.[238] She argues, also, that beauty requires health and capacity, and connects this to a moral purpose: 'exercise and cleanliness appear to be not only the surest means of preserving health, but of promoting beauty, the physical causes considered; yet this is not sufficient, moral ones must concur, or beauty will be merely of that rustic kind which blooms on the innocent, wholesome, countenances of some country people, whose minds have not been exercised'.[239] Wollstonecraft is indebted here to Shaftesbury's idea that the informing mind is essential to the physically beautiful. The good action, Wollstonecraft suggests, radiates to make the person beautiful, and so, 'when internal goodness is reflected, every other kind of beauty, the shadow of it, withers away before it – as the sun obscures a lamp'.[240] The statement alludes to two important themes in

Wollstonecraft's work: the idea that physical beauty is often overvalued, and that moral beauty is more important than physical beauty.

Wollstonecraft's moral view of beauty is reinforced by her discussion of the grace of Grecian statues, in comments which engage with Burke. Burke argues that the Greeks were wrong to think that measuring the proportions of the human body was a way of producing beauty. Wollstonecraft agrees and suggests that, although in the case of Greek statues 'beautiful limbs and features were selected from various bodies to form an harmonious whole', and this might be beauty, the resulting whole is not a portrait of nature and so amounts to merely a 'model of mankind'.[241] For Burke, the measuring of body parts does not account for the idiosyncrasies of beauty, and so he produces a number of more general qualities (such as softness) that give more latitude. Burke explicitly denies a link between beauty and the expression of a morally good disposition, and he dismisses the idea that virtue can have an aesthetic property. The beauty of virtue, he writes, is but a 'whimsical theory', even though it is one that has persisted for centuries in western thought.[242] Wollstonecraft, however, sees the moral aspects of beauty as working together with the physical:

> To render the person perfect, physical and moral beauty ought to be attained at the same time; each lending and receiving force by the combination. Judgment must reside on the brow, affection and fancy beam in the eye, and humanity curve the cheek, or vain is the sparkling of the finest eye or the elegantly turned finish of the fairest features: whilst in every motion that displays the active limbs and well-knit joints, grace and modesty should appear.[243]

For Wollstonecraft, beauty is as much the result of reflection, affection, compassion, and humanity as it is the product of decisions about what is aesthetically pleasing.

Wollstonecraft briefly considers the problem of the beautiful person who is not virtuous. She suggests, for instance, that the aesthetic evidence of vice (deformity) and virtue (beauty) is sometimes not present on the body. In this case, the aesthetic quality belongs to a moral attribute rather than to the body. So, for example, the superficial young men of a country town 'whose only occupation is gallantry' have polished manners that 'render vice more dangerous, by concealing its deformity under gay ornamental drapery'.[244] Wollstonecraft makes the same observation in the case of the moral beauty of women. A woman who is able to earn her own money is more respectable than 'the most accomplished beauty', because the 'beauty of moral loveliness, or the harmonious propriety that attunes the passions of a well-regulated mind' makes her withdraw 'from the giddy whirl of pleasure, or the indolent charm that stupefies the good sort of woman it sucks in'.[245] The woman's physical beauty is not supported by her beauty of character; beauty is solely the aesthetic property of her virtue.

Like Godwin, Wollstonecraft has not fully worked through the implications of a combined moral and aesthetic theory, however; and this is especially evident in the absence of comments on deformity. She does not articulate a theory of deformity that would naturally be the opposite of her more fully developed theory of beauty, even though she certainly subscribed to the conventional idea of beauty and deformity as opposites. This may be due to a lack of interest in the subject – beauty clearly fascinates Wollstonecraft more – or it may be that the implied consequences of her views on physical beauty made her uneasy when directly expressed. The implications for deformity, as the aesthetic and moral opposite of beauty, are incompatible with the compassion, sympathy, and sensibility Wollstonecraft expresses elsewhere when considering deformity. For example, when Mary, Caroline, and Mrs Mason meet a deformed woman whose lack of teeth makes her drawl, Mrs Mason chastises Mary for ridiculing the woman, and censures both children for staring her 'almost out of countenance'.[246] She remarks that the children must make a habit of looking away, and of thinking 'of others and what they will suffer on all occasions'.[247] Wollstonecraft's condemnation of those who ridicule deformed people is also evident in her translation of Christian Gotthilf Salzmann's children's book, *Moralisches Elementarbuch* (1782). Here, another Mary is advised by her father that 'above all, we ought never to laugh at bodily deformity or poverty, because persons so afflicted have often more good qualities than rich and handsome people, who have not had misfortunes to teach them how to improve their understandings, and love their miserable fellow creatures'.[248] A more direct translation would be: 'one ought not to make fun of a person because of some defect or other, because they could have many qualities in spite of this'.[249] Salzmann highlights the qualities of the deformed person; Wollstonecraft highlights the defective education, class privileges, and that laughing at deformed people is as heartless as laughing at poor people.

Wollstonecraft's unarticulated views on the opposite of beauty are also incompatible with her suggestion that deformity provides women with an opportunity to separate themselves from a world in which they are not valued for their minds. In *Original Stories*, she draws a moral lesson from the story of a vain woman who loses her beauty to smallpox. The unnamed woman listens to her friends 'lament the depredation that dreadful disease had made in a fine face'.[250] While the woman is miserable for a time, 'the natural vivacity of her youth overcame her unpleasant feelings'.[251] When her eyes are sensitive to light, she applies herself to music 'and made a surprising proficiency'; and once they become less sensitive, she 'grew fond of reading'.[252] Wollstonecraft uses the tale as an illustration of how the distraction of superficial things, once removed, can open up self-improving possibilities. The woman's deformity helps her to discover 'that virtue, internal beauty, was valuable on its own account, and not like that of the person, which resembles a toy, that pleases the observer, but does not make the possessor happy'.[253] Frances Burney later takes up this theme in *Camilla* (1796).

## Conclusion

When Wollstonecraft discusses the weak woman, she slips between concepts of illness, luxury, irrationality, imbecility, and misogyny. Her work reveals much about weakness as a category of exclusion before disability emerged as a concept. She defines female weakness as having negative personal and social consequences. Foremost among these is the idea that dependent women are unable to pursue physically and intellectually active lives due to misogynistic cultures. Wollstonecraft argues that in submitting to these cultures, women sacrifice their dignity and their natural rights. Once their capacities are developed and redirected, she suggests, they will become useful, happy, independent, free, and virtuous beings, and they will increase the possibilities for social progress for the population more broadly. The central point of *A Vindication of the Rights of Woman* is that the economic and social dependence of middle- and upper-ranking women is generated by the legal and cultural suppression of their intellectual and physical utility. Wollstonecraft thinks of this type of inutility as inauthentic incapacity; it is either avoidable or feigned. She is, however, often not careful to distinguish between inauthentic and authentic impairment. Significantly, Wollstonecraft argues that the inability of women to function in ways that benefit them or society is the result of a preference for an aesthetic of female social dependence. Women are deemed aesthetically appealing, she argues, because of their weakness. Society, she argues, cannot maintain physical and intellectual impairment as an aesthetic, and she suggests that women should be shamed by their weaknesses rather than assisted in promoting them as attractive. For Wollstonecraft, the current time is an age of feebleness in both men and women, where 'bodily strength from being the distinction of heroes is now sunk into such unmerited contempt that men, as well as women, seem to think it unnecessary: the latter, as it takes from their feminine graces ... and the former, because it appears inimical to the character of a gentleman'.[254] There is, however, one striking moment when Wollstonecraft realizes in a different context that governments need to protect people from being oppressed by those who are more powerful. She writes that, 'Nature having made men unequal, by giving stronger bodily and mental powers to one than to another, the end of government ought to be to destroy this inequality by protecting the weak. Instead of which, it has always leaned the opposite side, wearing itself out by disregarding the first principle of it's [sic] organization.'[255]

Wollstonecraft's critics have denounced her characterization of women as weak as being misogynistic, but assume that there is no difficulty with characterizing weakness as a social problem. It is relatively new for scholars to question the disparagement of impairment in the discourse of emancipation. Scholars have been slow to recognize that *A Vindication of the Rights of Woman*, is as much a call to reinvigorate the body and to cure women of impaired femininity as it is a call to free them from political and social enslavement. Rosemarie Garland Thomson suggests that we avoid disability because 'our collective cultural consciousness emphatically denies the knowledge of vulnerability, contingency, and mortality', and that 'our bodies need care; [and] we all need assistance'.[256] She calls for a 'methodology of inclusion',[257] and observes that 'integrating disability as a category of analysis and a system of representation deepens, expands, and challenges feminist theory'.[258] There are many reasons why critics have not explored the ableist ideology evident in Wollstonecraft's work. 'Feminist theories', for instance, 'all too often do not recognize disability in their litanies of identities that inflect the category of woman.'[259] Garland Thomson urges feminist critics to recognize ability/disability as an all-pervasive binary that 'stigmatizes certain kinds of bodily variations'.[260] This binary structures 'institutions, social identities, cultural practices, political positions, historical communities, and the shared human experience of embodiment'.[261] Wollstonecraft's strength/weakness binary is similarly pervasive. Her emancipation arguments devalue the weak body by stressing its cultural dependence and imputing to it inauthenticity. A weak woman is indistinguishable from a victim of, or a slave to, misogynistic cultures; a strong woman is free, capable of virtue, and is socially useful.[262] As Garland Thomson suggests, 'understanding how disability [or pre-disability] functions along with other systems of representation clarifies how all the systems intersect and mutually constitute each other'.[263] It is important to understand Wollstonecraft's work as a product of its time, but it is clear from modern critical engagement with her work that while readers are aware of the potential for understanding her attack on the culturally feminine woman as misogyny, they are not aware of her ableism.

CHAPTER 3

# Wordsworth's 'The Discharged Soldier' and the Question of Desert

When Emperor Alexander I of Russia sat next to Sir Walter Scott at a dinner in 1815, the first question he asked him was: 'In what affair were you wounded?'[1] Discomforted, Scott replied that his was a 'natural infirmity; upon which the Emperor said, I thought Lord Cathcart mentioned that you had served'.[2] Their host looked a little disconcerted, since the Emperor had incorrectly assumed that Scott's post-polio limp was a war wound. Scott continued, "Oh yes; in a certain sense I have served – that is, in the yeomanry cavalry; a home force resembling the Landwehr, or Landsturm'", and, on further petitioning, he gave an account of "'some slight actions – such as the battle of the Cross Causeway and the affair of Moredun-Mill'".[3] This was, as Scott 'saw in Lord Cathcart's face, quite sufficient, so he [Scott] managed to turn the conversation to some other subject'.[4] Scott may not have been wounded in a battle, but his service deflected the embarrassment caused by the Emperor's assumption that male impairment is usually military, and that military impairments are deserving of recognition as honourable.

Scott's conversational situation is part of a phenomenon that has recently been studied in legal, pedagogical, and sociological contexts.[5] In certain social settings, people are called upon to tell the 'origin story' of aspects of their bodies that make them visually distinctive. Origin stories incorporate the moment of diagnosis or acquisition, but they are also about 'a set of relationships and experiences ... that go far beyond the brief interaction'.[6] They are what David Engel calls 'defining moments in which roles, norms, and meanings become unambiguously apparent'.[7] Origin stories contain within them 'embedded' narratives that are 'a way to ensure that [the] archetypal values and outcomes of the myth will triumph over pain, opposition, and disorder'.[8] These narratives are, Engel observes, 'part of the process of constructing a world in which' the disabled person can live, and they encode 'the dominant ideological systems in a society' and a society's counter-cultural narratives.[9] While Engel's stories belong to a very different social group (modern American parents of children with disabilities), they share something with eighteenth-century and early nineteenth-century disabled soldier origin narratives: they 'are rich with implicit references' that connect the origins of the disability with conflicts that are later resolved.[10] They are selective tales that in some sense explain how disability should be understood.

Engel defines the term 'origin stories' (or 'origin myths') as narratives that are distinctively about 'how something "began to be"'.[11] For Engel, this account of 'beginning' is about a particular day when someone was diagnosed with a disability, and the diagnosis is presented as a transformative event. He suggests that the origin story, however, is always a life story rather than a story about a moment, as it embeds aspects of later events. His term 'embedded narratives' refers to the implicit details within an account of the past that relate to the current situation. For example, a family's later setbacks are projected onto the original moment of diagnosis: 'parents emphasize certain narrative themes in the origin myths because their more recent experiences ... have focused their attention on some aspects of the original diagnosis more than on others'.[12] Engel stresses the binary relationships in these scenarios. The medical professional is opposed to the parent; science is opposed to common sense; objectivity is opposed to subjectivity; and hierarchical authority and expected submission are opposed to equality and participation. These are, essentially, conflicts in which a parent figure (exhibiting common sense, subjectivity, and a participatory ethic) is an advocate for their child, and battles against a health professional (who is scientific, supposedly objective, and authoritative).

Fictional stories about disabled[13] servicemen come in many forms and appear in many literary genres, but the majority narrate the origin of the disability. These narratives are retold by a disabled serviceman to an apparently able-bodied interlocutor, and include some account of how an impairment was acquired. Although they are usually not direct petitions for assistance, these stories embed reasons why the soldier or sailor is currently deserving of assistance, or in some way motivate the listener to help. They are about the endurance of multiple hardships, and they make in one way or another a case for moral desert. The stories usually establish a 'desert base' (to borrow a term from Joel Feinberg) for some kind of compensation.[14] In this respect the stories have a specified embedded purpose beyond that established in Engel's paradigm (which is not about compensation). Engel's paradigm is, nevertheless, helpful here because it signals that stories about the origins of impairment are also stories about justification. As disabled servicemen were entitled to governmental support, their stories often contain elaborate explanations as to why the serviceman has not qualified for this support; and, if he has not qualified, outline why he is nonetheless deserving of support. Thus the narratives operate as some kind of vindication of the soldier against the governmental disqualification from entitlement, and also demonstrate the soldier's moral worth. Engel's diagnostic stories are likewise concerned with moral evaluation. The parents demonstrate their concern and advocacy for their child; they make the case that their children are deserving of better treatment; and they emphasize their own position as a supporter of the child.[15]

In disabled servicemen stories, the presentation of desert is, in principle, either established through the content of the soldier's narrative (*intrinsic desert*), or through grounds that are external to the content of the soldier's narrative, such as visual evidence of apparent indigence (*extrinsic desert*). Additionally, the recounting of the narrative itself may generate desert, as the performance constitutes a form of entertainment that may deserve a compensation (*performative desert*). Intrinsic, extrinsic, and performative desert are sometimes at work in the same narrative, and are merely presentations of the desert claim, rather than modes that affect the moral status of the claim itself. Obligation to compensate according to desert (in non-altruistic circumstances) usually occurs in three ways: when a debt has been incurred (*repayment*); when there is an exchange (*quid pro quo*); or when there is a fault (*compensation for injury*). Desert claims do not always imply that there is any sense in which a bystander is morally liable for compensating desert. Altruistic giving is a kind of compensation that occurs without liability, and which may, on the face of it, appear undermotivated. One way in which altruism can be provoked is in the appeal to *sympathy*, and possibly to the *virtues* of the giver more generally. This does not generate a particular liability in the giver, but it does explain why the giver gives in cases of desert without obligation. One way in which such an altruistic situation might arise is when there is extrinsic desert without intrinsic or performative desert.

The case of the disabled soldier is often presented in terms of altruism. In this genre, *sympathy* and/or *virtue* sometimes explain the motivation to respond to a desert claim. In the case of altruistic giving in disabled servicemen stories, however, there may be other motivating factors too. Four are relevant here. Firstly, *friendship* (or family kinship) generates motivation. Sometimes, the acknowledgement of a prior relationship between the listener figure and the serviceman explains why the listener is likely to give. For example, the narrators of the disabled servicemen stories in the work of Oliver Goldsmith, Henry Mackenzie, and Robert Bage are already known to their soldier figures. Secondly, and relatedly, *fellowship* generates motivation through the possession of shared qualities or features. Fellowship works in a similar way to friendship. The service-man may possess similar characteristics to the listener and these may motivate a response. Thirdly, *proximity* generates motivation. For example, one may be motivated to help someone by being the only person nearby able to relieve distress, or simply being the nearest person. In all of these instances, having the capacity to give is a necessary condition for giving (for example, you need to have money to spare). Finally, a direct *request* may motivate a response. The virtues of the interlocutor are also pertinent. If the interlocutor is virtuous, and has evaluated the soldier as virtuous, the interlocutor's character is an intensifier of the soldier's deservingness.

### Desert and Rewards in Disabled Servicemen Narratives

It is notable that in many disabled servicemen narratives the simple facts of indigence and injury are not sufficient to establish desert. Virtue is a typical trait that makes a soldier's case deserving. There are many examples of this in the disabled servicemen stories. The virtues expressed in such stories include a wide range of qualities, such as being hard-working, honest, resilient, adaptable, brave, selfless, loyal, frugal, humble, sympathetic, and self-reliant. Goldsmith's serviceman, in 'The Distresses of a Common Soldier' (1760), is virtuous simply because he is uncomplaining. Gold-smith comments that 'the meanest of our common sailors and soldiers endure without murmuring or regret, without passionately declaiming against Providence'.[16] Old Edwards, the soldier in Mackenzie's *The Man of Feeling* (1771), is deserving because he has fought for his country. Harley, the novel's hero, has 'the highest esteem for' the character of a man who has served in this way.[17] Bage's soldier, John Morgan, in *Mount Henneth* (1782), is deserving because he is brave. Morgan says of his amputation, 'this was the most lively sensation I have ever experienced, but then it was glorious, and soldiers should be content'.[18]

Often, the serviceman's narrative (the intrinsic desert claim) is not externally verifiable. A soldier may tell his tale and the listener must decide from the evidence in the story whether the man is worthy. Some narrators get around this problem by introducing methods of independent verifica-tion. For example, they reveal that they knew the soldier years before, and that he proved to be virtuous then and so is likely to be virtuous now. Goldsmith's soldier, for example, is 'a poor fellow, whom I knew when a boy'.[19] The narrator 'knew him to be honest and industrious when in the country'.[20] Independent verification strengthens desert. Desert on the basis of virtue is sometimes also verified by visual appearance. For example, a soldier is thought to be deserving because he appears to have the physiognomy of an honest man, or because his poverty and clothing justify his tale. Sometimes these methods of verification also serve as motivators to act altruistically. Prior knowledge of a man's virtue is a friendship motivator as well as a means of verification.

Disabled servicemen may be deserving because their adverse circumstances were unavoidable, or because they were not responsible for the adversity. For example, prior to his military career, a soldier may have had bad luck, have experienced poverty due to poor harvests, or have been the victim of a miscarriage of justice, oppressive landlords, impressment, or unemployment. The amputation of Morgan's arm is presented as an instance of poor luck, because the surgeon 'sawed off my arm, and seared up the stump' in order 'to save time' rather than because it was strictly necessary.[21] These events may also highlight virtues displayed during adverse experiences. The soldier may respond in a particularly admirable way to the experience of unfavourable events. Desert according to adverse circumstances also applies in situations where there is a context that prevents a soldier working when they could, or where there is no bodily or mental capacity for work. Incapacities may result from age, or function impairment; or they may be unspecified. In a way that parallels Engel's origin stories, events that occur prior to military service and prior to the impairment often involve many adverse circumstances that are supportive of desert claims even if these become apparent only later, when the account of military service, impairment, and disqualification from pension entitlement is given. For example, William Combe's soldier is unable to apply for relief at Chelsea, even though he has 'been in twenty engagements and dangerously wounded seven times', because his 'only friend Major MORRISON, died just before I was discharged; – and so many applied to be admitted, that, for want of a friend, I was passed over'.[22]

Desert claims operate in a number of ways. For example, the kinds of things that count as desert bases (e.g. virtues and adverse circumstances) are affected by circumstances (modalities) that intensify or weaken these bases. This section will concentrate on intensifiers in desert claims as these are common in disabled servicemen narratives. For example, some desert claims may be comparative. One person's desert may increase when they are compared with someone else. For example, someone who has been unlucky in their experience of adverse circumstances may increase their desert claim when compared with someone who has been luckier; or someone who has a number of incapacities may be treated as more deserving than someone who has fewer incapacities. This comparative mode pays attention to the properties of an individual, or to the actions that individual has performed, or to the context, and compares them with the properties or actions or context of another, in order to anchor a hierarchy of desert claims.[23]

There are a number of intensifiers in Goldsmith's 'The Distresses of a Common Soldier', for instance. Goldsmith begins his tale with a theory of comparative desert. He observes that more attention is given to the sufferings of great people.[24] By comparison, the disabled soldier, who is 'without friends to encourage, acquaintances to pity, or even without hope to alleviate his misfortunes', is more deserving than he might have been because he responds with 'tranquillity and indifference' when his situation is overlooked.[25] Some desert claims may be accumulative. A soldier who has multiple desert bases may increase the strength of his desert claims by virtue of their quantity. Goldsmith's soldier loses his father at five years old, is sent to the workhouse and is made to work ten hours a day for food, is apprenticed to a farmer who dies, becomes an itinerant labourer, and is transported and forced to work on a slave plantation for seven years for accidentally killing a hare. On his return, he is press-ganged onto a ship, and is wounded in the breast and discharged. The soldier becomes sick and is given forty pounds, but is pressed again before he sets foot on the shore. His next ship is captured by the French, who take the money and imprison him. He escapes on a privateer, is captured again, and is freed by another ship. The man suggests that the timing of his impairment was his misfortune: 'if I had had the good fortune to have lost my leg and the use of my hand on board a king's ship, and not a-board a privateer, I should have been entitled to cloathing and maintenance during the rest of my life, but that was not my chance'.[26] The impairment would have been considered an asset, if it had occurred at another time in the man's life.

Mackenzie is also a master of the accumulative desert base. Edwards embeds the story of his suffering at the hands of an unjust London steward, the arrest of his son, the death of his dog, and the loss of his savings prior to his service. The story of his fight against the torture of an Indian man explains his court martial and the loss of his pension, and again establishes his worth as a defender of the humane treatment of a colonized people. Edwards is sentenced to 300 lashes, which is reduced to 200 because he has received wounds to the arm and leg while in the service. Nevertheless, this counts as an excessive punishment, and makes him deserving. Additionally, Edwards's heroism increases his desert: his career as a soldier is motivated by his intention to save his son's life (by going in his place), but he is unfortunate in that his son and daughter-in-law die as a consequence of 'bad crops and bad debts'.[27] The extremity of the desert base may increase a claim, as is highlighted in the Navy's compensation system for injury. According to Daniel Ennis, 'the Admiralty had a pay scale for pensions based on the severity of the injury. The life-time pension for a lost arm in the mid-eighteenth century was five shillings per day. By Nelson's time, the compensation for a lost arm was a lump-sum payment of £100'.[28]

The extent to which desert can be used as an example to others to act well is also a modality.[29] Goldsmith's soldier, we are told, 'deserves admiration, and should be held up for our imitation and respect'.[30] The narrator of *The Man of Feeling* is thankful to have heard Edwards's story. 'Father of mercies! I also would thank thee, that not only has thou assigned eternal rewards to virtue, but that, even in this bad world, the lines of our duty, and our happiness, are so frequently woven together.'[31] The serviceman often serves as an example of someone who has endured hardship resiliently, and who has value as a model of how to behave.

A serviceman may be deserving of reward because he has told a good story. A payment for a formal performance is not altruism, as a service has been performed for which there is an expected fee (*quid pro quo*), but an informal performance in which a stranger recounts his life narrative implies different rules. Combe's narrator, for instance, responds to a soldier's story as a kind of entertainment: 'I am fully convinced that the pleasure I received, in conversing with this old soldier, arose entirely from that sentimental disposition, which works up every thing it sees into a congeniality with some soft and amiable passion.'[32] Even though the listener is motivated by sympathy in Combe's narrative, at the heart of this account is a *quid pro quo* exchange (money or gratitude, either for the tale or for the fact that the tale has elicited a welcome sympathy).

The rewards for desert in disabled servicemen narratives usually take three forms: verbal (e.g. praise); material (e.g. money, housing, and food); or relational (e.g. friendship or sympathy). These are often combined. For example, Goldsmith's soldier receives money and the respect of his listener, who ends the story: 'thus saying, he limped off, leaving me in admiration of his intrepidity and content; nor could I avoid acknowledging, that an habitual acquaintance with misery serves better than philosophy to teach us how to despise it'.[33] Harley gives praise and love, when he asks of the serviceman, '"let me hold thee to my bosom; let me imprint the virtue of thy sufferings on my soul. Come, my honoured veteran! let me endeavour to soften the last days of a life, worn out in the service of humanity: call me thy son, and let me cherish thee as a father"'.[34] Edwards is not in need of material compensation as he has two hundred pieces of gold from an Indian whom he saved from torture. Harley, nevertheless, gives him a small farm as recompense for the sufferings he has undergone, and Edwards lives frugally and contentedly with his surviving grandchildren. Bage's soldier, Morgan, is given money to 'refresh himself' before returning to Henneth Castle to give his story, and is later granted 'a comfortable settlement, for life, in Henneth castle, the chosen abode of love, friendship, and benevolence'.[35] Combe's soldier is 'sure of having a comfortable meal or two' at several squires' houses, and regards this as 'a great blessing'.[36] The soldier usually expresses gratitude or gives a benediction. Edwards's response is 'gratitude and piety'.[37] Morgan's response is 'God bless your honour'.[38]

## Critical Context: The Sympathetic Approach to Wordsworth's 'The Discharged Soldier'

Situating Wordsworth's 'The Discharged Soldier' within the context of disabled soldier origin stories and the questions of desert that these stories raise casts new light on some otherwise puzzling features of the poem.[39] For example, critics often find the encounter between the speaker and the soldier to be unsatisfactory.[40] Critics have hitherto focused on sympathy as a way to understand it. James Averill argues, for instance, that the poem is a 'dramatization of a response to suffering', and that 'the motives [for responding] are intended to be intuited, but that they clearly revolve around the notion of sympathy'.[41] Averill suggests, moreover, that there is enough in the 'painful simplicity of the description' to make the reader sympathize (*extrinsic desert*), and that 'the underlying assumption of the poem is that the reader shares a common bond of sympathy with the author and all civilized men' (*fellowship*).[42] For most critics, however, several features of the narrative create an emotional distance between the speaker and the soldier, such as their unequal relationship.[43] Matthew Brennan suggests that Wordsworth's speaker shows 'condescending superiority and an immature disgust for lower, destitute beings'.[44] Commentary on perceived differences between the soldier and the speaker is often based on a premise that the soldier is in some sense a projection of the speaker. Brennan builds on Warren Stephenson's reading of the soldier as an alter ego, interpreting the poem as an 'archetypal story of self-discovery and psychological growth ("individuation"), in which the poet-to-be reaches the threshold of overcoming an inferiority through confrontation with the soldier – his alter ego or shadow, which was previously submerged in his unconscious'.[45]

Critics sometimes suggest that there is an emotional distance between the speaker and the soldier because of the speaker's inability to express appropriate feelings (indignation or sympathy) during the encounter with the soldier. Stephenson notes a reluctance in the poet with regard to expressing feelings of sympathy and comments that 'any honest reading of the' encounter 'will impress one with a sense of the powerful ambivalence with which Wordsworth regards the veteran'.[46] Brennan warns that 'the poet's sympathy should not be emphasized too strongly, for the ... youth's reaction to the poor veteran is not sympathy but "specious cowardice" – he cold-bloodedly gawks at the miserable man as if he were a circus freak; and even when he does act charitably, he does so in a condescending, reproachful way'.[47] Simon Bainbridge observes that 'what is striking in Wordsworth's presentation of the soldier's telling of his tale is ... its failure to produce the conventional poetic responses of sympathy or indignation on the part of the poet'.[48] Moreover, the narrator remains distant from the act of giving (he asks someone else to give). Mark Offord argues that 'not only has there been no genuine exchange, there has not even been any real giving'.[49] He calls the speaker's actions at the end of the poem, 'Wordsworth's act of insufficient charity'.[50] The narrator appears to critics to lack an overt motive for giving. Adam Potkay, for instance, reads the poem as exploring 'the challenge of unexpected and unpredictable encounters, with strangers whose claims on us are imperfect'.[51]

Several critics comment that they are certain that the poem produces sympathy in the reader, but that they are uncertain about what generates this. The frustrating nature of the poem is routinely seen as *disabling* the reader with its awkwardness or non-communication. Beth Darlington comments that the poem has 'a sense of baffling significance, a frustrating urgency that induces dumbness'.[52] Although Brennan understands the speaker as condescending and unempathetic, he oddly disaffirms this, describing the poem as having 'a moral purpose in which the exalted Poet identifies his feelings with the pain of the poor and deserted, and thereby pleasingly evokes our sympathy'.[53] Other critics read the poem as expressing opposing views of sympathy. Nancy Yousef, for instance, places the poem in the context of what she sees as 'key contradictions in eighteenth-century theories of moral sentiment'.[54] Yousef argues that the tension in Wordsworth's poem, between 'assumptions of fellow feeling (on the one hand) and unresolved questions about the possibility of knowing other persons (on the other)', is part of a central and 'deeply troubling . . . epistemological problem' that emerges from confusions in eighteenth-century theories of moral sentiment, such as those seen in Shaftesbury and Smith. The issue is that sympathy by itself seemingly provides no morally normative guidance for ethical decision-making.[55] Yousef describes the encounter as 'a curiously disappointing' meeting 'in which sympathetic expectations are roundly frustrated'.[56] According to William Richey, it is because of Wordsworth's failure to solve the contradiction between sympathy and moral duty that he 'appears to be doing everything he can to *prevent* his readers from identifying with . . . [a] seemingly perfect candidate for sympathy'.[57] Whatever we make of these appraisals of the problem of sympathy in Wordsworth's poem, it seems reasonable to suppose that, since sympathy appears not be the primary focus of the poem, the poem's emphasis is elsewhere.

This chapter argues that despite the focus on sympathy in the critical conversation, the primary focus of the poem is on the problem of desert, and that this is a traditional topic for this kind of encounter. Placing Wordsworth's poem in the context of disabled servicemen stories reveals that the poet is aware of the desert bases that are typically used in this genre, of extrinsic and intrinsic desert claims, of the different ways of creating motivation in cases of altruism, and of the need to have the capacity to give. The issue of whether the soldier's claims are deserving, and of whether the speaker's response is appropriate, is only resolvable once we establish the nature of Wordsworth's implied theory of desert.[58] Wordsworth's soldier's story is short and factual, and, although it contains elements of a desert base, the story is not the motivator for the reward. Indeed, it is regarded by the speaker in the poem as being told in a disengaged, disinterested, and overly brief manner. Additional components of the story take us out of the realm of altruism motivated by sympathy or virtue and into the realm of altruism motivated by appeals to friendship, fellowship, and proximity, as is traditional in disabled servicemen narratives. The speaker thus affirms the soldier's extrinsic desert, and is moved to act altruistically by his friendship (he twice calls him 'comrade'), his fellowship (he is likewise a weary solitary), and his proximity (they are the only people on the road). He agrees that the soldier does not need to tell his story in order to establish a desert claim, but he asserts nonetheless that the soldier should generate a motivation through a request. He tells the soldier to *demand* the succour that his state requires. He may even imply that an obligation is due as a consequence of a request (and thus that this is not altruism at all).[59] The soldier counters this assertion with the response that he should not have to ask. He expects others to act on his appearance (*extrinsic desert*). Both the speaker and the soldier favour extrinsic desert (that is, desert based on what is apparent and not on the soldier's account of himself): the speaker because he acts on it, and the soldier because he relies on it. The speaker, however, is aware that other people may not respond to extrinsic desert and advises the soldier to make a petition to motivate people to act altruistically.

Significantly, Wordsworth shows his sophistication in making the poem self-reflexive. Not only is the speaker's discussion with the soldier *about* the most effective motivations in altruistic circumstances, the poem as a whole inserts elements in the speaker's account of the moments before the two meet that hint at the motivating factors (as we see in Engel's account of embedded hints). The poet also helps us to understand some of the confusion that the unusual appearance of the soldier may generate. His trouble with his initial reactions to the soldier's appearance models for us the aspects of a situation that may demotivate. He uses these responses as a false start. For the reader used to reading disabled soldier origin stories, however, the poem is about a prima facie case of desert, in which the speaker recognizes the soldier's *extrinsic desert*, and is motivated to help by friendship, fellowship, and proximity. This reading explains a number of oddities about the poem, including the speaker's hesitancy over ascribing needs for which he has no verifiable evidence; the kind of desert case the speaker makes to the cottager whose assistance he calls on; and some of the changes that Wordsworth made to the poem over time. All of these point us in the direction of reading the poem as an account of desert rather than of sympathy.

## Aesthetic False Starts

The beginning of 'The Discharged Soldier' is usually presented as a puzzle, if it is noticed at all. Adam Potkay suggests that the 'meditative description' in the opening moments before the speaker describes his meeting with the soldier 'seems strangely divorced from any narrative purpose'.[60] C. F. Stone comments that 'the first verse paragraph is often troubling for critics' because of the 'narrative awkwardness' in representing the speaker as an unworthy recipient of the natural scene.[61] The opening is less of an enigma, however, if we see it as grounding the relationship between the speaker and the soldier. The speaker's senses slumber, he is exhausted from work, he feels unworthy, and he is solitary. He feels unprepared to engage emotionally with the beauty he anticipates he will experience in his walk in the countryside. His solitariness and weariness, however, suggest an affinity and a fellowship with the soldier, who also exhibits these detached qualities, and these are altruistic motivators. In identifying himself as a 'worn out' and 'exhausted' worker, the speaker shares the condition of incapacity with the soldier he has yet to meet.[62] The close connection between the soldier and the speaker is also developed through a series of images that explore the common ground, often contrasting ability and inability only to dismantle the distinctions later on. The opening celebrates ambulatory ability in the declamatory and truncated, and ultimately ironic first line, 'I love to walk', only to question it immediately.[63] This line is followed with a halting enjambment, by the clause 'Along the public way'.[64] Although meant as a continuation, the line change creates a moment when the reader is forced to manage the transition. It implies a moment of pause. The speaker's celebration of pedestrianism, able-bodiedness, and independence is quickly undermined by the subsequent description of the difficulty of the climb, where the expectation of vigour is countered by the speaker 'slowly'[65] mounting 'up a steep ascent'[66] on a road so waterlogged that it 'seemed before my eyes another stream'.[67] The watery road leaks into the brook in the valley, further foreshadowing the encounter that is yet to come. The speaker's solitary struggle up the muddy hill is an embedded narrative that makes his body more closely akin to that of the soldier. The speaker signals the significance of desert in other ways in his pre-encounter state of mind, too. He highlights the relief he receives from the tranquillity of the scene 'in my own despite'.[68] So, in spite of not *apparently* being deserving ('all unworthy'), he is, nonetheless, the recipient of a gift.[69] This again foreshadows the encounter to come. The gift restores him to a sense of 'self-possession'[70] which is 'felt in every pause / And every gentle movement of my frame'.[71] He begins with a sense that he cannot respond worthily to a visually aesthetic experience, and ends with happily experiencing mental images inspired by sounds.

This kind of narrative preamble is not uncommon in disabled serviceman narratives, and bears a strong resemblance to the opening to Harley's encounter with Edwards in Mackenzie's *The Man of Feeling*. Harley, who begins his journey home by stagecoach, decides he would prefer to walk, because it leaves 'him at liberty to chuse his quarters, either at an inn, or at the first cottage in which he saw a face he liked', or to sleep outside.[72] He follows a 'little frequented' overgrown path.[73] Receptive to the twilight scene, Harley is 'induced ... to stand and enjoy it; when, turning round, his notice' is 'attracted by an object, which the fixture of his eye on the spot he walked had before prevented him from observing'.[74] He does not recognize Edwards, his boyhood friend. As Edwards wakes in confusion, Harley turns and walks on, concerned that he has caused distress. He glances back to see the old man has followed him. Weighed down by his heavy knapsack, Edwards 'halted on his walk, and one of his arms was supported by a sling, and lay motionless across his breast'.[75] Edwards asks for the hour, concerned that he has not allowed himself enough time to get to the next village. Harley offers to carry his knapsack, as it would be 'the most honourable badge I ever wore', were Edwards to accept the help.[76]

When Harley meets Edwards, he first describes him aesthetically. He is 'an old man, who from his dress seemed to have been a soldier'[77] and looks like 'one of those figures which Salvator would have drawn'.[78] 'The surrounding scenery' is similar to 'the wildness of that painter's backgrounds'.[79] Harley's aesthetic false start (he responds to Edwards as if he is in a picture) distracts him from realizing that he knows the man. When the two talk, however, the picturesqueness of the old man becomes insignificant. Rather, the focus is on the details of his origin story, on his desert claims, and the question of how to formulate a practical response to his situation. In this genre, the first impressions of a serviceman frequently concern his visual appearance, and this contributes to the sense of the serviceman's deservingness. The visual evidence is contingent upon the story, however. These narratives are essentially about the relief of a man who cannot work, and they treat impairment as a functional rather than an aesthetic category. Narrators who approach the visual component aesthetically usually transition to an abilities-based response.

Wordsworth follows MacKenzie's model loosely. Like Harley, Wordsworth's speaker has gone in search of the freedoms and aesthetic pleasure of nature. He begins with an aesthetic response to the man's appearance, which may imply a gothic gaze ('ghostly figure').[80] He describes the soldier as an 'uncouth shape': aesthetically odd, strange, or unusual.[81] This is a false start because the speaker is not immediately motivated to altruism. He is, instead, afraid. It is, however, a 'specious cowardice'.[82] Here he embeds his later partiality, commenting from the perspective of his subsequent knowledge that there was no need to fear. The undeniably gothic aura surrounding the initial encounter with the serviceman establishes the soldier as the 'Other'. This effect is soon undermined, however, by the soldier himself becoming unsettled by the gothic nature of the scene that surrounds him.[83] The gothic gaze that initially constructed the soldier as the Other signals the similarity, even solidarity, of the soldier and the narrator.

Both MacKenzie's and Wordsworth's interlocutors stop and stare at their soldiers. Harley guesses much about the sleeping man from observing him. Although Wordsworth's soldier is awake and in the shadows, his unseen speaker tries to work out why the man is there without engaging with him. Wordsworth dwells for longer than MacKenzie on his description of the soldier's body and clothes. Both speakers feel that they deserve blame for their initial reactions to the soldier: Harley for having startled the sleeping man, and Wordsworth's speaker for having stared too long. The speaker feels a sense of self-reproach for having prolonged his gaze: 'Not without reproach / Had I prolonged my watch'.[84] Critics sometimes read this staring as voyeurism. David Bromwich suggests, for instance, that 'the man had left an uncomfortable residue of some trait of Wordsworth himself; and [that] the image of himself watching gave a hint of a quality in his poetry that he would rather have kept hidden'.[85] We can also see this moment as a hint at the importance of moral desert. Self-reproach is a deserved reaction to staring, even if this staring is in some respects an attempt to establish evidence for extrinsic desert. The narrator's sense of having injured the soldier by intrusive looking may suggest he has generated some kind of obligation towards him.

In calling the soldier an 'uncouth shape',[86] Wordsworth uses the same aesthetic language that he uses in *The Convention of Cintra* (1809). Here, he asserts that the French army did not deserve protection as they exited Portugal after their defeat. A deal was done that allowed the French to leave with their equipment and stolen plunder, and without having answered for the atrocities that, Wordsworth suggests, were committed there. In an elaborate metaphor that connects the strangeness of a deformed body with the strangeness of the deal, Wordsworth writes that the agreement struck the British people as

> *strange and uncouth*, exhibiting such discordant characteristics of innocent fatuity and enormous guilt, that it could not without violence be thought of as indicative of a general constitution of things, either in the country or the government; but that it was a kind of *lusus naturae* in the moral world – a solitary straggler out of the circumference of nature's law – a monster which could not propagate, and had no birthright in futurity.[87]

Wordsworth suggests here that Britain, as the country that allowed this to happen, let a monster threaten the future. He comments on this figure again later in the essay, suggesting that, when the government gave the impression that the convention was a cause for celebration, 'the evil appeared no longer as the forlorn monster which I have described. It put on another shape, and was endued with a more formidable life – with power to generate and transmit after its kind'.[88] The soldier is the 'uncouth shape' that appears at first glance to be worthy of rejection, but whose desert is later made apparent; the convention of Cintra, however, remains monstrous in Wordsworth's estimation.

## The Discharged Soldier's Deservingness

Wordsworth's speaker includes a number of signifiers of extrinsic desert, some of which belong to the aesthetic false start. While he is observing the soldier, before he converses with him, the speaker lingers over aspects of the soldier's visual appearance – particularly the clues that point to his identity as a soldier, and the evidence of his physical state. The soldier appears to have a number of impairments that are described in vague terms. He rests on a milestone groaning, his form has 'A meagre stiffness', and 'You might almost think / That his bones wounded him'.[89] His cheeks are 'sunken',[90] he has a 'wasted'[91] face, and his legs are so 'shapeless' they make the speaker 'Forgetful of the body they sustained'.[92] These all point to desert arising from adverse circumstances, in which the appearance of sickness, weariness, and solitude (and possibly hunger and poverty) intensify the soldier's deservingness.[93] Wordsworth further increases the sense of the soldier's deservingness in 1850, by suggesting that he has been on the road for three weeks rather than ten days.[94]

In MacKenzie's narrative, the switch from aesthetics to functionality is smooth, because Edwards's elaborate and affecting story distracts the reader with the desert claims elaborated on in the origin story. The story of Wordsworth's soldier, however, is simple, short, and told without feeling. Here Wordsworth redirects the soldier's deservingness away from its usual territory: virtuous past actions, an entertaining story, or a detailed list of adverse events. Instead, the poem is about learning to take account of extrinsic desert, and the importance of recognizing fellowship and proximity as motivators to altruistic giving. Of the soldier's military service (whether he 'endured ... war, and battle'),[95] we learn only that he had gone 'to the tropic isles' and had come back.[96] Little is presented beyond the observable effects of adverse circumstances. Extrinsic desert is evident, then, simply from the soldier's apparent function impairment and indigence, coupled with his status as a former serviceman. The poem offers nothing further to establish his worthiness for compensation and neither the emotion of the speaker nor that of the soldier is required to support or to intensify the soldier's deservingness.

Wordsworth complicates this. The speaker makes it very clear that he is not certain that a need is present. When he arranges a bed for the soldier, he suggests, without making assumptions, that the cottager 'will give' him 'food (*if food you need*)'.[97] The soldier's injuries only *seem* to be present, and the speaker stresses both the contingency of his statements and that their provability is not necessary for a benevolent response. Like Harley, Wordsworth's narrator does not need to be satisfied beyond perceived desert; but Wordsworth's speaker is self-conscious about his doubtful readings of the signs. His soldier '*appeared* / Forlorn and desolate',[98] '*appeared* / To travel without pain',[99] 'You might *almost* think / That his bones wounded him',[100] and he makes 'murmuring sounds, *as if* of pain'.[101] Although the speaker stresses that he cannot see the soldier clearly, he does not question the soldier's deservingness. Wordsworth's subtlety has been missed. The speaker's sense of contingency signals that the soldier deserves his reward without the need for verification or for a desert case to be fully made.

Additionally, Wordsworth sets aside the idea of a performance creating an obligation in the listener (*quid pro quo*), and, in omitting the expected emotional story (*intrinsic desert*), he dismisses the opportunity for the soldier to demonstrate the effect of his adverse circumstances on his wellbeing. Expressing the pain of recollection is a significant sympathy generator. Wordsworth's soldier presents his tale offstage with 'a strange half-absence, and a tone / Of weakness and indifference, as of one / Remembering the importance of his theme / But feeling it no longer'.[102] This absence can be read in two ways: it may be an argument for the necessity of sympathy generators (contrary to my reading); and it may be an intensifier of the soldier's deservingness. For the latter reading, we need to understand the adverse events to be so affecting that the soldier cannot engage his emotions when telling the tale.

The soldier's lack of emotion, and thus his seeming undeservingness, is reinforced by his private but audible complaints. His 'murmuring voice of dead complaint'[103] stops when he sees the speaker ('He ... ceased / From all complaint').[104] Although the speaker makes a point of noting that the soldier does not complain to him, and describes his replies as spoken in 'a quiet uncomplaining voice',[105] there is an undercurrent of complaint in the poem. The soldier's murmur of complaint is echoed by other elements of the landscape: the stream which 'murmured in the valley',[106] the cottager who will not 'murmur should we break his rest',[107] and the dog howling to the 'murmur of the stream'.[108] The quantity of unarticulated complaints, their transference to other objects and people, and their negation (the cottager will not murmur, and the soldier stops his groans), remind us that the soldier could complain, but does not. The soldier could gain virtue from his stoicism in not voicing complaint, but the murmuring may also indeed suggest complaint, and the soldier is not required to be stoical in order to be deserving. Wordsworth comments directly on the honour and virtues of servicemen in *The Convention of Cintra*, when he suggests that 'there was scarcely a gallant [British] father of a family who had not moments of regret that he was not a soldier by profession', and that every serviceman 'from the General to the private soldier' had the 'virtues which might be expected from him as a soldier'.[109]

## Rewarding Desert

The interchange between the speaker, the soldier, and the cottager at the end of the poem is important for reinforcing the idea that the poem is about desert rather than sympathy. There are three moments to consider: the speaker's account of the cottager to the soldier; his petition to the cottager on behalf of the soldier; and his advice to the solider on what to do when they part company. The first persuades the soldier to trust the cottager as a person who will be motivated to act; and the second provokes the cottager to altruism. Wordsworth altered these sections of the poem several times, perhaps indicating that he was concerned about the problem of desert. In the 1798 version, the cottager is a labourer who is an 'honest man and kind', and is thus to be depended upon.[110] The labourer's own virtue, it is implied, will prompt his recognition of the soldier's desert. In this version, the speaker motivates the cottager by claiming friendship with him, by outlining the soldier's desert (sickness, hunger, and lack of shelter). He indicates, too, the expected reward

> 'My friend, here is a man
> By sickness overcome. Beneath your roof
> This night let him find rest, and give him food.–'[111]

The speaker is careful, nevertheless, not to presume that the cottager is in a financial position to give, and so offers money to compensate the cottager: '"This service if need be I will requite".'[112] The speaker himself is not in a position to provide succour, because he is not near his home – a fact that Wordsworth makes clearer in 1805 when he changes the final line from 'And so we parted' to 'Then sought with quiet heart my distant home'.[113] The cottager unlocks his door, and the speaker is 'Assured that now my comrade would repose / In comfort'.[114] At the end of the poem the speaker repeats the reference to the soldier as his 'comrade' when describing the soldier touching his hat, again emphasizing their fellowship.[115]

In 1805, the speaker gives a different account of the cottager. He no longer emphasizes the cottager's virtues (honesty and kindness). He asks the soldier to 'take it on my word'[116] that the cottager will not complain about being woken at night, and that the cottager will give him 'food and lodging for the night'.[117] Wordsworth also alters the narrator's comment from an assurance about the cottager ('he will give you food [if food you need])'[118] to an instruction to the cottager ('give him food, / If food he need'),[119] and he removes the offer of compensation to the cottager. The removal of the offer to 'requite' compensation may be explained by Wordsworth rethinking the plausibility of indicating that the two are friends.[120] If the speaker is the friend of the cottager, then he is likely to be aware of his means, or the two may have an unspoken understanding that the speaker would not allow the cottager to suffer financial hardship on his behalf. At the conclusion of the tale, the soldier, in 1805, is no longer a comrade touching his hat, but is merely 'the soldier'.[121] He retains his status as 'comrade', however, when the speaker refers to his assurances about the cottager.[122] In 1850, Wordsworth removes his account of the cottager altogether. The speaker asks the soldier to '"Come with me"', but does not specify where or to what end.[123] This may emphasize the sense of fellowship between the speaker and the soldier, or it may highlight the thematic emphasis on the lack of need for explanation. Additionally, the speaker's direct speech to the cottager is removed in 1850, and, instead, the speaker reports that he 'earnestly to charitable care / Commended him as a poor friendless man, / Belated and by sickness overcome'.[124] In the final iteration, Wordsworth characterizes the soldier's deservingness as his friendlessness, the late hour, and his incapacity; he removes the word 'comrade' entirely in this version, and the soldier is referred to less familiarly as 'the traveller'[125] and 'the soldier'.[126]Although the friendship words are not present in the later versions, the narrator nevertheless indicates a stronger sense of his fellowship with the soldier than is implied in the first version.[127] Fellowship arises, particularly in the 1850 *Prelude*, from shared experiences of solitude, and it assists in the speaker's motivation to act. The 1850 version also contains a philosophical excursus on the positive benefits of solitude for busy and exhausted people. The speaker observes that people who are alone remind us of this benefit. Both men feel the healing and benign power of solitude. The earlier versions of the incident do not contain a reference to solitude as a 'great Power', but there are references to solitude in the description of the night, and in the peace surrounding the speaker. Fellowship through solitude is thus implied in the earlier versions.

The speaker's advice to the soldier on what to do after they have parted also concerns desert. In 1798, he entreats the soldier to 'Demand the succour which his state required'[128] 'at the door of cottage or of inn';[129] and says of him that "twere fit / He asked relief or alms'[130] and not to 'linger in the public ways'.[131] Wordsworth, however, is less specific about where to ask for relief in the later versions, and the soldier is advised to 'ask for timely furtherance, and help / Such as his state required'.[132] The undefined reference to the soldier's 'state' may refer to his physical condition, his homelessness, hunger, or to his status as a former soldier, or to all of these. In entreating the soldier to petition, the speaker is clearly concerned with the soldier's role in motivating an altruistic response. Demanding what you need is obviously more forceful than asking for assistance, and the change may indicate that Wordsworth has become more confident that the altruism is not under-motivated. Significantly, by changing 'demand' to 'ask', he removes any temptation to read this as a question of obligation. In all versions, the soldier asserts in response to this advice that he does not need to ask (*extrinsic desert*): "'My trust is in the God of Heaven, / And in the eye of him that passes me!'"[133] Like the soldiers in the other disabled servicemen narratives, the discharged soldier does not beg. This is most likely because begging will invalidate his governmental entitlements.[134]

In this reading of 'The Discharged Soldier' and its later versions, I have set aside the problem of sympathy that has vexed so many commentators in favour of a reading that focuses on the problem of motivation in altruistic giving. Sympathy is not wholly lacking in the poem, however.[135] The narrator states, before the encounter, that he is 'disposed to sympathy'[136] and, at the end of the poem, both the soldier and the narrator show some kind of mutual understanding that may indicate sympathy:

> and in a voice that seemed
> To speak with a reviving interest
> Till then unfelt, he thanked me; I returned
> The blessing of the poor unhappy man,
> And so we parted.[137]

Nevertheless, a disposition towards sympathy is, of course, not the same as feeling sympathy, and Wordsworth omits the word 'sympathy' entirely in 1850. Sympathy is clearly not the theme of any version. There is a context for Wordsworth's side-lining of sympathy. Eighteenth-century theories of moral sentiments generally present sympathy as a deserved good that can only be given once a person has ascertained the details of a particular situation. Adam Smith observes, for instance, that reason and knowledge of a case are a prerequisite to sympathy.

> General lamentations, which express nothing but the anguish of the sufferer, create rather a curiosity to enquire into his situation, along with some disposition to sympathize with him, than any actual sympathy that is very sensible. The first question we ask is, What has befallen you? 'Till this be answered, tho' we are uneasy both from the vague idea of his misfortune, and still more from torturing ourselves with conjectures about what it may be, yet our fellow-feeling is not very considerable.[138]

According to Smith, sympathy requires detailed knowledge of a particular person and their circumstances. Wordsworth's speaker, however, cannot gain this knowledge from the soldier, and so he establishes different motivations for altruism. Wordsworth follows a Smithian line on sympathy in the 'Essays Upon Epitaphs', where he writes that the particular details of a person's life need to provoke sympathy and to be blended to produce sympathy.

> The general sympathy ought to be quickened, provoked, and diversified, by particular thoughts, actions, images, – circumstances of age, occupation, manner of life, prosperity which the deceased had known, or adversity to which he had been subject; and it ought to be bound together and solemnised into one harmony by the general sympathy.[139]

Critics have seen the poem as problematic because sympathy is neither expressed by the speaker nor motivated by the soldier. The poem deliberately sets up the situation in this way, however, and so it is perhaps more fruitful to see this problem as a different question about altruism. What are the appropriate motivators in situations where we do not know or cannot be certain of the circumstances (and therefore cannot generate the informed sympathy that Smith prizes)? In this case, motivation derives from the speaker being physically near and similar to the soldier, and from the soldier's appearance.

## Conclusion

Desert is significant for understanding the moral sentiment expressed in 'The Discharged Soldier', as it is the basis for moral and justice claims. The issue of how desert is presented has some bearing on how we understand the politics of the poem and on its biographical significance. The questions 'What does the discharged soldier deserve?' and 'On what basis does he

deserve it?' bring with them further questions. What does a society deem
necessary to give to someone who may be unentitled, but morally deserving? And, in cases in which an individual is moved to rectify the mismatch
between moral desert and entitlement, what is it that prompts them to act?
The poem suggests that an outpouring of sentimental emotion is required
neither by the speaker nor by the soldier for us to establish that the soldier
is deserving; and sympathy does not need to motivate altruism. The question is: Why make this case? Mark Offord suggests that Wordsworth is
prompted here 'less by a conscious philosophical ambition than by an
aesthetic drive to overturn the banal exchanges of sympathy in sentimental
literature – whose apparent spontaneity tended rather in its mechanisms to
follow the *quid pro quo* of the contract'.[140] I have argued, however, that the
poem has a legitimate philosophical purpose: the speaker is called to a
humanitarian response to a deserving person, motivated by fellowship,
proximity, and kinship, as is common in the genre in which the poet is
writing. The speaker is schooled by the soldier to trust in the effectiveness of
his appearance of deservingness. He is, nevertheless, uncertain that others
will act as he does towards the soldier without the details of an origin story;
but the soldier remains committed to his view that extrinsic desert (that
which appears to be the case) will provide him with what he needs.

Depicting impaired soldiers persistently as receivers of charity is not
unproblematic.[141] Disability studies alerts us to the restricted form of social
inclusion that designates people with disabilities as appropriate for charitable
support, and as deflecting discussion of rights into discussion of needs.[142]
Charity is dismissed by disability activists on the grounds that it renders
people with disabilities passive, and excludes, and stigmatizes. Tom Shakespeare comments that charity promotes disability as 'a tragedy, not a political
responsibility'.[143] Ellen Barton asserts, furthermore, that charity constructs
'simplistic and stereotypical representations of disability primarily by erasing
the complex experience of individuals'.[144] Narratives that associate disability
with charity, she suggests, 'maintain the stereotype that people with disabilities are the Other, not integrated into ordinary life, not allowed to define
independence and dependence in their own ways, not allowed to be different
in spite of their differences'.[145] 'The Discharged Soldier' gives us scope for
rethinking the sympathy-dependent ethos of charity. In seeking to explore
the connectedness of the discharged soldier and his interlocutor, and in his
exploration of the complexities of desert, Wordsworth circumvents the
cultural divisions between helper and helped, and between impaired and
not impaired, and he recognizes a self-evident deservingness that could be
conceptualized as a prelude to disability rights-based thinking.

# PART II

# Aesthetics of Deformity

## CHAPTER 4

# Picturesque Aesthetics
## Theorizing Deformity in the Romantic Era

> Poetry turns all things to loveliness: it exalts the beauty of that which
> is most beautiful, and it adds beauty to that which is most *deformed*;
> it marries exultation and horror, grief and pleasure, eternity and
> change; it subdues to union under its light yoke all irreconcilable
> things.[1]

When Percy Shelley wrote to Thomas Love Peacock about their disagreement on the nature of poetry – a disagreement caused by Peacock's *The
Four Ages of Poetry* (1820) – he expressed a hope that they would not
'imitate the great founders of the picturesque, [Uvedale] Price and [Rich-
ard] Payne Knight, who like two ill-trained beagles, began snarling at each
other when they could not catch the hare'.[2] The hare that Price and
Knight were chasing was the definition of the picturesque; and an important part of their disagreement centred on the question of whether
deformed people could be regarded as picturesque, and in this way
aesthetically pleasing. Shelley's suggestion, in 'A Defence of Poetry'
(1821), that representation adds beauty to 'that which is most deformed'
by linking together the 'irreconcilable' hints at his knowledge of the details
of this disagreement.[3] It also highlights the significance of deformity for
questions that are fundamental to aesthetic production and appreciation in
the Romantic era.

Tobin Siebers observes that while disability is not absent from aesthetic
history, it has been excluded in the sense that its role in the questions that
are fundamental to aesthetic production and appreciation has not been
made apparent. For Siebers, disability aesthetics names 'the emergence of
disability in modern art as a significant presence' in the twentieth century,
and it 'prizes physical and mental difference as a significant value in itself'.[4]
Disability aesthetics, as Siebers describes it,

> does not embrace an aesthetic taste that defines harmony, bodily integrity,
> and health as standards of beauty. Nor does it support the aversion to

disability required by traditional conceptions of human or social perfection. Rather, it drives forward the appreciation of disability found throughout modern art by raising an objection to aesthetic standards and tastes that exclude people with disabilities.[5]

As modern uses of the term 'disability' do not emerge until the nineteenth century, pre-disability concepts that are ancestral or analogous to disability, such as deformity, are significant for understanding in what sense, if at all, such a claim about the twentieth century as a significant moment in the aesthetic inclusion of people with disabilities is true.

## Eighteenth-Century Theories of Deformity

In eighteenth-century aesthetics, deformity is most commonly defined in relation to its effect, and is, according to most thinkers, the opposite of beauty.[6] Looking at people or objects with deformities causes the viewer to experience 'pain'[7] (Hume), 'disgust'[8] (Burke), and 'disappointment'[9] (Hutcheson). Shaftesbury associates deformity with 'calamity and ruin',[10] and Addison calls it 'disagreeable'.[11] Hume is an exception in thinking that being deformed causes self-dissatisfaction (or 'humility'), and that one's own deformed body has this effect because, unlike illness, deformity is 'peculiar' to the possessor.[12] In Hume's estimation, illness varies so greatly and is experienced so frequently and by so many people that it is 'never consider'd as connected with our being and existence'.[13]

    The earliest and most influential account of beauty and deformity in British philosophy is in Shaftesbury's *Characteristics* (1711). Although his discussion of the topic is scattered throughout this work, and is occasionally voiced in Socratic dialogue, it nevertheless amounts to a coherent aesthetic theory and a theory of taste,[14] and is generally thought to have played 'a seminal role in the development of British aesthetics'.[15] Jerome Stolnitz notes, for instance, that Shaftesbury was 'one of the most widely read authors of his time', because 'by the middle of the century "disinterestedness" had become a staple of British thought'.[16] Shaftesbury, a student of Locke's work, suggests that, since the mind begins as a *tabula rasa*, 'a taste or judgment' on an aesthetic issue 'can hardly come ready formed with us into the world', and the experience of beauty or deformity requires a combination of sensory perception and judgement.[17] Although the idea of beauty is not innate, Shaftesbury proposes that our disposition to experience the world aesthetically evolves as a natural process that is developed by knowledge of the systems to which objects belong.[18] Additionally, Shaftesbury asserts that there is a real standard of beauty that is located in the object of beauty itself, and not in the judgement of the observer.[19] He posits that beauty derives from the perception of harmony, proportion, and order; and that the parts of the object, whether natural or man-made, must relate to each other in such a way that they have 'a unity of design and concur in one'.[20] Shaftesbury's theory of beauty is explicitly tied to his understanding of moral beauty as 'the most natural beauty in the world'.[21] Beauty is synonymous with good, and with truth, he observes, and virtue is a type of beauty. Shaftesbury describes deformity as unnatural, and associates it with vice and as deserving of ridicule: 'nothing is ridiculous except what is deformed, nor is anything proof against raillery except what is handsome and just'.[22] Taking the view that God has the most beauteous body and is the source of all beauteous bodies, Shaftesbury quotes from Maximus Tyrius's *Orations* to 'express' this view: 'As beings partake of this [celestial beauty] they are fair and flourishing and happy; as they are lost to this, they are deformed, perished and lost.'[23] Regarding the converse, as James Chandler summarizes, 'a distorted the soul is said by Shaftesbury to arise from a distorted body'.[24]

Francis Hutcheson writes extensively on beauty and deformity, and, like Shaftesbury, his work owes a great deal to Locke. Hutcheson's *An Inquiry into the Original of Our Ideas of Beauty and Virtue* (1725) takes as its starting point Locke's distinction between primary and secondary qualities.[25] A primary quality exists without being perceived (such as shape and size), whereas a secondary quality (such as colour) requires a perceiver for its reality. Hutcheson understands beauty to be a secondary quality.[26] Importantly, he argues that a specific internal sense, the 'sense of beauty', is needed in order to perceive aesthetically. He distinguishes two kinds of beauty: *original* (or absolute) and *comparative* (or relative). The first is perceived in objects 'without comparison to anything external' and the second is perceived 'in objects considered as imitations or resemblances of something else'.[27] Original beauty is described as 'uniformity amidst variety'.[28] The ground of comparative beauty is the accuracy of the object considered as a *representation*. So, as Hutcheson points out, a true representation of something that wholly lacks beauty can be beautiful.[29] He suggests, nevertheless, that the beauty of the original object might increase the beauty of the representation.[30] Deformity comes into Hutcheson's discussion as the contradiction of beauty; it is simply the absence of beauty: 'deformity is only the absence of beauty, or deficiency in the beauty expected in any species'.[31] In this Hutcheson is in accordance with a long tradition of Neoplatonic and Christian thinking on the nature of evil (as a privation of good) that goes back to Augustine and Plotinus. As is standard, the emotional reaction to beauty is pleasure; but, Hutcheson explains, the emotional reaction to deformity is disappointment rather than pain.[32] This is because, unlike the external senses, the sense of beauty cannot be adversely affected – it cannot suffer 'pain, or positive pain or disgust, any further than what arises from disappointment'.[33] Hutcheson accepts that there are 'many faces which at first view are apt to raise dislike',[34] but maintains that this is not because of their failing to be beautiful; it is either because of the disappointment of an *expectation* of beauty or 'much more from their carrying some natural indications of morally bad dispositions'.[35] Hutcheson avoids taking a relativist position by arguing that differences in aesthetic judgement are the result of the accidental association of different ideas with various perceptions. These variables derive, for Hutcheson, from custom, education, and example.[36]

Hume generally holds the view that both deformity and beauty are not objective properties of bodies but simply subjective properties of the observer: 'pleasure and pain, therefore, are not only necessary attendants of beauty and deformity, but constitute their very essence'.[37] As he writes in 'Of the Standard of Taste', there is no 'real deformity'.[38] There is also no correct response to given bodily configurations: 'one person may even perceive deformity where another is sensible of beauty'.[39] Hume is some-times ambiguous about his subjectivism, however, and occasionally sug-gests that beauty and deformity are objective features of bodies that cause certain kinds of sentiments in the observer. For example, he writes that 'deformity is a structure of parts, which conveys pain'.[40] Hume is ambig-uous about his relativism as well, since he maintains that there are expert views or true judges who are the arbiters of taste.[41] Taste can be refined, and experience and practice in the art of assessing things aesthetically can produce a more 'acute perception of beauty and deformity' than that produced by someone less well informed.[42] Hume may mean, however, merely that people can be trained to better follow the aesthetic customs of a given society. Hume's relativistic subjectivism represents an extreme view in eighteenth-century aesthetics. At the other extreme are the views of those who believe not only that negative associations attaching to defor-mity are objective, but that deformity itself is an objective quality of a body. The most general division is between those who, like Hume, believe beauty and deformity to be subjective qualities, wholly dependent on and descriptive of the response of an observer, and those who adopt the majority view that beauty and deformity are objective properties, existing independently of observation. Among the Humeans, some, like Hume himself, are relativists, believing that aesthetic judgements are simply matters of individual taste; and others are subjectivists who reject relativism, claiming that there are absolute standards for aesthetic evaluations – much as someone might think that colours are observer dependent, but that there are right and wrong ways of perceiving objects. Hutcheson adopts a view like this. Hume's relativism opens up possibilities for the reinterpretation of the negative qualities associated with deformity, even though he retains, as a definitional truth, the negative evaluation of deformity that is widespread in eighteenth-century aesthetics.

Edmund Burke's influential *A Philosophical Enquiry* (1757) does not explicitly state that it is a response to Hutcheson, whom he does not name, but it is clear from his argumentation that Burke is responding to *Inquiry into the Original of Our Ideas of Beauty and Virtue*.[43] Burke assumes, in his discussion, that there is more or less universal agreement about what counts as beautiful: 'I never remember that any thing beautiful, whether a man, a beast, a bird, or a plant, was ever shewn, though it were to an hundred people, that they did not all immediately agree that it was beautiful, though some might have thought that it fell short of their expectation, or that other things were still finer.'[44] He concedes from the outset that the word 'beauty' is 'indiscriminately applied to things greatly differing',[45] but determines that this situation derives from defects in 'sensibility and judgment'.[46] Burke argues for a standard of beauty, suggesting that while we may argue over degree, we do not disagree over kind, even though the term 'beauty' is 'indiscriminately applied to things greatly differing'.[47] He does not, however, propose the usual standard of beauty, suggesting that the generally accepted 'measure of relative quantity'[48] reduces beauty to a matter of 'calculation and geometry'.[49] He takes the rose as his example: its infinite variety demonstrates that beauty is more than a standardized set of proportions. For Burke, beauty is a variable in the sense that there are many ways in which something can be beautiful. While he allows that there are plenty of beautiful people whose bodies do not follow classical proportions, he concludes that there are qualities in objects that point to beauty, such as smallness, smoothness, gradual variation, delicacy, clarity, fairness, and brightness. Burke rejects outright the idea that deformity is the opposite of beauty, and suggests that belief in this proposition may be behind the persistence of the idea that beauty can be defined according to proportionality. While Hutcheson defines 'deformity' as the absence of beauty, Burke suggests that it is the absence of the '*compleat common form*',[50] and claims that ugliness (not deformity) is the opposite of beauty. For Burke, ugliness is 'in all respects the opposite to those qualities that we have laid down for the constituents of beauty'.[51]

While he does not subscribe to the view that proportionality determines beauty, Burke invokes the proportion argument in order to sustain his view of deformity. He makes an additional case for seeing beauty and deformity as independent of each other on the grounds that both beauty and deformity are uncommon: 'The beautiful strikes us as much by its novelty as the deformed itself.'[52]

Of the picturesque theorists, however, at least William Gilpin and Uvedale Price conceptualize picturesque deformity as giving aesthetic pleasure; and while they retain unqualified deformity as a separate and pejorative category, they undertake a range of complex theoretical manoeuvres in order to maintain the possibility that something deformed can give pleasure. In contrast to Hume, who holds that deformity is just an aesthetic response to an object, the picturesque theorists presuppose deformity to be a feature of an object independently of any observer, and their discussion focuses on the possible aesthetic responses to this feature. Hutcheson's idea of original and comparative beauty may have some influence on these writers, but Addison's views on representation (which I shall outline below) are a more direct source. Burke may have provided an impetus to question the beauty–deformity binary, and may well be the picturesque theorists' source for Addison.

## William Gilpin, Representability, and Picturesque Beauty

Accounts of the picturesque appear in books on art, travel, and gardening, as well as in poetry and fiction. The discussions of this topic engage with theories about perception, taste, and cultural specificity. Picturesque theory largely concentrates on the artistic qualities of natural landscapes, on the ways in which landscapes can be improved artificially, and on the imitation of nature in paintings. Picturesque theorists frequently discuss the qualities of the work of artists such as Rubens, Salvator Rosa, and Guido Reni. It is in the descriptions of this work that much of the consideration of picturesque people takes place. Blind men, old people, gypsies, hermits, and banditti are commonly mentioned in relation to their representation in paintings. There are also occasions on which the theorists consider the aesthetic quality of the real people they encounter on their travels. Picturesque theory is largely about landscape, so the commentary on people is usually something of an afterthought: people are, to some extent, accessories that decorate a landscape. Because the main theorizing about the picturesque occurs in this way, the discussion often raises the question of the relative aesthetic value of people, animals, and inanimate objects (including landscapes and buildings). Ideas about picturesque people become entangled with the central questions for picturesque theory in general, such as the nature of the relationship between deformity and the picturesque, and the mechanism by which deformity can be dissociated from negative characteristics. Gilpin, Price, and Knight all address these problems in different ways.

Gilpin, early in his career, offers a simple and combined solution to three central questions that concern the philosophers of the picturesque: (1) Do people, animals, and inanimate objects all have the same kinds of aesthetic value? (2) What is the nature of the relationship between deformity and the picturesque? (3) How to do we explain the aesthetic appeal of deformity? Gilpin defines the picturesque as 'a term expressive of that peculiar kind of beauty, which is agreeable in a picture'.[53] He highlights, then, a feature of an object that is apt, in a particular way, to be represented: picturesque objects are those 'which please the eye from some quality, capable of being *illustrated in painting*'.[54] The picturesque nature of certain objects results from their intrinsic qualities; and these intrinsic qualities, since they ground a certain kind of representability, enable Gilpin to use the same descriptive terms for people as he does for animals, buildings, and landscapes. We see the picturesque in the 'elderly man, strengthening his steps with a long measuring wand', and in the 'worn-out cart horse' that is admired more than the thoroughbred 'led out of the stable in all his pampered beauty'.[55] Gilpin writes that 'we judge of beauty in castles, as we do in figures, in mountains, and other objects'.[56] The objects that are representable in the relevant way are things that are irregular. The 'picturesque eye' looks at 'the waving corn field, and the ripened sheaf ... with disgust. It ranges after nature, untamed by art, and bursting wildly into all it's [sic] irregular forms'.[57] Irregularity, roughness, and, as Gilpin puts it in 'On Landscape Painting, A Poem' (1792), '*parts disjointed*; nay, perhaps, *deform'd* are, especially, art's 'chief excellence'.[58]

In introducing the idea of picturesque beauty, Gilpin, like Burke, disrupts the beauty–deformity binary. The picturesque is a 'species of beauty' for Gilpin, and he frequently talks about 'picturesque beauty'. The phrase occurs in the titles of several of his books.[59] This is, however, a kind of beauty that relies on the characteristics of deformity, even though Gilpin is careful to distinguish the picturesque from deformity. For example, he sometimes speaks of objects that would be deformed if they were not picturesque.[60] Beauty typically arises for Gilpin, as it does for Burke, 'from that species of elegance, which we call *smoothness*, or *neatness*', and is seen in the 'lovely face of youth smiling with all it's [sic] sweet, dimpling charms'.[61] Gilpin also follows Burke in rejecting the view that the concept of beauty is universal across all objects. Gilpin observes that 'ideas of beauty vary with the object, and with the eye of the spectator'.[62] Picturesque beauty describes 'the human face in it's [sic] highest form', and is seen in 'the patriarchal head' with its 'forehead furrowed with wrinkles', in the 'prominent cheek-bone', the 'shaggy beard', an 'austere brow', and the '*rough* touches of age'.[63] Picturesque grace is 'an agreeable form given, in a picture, to a clownish figure'.[64] When talking of the picturesqueness of the ruins of Valle Crucis Abbey, near Llangollen, Gilpin discerns that 'Beauty is derived from two sources; from objects themselves, and from their contrast with other objects. In contrast even deformity may be one of these sources; and produce beauty, as discords in music, produce harmony'.[65] The picturesque can combine beauty and deformity in ways that are harmonious. Additionally, the arrangement of a thing's intrinsic components – its internal relationships – also contribute to its representability.

Gilpin's deformity aesthetics enables him to write in an untroubled way about ruins and people as having the same aesthetic values. His most elaborate account of a picturesque person occurs in the description of Tintern Abbey in *Observations on the River Wye* (1782). Here he calls the abbey 'the most beautiful and picturesque view on the river', and one which is more picturesque close to than it is from a distance.[66] He laments that someone has tidied up the 'rough fragments'[67] that must have been scattered around, but is pleased with its irregularity, the lack of roof, the 'mosses of various hues',[68] and that 'Nature has now made it her own'.[69] Having described the ruins of the abbey, its form and situation, Gilpin moves his aesthetic gaze to the 'poverty and wretchedness' of its inhabitants.[70] Modern critics of picturesque theory have long noted that the aestheticization of poverty, seen in the admiration of gypsies, bandits, beggars, and hermits, reveals a disengaged emotional, political, and moral sense. Gilpin openly admits that 'moral, and picturesque ideas do not always coincide. In a moral light, cultivation, in all it's [sic] parts, is pleasing', so that it would be better to see farmland and civilized dwellings. The picturesque demands people living in poverty, however, and their representability is all that matters.[71] Nevertheless, Gilpin occasionally shows both moral and aesthetic interest in the picturesque people who become the objects of his appreciation.

In his account of Tintern Abbey, Gilpin focuses on a woman whose body contributes to the aesthetic experience of the abbey: 'She could scarce crawl; shuffling along her palsied limbs, and meagre contracted body, by the help of two sticks. She led us, though an old gate, into a place overspread with nettles, and briars; and pointing to the remnant of a shattered cloister, told us that was the place. It was her own mansion.'[72] Gilpin elides the body of the woman with the building. Very much part of the location, the woman lives in 'a cavity, loftily vaulted, between two ruined walls; which streamed with various-coloured stains of unwholesome dews'.[73] He finds himself listening to her story, while observing the 'wretched bedstead, spread with a few rags', the 'chilling damps', the water 'which trickled down the walls', the low light, 'enough to discover the wretchedness within', and the earth floor 'yielding, through moisture, to the tread'.[74] He is surprised by two things: that he and his companion are interested in her story ('We did not expect to be interested: but we found we were'[75]), and that the conditions in which she is living have not affected her more than the loss of 'the use of her limbs'.[76] Gilpin envisions the woman, her poverty, and the abbey in one view: the ruin, the 'loathsome … human dwelling', and the 'palsied limbs'.[77] The woman's body is part of the aesthetic appeal of the architectural scene; and Gilpin uses the same discourse for both. Even the tale the woman tells of 'the monk's library' is 'the story of her own wretchedness'.[78]

## Uvedale Price, the Aesthetic Continuum, and Striking Peculiarity

Uvedale Price, in his monumental work *An Essay on the Picturesque, as Compared with the Sublime and the Beautiful* (1794), distinguishes himself from Gilpin in preferring to define the picturesque independently of painting and of representation, and in making a distinction between beauty and the picturesque. Price takes issue with these latter two being 'ever mixed and incorporated together' into a single term in Gilpin's work.[79] Beauty and picturesqueness are, Price claims, 'founded on very opposite qualities; the one on smoothness, the other on roughness; – the one on gradual, the other on sudden variation; – the one on ideas of youth and freshness, the other on that of age, and even of decay'.[80] Price concedes, however, that the picturesque can be blended with the sublime or with beauty, that picturesqueness is 'more happily blended with them both than they are with each other', and that 'its charms to a painter's eye are often so great as to rival those of beauty itself'.[81] For Price, the picturesque is a way of describing many things that have 'qualities the most diametrically opposite' to beauty, but which are not deformed. 'The connection between picturesqueness and deformity cannot be too much studied', Price observes, and he spends a great deal of time refining the relationship.[82] Price creates for himself the same problem raised by Gilpin: using the characteristics of deformity to define picturesqueness as agreeable, while at the same time denouncing deformity as disagreeable.[83] Representability solves two problems for Gilpin: (1) it separates the characteristics of deformity from any negative aesthetic evaluation, and (2) it allows both animate and inanimate objects to be picturesque.

Price also provides distinct answers to these two issues. His solution to the first is set out in *An Essay on the Picturesque*. Here he places beauty, picturesqueness, sublimity, and deformity on an aesthetic continuum in which the picturesque is somewhere between the beautiful and the sublime. 'Picturesqueness', Price suggests, 'appears to hold a station between beauty and sublimity', and is 'perfectly distinct from either'.[84] It is distinct in its effect: while beauty pleases and the sublime astonishes, the picturesque inspires 'curiosity'.[85] Additionally, Price sets out a separate but related scale that moves from ugliness to deformity. This scale makes ugliness the correlate of beauty, and deformity the correlate of the picturesque. In Price's words, 'deformity is to ugliness what picturesqueness is to beauty; though distinct from it, and in many cases arising from opposite causes, it is often mistaken for it, often accompanies it, and greatly heightens its effect'.[86] The picturesque is a less extreme form of deformity, however. Price suggests that an 'excess of those [qualities] which constitute picturesqueness produces deformity'.[87] In a remarkable passage, he asks us to consider the features of 'our own species' and imagine the face of a beautiful woman gradually developing into picturesqueness, and then into deformity.[88]

> conceive the eyebrows *more* strongly marked – the hair rougher in its effect and quality – the complexion more dusky and gipsy-like – the skin of a coarser grain, with some moles on it – a degree of cast in the eyes, but so slight as only to give archness and peculiarity of countenance – this, without altering the proportion of the features, would take off from beauty what it gave to character and picturesqueness. If we go one step farther, and encrease the eyebrows to a preposterous size – the cast into a squint – make the skin scarred and pitted with the small pox – the complexion full of spots – and encrease the moles and excrescencies, – it will plainly appear how close the connection is between beauty and insipidity, and between picturesqueness and deformity, and what 'thin partitions do their bounds divide'.[89]

Price's point is that the 'general features' remain the same in the case of beauty, deformity, and the picturesque, but the superficial qualities are enough to make something beautiful, picturesque, or deformed.[90]

Significantly, only a 'thin partition' divides picturesqueness from deformity. Deformity is distinct from the picturesque, but shares elements with it. In spite of the appeal of the picturesque, however, beauty nevertheless remains 'the most pleasing of all ideas to the human mind', for Price, and he finds it 'very natural that it should be most sought after, and that the name should have been applied to every species of excellence'.[91] There is, then, a hierarchy of value implied by the continuum from beauty to picturesqueness. Having rejected picturesque beauty as a nonsensical combination that attempts to reconcile the irreconcilable, Price argues that the picturesque is instead a stage on a continuum that ranges from beauty to deformity. He follows Burke in linking 'ugliness' to deformity, and asserts that 'ugliness, like beauty, in itself, is not picturesque, for it has, simply considered, no strongly marked features'.[92] The important difference between ugliness and picturesqueness is the striking quality. Additionally, Price follows Burke in defining deformity as a deviation from an original: it is 'something that did not originally belong to the object in which it exists; something *strikingly* and unnaturally disagreeable, and not softened by those circumstances which often make it picturesque'.[93]

The concept of picturesque beauty, as something that is both appropriate for a painting and inclusive of deformity, enables Gilpin to give deformed people and deformed things the same aesthetic value. There need not be a distinction between person and thing, or even between represented object and representation, when the most important quality is the suitability for representation. Price rejects Gilpin's centralizing of representability, but agrees with Gilpin that it is possible to use the same discourse to describe the aesthetic appeal of the ruin and the person. The picturesque, when we apply it to people, Price observes, is seen in 'beggars, gypsies, and all such rough tattered figures', and these figures 'bear a close analogy, in all the qualities that make them so, to old hovels and mills, to the wild forest horse, and other objects of the same kind'.[94] Price makes this analogy between people and buildings numerous times. For instance, he notes that Salvator Rosa's Belisarius, who is depicted as old and blind, is as good an example of 'picturesqueness and decayed grandeur as the venerable remains of the magnificence of past ages'.[95] Moreover, Price regards an old woman in make-up as like a 'building daubed over and plaistered'.[96] For Price, the picturesque is as appropriate a term for 'an old rugged mossy oak' as it is for 'one of Rembrandt's old hags'.[97] In order to account for the use of the same discourse for both people and things, Price suggests that the appeal of deformity in the picturesque derives from its striking quality.

Price suggests, in *A Dialogue on the Distinct Characters of the Picturesque and the Beautiful in Answer to the Objections of Mr. Knight* (1801), that picturesque objects strike one whatever their origins. While speaking through a fictional persona who, he claims, holds his own opinions, Price observes that 'an object peculiarly and strikingly ugly, is picturesque' because one would be struck by it in a painting just as one is struck by it in nature.[98] The aim of the artist, he suggests,

> is to fix the attention; if he cannot by grandeur or beauty, he will try to do it by deformity: and indeed, according to Erasmus, 'quae naturâ deformia sunt, plus habent et artis et voluptatis in tabulâ' [those things which are deformed by nature are more artful and desirable in a painting]. It is not ugliness, it is insipidity, however accompanied, that the painter avoids, and with reason; for if it deprives even beauty of its attractions, what must it do when united to ugliness?[99]

Price supports Erasmus's apothegm by suggesting that deformity is not only a subject for art, but is more desirable than other subjects. For Price, 'deformity, like picturesqueness, makes a quicker ... impression [than ugliness], and strongly rouses the attention'.[100] In this way, Price is able to talk about the represented object and the representation (of people, animals, landscapes, and buildings) as all part of a group of things to which the same positive aesthetic value can be applied.

William Hazlitt notices Price's use of the striking, and himself defines the picturesque as both an 'ideal deformity' and 'that which stands out, and catches the attention by some striking peculiarity'.[101] In defining the picturesque as the object of the arrested gaze, Price anticipates Rosemarie Garland Thomson's observation about disability, that when a 'stare is a response to someone's distinctiveness', it 'creates disability as a state of absolute difference rather than simply [as] one more variation in human form'.[102] Hazlitt suggests that the eye pauses over something picturesque because it has 'prominence and a distinctive character' of its own.[103] Hazlitt also suggests, like Percy Shelley, that the representation of objects renders them beautiful. Hazlitt writes that 'imitation renders an object, displeasing in itself, a source of pleasure, not by repetition of the same idea, but by suggesting new ideas ... Art shows us nature, divested of the medium of our prejudices'.[104] He notes, too, that novelty is effective in challenging prejudicial responses to deformity, a point that is also raised by Addison when he observes that when we see something '*new* or *uncommon*', the imagination is pleased because it is given 'an agreeable surprise'.[105] Novelty is, for Addison, sufficient to allow deformity to give pleasure: it 'bestows Charms on a Monster, and makes even the Imperfections of Nature please us'.[106]

### Richard Payne Knight and Aesthetic Distancing

Richard Payne Knight offers a further account of the relationship between beauty, deformity, and the picturesque that owes much to the theories of Gilpin and Price. In *An Analytical Inquiry into the Principles of Taste* (1805), Knight follows Gilpin in centralizing the relationship between painting and the picturesque, defining the picturesque in a Gilpinian manner, as that 'which nature has formed in the style and manner appropriate to painting'.[107] Like Gilpin, he regards the picturesque as only pleasing to those who are 'conversant with the art of painting, and sufficiently skilled in it to distinguish, and be really delighted with its real excellences'.[108] Furthermore, he includes a strong account of the cultural specificity of judgements about beauty and deformity. For instance, the pleasing effect of symmetry is, for him, dependent 'upon the association of ideas, and not at all upon either abstract reason or organic sensation', and is the result of 'arbitrary convention'.[109] The appeal of deformity is ultimately found in 'the minds of the spectators', and not in 'any characteristic distinctions inherent in [the bodies] themselves'.[110] Knight follows Price in presenting the picturesque as distinct from beauty; beauty is, Knight argues, a term 'applied indiscriminately to almost every thing that is pleasing, either to the sense, the imagination, or the understanding'.[111] Knight asserts that 'many objects, that we call picturesque, certainly are not beautiful; since they may be void of symmetry, neatness, cleanness, &c; all which are necessary to constitute that kind of beauty, which addresses itself to the understanding and the fancy'.[112] Nevertheless, beauty is a quality that Knight frequently associates with the picturesque, and we find him using the phrase 'picturesque beauty' occasionally.[113] This is likely to be because Knight does not define beauty in a conventional manner. Beauty is, for Knight as it is for Hume, a subjective property, a reaction to an object, not something residing in the object itself. In Knight's estimation, the word 'beauty' changes meaning 'accordingly as it is applied to objects of the senses, the imagination, or the understanding'.[114]

While Gilpin uses representability to enable him to talk about people, animals, landscapes, and objects using the same aesthetic values, and Price uses the quality of being striking, Knight observes that there is a difference between something that is real and something that is represented (an

aesthetic distance), and that we need a different account of deformity for
each of these. Giving separate consideration to the real and the represented
has a significant effect on the way in which the aesthetic appeal of
deformity is accounted for. Knight argues, like Percy Shelley, that art has
a transformative power that makes deformity aesthetically pleasing. The
difference between the pictorial version of something and the thing that it
represents plays an important role in separating deformity from negative
characteristics. Knight uses the aesthetic distancing that takes place in
viewing an artistic version of something to explain the positive evaluation
of deformity in the case of the picturesque. Ruminating on what makes
deformity acceptable in art, Knight is concerned that by calling beggars
and 'extravagant monsters' beautiful, he will be accused of 'calling a
dunghill *sweet* because I assert that it contains sugar'.[115] He replies to this
by making the case that representation can separate disagreeableness from
beauty: 'the beautiful tints and lights and shadows, when separated, in the
imitation, from the disagreeable qualities, with which they were united,
are as truly beautiful as if they had never been united with any such
qualities'.[116] Aesthetic distancing enables Knight to see the attraction of
picturesque deformity in art because art transforms deformity.[117]

Knight's dunghill example is probably taken from Addison's *Spectator*
(1712), or possibly from Burke's *A Philosophical Enquiry*, in which Burke
states briefly that 'A cottage, a dunghill, the meanest and most ordinary
utensils of the kitchen are capable of giving us pleasure'.[118] Addison
suggests that one can take aesthetic pleasure in something that is deformed,
provided that it is appropriately described or represented: 'any Thing that
is Disagreeable when look'd upon, pleases us in an apt Description'.[119] He
asserts that representation has an important effect in removing the negative
associations from deformity. Pleasure is to be found in the 'Agreeableness
of the Objects to the Eye, and from their Similitude to other Objects', and
this similitude makes it possible to take aesthetic pleasure in something
that is deformed.[120] For Addison, there is no difficulty in responding to
objects and people using the same terms, as 'Almost every thing about
us'[121] can raise 'an agreeable Idea in the imagination',[122] and even 'the
Description of a Dung-hill is pleasing to the Imagination, if the Image be
presented to our Minds by suitable Expressions'.[123] The dunghill does not
delight, but the aptness of its description does. Knight agrees with Addison
that something that is disagreeable in reality can be agreeable in a representation: it is, in this case, the art work and not the object itself that is
beautiful. Burke's treatment of the issue is similar. He suggests that the
pleasure that arises from imitation derives from 'the resemblance which the

imitation has to the original', but that the pleasure does not *solely* derive from resemblance.[124] Burke refines Addison's example of the dunghill by suggesting that 'when the object represented in poetry or painting is such, as we could have no desire of seeing in the reality; then I may be sure that its power in poetry or painting is owing to the power of imitation, and to no cause operating in the thing itself'.[125] Here, it is the representation alone that has the positive aesthetic quality.[126]

Knight's theory that representation makes deformity aesthetically pleasing is similar to Gilpin's. Similar, but not the same, because Knight highlights the mimetic relationship between the original and the representation as one that distances the spectator from the real qualities of the original. Knight also regards deformity in art as different from deformity in real life, whereas Gilpin does not. Knight's theory also diverges from Gilpin's by explicitly excluding deformed people from his list of picturesque figures in art. He suggests that, while 'irregularity of appearance is generally essential to picturesque beauty, no painter has ever thought of making a man or animal more picturesque, by exhibiting them with one leg shorter than the other; or one eye smaller than the other'.[127] Even though Knight suggests that deformed people are generally excluded from art, he takes the debate in a strikingly new direction when he proposes that real deformed people can be attractive, as will be explored in the next section. Knight's position on this issue has an important context: it is part of the public disagreement he had with Price that Shelley alludes to in the letter to Peacock cited at the beginning of this chapter.

### Uvedale Price, Richard Payne Knight, and the Parson's Squinting Daughter

The controversy in print began in earnest with the publication of Price's *A Dialogue* (1801), which is a response to Knight's note to the second edition of his poem, *The Landscape* (1795).[128] Price's *A Dialogue* takes the form of a fictional conversation between Mr Hamilton, who speaks for Price *in propria persona*, Mr Howard, a 'supposed partizan of Mr. Knight's opinions', and a fictional Mr Seymour, who 'has little acquaintance with the art of painting, or with the application of its principles to that of gardening, or to natural scenery'.[129] While on a brief walking tour, the three characters arrive at a parsonage that has 'differently shaped windows and chimneys ... rooms in odd corners ... [and] roofs crossing each other in different directions', and they discuss how it may be understood to be aesthetically pleasing.[130] Hamilton (Price) responds that 'irregularity is one of the principal causes of the picturesque; and [that] as the general appearance of this building is in a very great degree irregular, so far it is highly picturesque'.[131] The discussion pauses as the parson comes 'into the garden, with his daughter; and being an old acquaintance of Mr. Hamilton's', he shows the group the house and grounds.[132] As the men depart to look at a nearby mansion, Seymour comments that the parson's daughter bears a strong similarity to the parsonage, and that the conventions of beauty do not account for the aesthetic appeal of both the woman and the house.

> 'The good old parson's daughter is made upon the model of her father's house: her features are as irregular, and her eyes are somewhat inclined to look across each other, like the roofs of the old parsonage; but a clear skin, clean white teeth, though not very even, and a look of neatness and chearfulness, in spite of these irregularities, made me look at her with pleasure; and, I really think, if I were of the cloth, I should like very well to take to the living, the house, and its inhabitant...'[133]

Seymour, who is not conversant with the picturesque, argues simply that the woman and the house are appealing because they have enough beauty to make them attractive. He teases Hamilton (Price) by supposing that Hamilton would think the woman was insufficiently deformed to count as picturesque and therefore appealing. Seymour says, '"You Hamilton, I suppose, were thinking, how age and neglect would operate upon her as upon the house, and how simply picturesque she would become, when her cheeks were a little furrowed and weather-stained, and her teeth had got a slight incrustation."'[134] Hamilton replies that he was thinking 'how great a conformity there is between our tastes for the sex, and for other objects'.[135] Although making light of his views, Price echoes, through Hamilton, his idea that the same discourse should be used when describing the aesthetic value of people and things; and he confirms, through Knight's persona, that Knight does not hold the same view. Price gives Howard (Knight) the view that men do not reason well when they consider attraction between the sexes. According to Price, Knight believes that aesthetic judgements about real people with deformities are influenced by the potential for sexual attraction.

Knight does indeed disagree with Price on this question in *An Analytical Inquiry* (1805). Here Knight observes that real people with deformities are aesthetically appealing to the people who love them, because they have 'charms and graces, where ordinary discernment can only see faults and defects'.[136] He suggests that a woman 'with even greater personal defects than either hobbling or squinting, may, by the influence of sexual and social sympathies, be extremely interesting and attractive',[137] and he cites the example of the 'lovely and amiable Duchess of La Valière', a mistress of Louis XIV, who 'is said, not only to have had bad teeth, but also, in consequence of an accident in her childhood, to have limped or hobbled in her gait; which, nevertheless, *seemed* to add to, rather than take away from the graces of her person'.[138] Knight observes that while the 'irregular movements of the monarch's lovely mistress, or the irregular looks of the parson's blooming daughter, may have been very charming to those, who were predisposed by other charming qualities of tint, form, or expression, to be pleased with them', they are 'not at all after the manner of painting', and these 'irregular charms' of the women reside 'in the minds' of the people they know.[139] When they are represented, however, 'imitative art separates these faults and defects from the magic, which recommends them in real life'.[140] These women, Knight suggests, perhaps referencing Price's continuum, do not belong in the 'general intermediate repository of the picturesque', even though they are striking.[141] They are aesthetically (and sexually and socially) pleasing, and deformed, but not picturesque. In Knight's estimation, the parsonage is a separate issue because the aesthetic assessment of a building is 'independent of the medium of affection, passion, and appetite through which [a lover] views them'.[142]

Seymour, in Price's *Dialogue*, observes that 'qualities that are analogous to beauty' make the parsonage and the parson's squinting daughter appealing.[143] Knight takes up this point in *An Analytical Inquiry*, suggesting that the charm that gives the woman her appeal is an equivalent to beauty because 'when a squinting woman' is 'invested with a sufficient portion of sexual charms to render her capable of exciting affection and desire, those charms suddenly become *qualities analogous to beauty*'.[144] Seymour's observation that Price would have preferred a more deformed woman is also discussed by Knight. Knight attacks Price's example of the squinting woman on the grounds that he believes it is not a proper case of deformity, and he offers what he thinks of as a clearer example.

> My friend, Mr. Price, indeed, admits squinting among the irregular and picturesque charms of the parson's daughter, whom (to illustrate the picturesque in opposition to the beautiful) he wishes to make appear lovely and attractive, though without symmetry or beauty. He has not, however, extended the details of this want of symmetry and regularity further than to the features of the face; though to make the figure consistent and complete, the same happy mixture of the irregular and picturesque must have prevailed through her limbs and person; and consequently she must have hobbled as well as squinted; and had hips and shoulders as irregular as

her teeth, cheeks, and eyebrows. All my friend's parental fondness for his system is certainly necessary to make him think such an assemblage of picturesque circumstances either lovely or attractive; or induce him to imagine, that he should be content with such a creature, as a companion for life; and I heartily congratulate him that this fondness did not arise at an earlier period, to obstruct him in a very different choice.[145]

Knight alludes here to Price's wife Caroline, a society beauty who was painted by Sir Joshua Reynolds. The attack was particularly cruel as Knight was intimate with Price's family and knew that their first child, also Caroline, who was eighteen when this was published, was considered to be deformed. Joseph Farington records in his diary on 13 October 1806 that Price's daughter had in the past 'been confined' for her insanity and 'is deformed and has many singularities'.[146] Wordsworth, when he dined with the Prices at his friend Samuel Rogers's house in May 1812, sneered to his wife in a letter, that

nothing could be more deplorable than the rest of the Party: Miss P[rice].– a little deformed Creature, with a most strange enunciation, sitting by Mr Jekyll a celebrated Wit, and quite pert and to use a coarse word ever rampant upon him. She is, as Sir G.[eorge] Beaumont observed in expression and countenance and manner just like the bad Sister who does all the Mischief in a Faery tale.[147]

Price replied to Knight's criticisms in his appendix to *Essays on the Picturesque* (1810), commenting pedantically that the parson's daughter had 'eyes *somewhat inclined* to look across each other', and that 'this slight *inclination*, my adversary, has exaggerated into a squint'.[148] In his redirection, Price asserts that an 'inclination to deviate' is something that is 'scarcely to be perceptible at first sight', and that it may give a woman 'an archness and a peculiarity, which may accord with the general character and expression of the countenance, and like other peculiarities, suit particular tastes'.[149] He dismisses squinting, however, as 'among the worst of deformities', and rejects the description as something that 'belongs to Mr. Knight's comment, not to my text'.[150] The response is intellectually – though perhaps not emotionally – surprising, representing as it does a distinct retreat from Price's earlier and more radical aesthetic. Here Price seems to recast something that he had earlier regarded as picturesque as something deformed, and seems now to deny that he could ever have taken pleasure in any such thing. Although he is piqued enough to make the correction, Price cautions us from taking his 'jocular' discussion of the parson's squinting daughter in *A Dialogue* to be a serious position, appropriate for a philosophical treatise.[151] He nevertheless adds a further justification for Seymour's attraction to the parson's squinting daughter: personal taste. He suggests that if it is true that

> a woman with irregular features, with a slight cast in her eyes, with uneven teeth, but those teeth white and clean, and with her complexion fresh and clear, may, to many tastes, be often more attractive than a woman regularly handsome; and if a house under circumstances as nearly similar as the two cases will admit of, may also be preferred by many, to houses of regular architecture, – then Mr. Seymour, whether he were jocular or serious, might be allowed to profess his willingness, under certain circumstances, to take to the house and its inhabitant.[152]

Price ultimately dismisses the reasons for the preference as irrelevant, suggesting that 'Mr. Knight may attribute such a liking (for that is the most it can be called) to what motives he pleases; but he must allow that fondness for a house, cannot arise from "social and sensual sympathies"'.[153] In this way, Price takes the argument back to the central issue of whether it is possible to talk about people and objects using the same aesthetic value. These sallies have the tone of a disintegrating friendship that has degenerated into tit-for-tat attempts to explain misunderstanding and wilful misinterpretation, but they continue the discussion of important questions within picturesque theory: how to account for the aesthetic appeal of deformity, and whether that appeal extends to real deformed people.

## Conclusion

Tobin Siebers's claim that 'the emergence of disability in modern art as a significant presence' in the twentieth century is the beginning of a disability aesthetics is not challenged by picturesque theory, but we should acknowledge that deformity aesthetics is a significant re-evaluation of aesthetics away from the traditions of beauty.[154] Deformity aesthetics occurs in the Romantic period in many and varied ways. We see it in the form and subject matter of the Romantic fragment poem, in Gothic literature, ballads, and encounter poems, and in the widespread interest in non-idealized people and their bodies. Coleridge's poem 'Christabel' (1801) is both a fragment and about deformity. Geraldine's deformed 'bosom and half her side' are described as shocking and unnameable: 'A sight to dream of, not to tell!'[155] Josiah Conder, reviewing it in 1816, writes that the poem 'might be compared to a mutilated statue, the beauty of which can only be appreciated by those who have knowledge or imagination sufficient to complete the idea of the whole composition'.[156] Conder's comments are close to Gilpin's iconoclastic statement about dismantling the classical ideal: 'a piece of Palladian architecture may be elegant in the last degree. The proportion of it's [sic] parts – the propriety of it's [sic] ornaments – and the symmetry of the whole, may be highly pleasing', but 'should we wish to give it picturesque beauty, we ... must beat down one half of it, deface the other, and throw the mutilated members around in heaps'.[157] With this statement, Gilpin rejects symmetry, regularity, harmony, and a traditional understanding of beauty. Commenting on the fragment poem, Anne Janowitz suggests that 'the model for something either unfinished or broken came to be understood as both *a* genre within Romantic poetry and as *the* paradigm genre of Romantic literature'.[158] Janowitz reads the Romantic fragment poem as 'an affirmation of the ideal, and as such, it necessarily undervalues its own achievement in the face of its unachieved ideal completion, its "beyond"'.[159]

The picturesque theorists are also concerned with justifying negative evaluations of deformity. Addison's suggestion that we find pleasure in 'Similitude' provides an important mechanism for picturesque theorists to justify the appeal of deformity. We also find this manoeuvre in Romantic aesthetics. Wordsworth uses it in the preface to *Lyrical Ballads*, when he defends the simplicity of his subject matter and form. He writes that the mind derives pleasure 'from the perception of similitude in dissimilitude, and dissimilitude in similitude', suggesting that representation is itself a recommendation for any subject matter.[160] In making a case for deformity aesthetics, however, we should acknowledge that the language of incompletion and dysfunction, used in the discussion of deformity, is pejorative. This language is the thing that picturesque theorists value, however. We should also be careful not to overstate the embrace of deformity, as the exceptionalism that picturesqueness provides is sometimes, even if it may be only nominally, exclusive of deformity. Picturesque aesthetics is nevertheless an important attempt to redefine incompletion and dysfunction as concepts, and to find beauty in them, and it challenges neoclassical ideals in which standards of beauty are preferred.

## CHAPTER 5

# Relational Deformity in Frances Burney's Camilla

A courtship novel about young people is an unlikely work of aesthetics. Frances Burney's *Camilla* (1796) is, nevertheless, preoccupied by definitions of beauty and deformity, and it is surprising how much philosophical resonance is present in it. While we cannot know for certain the extent of Burney's philosophical reading, her work demonstrates keen awareness of the eighteenth-century debates on aesthetics, and was viewed at the time as making a contribution to them. Burney is one of handful of novelists who examine the formation of personal identity through a deformity, and one of the earliest to experiment extensively with the idea that a deformed body does not cause or indicate a deformed mind. Her novel is also remarkable for its extensive exploration of the emotions of a deformed person in relation to their deformity. Burney separates bodily impairment from the social construction of disability, tracing Eugenia Tyrold's transition from a state of ignorance about the social significance of her deformity to her development of new understanding of it. Moreover, Burney centralizes the formation of identity out of the private and the social, demonstrating that the private and social are both dynamic and performative. A considerable part of the novel is devoted to exploring the possibility of a non-stigmatized notion of deformity, according to which deformity need not generate a negative reaction, and does not necessarily disadvantage its subject. The inclusion of a deformity/disadvantage distinction makes Burney's work distinctly unusual, as it anticipates the impairment/disability binary of the social barriers approach to disability. Additionally, in *Camilla*, deformity is a relational and dynamic concept that exposes the intersectionality between deformity and other restrictive social identities of the time. The disadvantages linked to deformity derive largely from discriminatory attitudes bound up with culture, taste, economic circumstances, gender, rank, and education. Evaluative variability in aesthetic response is often explained by context. Burney promotes a *relational* approach to deformity (and beauty), demonstrating that aesthetic evaluation is not fixed, but is relative to the positioning of the subject and the observer.[1]

The idea that philosophical aesthetics is a legitimate context for Burney is gaining some critical currency. Melissa Pino notes that 'several scholars have responded with varying degrees of bemusement and disbelief' to the suggestion that the author might have had access to eighteenth-century philosophy without 'a formal classical education', and to the possibility that she would have been capable of engaging in 'well-informed dialogue' on the subject.[2] Pino argues convincingly that Burney's world was 'flush with ideas about beauty',[3] that her characters are 'aestheticians',[4] and that it would easily be possible for someone of her intellect, irrespective of her youth and education, to 'respond intelligently to a complex of ideas whose contributors included Burke, Locke, and Hume'.[5] Gabrielle Starr takes a similar line, commenting that Burney's 'work spans a key moment in the history of aesthetics', and that 'she explores the contradictions surrounding how we value what is or was beautiful'.[6] While these critics have concentrated on her other novels, Burney's knowledge of the aesthetic debates on the nature and perception of beauty and deformity is central to *Camilla*.[7] Such philosophical knowledge may have been available to her via a number of routes. She need only have opened Ephraim Chambers's *Cyclopaedia* (1786) to have read a detailed and accessible summary of Hutcheson's influential definition of deformity, for instance. It is very likely, too, that Burney had read Burke's *A Philosophical Enquiry*.[8] Burke, who was personally known to Burney, was a great admirer of her work, and was one of the subscribers to the first edition of *Camilla*.[9]

## Relational Deformity in *Camilla*

Much of *Camilla* concentrates on the personal and social effects on Eugenia of the revelation of the consequences of deformity.[10] Eugenia acquires a spinal injury in childhood that results in a limp and restricted growth when she is dropped by her uncle, Sir Hugh. She is also scarred by smallpox, caught when her uncle disregards the instructions of her parents and takes her to a nearby fair. At Sir Hugh's request, Eugenia's family reluctantly agrees to shelter her from any awareness of the way in which her deformities might be viewed negatively in a social context. The family has a small circle of acquaintance in rural Hampshire, and manages to keep Eugenia in a state of 'utter ignorance' for fourteen years.[11] Sir Hugh fears that Eugenia's deformities 'should make her hate him, for being their cause', and instigates the situation 'for fear they would vex her'.[12] For a time, Eugenia has physical impairments and deformities, which she is aware of, but has them in the absence of any negative evaluation, or notion of deficit. When her social context is revealed, Eugenia comes to think that her life prior to understanding the social significance of deformity as a deception. Eugenia experiences shame, embarrassment, anger, agoraphobia, and melancholy as a consequence of the revelation of the significance of her deformities. She despairs that her family have let her believe that 'thousands resembled me! ... assuring me I had nothing peculiar to myself, though I was so unlike all my family', and she accuses them of 'deluding' her about her 'unhappy defects, and then casting me, all unconscious and unprepared, into the wide world to hear them'.[13] Direct prejudice initially comes from the lower classes. Market women ask her whether she walks 'upon her knees', they suggest that she could wear children's clothes, and speculate that her dress could be made from a handkerchief.[14] A boy likens her to a scarecrow, and Mr Dubster, a social climber who is unaware of conventions of politeness, says to Eugenia: 'you're not much above the dwarf as they show at the Exeter 'Change? Much of a muchness, I guess'.[15] Eugenia's gait, her smallpox scars, and her height all become the subject of ridicule; and seclusion from this kind of prejudice leaves her without the emotional resources to protect herself. She is angry at not having been prepared with 'lessons for fortitude'.[16]

Burney acknowledges a Humean emotional landscape in Eugenia's reactions to her deformity: she experiences self-consciousness and shame. Eugenia is a possible bride for her absent cousin, Clermont Lynmere, who is vain, unscholarly, and girlishly beautiful. Their encounters emphasize how much her sense of self becomes connected with shame. On his first return, Clermont unintentionally humiliates Eugenia by walking past her in the grounds without imagining that she could be one of the ladies of the house. For Eugenia, 'the notion of having a figure so insignificant as to be passed, without exciting a doubt [who] she might be, was cruelly mortifying'.[17] Burney notes the common link between deformity and ridicule. Furthermore, 'Indiana, when she saw her brother as handsome as her cousin was deformed, thought the contrast so droll, she could look at neither without tittering; Lavinia [Eugenia's sister] observed, with extreme concern, the visible distress of Eugenia.[18] This is the occasion on which Eugenia experiences 'for the first time, a sensation of shame for her lameness, which, hitherto, she had regularly borne with fortitude, when she had not forgotten from indifference: neither did she feel spirits to exhibit, again, before his tall and strikingly elegant figure, her diminutive little person'.[19] Clermont's negative reaction alters Eugenia's perception of herself: 'Eugenia had never yet thought herself so plain and insignificant, and felt as if, even since this morning, the small-pox had renewed its ravages, and she had sunk into being shorter.'[20] When Eugenia begins her memoirs, at the end of the novel, this relational view of deformity is emphasized. She describes herself as 'one from whom fate has withheld all the delicacy of vanity'.[21] She laments her 'loss of beauty' not because of vanity, but because she has learnt how much value society has placed on beauty.[22] Eugenia's father regards her unhappiness as caused by misdirected self-regard, however. Her father's warning about her vanity, and advice to 'make a conquest' of herself centres on a quotation from Steele: that 'a too acute sensibility of personal defects, is one of the greatest weaknesses of self-love'.[23] The tenor of Steele's essay at this point is that self-acceptance is warranted in the case of ugliness: 'Since our Persons are not of our own Making, when they are such as appear Defective or Uncomely, it is, methinks, an honest and laudable Fortitude to dare to be Ugly.'[24] Mr Tyrold thinks Eugenia can change her evaluation of herself simply by thinking of herself in a different way. The negative quality she attaches to her deformity is subjective, he surmises, and it can be changed with no alteration in objective reality at all.

*Camilla* also explores how negative perceptions of deformity can be mitigated or intensified by other circumstances. Eugenia's deformities are inflected by class and money, and by race and gender. The issue of Eugenia's beauty is made paramount because she is a wealthy and unmarried white woman of high social rank. Her family hope that their money can alleviate the social disadvantages of deformity. We see an example of this in Eugenia's first experience of prejudice. When market women make fun of her, they are 'quieted and dismayed' and offer 'some awkward apologies' when they learn that she is heir to a fortune.[25] Sir Hugh makes Eugenia his heir in order to counteract what he sees as a loss. He puts his desires metaphorically: 'a guinea for every pit in that poor face will I settle on her out of hand'.[26] Eugenia's sister, Camilla, is also a vehicle for the novel's lesson that money affects how appearance is treated. For example, when Camilla offers to pay her brother Lionel's debts, he says to her: 'you are an excellent girl. If you were as old and ugly as [the governess] Miss Margland, I really believe I should think you young and pretty'.[27] The role of money is not always positive, however. Eugenia's inheritance makes her the target of fortune-hunters. As her father puts it: 'Eugenia is … dangerously circumstanced, in standing so conspicuously apart, as a prize to some adventurer.'[28] This is precisely what happens. Alphonso Bellamy, after failing in his attempts to woo her, eventually kidnaps Eugenia and forces her to marry him.[29]

Sir Hugh serves as an important comparison with Eugenia, as his illnesses and physical capacity are regarded differently from hers because of their difference in age and gender. Although the descriptions of Sir Hugh's physical movements often echo those of Eugenia, he is never regarded in aesthetic terms, and his incapacity is treated as functional. He limps as a consequence of having received a 'wound in his side' from falling from a horse. In the early stages of his recovery, he feels himself 'at once deprived of all employment, and destitute of all comfort' and 'active diversions'.[30] His lack of 'sedentary resources' prompts a belated attempt at a classical education.[31] Sir Hugh later acquires gout in his hip, stomach, and right hand, and is described by the narrator as 'hobbling rather than walking'.[32] Burney spends a surprising amount of time explaining how Sir Hugh moves around. He has walking sticks, a garden chair follows him when he takes a walk in the grounds of Edgar Mandlebert's house, and he arranges a phaeton to take Eugenia with him to Church, though he eventually walks. In one scene, both Sir Hugh and Eugenia use similar aids: 'they proceeded very slowly, the baronet leaning upon Dr. March-mont, and Eugenia upon Dr. Orkborne'.[33] In another scene he accepts 'the arm of Edgar to aid his stick in helping him home'.[34] Sir Hugh views his slow movement as 'no fault of mine'.[35] His comment references an earlier narratorial statement on Sir Hugh's view of illness – that he 'had no notion of people's taking diseases upon themselves' – something that we later see Indiana do when she feigns delicacy at a ball in order to recapture Mr Melmond's attentions.[36] As Margaret Doody has pointed out, the issue of mobility is a preoccupation of the text more broadly. Doody notices that everywhere in Mr Dubster's semi-finished house 'we see an indicative problem with *steps*. There are no logical or convenient means of moving continuously from place to place'.[37]

Although deformity and incapacity are treated differently according to gender, Burney complicates this by presenting Sir Hugh as effeminized by his physical conditions. At one point the children even dress him as a woman. This may hint at an incompatibility of masculinity and weakness that Burney balances with its opposite in the case of Sir Sedley Clarendel. Sir Sedley drops his foppish persona when injured rescuing Camilla from a carriage accident. His convalescence prompts him to 'rediscover his natural courage', drop 'the effeminate part he was playing', and become reflec-tive.[38] Like Sir Hugh, he recognizes that incapacity makes him rely on his intellectual resources. Ironically, Sir Sedley is temporarily 'reduced' to becoming 'reasonable' and 'natural'.[39] Mrs Arlbery, a witty widow, observes of Sir Sedley that deformity would enhance his character: 'deface

and maim his features and figure, and by letting him see that to appear and
be admired is not the same thing, you will render him irresistible'.[40]
Incapacity in the case of effeminization, however, does not lead to male
incapacity being recast as deformity.

Eugenia's education becomes an additional social hindrance that adds to
the perception of her as deformed. Clermont is alarmed, not only by
Eugenia's appearance, but by the gendered problems caused by her bookishness: 'this learning is worse than her ugliness; 'twould make me look like
a dunce in my own house'.[41] 'What have I to do with marrying a girl like a
boy?' he exclaims after a long yawning fit.[42] The narrator ironically
balances this gesture at masculinity with the suggestion that he looks like
a girl: 'Clermont Lynmere so entirely resembled his sister in person, that
now, in his first youth, he might almost have been taken for her, even
without change of dress . . . what in her was beauty in its highest delicacy,
in him seemed effeminacy in its lowest degradation.'[43] Importantly, Eugenia's education is seen as freakish: 'the misses, in tittering, ran away from
the learned lady; the beaux contemptuously sneering, rejoiced she was too
ugly to take in any poor fellow to marry her. Some imagined her studies
had stinted her growth; and all were convinced her education had made
her such a fright'.[44] When a similar education is proposed for Indiana, her
governess warns of 'the danger of injuring beauty by study'.[45] As she
embarks on her cathartic memoirs at the end of the novel, Eugenia enters
into the life of the mind that will 'amuse her solitude'.[46] The memoirs
begin with a lament that few men would want to marry an 'heiress to
whom fortune comes with such alloys'.[47] At the end of the novel, Eugenia,
a 'practical philosopher',[48] signals her intention to write her memoirs as a
way to confirm what she calls her 'philosophical idea'[49] about beauty and
deformity.

We see something of the slipperiness of the evaluation of deformity in a
striking scene that echoes Shaftesbury's idea that beauty is connected to
mental capacity. Shaftesbury maintains that, just as a person with an
intellectual impairment could not produce a beautiful object, since a
beautiful mind is not present, so a person with an intellectual impairment
could not be beautiful: 'for what is a mere body, though a human one and
ever so exactly fashioned, if inward form be wanting and the mind be
monstrous or imperfect, as in an idiot or savage?'[50] Beauty must include
'beauty of the mind'.[51] According to Shaftesbury, even though we think
the 'outward features' of someone are what we admire, the outward
features are a 'mysterious expression and a kind of shadow of something
inward in the temper', and it is the inner beauty that we admire.[52]

Eugenia's father takes her to see a local woman who is described both as a madwoman and as an idiot. At first glance the woman is 'young, fair, of a tall and striking figure, with features delicately regular' – the standard of beauty.[53] Seconds later, her behaviour reveals her impairment, as she bursts 'into a fit of loud, shrill, and discordant laughter . . . began turning round with a velocity that no machine could have exceeded', and, as the narrator graphically puts it, 'the slaver drivelled unrestrained from her mouth, rendering utterly disgusting a chin that a statuary might have wished to model'.[54] The unnamed woman strikes 'her head with both her hands, making a noise that resembled nothing human'.[55] Mr Tyrold counsels Eugenia to find herself fortunate that she has intellectual capacities. Eugenia initially counters her father's lesson with the argument that self-awareness makes reason without beauty harder to bear than the reverse: the mentally impaired woman 'was born an idiot, and therefore, having never known brighter days, is insensible to her terrible state'.[56] Mr Tyrold's lesson hits home, nevertheless, and Eugenia sees this 'melancholy sight'[57] as a cure for her supposed pride:

> your prescription strikes to the root of my disease! – shall I ever again dare murmur! – will any egotism ever again make me believe no lot so hapless as my own! I will think of her when I am discontented; I will call to mind this spectacle of human degradation – and submit, at least with calmness, to my lighter evils and milder fate.'[58]

Eugenia accepts Mr. Tyrold's instruction 'that beauty, without mind, is more dreadful than any deformity', and is disciplined into finding herself more fortunate.[59] She describes herself as 'your vanquished Eugenia!'[60] Eugenia is unable to see that both she and the mentally impaired woman are the subject of prejudicial social judgements, however, and she is reconciled to her own deformity precisely by relativizing the beautiful woman's cognitive impairment. Andrea Haslanger reads Mr Tyrold's 'pat reinforcement' of 'intellection' as 'a balm for deformity' as one that 'rings false'.[61] Felicity Nussbaum, however, is convinced by it, suggesting that Eugenia 'transforms her self-pity into a contented acceptance of her father's' view of beauty without mind, and 'accepts her new role in inhabiting an anomalous body'.[62] I suggest that Eugenia is disciplined at this point, and takes longer than this scene to rehabilitate her sense of self.

Aside from Hartley and Steele, there is little discussion of the separation of deformity from its social disadvantages in the formal debates of the eighteenth century. The possibility of separating deformity from social disadvantage is explored briefly in Sarah Scott's novel *Millenium Hall*

(1762), however. *Millenium Hall* was a popular novel and may have been one of Burney's sources for *Camilla*. Margaret Doody notes that 'Scott was known to Burney, but not as well as her more famous and imposing sister, Elizabeth Montagu'.[63] Scott describes, in *Millenium Hall*, a secluded refuge for deformed women. Recognizing the intersectionality of different factors in determining the treatment of deformity, Scott's narrator reflects on the tendency in the world at large to enslave, display, and ridicule people who 'either fall short, or exceed the usual standard', if 'they happen to have the additional misfortune of poverty'.[64]

Burney's contribution to these aesthetic debates was recognized by Sara Coleridge, the daughter of Samuel Taylor Coleridge. Writing in the 1820s, Coleridge comments that the fashion for beauty is as strong as it was in the 1790s. 'This is', she writes of her current time, 'the age of Taste.'[65] She makes a number of salient observations that undermine beauty's ascendency: beauty does not increase happiness; beauty of person and beauty of character are unrelated; beauty encourages vanity; and beauty should not be the standard by which women are measured (they should be measured by character, piety and 'inward ... excellence').[66] Coleridge affirms that beauty is a contested and unstable category because it is transient and culturally specific. One of the earliest writers to recognize Burney's contribution to these issues, Coleridge singles out *Camilla* as evidence for the plausibility of the notion that beauty does not contribute to happiness: 'the plain girl, as Miss Burney shews in the character of Eugenia, till her attention is rudely called to the subject, feels no very keen regret concerning her want of beauty: – she views her coarse skin & homely shape & visage in general without a sigh'.[67] *Camilla* also received praise from Mary Wollstonecraft, who found Eugenia to be 'one of the most interesting personages' because of 'the loss of her beauty, and the circumstances to which this misfortune gave birth'.[68] Wollstonecraft regards Burney, nevertheless, as sometimes writing 'too slightingly of this privilege of nature [beauty], but this, if an errour, is erring on the right side'.[69]

Burney's relational approach to deformity may owe something to Hume's relativist subjectivism. The titles of her paired chapters 'Strictures on Deformity' and 'Strictures on Beauty' echo Hume's 'Of Beauty and Deformity' in *A Treatise of Human Nature* (1739–40). Burney was both attracted to and repulsed by Hume, calling him 'that dangerously renowned philosopher; whose judgment of men was as skilfully inviting, as his sophistry in theology was fearfully repelling'.[70] Commenting on the part Hume played in a controversy over her father's career aspirations, Burney remembers him as 'a man who was then [in the 1760s] almost universally held to be at the head of British literature'.[71] Burney may also be indebted to David Hartley in her thinking on deformity. Hartley is interested in the effect of deformity on a person who might have it, rather than merely the effect of deformity on the observer, though he develops his account without accepting Hume's subjectivism. Hartley locates the disadvantages associated with deformity in the social context of the person. In so doing, he makes not deformity but the associated disadvantages relative. He dismisses the worries one might have about being deformed as merely concerns about how one is seen by the world. Once away from the world, he suggests, the concept of objective deformity is easily dissociated from its subjective and displeasing elements. Hartley comments that it is merely because of custom that

> the Fear of *being* or *being thought* deformed, should be a Thing to which the Imagination has the greatest Reluctance. And the Reputation of Beauty, with the Scandal of Deformity, influences so much the more, as Beauty and Deformity are not attended with their respective pleasing or displeasing Associates, except when they are made apparent to, and taken notice of, by the World. So that here the original Desire is rather to *be thought* beautiful than to *be* so.[72]

Hartley's point is brief, but significant: deformity appears to be negative only when one is being observed: that is to say, when it has a social context.

## Relational Beauty in *Camilla*

As is the case for deformity, Burney has much to say about the gendered standard of beauty in *Camilla*, and about the instability of its evaluation. In the opening chapter, Sir Hugh, arriving in Hampshire with his niece Indiana Lynmere, meets his other nieces and immediately ranks them in order of their beauty.[73] The entire exercise is a question of taste. Sir Hugh, 'whose breast was laid open to the world with an infantine artlessness', is aware that he must appear to be cultured, but by discussing their beauty in front of his nieces reveals that he is, as the narrator says, 'wholly uncultivated, and singularly self-formed'.[74] He is particularly 'struck with the beauty of . . . Camilla'.[75] Never consistent for very long, Sir Hugh quickly reassesses them and decides that Camilla is not 'so pretty as her little sister Eugenia, nor much better than t'other sister Lavina; and not one of the three is half so great a beauty as my little Indiana'.[76] When he next sees them, he switches back to Camilla as his standard of beauty, suggesting that while Indiana's beauty is 'the most complete', Camilla's has 'a variety that was captivation'.[77] Camilla's vivacity, her 'animated voice', 'light-springing figure', 'playful countenance', 'sportive sounds', and the 'elasticity' of her 'form and mind' ultimately make her the superior beauty in Sir Hugh's view.[78] This is, in part, a play on Sir Hugh's indecisiveness and lack of taste, but it is also a hint that, in *Camilla*, the standards of beauty and deformity are unstable and context-dependent. With the character of Indiana, Burney is particularly interested in the idea of the transcendent quality of physical beauty. When the Oxonian poet, Frederic Melmond, sees Indiana for the first time, he is 'struck with amazement', as if entering the presence of a god.[79] 'He started back, bowed profoundly ... and then riveting his eyes, in which his whole soul seemed centred, on her lovely face, stood viewing her with a look of homage, motionless, yet enraptured.'[80] Indiana's beauty jolts him from his theatrical enthusiasm for Thomson's 'Spring' an into a quasi-religious experience: 'his fervent mind fancied her some being of celestial order'.[81] Indiana makes the journey from transcendent 'idol' to mere 'automaton' very quickly, however.[82] Edgar sees her as lacking 'finely subtle sensations', and by the end of the novel Melmond comes to think as Edgar does, that moral beauty is of more value than physical beauty.[83] Melmond realizes, like Othello, that 'he had thrown away, in Eugenia, *a gem richer than all her tribe!*'[84]

There are many occasions on which beauty varies according to context. In one scene, all the ladies at a ball are required to wear the same kind of dress, a 'uniform' of 'clear fine lawn, with lilac plumes and ornaments'.[85] This directive appears to be an attempt to reduce the variables that make it hard to judge beauty consistently. The women will be judged according to a single standard of dress, as they cannot use the advantages that individual styles could bring them. Indiana wins this competition: she 'was the first object to meet every eye, from the lustre of her beauty, and the fineness of her figure, each more than ever transcendently conspicuous, from the uniform which had obliged every other female in the room to appear in exactly the same attire'.[86] Moreover, she uses Eugenia as her foil to emphasize her beauty further: 'the contrast here to the spectators was diverting as well as striking, and renewed attention to her own charms, when the eye began to grow nearly sated with gazing'.[87] This is not beauty as an absolute, but beauty as a variable whose degree is affected by context.

For Edgar, however, Camilla's beauty is enhanced by an inner morality. When Camilla speaks kindly to Lavinia, Edgar thinks that Camilla 'looked almost as pretty' as Indiana, and when she expresses her contentment with giving up her inheritance, Edgar thinks her 'grown a thousand times more beautiful than Indiana'.[88] By contrast, Indiana is described as selfish in her concern for her own legacy; and her beauty, although universally admired as a standard, is relegated to a lower level in Edgar's hierarchy. Camilla's generous and lively personality combines with her outward features to make her the most beautiful woman in the family, according to Sir Hugh and Edgar. Edgar frequently notes how Camilla's beauty intensifies with the degree to which she acts morally or demonstrates virtue. Burney is in accord with Shaftesbury in her appreciation of moral beauty. Shaftesbury describes deformity as unnatural, and associates it with vice, disease, loss, disharmony, 'calamity and ruin'.[89] While Shaftesbury argues that moral and virtuous actions are not sufficient to make someone beautiful, he thinks these actions have a beauty of their own. Inward beauties, he writes, 'are the most real and essential, the most naturally affecting and of the highest pleasure as well as profit and advantage'.[90] Likewise, 'the most natural beauty in the world is honesty and moral truth'.[91] For Shaftesbury, beauty is synonymous with good, and so the positive reaction one has to observing beauty is similar to the reaction one might have to observing a moral action or person.[92] Moreover, the beauty of a virtuous action consists in its being impartial, free from self-interest, and performed by someone with the capacity to reflect upon it. There is, Shaftesbury argues, a harmony and grace of character that indicates a person who loves virtue for its own sake and not for personal, social, or religious reward.

Eugenia possesses a kind of beauty that derives from her moral disinterestedness. The narrator observes that neither 'disease nor accident had power over her mind; there in its purest proportions, moral beauty preserved its first energy'.[93] Edgar, the most Shaftesburian character, perceives Eugenia's moral disinterestedness as beauty. Of her disinterestedness, Edgar says, "'she is perfectly free ... from self! she is made up of disinterested qualities and liberal sensations. To the most genuine simplicity, she joins the most singular philosophy; and to knowledge and cultivation, the most uncommon, adds all the modesty as well as innocence of her extreme youth and inexperience'".[94] Eugenia's moral beauty cannot increase her physical beauty, but it is a form of beauty. When she sacrifices part of her fortune to Indiana and Melmond, Eugenia displays heavenly beauty. The narrator describes Eugenia 'with a bright beam upon her countenance, which, in defiance of the ravaging distemper that had altered her, gave it an expression almost celestial. It was the pure emanation of virtue, of disinterested, of even heroic virtue'.[95] As Melmond discovers to his regret, this kind of beauty requires 'mental eyes' in order to see it.[96] Dr Marchmont, Edgar's former tutor, has already noticed this quality in Eugenia, observing much earlier that she 'joins so much innocence with information, that the mind must itself be deformed that could dwell upon her personal defects, after conversing with her'.[97] The reward of Eugenia's virtue is to have her impaired body de-stigmatized: 'while her voice was heard, her figure was unobserved; where her virtues were known, they seemed but to be enhanced by her personal misfortunes'.[98] The novel thus undercuts any traditional association of deformity with moral turpitude, and the 'beauty of piety' that Eugenia displays extends to all of the 'virtuous Tyrolds' by the end of the narrative.[99]

## Conclusion

Although mobility impaired, Eugenia, Sir Hugh, and Sir Sedley do not belong to a common category. The word 'lameness', however, is used for the impairments of both Sir Sedley and Eugenia, and is a polite usage. 'Lame', however, seems only to be used in *Camilla* in impolite discourse.[100] There are two references to 'cripple' in *Camilla*, and the usage is also associated with ill-educated and impolite characters. 'Lame' and 'cripple' are both capacity terms. The flighty Miss Dennel defines an old woman as 'being a cripple, and blind, and deaf, and dumb, and slavering, and without a tooth'.[101] Mr Dubster observes to Eugenia that there is a difference between her situation and that of a man who depends on physical strength to earn a living: 'it's but a hard thing upon a man to be a cripple in the middle of life. It's no such great hindrance to a lady, so I don't say it out of disrespect; because ladies can't do much at the best'.[102] Eugenia is not concerned about her impaired functionality, however. For example, Camilla says of Eugenia, when asking Edgar to partner Eugenia in a dance, that 'her lameness is no impediment; for she never thinks of it. We all learnt together at Cleves. Dancing gives her a little more exertion, and therefore a little more fatigue than other people but that is all'.[103] At this point in the novel, Edgar, Camilla, and Eugenia pay no attention to the aesthetic component of Eugenia's impairment, and only recognize the functional component. Edgar is notable for his disregard of the negative social significance of deformity. Aside from the general acceptance of deformity as an issue of aesthetics rather than function, Eugenia's gender and station in any case ensure that her deformities are perceived aesthetically.

The pejorative terminology that we see in *Camilla* is sometimes used unquestioningly by Burney's critics, and there has been little attempt to maintain the distinctions between terms relating to deformity and those relating to capacity. Carol Ann Howells's comment that Eugenia 'becomes a cripple after falling off the see-saw' leads her to miss the distinction between function and aesthetics.[104] David Shuttleton calls Eugenia 'crippled' and 'severely disfigured' without commenting further on these terms.[105] Jason Farr is more interested in function than aesthetics, and describes Eugenia as 'a highly educated, physically disabled young woman' with a 'broken', 'crippled', and 'undersized' body.[106] Felicity Nussbaum includes an unusually large number of pejorative terms and many unnecessary reiterations of descriptions of Eugenia's appearance in her discussion of the novel. Eugenia is 'the novel's maimed character . . . rewarded for her pock-marked face by the coins first struck for use in the slave trade';[107] 'the lovely daughter of a country parson' transformed into 'a pock-marked humpback' who 'contracts a serious and disfiguring case of smallpox';[108] 'afflicted by smallpox and permanently scarred';[109] 'her crooked body . . . becomes an obvious affront to the prevailing standards of beauty and symmetry';[110] she is 'the multiply defective, "diminutive and deformed" Eugenia';[111] 'a blemished, crippled learned lady once she contracts smallpox and falls from the teeter-totter';[112] 'ugly and misshapen by accident';[113] 'severely deformed and ugly in the eyes of the world';[114] 'more defective than the generality of the sex';[115] 'ugly and deformed';[116] with a 'scarred face and unsightly back'.[117] As we see with Wollstonecraft's critics, a pejorative discourse has emerged around the discussion of Eugenia.

*Camilla* is a significant text in the literary history of pre-disability because Burney explicitly separates deformity from its social meanings, tracing Eugenia's complex transition from someone isolated from negative judgements on deformity to someone who is made brutally aware of the social consensus about the disadvantages of deformity. Reading this text alongside the aesthetic debates of the eighteenth century reveals how connected some of the issues Burney discusses are to the fundamental questions that preoccupy the philosophers of the period. *Camilla* does not offer the utopian enclosure for deformed women that we see in *Millenium Hall* – a 'criptopia' – but it does promote the advantages of the retired life (as a refuge from prejudice) and the benefits (and disadvantages) of educating deformed women.[118] Critics have paid attention to Eugenia's exceptionalism from traditional feminine roles, the part she plays in Burney's exploration of misleading bodies, and her emblematic status as an example of 'stoic self-command'[119] or 'female difference'.[120] Eugenia's importance for questions of taste and aesthetics has, nevertheless, been overlooked. Recently reclaimed as a disabled woman, Eugenia's aesthetic differences have been downplayed in the revisionist criticism in favour of her functionality.[121] The concept of deformity is much more aligned with questions of taste and aesthetics than it is with functionality and normalcy, however, and Burney places her emphasis on deformity. Burney and her contemporaries define deformity against beauty; and beauty is not seen as a norm, but as a perfect version or ideal. Eugenia's deformity ranges from liberating to exclusionary in critical readings that focus on Burney's portrait of women's circumscribed social roles.

Whatever the level of Burney's familiarity with the philosophical discussions on deformity, it is clear that she uses a critical discourse associated with aesthetics and questions of taste that enables us to place her work in the context of these debates. She challenges the idea that deformity and beauty are absolute standards, that the disadvantages that accrue to deformity are what defines it, and that these disadvantages are in any way stable. Where deformity is concerned, to judge by appearance is to 'play the fool',[122] as the plain-speaking Mr Westwyn puts it, and several of Burney's characters come to this understanding. The acknowledgement that disability has a relational and interactive context, and is not solely located in the individual, is widely thought to be a recent concept that grew out of the disability rights movement of the 1990s. If we search for a social barriers approach to disability in the eighteenth century, we will not find it. Burney's *Camilla* demonstrates, however, that relational approaches to *deformity* pre-date relational approaches to disability by two hundred years.

CHAPTER 6

# Monstrous Sights
## Mary Shelley's *Frankenstein*

Must eyes be all in all, the tongue and ear
  Nothing?[1]

The visible is the central and unrivalled repressed of romanticism.[2]

Engagement with the visible, even in its absence, is everywhere in
Romanticism.[3]

'Deformity' and 'monstrosity' are the principal group terms for physical
difference in *Frankenstein*. Most critics treat them as straightforwardly
interchangeable, but this interchangeability arises in at least two distinct
ways. Each is substitutable for the other, and physical monstrosity and
deformity are substitutable for moral monstrosity and deformity. Although
the terms are equivalents in *Frankenstein*, it is worth noting that 'monstrosity' is generally a physiological and mythological category, whereas as
'deformity' is generally an aesthetic category. Both terms are used in
physiological and aesthetic discussions, however.[4] Additionally, 'monster'
is also a name, a designation, or a species.[5] James Chandler calls the novel
'modernity's highest-profile treatment of the question of monstrosity and
one that is ... thoroughly steeped in eighteenth-century notions of
sympathy and sentiment'.[6] I argue that Shelley is more concerned with
how characters come to their judgements about monstrosity/deformity
than she is with defining these concepts.

Using the definitions of 'monstrosity' in the work of Edmund Burke
and Francis Bacon as comparisons (since these thinkers are the most
influential theorists of monstrosity and deformity), this chapter will begin
by explicating what is called here Shelley's combined monstrosity-and-
deformity concept (monstrosity/deformity), and examine some of the
critical responses to the novel that address the issue of definition. It will
then discuss how critics have responded to the issue of what monstrosity
and deformity represent in the novel, and will end with a discussion of the
novel's engagement with modes of looking. It argues that *Frankenstein*

focuses on transformative vision (or moments when ways of looking change) in its account of monstrosity/deformity. I take my cue from William Wordsworth, who offers several paradigms for transformative vision and blindness, and from William Galperin's interpretation of Wordsworth's theory of vision.

Any conceptual discussion of monstrosity and deformity in *Frankenstein* is by necessity complicated by the narration of the story by its characters. The narrative filter makes it impossible to know, even at the point of the creature's birth, whether the term 'monster' refers to physical or moral monstrosity or to both. For example, when Victor says, 'I beheld the wretch – the miserable monster whom I had created', he may imply the moral monster that the creature will become, or that the creature is a physical anomaly, or even that he is both physically and in some sense morally monstrous at birth.[7] Similarly, the creature's own account demonstrates that the relevant concepts operate on multiple levels at the same time. For instance, he looks at himself in a pool, having not yet committed any crimes, and becomes 'fully convinced that I was in reality the monster that I am'.[8] This leaves us with difficult questions about what this response might mean. A discussion of monstrosity and deformity as categories in *Frankenstein* needs to take account of the blurring of designation and description, and of the problem caused by the narrative arrangement.

## The Monstrosity/Deformity Concept in *Frankenstein*, and in the Critical Reception

If one were to construct a definition of Shelley's concept of monstrosity/deformity using the characteristics of the creature in *Frankenstein*, the definition would probably look something like this: it is a feature of an artificially created human-like being of gigantic stature and unusual strength and endurance, whose exceptionally disfigured appearance shocks or frightens all those who see it. Although definitions based on acknowledged examples engender a hermeneutic circularity that is difficult to overcome, several critics have offered definitions of 'monstrosity', of which some draw on the physiological history of the term, and others on the mythological. Percy Shelley's is one of the earliest to hint at the creature's physiological monstrosity. He describes the creature as an 'anomaly' in his review of the novel.[9] Peter Brooks does the same. For Brooks, a monster is 'that which cannot be placed in any of the taxonomic schemes devised by the human mind to understand and to order nature. It exceeds the very basis of classification, language itself: it is an excess of signification, a strange by-product or leftover of the process of making meaning'.[10] Brooks argues, further, that, as a combination of 'natural and supernatural', the creature 'puts normal measurements and classifications into question'.[11] He makes the case both that the creature (as monster) is beyond classification – beyond reduction to the verbal – and that the creature has the potential to use language to escape his oppression: 'the symbolic order of language appears to offer the Monster his only escape from the order of visual, specular, and imaginary relations, in which he is demonstrably the monster. The symbolic order compensates for a deficient nature: it promises escape from a condition of 'to-be-looked-at-ness'.[12] For Brooks, the creature as monster is the victim of looking; his defining characteristic is his indefinability, and the definition of 'monster' is the 'vital enigma' of *Frankenstein*.[13] The stable sense of the term may be simply that the monster is in the class of things that cannot be defined.

The idea of a monster as an anomaly is also present in Burke's *A Philosophical Enquiry into the Origin of Our Ideas of the Sublime and Beautiful* (1757).[14] Monstrosity, Burke suggests, is something 'unusual',[15] by being a deviation from the 'proper species'.[16] Although Burke's brief discussion of monstrosity is in a work of aesthetics, monstrosity is not generally regarded as an aesthetic category.[17] Nevertheless, Burke uses a physiological discourse to make an aesthetic point, as his comment is part of a discussion of the aesthetic difference between a small man and a giant – a comparison that was frequently made in the early equivalents of freak shows, such as Bartholomew Fair. In his statement on this, Burke is cautious about the idea that monstrosity is a deviation from the proper species, since 'no species is so strictly confined to any certain proportions, that there is not a considerable variation amongst the individuals'.[18] This clarification is necessary because Burke has committed himself to the premise that aesthetic qualities cannot be standardized or measured. 'The large and gigantic, though very compatible with the sublime, is contrary to the beautiful. It is impossible to suppose a giant the object of love. When we let our imagination loose in romance, the ideas we naturally annex to that size are those of tyranny, cruelty, injustice, and everything horrid and abominable.'[19]

For Burke, a man of two or three feet in stature, who is 'otherwise endowed with the common qualities of other beautiful bodies', would be considered beautiful and loved.[20] The small man is, on Burke's theory, not in any sense deformed, even though he is deemed monstrous because of the rarity of his body size. For Burke, rarity, and not size, is the defining feature of monstrosity. Mary Shelley's idea of the giant as monstrous,

anomalous, unloved, and sublime accords with Burke's, even if the gigantic is extrinsic to Burke's understanding of monstrosity.

Burke keeps the concepts of monstrosity and deformity distinct; and
this is where we see some similarities and some differences between Shelley
and Burke, and some inconsistencies in Shelley's account. Firstly, Shelley's
view accords with Burke's in his assertion that deformities 'are sure to
disgust' and cannot be the object of love.[21] While Burke describes monstrosity as a deviation from the proper species, he also describes deformity
as arising 'from the want of the common proportions'.[22] Proportionality is
an important element in the description of the creature, though the
accounts of it are inconsistent. According to Victor, the creature's limbs
are 'in proportion'.[23] Walton observes, however, that the creature's form is
'gigantic in stature, yet uncouth and distorted in its proportions', and so it
is difficult to decide on whether the novel follows Burke on this issue.[24]
Burke's description of the relationship between ugliness and the sublime,
however, is close to Shelley's account. Burke suggests that ugliness is
'consistent enough with an idea of the sublime', but he 'would by no
means insinuate that ugliness itself is a sublime idea, unless united with
such qualities as excite a strong terror'.[25] Ugliness is, in Burke, everything
that beauty is not. Burke suggests, nevertheless, that 'a thing may be very
ugly with any proportions, and with a perfect fitness to any uses'.[26]
Shelley's creature is both sublime and ugly.[27] Indeed, his face is 'of such
loathsome, yet appalling hideousness' that Walton shuts his eyes involuntarily and dares not look at it again, as 'there was something so scaring and
unearthly in his ugliness'.[28] Moreover, Shelley's characters express the view
that deformity is disharmonious. The creature's individually beautiful parts
become deformed when assembled. Contrast also plays a part in the
description of ugliness. The creature's 'lustrous, black, flowing' hair and
'teeth of a pearly whiteness' were 'luxuriances' that made the 'dun white'
eye sockets, 'shrivelled complexion, and straight black lips' a 'more horrid
contrast'.[29] This disharmonious whole is increased in ugliness by the
creature's animation. As is the case in eighteenth-century philosophical
responses to deformity, in *Frankenstein* the observers' emotions are an
important indicator of whether deformity is present. Shelley follows Burke
in highlighting disgust. Burke claims that those who 'want the usual
proportions' are 'sure to disgust, though their presence [i.e. the presence
of the usual proportions] is by no means any cause of real pleasure'.[30] The
creature describes himself as 'a monster so hideous that even you [Victor]
turned from me in disgust'.[31] Perhaps the biggest difference between
Shelley and Burke is on the question of the relationship between aesthetics

and morality, however. Burke decides that aesthetic judgements do not inform us of moral character, whereas Shelley is committed to aesthetic and moral interchangeability.

The language of anomaly, and in particular of anomalous origins, is important in modern definitions of monstrosity. Chris Baldick suggests, for instance, that the creature is akin to classical monsters that were 'composed of ill-sorted parts, sometimes combined from different creatures ... sometimes merely multiplied to excess'.[32] Abigail Six and Hannah Thompson concur, suggesting that a monster could be a collection of different parts, such as 'the body parts of different animals' or 'like the Minotaur', a 'mix human with animal elements'.[33] Monsters, they claim, 'have a long-standing association with being enormous'.[34] Six and Thompson also define the term through its etymology. The term collapses 'two Latin derivations in the popular imagination: *monere* "to warn" and *monstrare* "to show"'.[35] They suggest that monsters are a 'visual symbol of something important and usually ominous'.[36] John Block Friedman adds that monsters are 'largely malign' and represent 'the darker side of nature and culture'.[37] The critical consensus on the definition of 'monster', however, has been that, as Patricia MacCormack observes, 'there is no single taxonomical category of monster'.[38] On the question of monstrosity, we can be certain about only a few things in *Frankenstein*. Deformity and monstrosity generate similar affective responses and are referred to interchangeably. Some of the characters' responses to monstrosity/deformity appear to be aesthetic, and some are not obviously so (such as fear of danger as a result of the creature having superior strength). Some appear to be instinctive and others appear to be cultural.

Developments in disability studies have brought new perspectives to the discussion of bodily difference, and critics have begun to trace the historical and cultural development of the disability concept in relation to *Frankenstein*.[39] Reclaiming an account of monstrosity that links it with revolution, David Mitchell and Sharon Snyder imagine the novel as 'an allegorical moment in literary history where those constructed as physically deviant assail those who would create them in that image'.[40] They assert that 'the study of disability must understand the impact of the experience of disability upon subjectivity without simultaneously situating the internal and external body within a strict mirroring relationship to one another'.[41] Julia Miele Rodas finds in '*Frankenstein*, the presence of "an autistic voice"' through the 'dialogue between potent silence and exquisitely framed expressive bursts'.[42] Like William D. Brewer, Rodas understands the novel as a 'tension between the impulse to communicate and the urge to retreat into isolation and death'.[43] Additionally, Fuson Wang has observed that 'to recover *Frankenstein* for disability studies is a steep uphill battle'.[44] He argues against first-wave disability studies' attempts to politicize an 'ableist past', advocating instead a historically aware reading of disability in *Frankenstein* that avoids 'ripping into the text with an urgent politics of anachronistic resentment'.[45] Wang, like others, retains the use of the disability concept in his discussion of *Frankenstein*, setting aside the opportunity to explore historically appropriate group terms such as 'deformity' and 'monstrosity'.

Six and Thompson briefly explore a Baconian reading of the creature's monstrosity. Although Bacon's essay, 'Of Deformity' (1597), which is their source, does not use the term monster, it is still relevant to Shelley's monstrosity/deformity hybrid concept. They suggest that, 'for Bacon, as for Shelley, physical monstrosity is the indirect cause of moral monstrosity, because the latter is attributable to the cruelty unjustly meted out to those whose appearance falls outside what a particular society deems normal.'[46] Further ideas in Bacon's essay are pertinent to the novel's account of monstrosity/deformity. Firstly, the idea that deformed people wish to avenge themselves because of their deformities. They are, Bacon writes, 'commonly revenged of Nature: For as Nature has been unkind to them; so they, on the other hand, are cross to Nature, being most of them (as the Scripture saith) *void of Natural Affection*'.[47] Secondly, Bacon suggests that the outside of the bodies of deformed people matches their minds: 'there is a Consent between the Body and the Mind: And where Nature erreth in the One, She ventureth in the Other'.[48] Thirdly, deformity is a 'perpetual Spur' for people as they strive 'to rescue' themselves 'from Scorn'.[49] Fourthly, Bacon observes that it is better 'to speak of Deformity, not as a Sign, which sometimes deceives; but as a Cause which seldom faileth of the Effect'.[50] Finally, Bacon views physical deformity as the *inevitable* cause of moral deformity. The creature may reference the latter view in the transparent pool scene, when he talks of the 'fatal effects of this miserable deformity'.[51] The novel alludes to fatal effects[52] many times with regard to several characters, however, and the theme of inevitability may be Godwinian rather than Baconian. Baconian deformity is compatible with Percy Shelley's Godwinian idea that the creature's crimes flow from his mistreatment: 'Treat a person ill, and he will become wicked.'[53]

Aside from the two main group terms, deformity and monstrosity, *Frankenstein* suggests that the creature is of an unnamed species separate from humankind. Shelley may have been influenced in this choice of language by her reading of Burke, or by Erasmus Darwin's *Zoonomia*

(1794), which is referenced in the preface to the first edition. Darwin notes that many 'monstrous births ... are propagated, and continued as a variety at least, if not as a new species'.[54] The attribution of the creature's species is important for our understanding of whether he is a deformed human (deviating from an expected form) or a being whose deformity is characteristic of its kind. Maureen McLane suggests that species in *Frankenstein* 'seems to follow a logic of appearance', and argues that it 'seems less a scientific category denoting classes of beings which reproduce their like over time than a perceptual-social category which organizes the possibility of contact among beings'.[55] The creature's namelessness, and the epithets used to describe his physical and moral monstrosity, certainly facilitate our impression of him as non-human.[56] Victor begins his scientific endeavour with the idea of 'the creation of a human being', but suggests immediately that the mode of creation will mean that this will be 'a new species', and it 'would bless me as its creator and source; and many happy and excellent natures would owe their being to me'.[57] The mode of creation will, it seems, designate this person a separate species. Moreover, the creature identifies himself as belonging to another species: 'my companion must be of the same species, and have the same defects'.[58] McLane notes that this is an acquired sense of separateness rather than an instinctive one, observing that 'when the monster gives the account of his own life, he makes clear that he did not naturally understand himself to be excluded from human fellowship'.[59] His declaration of 'everlasting war against the [human] species' is a reinforcement of his separateness as much as it is a consequence of being treated as separate.[60]

The creature defines his species separateness as deriving from deformity and defect. He says, 'man will not associate with me; but one as deformed and horrible as myself would not deny herself to me. My companions must be of the same species, and have the same defects. This being you must create'.[61] Victor is concerned that the creature will be 'exasperated by the fresh provocation of being deserted by one of his own species'.[62] The creature, nevertheless, would pass any test of humanity based on capacities. He can do all of the things a human being can do. He looks like a human being, and talks and reads like a human being. There is thus a conundrum at the heart of Shelley's use of deformity and defect to define a separate species. As a unique being, the creature cannot deviate from a proper form. He is the proper form. It may be that he occupies a double position: he is both a new species[63] and a deviation from a species. Shelley echoes this ambiguity when the creature says to Victor, 'I ought to be thy Adam, but I am rather the fallen angel.'[64] Whatever the origins of the term 'monstrosity', there is often an interplay between monstrosity and humanity. As John Friedman points out, there are 'shifting boundaries between monstrosity and humanity'.[65]

The uncertainty about the significance of the creature's designation as a separate species is evident in the critical responses. Chris Baldick suggests, for instance, that the 'most disturbing thing about him, indeed, is that he has fully human feelings'.[66] Anne K. Mellor is convinced of the creature's humanity, however: 'Mary Shelley saw the creature as potentially monstrous, but she never suggested that he was other than fully human.'[67] Building on the work of disability theorists Jeffrey A. Brune and Daniel J. Wilson, Jared Richman understands the novel to be about passing as human.[68] Maureen McLane suggests that Shelley dismisses Godwin's determinant of the division between human and animal, the ability to read, as insufficient.[69] McLane makes it clear, however, that 'the meaning of "species", like the meaning of monster, is not self-evident and indeed remains suspended through most of the novel'.[70] The species language is further complicated by language associated with race.[71] Victor fears that the creature might propagate a 'race of devils', for instance.[72] Additionally, Walton uses language suggestive that the creature has a foreign and inferior status: he 'seemed to be a savage inhabitant of some undiscovered land'.[73] H. L. Malchow argues that 'Shelley's portrayal of her monster drew upon contemporary attitudes towards non-whites, in particular on fears and hopes of the abolition of slavery in the West Indies.'[74] Furthermore, John Clement Ball observes that 'just as Africans were historically treated by Europeans as inferior, primitive beings, he [the creature] is rejected as a sub-human "other"'.[75] The novel frequently uses the discourse of slavery and abolitionism, and, as Ball suggests, 'warns about the immorality and danger of' condemning people to "peripheral otherness"'.[76]

In many readings, monstrosity/deformity represents moral or psychological failings, or punishment, or various kinds of alienation or political unrest; and Victor is the contemptuous cause of a disastrous effect (the creature).[77] In these readings, monstrosity and deformity take shape as concepts within the allegories to which they correspond. Responses range from those that assume that the creature is a moral and physical monster from the beginning, to those that explore the questions about causation and inevitability (physical monstrosity leading to moral monstrosity) which persist in the discussions of deformity from the early modern period. Critics who take a sympathetic approach to the creature also regard physical and moral monstrosity and deformity as interchangeable. Bruce Wyse, for example, observes that the creature as monster 'stands in for all those physically different human beings unjustly misrecognised, devalued, and excluded, subject to the social projection of dread and disgust, in short, dehumanised'.[78] We might ask, as Amy Vidali does in the case of disability, however, whether there is scope in *Frankenstein* to think beyond deformity/monstrosity as 'something only "used" or "represented" by metaphor'.[79] Much of the commentary on monstrosity in *Frankenstein* centres on the idea that monstrosity is in some sense a projection of something else. These readings elide physical and moral monstrosity without attention to this elision; they also connect corporeal and mental alterity. Here, the creature's origins and actions determine his tragic moral career, and Victor's ambitions derive from some kind of mental failure (e.g. narcissism). The extent to which the novel offers a critique of the social disablement of people with atypical bodies, and of their construction as aberrant by people who choose to or are accustomed to seeing them that way, is often lost.

Mary Poovey, one of the critics who favours the projection account of monstrosity, argues that the creature symbolizes the 'monstrosity' of Victor's ego, and asserts that, even when benevolent, the creature is a monstrous 'projection' of Victor's imagination.[80] Poovey views the creature's identity as monster as inescapable: 'the monster is "made", not born', he is 'the product of the unnatural coupling of nature and the imagination'.[81] D. L. Macdonald and Kathleen Scherf follow a similar line, commenting that 'the monster is an ugly image of Victor's narcissism, the pride that leads him to style himself as creator'.[82] Six and Thompson suggest that if we read the creature 'as an independent being who can be analysed in isolation from the character of his creature' then we would think along the lines of Percy Shelley that the 'direct moral of the book consists [in]: Treat a person ill, and he will become wicked'.[83] The creature's moral monstrosity is the consequence of his ill-treatment, which is in turn a consequence of his supposed physical monstrosity. The alternative – the idea that the creature is a projection of Victor's personality – Six and Thompson argue is 'an equally suggestive but different relationship between physical and moral monstrosity'.[84] They assert that, once the creature is 'read as the embodiment of an aspect of Victor's nature', Victor's moral monstrosity is inseparable from the creature's 'physical monstrosity'.[85] They highlight Victor's 'excessive thirst for knowledge' and 'Promethean arrogance' as 'the cause[s] of the creature's existence', arguing that this is 'in turn ... inseparable from its [the creature's] physical monstrosity'.[86] The account of monstrosity as a projection of something that it figuratively resembles is particularly prevalent in criticism inflected by psychoanalysis. Dean Franco, for example, reads the creature as a Lacanian 'trope, both in terms of his [the creature's] own subjectivity, as well as his position as a signifier in Victor's symbolic order'.[87] The creature is a sign, and 'Victor is the one who pronounces him'.[88] The scene in which the creature is rejected by the De Lacey family signals, according to Franco, the 'foreclosure of speech' and the creature's alienation 'from the signifying chain' of language.[89] The projection idea of monstrosity centres on negative associations attached to atypical bodies that are undoubtedly present in the novel, though these ideas are rarely explicated within a wider sense that these are oppressive cultural norms.

The idea of the monstrous body also serves to illustrate for critics of *Frankenstein* important elements in the history of ideas. Chris Baldick suggests that physical monstrosity is repeatedly associated with the chaos of civil unrest, and is a response to the French Revolution. Baldick writes that 'when political discord and rebellion appear, this "body" is said to be not just diseased, but misshapen, abortive, monstrous'.[90] While still accepting that the monstrous body is connected to Victor's deviance and the deviance of the creature's actions, Baldick argues that the 'Frankenstein myth' (the myth of the large monster that in some sense symbolizes the body politic or the mob) appears regularly 'when revolution and regicide reappear on the agenda of European history'.[91] Fred Botting similarly views the creature as a metaphor for the French Revolution, though his account of the construction of the monstrous body is more specific. He reads the creature's anatomy as echoing 'the "assemblage" of disparate elements drawn from a number of French theorists'.[92] Adopting a similar approach, Lee Sterrenburg suggests that the novel refers to the 'monstrosity' of Godwinian reform.[93] Moreover, the monstrous body serves a proto-feminist agenda in that its deviance, for some critics, accords with the idea of Eve's punishment. Sandra Gilbert and Susan Gubar suggest, for instance, that Shelley's creature exemplifies the idea that an irregular birth is the offspring of original sin: 'Eve's moral deformity is symbolized by the monster's physical malformation, the monster's physical ugliness represents his social illegitimacy, his bastardy, his namelessness.'[94] Alan Bewell transfers this idea of reproductive projection to medical and folk notions concerning maternity, arguing that *Frankenstein* perpetuates mythology about maternal impression (the idea that 'a pregnant woman's imagination' could 'revise the features of a child').[95] Bewell finds the novel to be a 'cautionary tale' about 'how an individual who pays scant heed to either the biological or imaginative conditions of human reproduction gives birth to a monster'.[96] Although critics struggle with defining the creature, his monstrous/deformed body is received critically as an allegory of incautious behaviour, political violence, iconoclastic thinking, and religious punishment. The creature's uncategorizable status is part of the sustained response to the defamiliarization that he encounters.

## Visual Theory and *Frankenstein*: Wordsworthian Modes of Looking

Rosemarie Garland Thomson's work on the role of looking in the formation of disability is important for sensitizing us to the ways of looking that bring with them a prejudicial understanding. Pre-disability texts, however, suggest that prejudicial ways of looking when applied to bodily difference may delineate group categories other than disability – such as deformity or monstrosity. So much critical attention has been centred on the physical body of the creature and what it represents that the attention Shelley gives to examining ways of looking at monstrosity is usually ignored. Modes of looking have been extensively theorized in the subfield of visual studies. Visual studies examines the role of looking in disciplining, stigmatizing, gendering, sexualizing, colonizing, disabling, and racializing people. Visual studies is particularly interested in moments when, as Sophie Thomas puts it, '"seeing" (and not seeing) become a preoccupation that is simultaneously material and thematic'.[97] The art historian W. J. T. Mitchell characterizes this interest as a pictorial turn. Mitchell suggests that in several disciplines there has been an increasing 'realization that *spectatorship* (the look, the gaze, the glance, the practices of observation, surveillance, and visual pleasure) may be as deep a [critical] problem as various forms of *reading* (decipherment, decoding, interpretation, etc.)'.[98] For Mitchell, 'visual experience or "visual literacy" might not be fully explicable on the model of textuality'.[99] Foucault's theories of looking are paramount in the discussion. Mitchell remarks that we can identify the pictorial turn with, among other things, 'Foucault's insistence on a history and theory of power/knowledge that exposes the rift between the discursive and the "visible", the seeable and the sayable, as the crucial fault-line in "scopic regimes" of modernity.'[100] Foucault explores the power of looking in a clinical context as a trope for the increasing professionalization of medicine and dependency on the power of scientific processes of assessment that rely on sight. In visual studies that include consideration of disability, discussions often emerge out of two strands of Foucault's work: his theory, in *Discipline and Punish*, that the carceral society regulates bodily norms, and demands individual productivity through surveillance; and his investigation, in *The Birth of the Clinic*, of epistemological myth-making that converts seeing into knowing. Foucault reveals the power relationships encoded within looking and the exclusionary ideologies that they support.

Garland Thomson's work on staring draws attention to the role of looking in the formation of disability.[101] Staring registers the new and the unexpected through its recognition of difference, and it 'gives meaning to impairment by marking it as aberrant'.[102] The disabled body is the 'to-be-looked-at' and at the same time the 'not-to-be-looked-at'.[103] Staring is, for Garland Thomson, a discriminatory 'ocular intrusion' for 'people who cannot achieve inconspicuousness'.[104] It 'registers the perception of difference and gives meaning to impairment by marking it as aberrant'.[105] To be the object of a stare, to become a spectacle,[106] is to be both 'visually conspicuous' and to be 'politically and socially erased'.[107] Lennard Davis similarly defines disability as the product of looking. Disability is, he claims, 'a disruption in the visual, auditory, or perceptual field as it relates to the power of the gaze. As such, the disruption, the rebellion of the visual must be regulated, rationalized, contained'.[108] Garland Thomson observes, further, that 'the conviction that visual observation is the source of truth supports the entire enterprise of science. Scientific observation and its twin, medical diagnosis, require sustained, intense looking that is imagined as untainted by the viewer's subjectivity'.[109] In *Frankenstein*, however, the intensity of looking goes beyond the subject of scientific observation; it is present in the ways in which characters come to decisions on truth more broadly, and in the ways in which they perceive reality. Looking is important in defining social relationships, social identity, moral and legal culpability, and narrative authority. The gaze in *Frankenstein* is an oppressive, stigmatizing, disciplinary act implicated in the definition of scientific endeavour.

William H. Galperin remarks, in *The Return of the Visible in British Romanticism*, that there is an 'antipathy to the visible in romantic literature'.[110] For Galperin the visible in Wordsworth's work returns in unfamiliar form, like the repressed uncanny. Romanticism's 'characteristic fear of visible images'[111] and its resistance to spectacle, Galperin argues, is evident in the projection of the self to the point at which 'the "I" demonstrably supplants the *eye* as the prime agent of perception in romantic aesthetics'.[112] The visible returns, he claims, not in a linear or chronological sense, but in the sense that it is present but repressed. The repressed unfamiliar is adopted as the familiar, as the *I* informs the way of looking. Galperin offers a number of paradigm cases of the return of the visible in his discussion of Wordsworth's *Prelude*, but two stand out as paralleling a similar return in the events of *Frankenstein*. These are the poet's childhood memory of seeing the dead body of a drowned man at Esthwaite, and his encounter with a blind beggar on the streets of London.

In the first scene, Wordsworth describes himself at eight years old returning to the place where the day before he had seen a pile of clothes left behind by a swimmer. He watches as men poke poles in the water to recover the body. 'At length, the dead man, mid that beauteous scene / Of trees and hills and water, bolt upright / Rose with his ghastly face – a spectre shape / Of terror even.'[113] The young boy recalls feeling 'no vulgar fear'[114] at this gothic sight, because his 'inner eye had seen / Such sights before among the shining streams / Of fairyland, the forests of romance'.[115] The dead man, whom the poet chooses not to mention was a schoolteacher, is, according to Galperin, 'an adversary once banished and subsequently reassimilated in the struggle with and against authority'.[116] For Galperin, the teacher failed 'to heed the lessons of his vocation in taking sufficient measure of the natural, physical world'.[117] He is symptomatic of the visible returning 'as a contradiction – as "something" whose "familiarity" is a function of its repression and continued strangeness'.[118] Wordsworth's loose syntax at this point in the poem produces an important ambiguity. It is not clear whether the face was terrified or terrifying. Nevertheless, the poet's imaginative lens (his perceiving 'I'), mediated by his reading of romantic fairy tales, indicates, Galperin argues, 'an alternative mode of perception: a way of regarding the world now that, according to the logic of the poem and its claim for a sovereign subjectivity, must also be resisted'.[119] Galperin does not discuss *Frankenstein*, but this description of the spectacle of the dead man resonates with the novel. Cynthia Chase reads these lines from Wordsworth as a commentary on the interplay between the allegorical and the literal: 'the emergence of the drowned man becomes the uncanny appearance of, in the real world, of a figure, a "romance", a fiction – but an intact and familiar figure, "hallowed", as Wordsworth says, with the prestige of art'.[120] The imaginative boy familiarizes the unfamiliar, and his I supplants his eye as the prime agent of perception.[121]

Wordsworth's encounter with the blind beggar in the *Prelude* is, Galperin suggests, a 'key instance of specular exchange, which is both a resistance to and, more importantly, a resistance *by* spectacle'.[122] The poet has recently described passing the unknowable masses in the streets of London. For him they appear as a supernatural vision, 'A second-sight procession'.[123] A blind man abruptly comes into view, wearing a paper explaining his story. Looking at his 'sightless eyes' makes the poet feel self-conscious, and 'As if admonished from another world'.[124] The poet's self-consciousness arises from not having his gaze returned. It is an unexpectedly voyeuristic moment. Galperin suggests that the sight of the beggar is 'so special and so prescient' because it foregrounds blindness and, paradoxically, enables the poet 'to see through blindness'.[125] For Galperin, the blind beggar is the visible presence of 'otherness' that is 'at once a function of and a challenge to the speaker's self-consciousness: a consciousness that, commensurate with a blindness brought suddenly into visible relief, is less specular and more spectacular and self-reflexive'.[126] The familiar sight of blind people on the streets reasserts itself as both familiar and unfamiliar, and the written account of the man's experience assists in transforming the perceiving eye into the perceiving I. As Galperin remarks, 'the spectacle of the beggar is by turns the spectacle of oneself'.[127] Neil Hertz finds in this moment a triangulation of 'the poet's self in relation to his double, who is represented, for a moment, as an emblem of minimal difference fixed in relation to itself'.[128]

Galperin's analysis of the drowned man and the blind beggar highlights the movement from the passive and 'specular' mode of perception 'to *some other* way of seeing'[129] – one 'more spectacular and self-reflexive'.[130] The transition thus individualizes and embodies the move from passive Platonic to active Plotinian modes of perception that M. H. Abrams, in *The Mirror and the Lamp*, supposes to distinguish the Romantic period from its neoclassical predecessor: a move from imitation (mirror) to expression (lamp).[131] Abrams argues that Romanticism uses the model of 'a projective and creative mind',[132] and that the 'perceptual mind' projects 'life and passion into the world it apprehends'.[133] Abrams's broader point is that the 'change from imitation to expression, and from the mirror to the fountain, the lamp, and their related analogues', was 'an integral part of a corresponding change in popular epistemology – that is, [the change] in the concept of the role played by the mind in perception'.[134] He situates the origins of this change in the influence of Plotinus via the Cambridge Platonists, 'whom Wordsworth has read, and Coleridge had studied intensively'.[135] As Abrams summarizes, 'Plato was the main source of the philosophical archetype of the reflector, Plotinus was the chief begetter of the archetype of the projector'.[136]

*Frankenstein* is an instance of the return of the visible in the sense that the novel's central tragedy is the creature's repeated failed attempts to transform adverse ways of looking at him, and the failure of other characters to be receptive to alternative ways of looking at him. The creature searches for the right kind of gaze – a gaze from a projective personality (a perceiving I) that is capable of looking without fear or revulsion, and who can receive the unfamiliar as familiar. The novel reinforces the creature's tragedy by reiterating instances in which the uncanny is familiarized and vision is changed (as in Wordsworth's encounters with the blind beggar and the drowned man). Additionally, the creature's monstrous/deformed body is characterized as impossible to remove from the eyes of those who see him. Gazes directed at the creature are averted, mediated, or in some way replaced. He hopes, nevertheless, to persuade characters to engage in what Garland Thomson calls an 'ethics of looking'.[137] Tragically, their gaze never re-visions monstrosity/deformity.

### Transformative Vision: Looking at Monstrosity/Deformity

With the exception of Monsieur De Lacey, all the characters in *Frankenstein* have the potential to transform their gaze.[138] Captain Walton and Victor Frankenstein are capable of looking at the creature sympathetically as they use this type of gaze on others.[139] William Frankenstein, Victor's younger brother, raises the prospect that a child may not be fully acculturated to an adverse way of looking; and the female creature might have looked with sympathy and familiarity, were she to have been animated, because she would have been of the same kind as the creature. Additionally, many of the characters transform their vision in circumstances other than an encounter with the creature. Robert Walton, for example, might have transformed the way he looked at the creature because he changes the way he sees several times. His preparation for the voyage, reading 'day and night', for example, increases his 'familiarity' with the uncanny region he intends to explore and he is interested in satisfying his 'intellectual eye'.[140] When his father forbids his seafaring, Walton's sight metaphorically changes (his 'visions faded'[141]) and he develops a different way of looking: he becomes 'a poet, and for one year lived in a Paradise of my own creation'.[142] Walton is, furthermore, in search of a projective personality, someone 'whose eyes would reply to mine', and 'whose tastes are like my own'.[143] His encounter with Victor provides a model for the creature's desire to meet with sympathetic friendship. Like the creature's, Victor's initial appearance is uncanny. He is strange, half-dead and brought back to life (the sailors 'restored him to animation by rubbing him with brandy').[144] Walton says, nevertheless, that he has never seen 'a more interesting creature: his eyes have generally an expression of wildness, and even madness'.[145] Although Victor is akin to a revivified dead body, which has uncannily replaced the expected sight of another returning dead body (the creature who has temporarily disappeared on the ice), his countenance is nonetheless viewed as revealing unparalleled 'benevolence and sweet-ness'.[146] Though described as mad, Victor is met by Walton's sympathetic gaze ('his constant and deep grief fills me with sympathy and compas-sion').[147] For Walton, Victor projects a 'celestial spirit, that has a halo around him, within whose circle no grief or folly ventures'.[148] Victor's uncanniness is erased by Walton's ability to transform his vision and look at him sympathetically.

Aside from the creature's appearance, Victor's account of his experiences (to Walton) prevents the creature's eloquence from altering Walton's gaze. When Victor finishes his story, Walton's response is horror. He writes to his sister, 'do you not feel your blood congealed with horror, like that which even now curdles mine?'[149] Victor instructs Walton not to listen to the creature, and directs his gaze away from the creature. The creature, Victor says, 'is eloquent and persuasive; and once his words had even power over my heart: but trust him not. His soul is as hellish as his form, full of treachery and fiend-like malice. Hear him not'.[150] In a scene reminiscent of *Richard III*, which Mary Shelley had recently read, Victor evokes a vision of the ghosts of the creature's victims, and asks Walton to 'call on the manes of William, Justine, Clerval, Elizabeth, my father . . . and thrust your sword into his heart'.[151] The ghosts are so alive that Walton comments that they 'are not the creations of his fancy, but the real beings who visit him from the regions of a remote world'.[152] When Walton meets the creature, his sight is overwhelmed. He recalls that he 'shut his eyes involuntarily, and endeavoured to recollect what were my duties with regard to this destroyer'.[153] Walton describes the creature as 'unearthly' and hideous, but he is nonetheless initially sympathetic: 'I was at first touched by the expressions of his misery.'[154] The creature, like Victor and Walton, is in search of someone who can interconnect with his own projections. He describes himself as 'once filled with sublime and transcendent visions of the beauty and the majesty of goodness', and, significantly, as having hoped to find 'beings, who, pardoning my outward form, would love me for the excellent qualities which I was capable of bringing forth'.[155]

As is the case for Walton, several aspects of Victor's character suggest that he has the potential for changing his way of looking at the creature. For example, he has been brought up unafraid of death or of darkness; he shares some common traits and experiences with the creature; and he is capable of imaginative vision (seen in his dreams and hallucinations). Victor also serves as a model for how eloquence can change sight. When he speaks to the sailors, they 'feel the power of his eloquence ... they believe these vast mountains of ice are mole-hills, which will vanish before the resolutions of man'.[156] Victor, however, has an aversion to unfamiliar faces that derives from his sheltered childhood, a preference for beauty, and a dislike of 'repulsive' physiognomies.[157] He also appreciates convergences of physical appearance and character. Victor's grief increases the negative affect of his visual experiences and he averts his gaze (or does not see) when he is emotionally distraught.[158] These elements point to his resistance to transforming his gaze when looking at the creature.

There are numerous instances in the novel where Shelley plays with another kind of transformative vision: the idea of replacement in visual perception, in which a vision of one thing substitutes for a vision of something else, or is mediated by something else. For instance, when Victor is too tired and ill to watch for the creature's sledge, Walton provides a sailor to 'watch for him, and give him instant notice if any new object should appear in sight'.[159] Moreover, the crew's first sight of the creature is mediated by telescopes. The instrument, replacing their natural vision, draws attention to '*some other* way of seeing'.[160] The men see 'a strange sight', 'an apparition', 'a being which had the shape of a man, but apparently of gigantic stature'.[161] The size of the being confuses their sense of perspective.[162] Significantly, telescopic sight does not lead immediately to horror. The men respond with excitement and 'unqualified wonder'.[163] We see this kind of transformative vision also when unexpected people replace those expected. For instance, the sailors initially think that they have seen the same man twice, but ultimately conclude that they have seen two different men: they expect to see the creature, but they see Victor. This switch prefigures the creature's later hopes to change the uncanny sight of a monster into the sight of a friend.[164] The reverse happens when Victor expects Mr Kirwin to bring the creature into his cell. Victor covers his eyes and is shocked to see his father when he uncovers them. Kirwin says he had imagined the sight 'would have been welcome, instead of inspiring such violent repugnance'.[165] The idea of looking at something differently is thematic and even structural. The three narrators offer three different perspectives. In addition to the emphasis on the potential for transformative vision and replacement sights, the novel repeatedly returns to the idea that some sights are unchanging. Victor mentions indelible sight in connection with the deaths of each of his loved ones and it is present in the creature's responses to rejection. Such sight emphasizes the tragedy of the creature's inability to encounter transformative vision.

Ways of looking are particularly important in the animation scene and in the transparent pool episode. In the former, we see a defamiliarization of the creature's appearance (Victor's sudden revulsion), gaze aversion (Victor leaves twice), replacement sights (Victor's dream of Elizabeth becoming his dead mother), imaginative vision (Victor falls asleep twice), and the material eye (a recurrent symbol of the potential for transforming vision). Victor's gaze, however, does not re-vision monstrosity, and the scene ends with indelible sight. Victor imagines the horrific image of the creature is in every street, and he recalls that 'the form of the monster on whom I had bestowed existence was for ever before my eyes, and I raved incessantly concerning him'.[166] Instead of transforming his vision, Victor sees 'a thing such as even Dante could not have conceived', and, via a quotation from the *Ancient Mariner*, 'a frightful fiend'.[167] Prior to the animation scene, Victor has spent a great deal of time constructing (and looking at) the unanimated corpse. Shelley, nevertheless, introduces an element of unexpectedness (defamiliarization) by suggesting that Victor's vision alters at the point of animation. He recalls that when he 'had finished, the beauty of the dream vanished, and breathless horror and disgust filled my heart'.[168] Victor runs into his bedroom 'unable to endure the aspect of the being' he had 'created' (gaze aversion).[169] After confronting the horror of what he has done, Victor falls asleep. Sleep brings imaginative and replacement vision: the nightmarish horror of the dead body returning turns into the horror of his dead mother returning as his beloved intended bride.

The creature has three important responses to Victor's gaze in the animation scene. He attempts to communicate verbally using 'inarticulate sounds';[170] he smiles ('a grin wrinkled his cheeks');[171] and he stares back. Garland Thomson notes that 'smiling, like staring, is a way to manage the uneven distribution of status in social environments'.[172] A grin ('to draw back the lips and display the teeth') can indicate, 'by way of a forced or unnatural smile, or of the broad smile indicative of unrestrained or vulgar merriment, clownish embarrassment, stupid wonder or exultation, or the like'.[173] Grinning is also 'an indication of pain or anger'.[174] The look is thus not easy to interpret. The creature's stare, however, creates discomfort in Victor: 'his eyes, if eyes they may be called, were fixed on me'.[175] Phoebe Ellsworth, whose work informs Garland Thomson's, suggests that 'gazing at a person's face is an extremely salient stimulus with interpersonal implications which cannot be ignored. The stare, in effect, is a demand for a response, tension will be evoked, and the subject will be motivated to escape the situation'.[176] Victor's response is to escape and rush down the stairs.

Victor's looking, in the animation scene, is not easily separable from his defining, however. He begins with a disclaimer about his inability to put what he sees and feels into language, and then does precisely that. Walton similarly calls the creature 'a form which I cannot find words to describe', but he immediately tries, calling the creature 'gigantic in stature, yet uncouth and distorted in its proportion'.[177] In his account of the animation, Victor conjures up a number of terms that begin the taxonomic problem of defining and describing a unique entity. He calls the creature a 'being' (a neutral term for something that exists), but also a 'miserable monster', a 'demoniacal corpse', a 'fiend', and a 'wretch'.[178] This excessive and pejorative naming makes it clear that he is evaluating and not merely looking. Nevertheless, some of the descriptions of body parts are positive and others are negative. The beautiful features (lustrous hair and white teeth) contrast with the 'watery eyes'.[179] This verbal dissection ironically echoes the itemization of female body parts in early modern love poetry. The incongruity is an important part of the negative appraisal of the creature's appearance, and Victor's inability to organize the inconsistencies may prompt his rejection. Victor is unable to sympathize.[180]

Ways of looking are equally prominent in the transparent pool scene. This scene begins with a comparison between deformity and beauty, followed by a recognition moment (where the creature identifies the reflection as belonging to him), and ends with gaze aversion, disbelief, belief, and mortification. The creature recalls that he

> had admired the perfect forms of my cottagers – their grace, beauty, and delicate complexions: but how was I terrified, when I viewed myself in a transparent pool! At first I started back, unable to believe that it was indeed I who was reflected in the mirror; and when I became fully convinced that I was in reality the monster that I am, I was filled with the bitterest sensations of despondence and mortification. Alas! I did not yet entirely know the fatal effects of this miserable deformity.[181]

Analysing the cause of his initial surprise, the creature suggests that he was afraid that the visual representation of his body corresponded to his outward appearance. He also does not believe that it does. In this moment, the creature's reflection and his idea of himself are mismatched. As soon as he recognizes that the visual representation is indeed him, he is convinced that the image equates to monstrosity and deformity. It is not clear whether he recognizes at this point that he is both a physical and a moral monster. The ambiguity is important. The 'I am' may refer to the moral monstrosity of the creature in his narrative present as a murderer telling his story, or to the physical monstrosity of the creature at this moment in the narration of his history (when he has committed no crime). Significantly, even the creature has trouble looking at himself in a sympathetic manner devoid of negative assumptions.

The creature understands his aesthetic difference in relation to the concept of beauty. His appreciation of the beauty and 'perfect forms' of the cottagers is derived from established cultural concepts of which he demonstrates awareness several times.[182] For example, he believes, or perhaps hopes, that Victor's younger brother, William, will not have acquired a visually aesthetic sense by the age of five: 'suddenly, as I gazed on him, an idea seized me, that this little creature was unprejudiced, and had lived too short a time to have imbibed a horror of deformity'.[183] The creature is inconsistent on this question, however. In one of his earliest memories, and before he has contact with people, he recalls that 'I was delighted when I first discovered that a pleasant sound, which often saluted my ears, proceeded from the throats of the little winged animals ... Sometimes I wished to express my sensations in my own mode, but the uncouth and inarticulate sounds which broke from me frightened me into silence again.'[184] His instinctive reaction to the beauty of birdsong as something pleasurable suggests, at least, that an aural aesthetic sense is not culturally acquired. The creature's confirmation of the equivalence between monstrosity and deformity and of the fatal consequences that he will later reveal, touches on the standard definition of deformity in terms of its negative effect on the observer. The creature feels despondence and mortification. Shelley here concurs with Hume in her presentation of deformity as causing self-dissatisfaction.

## Blindness and Not Seeing

Edward Larrissy suggests that the rhetoric connected to sight, and the interplay between sight and other sources of knowledge, is of central importance to Romanticism, and to *Frankenstein*.[185] Larrissy argues that the novel's blind man, Monsieur De Lacey, 'is highly significant for the meaning of the book' because 'he cannot react with prejudice to the creature's hideousness'.[186] He is significant too, Larrissy observes, because his blindness brings 'into sharper relief and opens up a play of meanings' that 'include large symbolic implications connected to Prometheus and Oedipus', and 'animal magnetism and electricity'.[187] Larrissy understands De Lacey as encouraging 'the reader to interpret incidental language about blindness and seeing, as well as references to eyes and eyesight'.[188] These references reveal the interconnectedness of tropes associated with blindness. For example, 'the idea of compensatory sensitivity to music merges with that of sensitivity to language and its resonances and associations'.[189] Monsieur De Lacey exemplifies the blind musician and the sensitive listener. There is also the possibility that he represents the impartial blind justice figure. Tobin Siebers notes that this latter 'trope…purposefully represses facts about blindness.'[190] According to Siebers, the blind justice figure usually takes the form of being metaphorically 'blind to the prejudices that bias judgment'.[191]

Shelley is sophisticated in her use of the blind musician, sensitive listener, and blind justice tropes, however. Rather than the expected idea that blindness renders one incapable of visually derived prejudice, De Lacey's comment on his blindness alludes instead to his inability to judge people's sincerity according to their faces, and of his need to use other means. Unlike the other characters, De Lacey judges the *content* of the creature's words. He says of himself, 'I am blind, and cannot judge of your countenance, but there is something in your words which persuades me that you are sincere'.[192] Monsieur De Lacey is not a widely discussed character, but he is usually understood as being without prejudice *because* of his blindness.[193] This view disregards his description of the way he comes to understand the creature's sincerity, and unnecessarily perpetuates the impartial justice trope. De Lacey will not make an aesthetic judgement based on sight, but this does not mean that Shelley wants to exclude the possibility of prejudicial judgements made on the basis of other sensory experiences, such as the sound of someone's voice, their accent, or the way in which they use words. There are allusions elsewhere in the novel to alternative ways of judging according to non-visual experience. For example, one of the reasons Victor gives for dismissing Professor Krempe is his 'gruff voice'.[194]

Some critics take a more extreme view, suggesting that De Lacey is in some way tricked because of his blindness. This interpretation may reference the cultural trope of the blind person as someone easily deceived, such as Januarie in Chaucer's *The Merchant's Tale* or Jean-Baptiste Greuze's 1755 painting, 'The Blind Man Deceived' (L'aveugle Trompé).[195] Poovey argues, for instance, that 'the monster tries to disguise its true nature by confronting only the blind old father'.[196] Jared Richman develops this line of thinking, suggesting that 'one might read the creature's attempt to pass as human as deceptive, but as an act of disability passing it registers as a strategy enacted by a marginalized figure seeking entry into a community from which he has been denied entry'.[197] De Lacey's acceptance of the creature is, for Richman, a moment of 'tacit disavowal of the visual as the essential measure of identity' and 'a pathway beyond the stigma of disability'.[198] Siebers is concerned, however, that 'passing preserves social hierarchies because it assumes that individuals want to rise above their present social station and that the station to which they aspire belongs to a dominant social group. It stamps the dominant social position as simultaneously normative and desirable'.[199]

Like the other characters in *Frankenstein*, elements in Monsieur De Lacey's background make it possible for him to sympathize with the creature. He is a French exile whose statelessness echoes the creature's own. Like the creature (at this stage in the narrative), he has been 'condemned although innocent';[200] he is a believer in 'brotherly love and charity';[201] and he says that he would gain 'true pleasure to be in any way serviceable to a human being'.[202] He is also poor, like the creature. The creature purposefully introduces himself to De Lacey in a moment that he hopes will lead to De Lacey's 'good-will and mediation'.[203] The old man has played the most beautiful music the creature has ever heard him play, and the music makes De Lacey radiate with happiness: his 'countenance was illuminated with pleasure', which gave way to 'thoughtfulness and sadness' and 'reflection'.[204] Blindness may be an alternative to the perceiving I, because, as it is imagined in *Frankenstein*, there is no perceiving eye to dissuade from a sympathetic encounter. De Lacey offers more than this, however. He offers transformational listening – a way of listening that the Genevan magistrate uses when hears Victor's request to arrest the creature. Victor comments that the magistrate 'heard my story with that half kind of belief that is given to a tale of spirits and supernatural events; but when he was called upon to act officially in consequence, the whole tide of his incredulity returned'.[205] The encounter between De Lacey and the creature represents the creature's greatest hope for acceptance. Percy Shelley selected the scene as 'one of the most profound and extraordinary instances of pathos that we ever recollect'.[206] He writes that he found it hard to read without tears streaming down his cheeks. The creature's encounter with blindness is visually transformational only in the sense that the domesticity of the cottage scene erupts into spectacular chaos. For the creature, however, this sight is indelible: 'the horrible scene of the preceding day was for ever acting before my eyes; the females were flying, and the enraged Felix tearing me from his father's feet'.[207]

Not-seeing and blindness, while separate phenomena, sometimes draw on the same cultural tropes, and are sometimes occasions for transformative listening. In the animation scene, not-seeing signals avoidance. In other places, not-seeing signals imaginative vision. Moreover, Shelley describes her writing process with a positive idea of imaginative sight as temporary non-sightedness.

> My imagination, unbidden, possessed and guided me, gifting the successive images that arose in my mind with a vividness far beyond the usual bounds of reverie. I saw – *with shut eyes* – but acute mental vision, – I saw the pale student of unhallowed arts kneeling beside the thing he had put together. I saw the hideous phantasm of a man stretched out.[208]

This statement draws on the cultural significance of the blind seer, the prophet who, because of their blindness, is capable of a compensatory insight.[209] The absence of sight is an alternative to transformative vision, and is a further iteration of the theoretical but unrealizable possibility that the creature will encounter sympathy. As Maureen McLane observes, 'the sympathetic blindness of Old De Lacey allows us to read normal human vision as ideologically blinkered ... Those with normal and normalizing sight will perceive the anomaly as a threat, as an invasion, and will, like Felix De Lacey, vigorously and righteously resist'.[210]

Not-seeing is a prompt for transformative listening. In their first conversation, Victor tells the creature to 'relieve' him 'from the sight of' his 'detested form'.[211] The creature puts his 'hated hands' over Victor's eyes and encourages him to 'hear my tale'.[212] The creature asks Victor to change his way of looking: '"How can I move thee? Will no entreaties cause thee to turn a favourable eye upon thy creature, who implores thy goodness and compassion."'[213] Not-seeing is also associated with defamiliarization and an inability to change a way of looking, however. The creature urges William to 'listen' to him.[214] The child, however, attempts to rid himself of the horrific sight: 'he placed his hands before his eyes, and uttered a shrill scream'.[215] This reaction recapitulates Victor's when asked about the cause of his sickness: '"Do not ask me", cried I, putting my hands before my eyes, for I thought I saw the dreaded spectre glide into the room.'[216] Before he murders him, the creature threatens William with indelible not-seeing: 'you will never *see* your father again'.[217] The murder initiates a number of intrusive gazes. The creature 'gazed' on his dead victim, 'fixed [his] eyes on the child' and then 'gazed with delight on' the 'dark eyes' of the miniature portrait of the boy's mother.[218] The portrait, a symbol of the beautiful form, deepens the response the creature has to sighted culture. He is conscious that the beautiful appearance of the boy's mother would change to disgust if she were to look at him: 'she whose resemblance I contemplated would, in regarding me, have changed that air of divine benignity to one expressive of disgust and affright'.[219] The boy who cannot look contrasts sharply with the creature who is fixated on looking.

## Conclusion

While critics have avoided discussion of the novel's engagement with modes of looking in relation to its use of deformity and monstrosity, they have discussed the creature's 'shuddering sense of deformity' as representative of his moral deformity or of the moral deformity of his creator, and have understood physical deformity and monstrosity as allegories of political unrest, racial difference, original sin, or womanhood.[220] In focusing exclusively on the monstrous/deformed body and its metaphorical meanings, however, we marginalize Shelley's interest in how looking constructs monstrosity/deformity, and, in particular, her interest in the creature's quest to find a sympathetic viewer. Jared Richman rightly suggests that 'disability studies has begun with a focus on the visual', and that scholars working in this field should 'continue the discussion of *Frankenstein* and disability with a consideration of monstrosity itself'.[221] Shelley, however, seems more interested in the negative consequences of the creature's deformity and monstrosity, and with the ways in which characters form their judgements about him, than with forming distinct definitions or consistent applications of monstrosity/deformity.

Visual studies is frequently concerned with the interplay between seeing and not seeing. For Galperin, the interplay is 'an antagonism . . . that is not simply negative or combative, but generative'.[222] He expresses something of the complexity involved in understanding looking: 'the epistemology of the *invisible* functions as a secret counterpart to the visible, structuring it, conditioning it, even doubling it'.[223] Invisibility informs the visible in the sense that the fragment informs our impression of the whole. Kate Flint suggests that the boundary between seeing and not seeing is about uncertainty. She appreciates 'the slipperiness of the borderline between the visible and the invisible, and the questions which it throws up about subjectivity, perception and point of view'.[224] Lennard Davis understands the borders of seeing and not seeing as an interface of binaries, arguing that we 'split bodies into two immutable categories: whole and incomplete, abled and disabled, normal and abnormal, functional and dysfunctional'.[225] These boundaries are not merely categorical, he argues, they are also part of how we understand what we see and do not see. Davis points out, for instance, the tension between the visible and invisible parts of the Venus de Milo's body. It is a torso that in some sense we aesthetically complete. He also notes the aesthetic filter. A real woman with no arms, Davis asserts, would meet with 'repulsion and fear', as 'the mutilated Venus and the disabled person, particularly the disabled person who is missing limbs or body parts, will become in fantasy visual echoes of the primal fragmented body – a signifier of castration and lack of wholeness'.[226] As Sophie Thomas comments, 'fragments ... mark the place where seeing becomes, for various reasons, impossible: either because the full object is no longer available for viewing (or reading), or because it never has and could never have been'.[227] For Flint, not seeing evokes the imagination (the I, not the eye), and there is a tension 'between different valuations given to outward and inward seeing; to observation on the one hand, and the life of the imagination on the other'.[228]

Visual studies has been slow to incorporate disability studies approaches, however,[229] and the visual dimension of *Frankenstein* is sometimes underplayed. For James Heffernan, the novel 'shields the reader from – or blinds the reader to – the shock of what Victor sees. He suggests that with one brief exception, all we are asked to visualize in our reading are reactions *to* the sight of the monster – not the sight itself'.[230] Fuson Wang also asserts that 'Shelley consistently forbids her reader to get a good look at the creature',[231] and suggests that 'the disabling of the visual narrative creates a significant and irrevocable gap in the empirical data set, a surplus of uncategorized information that frustrates and ultimately overwhelms the narrator's schemes'.[232] Wang echoes Peter Brooks, who argues that the creature as 'a verbal creation ... is the very opposite of monstrous: he is a sympathetic and persuasive participant in Western culture', and all of his 'interlocutors – including, finally, the reader – must come to terms with this contradiction between the verbal and the visual'.[233] Wang considers reading without visual information about the creature to be part of Shelley's positioning of the reader as blind. The novel asks us, he suggests, to 'read blindly and boldly with [Monsieur] De Lacey *for* instead of *against* difference'.[234] One might ask: What does it mean to get a good look at a literary creation? The creation scene contains a detailed description, and we are invited to imagine the creature. However extensive the descriptions, we would never *see* the creature. We read the creature; and this is an important element for engaging our sympathies as transformative readers/ listeners. Like De Lacey, we pay attention to the creature's words.

*Frankenstein* implies that sight is important for the formation of bodily differences, in the sense that it is the sensory tool that enables someone to engage with a particular set of prejudices about appearance. Blindness in this novel excludes a person from the visual experience of bodily difference, but there are ways of forming opinions other than through sight, and Shelley shows an awareness of this. The novel reveals the failure of transformative vision in the case of monstrosity and deformity, and invites sympathy for the object of such failure by its often positive portrayals of transformative vision in cases of the non-deformed and non-monstrous. The inseparability of moral and physical monstrosity renders self-explanatory the lack of sympathy for the creature that is expressed by the characters. In the *Prelude*, the movement from the *passive perceiving eye* to the *active perceiving I* leads to the erasure of the uncanny: the unfamiliar becomes familiar. Shelley's creature returns as an unfamiliar dead body seeking to inspire a specular transformation, a transformation that words might catalyse (as in Wordsworth's fairy tale and label) and blindness might enable. The creature remains frustrated, however, and eventually removes himself from sight. Monstrosity/deformity is the tragically unaccommodated uncanny in Shelley's account of transformative perception, but the novel nevertheless invites the reader to receive monstrosity and deformity transformatively.

# Conclusion

*Physical Disability in British Romantic Literature* diverges from current thinking in disability studies in three ways. Firstly, it argues that the metanarratives of disability that persist in disability studies (the *prodigy-to-pathology*, *recirculation*, *administration*, and *normalcy* theses) are dependent on anachronistic concepts of 'disability' that leave unacknowledged the multiple definitions that apply to disability concepts. I have not written at length on these metanarratives in this discussion, as I think they are refutable on principle, but I have instead concentrated on alternative accounts of pre-disability. I will, however, briefly conclude on the evidence drawn from these case studies that supports the case for setting aside these metanarratives.

The *prodigy-to-pathology* thesis proposes that modern disability emerged when disability ceased to be a moral problem (a sign of evil) and became a medical problem (the object of diagnosis). The most relevant material discussed here is in the chapter on *Frankenstein*. The creature is prodigious (in the sense of being treated as a sign of evil), but he is also the product of advanced medical experimentation. The extensive discussion in the novel of Frankenstein's ethical choices, and those of his creature, provides some evidence that monstrosity remains a locus for the discussion of moral and religious problems in the Romantic period, but no evidence for linear progression from prodigy to pathology.[1] The prodigy-to-pathology thesis is dependent on the term 'disability' as a unifying category – a term that is not part of this novel and which is not important to the period.[2] *Frankenstein* is not engaged in revising the term 'disability', but develops its own language of monstrosity and deformity. Shelley elides monstrosity/deformity and diverts the discussion away from definition and towards an ethics of looking. The novel is ultimately about the persistent alienation of the uncategorizable, and a crisis of identification. Frankenstein's creature offers some evidence for a modified *recirculation* thesis, however, in the sense that multiple discourses of deformity and monstrosity recirculate and intertwine.[3] *Frankenstein* argues for the tolerance of aesthetic difference, and, like *Camilla*, for a disassociation of deformity from disadvantage. Shelley's exploration of deformity, however, is quite different from Burney's, in that it is less an aesthetic re-evaluation of deformity and more a polemic that demonstrates what a society owes to people with deformities.

The central claim of the *administration* thesis is the idea that 'disability' emerges as a modern category in the development of the welfare system. This thesis is rooted in legislation and government regulation, the examination of which is beyond the scope of this study; but these laws and regulations are in themselves governed by political theories, and several writers discussed here engage with those theories. Godwin and Wollstonecraft address the role of ability in questions of social equity, distribution of resources, and human flourishing. The political theories of these writers demonstrate how important questions of capacity, ability, and strength were to the framing of citizenship. Deborah Stone identifies disability as the most problematic 'category of need' because of the difficulty of its verification, and because it was a political necessity for defining social obligations and privileges.[4] For Stone, disability arises because of the requirement to establish fair criteria for the distribution of social aid. The work of Godwin and Wollstonecraft provides some support for the *administration* thesis. Godwin's thinking about social contribution and equity does not produce the disabled group (in the sense of a group that is unable to work, and for which exceptions are provided), as he rules out any kind of social aid; and both writers concentrate on the eradication of incapacity rather than on social equity. Difficulties remain with the administration thesis, however, and we should be careful to use the term 'disability' in the sense that the administrators used it (i.e. referring to the inability to work), rather than to combine it with the modern term which includes a much broader range of people.

The *normalcy* thesis claims, amongst other things, that 'normalcy' (in the sense of conformity to the mathematically typical) and 'disability' are linked in their generation, and are interdependent terms; and that the unattainable 'ideal' is displaced by the abnormal/normal divide. As the appended chart of terminology connected with impairment and non-impairment shows, paired words are often generated hundreds of years apart (e.g. 'beauty' [1325] and 'deformity' [1450]; and 'able' [1382] and 'disable' [1500]). There are examples of binaries coming into existence at the same time (e.g. 'complete' and 'incomplete' [c. 1380]), but this is fairly unusual when it comes to disability-related terms. Furthermore, while it is usual to see the non-impairment word generated first, there are some important exceptions, such as 'insane' (1575) and 'sane' (1721). 'Normalcy' currently dates to 1857, whereas 'disability' dates to 1545. Questions remain as to which definition of 'disability' is part of the binary pair. The normalcy thesis also sets aside other standardizing terms that have been in use throughout history. The chapters on *Camilla* and on the picturesque challenge this omission, and demonstrate that many writers and philosophers discussed terminology related to concepts of the ideal and their opposites without using or implying the normalcy/disability binary. *Camilla* suggests, for instance, that beauty and deformity are not absolutes, but shifting concepts that are context dependent. Beauty, rather than normalcy, creates the problem of the deformed body in Burney's novel, and neither beauty nor deformity are fixed ideas. The picturesque theorists reveal that bodies described as deformed, picturesque or non-standard do not require the idea of a norm to explain them.

This book challenges the use of the modern concept of disability in discussions of the Romantic-era literature, and argues that additional value is gained by using group terms rooted in the period. Such terms help us understand the evolution of disability concepts. They also aid our reading of the literature of the period more broadly. The scarcity of the use of the word 'disability' in the period, and the difference in its meanings when compared with modern disability, suggests that we force similarities when we use it of historical periods. For example, the sophisticated deformity aesthetics in Burney's *Camilla* anticipates theoretical work concerning the relational aspects of disability that occurs in the disability theory in the twentieth century (the *disability/impairment* distinction). Period-specific terminology, such as 'deformity', allows us to see progression towards the social model of deformity much earlier than we see in the case of disability. While Godwin's idea of 'capacity' is perhaps too fine-grained for relevance outside political philosophy, it is nonetheless a concept that we find in other texts, and merits further study. For example, Elizabeth Bennet, responding to Mr Darcy's verbal portrait of the ideal woman, retorts, "'*I* never saw such a woman. *I* never saw such *capacity*, and taste, and *application*, and elegance, as you describe, united.'"[5] Austen appears to use 'capacity' here as a synonym for actual ability rather than potential ability, as Mr Darcy's descriptions are of accomplishments possessed by the ideal woman and, like Godwin, she makes a distinction between a capacity and its application. Furthermore, as the chapter on *Frankenstein* shows, the modern disability concept obscures the interplay between physical deformity (an aesthetic concept), monstrosity (a flexible category), and the associated moral deformities and monstrosities. The terms discussed here – 'capacity', 'weakness', 'disabled' (in the sense of discharged from the services due to injuries), 'deformity', 'picturesque', and 'monstrosity' – represent only the beginning. These are the terms that emerged from this set of writers, whose subject matter seemed to me to merit their inclusion. It is not intended to be exhaustive or foundational or even a central set of concepts. These are merely the concepts used in this collection of work. There is much additional work for me and others to do to recover other group terms such as 'cripple', 'lame', and 'valetudinarian', and especially to flesh out their class-inflected usage.

Finally, this book argues for a separation of discussions of ability and aesthetics, and between the physiological and aesthetic senses of deformity, again by demonstrating what is gained when we make these distinctions. We gain, for example, a more nuanced sense of the switch from aesthetics to functionality in disabled soldier narratives, and of the differences between arguments for charitable assistance based on aesthetics and arguments based on function impairment. Accounts of deformity in eighteenth-century philosophy are rarely troubled by questions of ability. Burney's *Camilla* rests on the distinction between aesthetics and ability, and it stresses the gendered social dimensions of this distinction. We have perhaps held on to the modern disability concept for so long in our historical literary critical work because it firmly unites our scholarship to where it rightly belongs, as part of the history of disabled people. It is now time to recover the concepts of the past in order to do full justice to this history.

# Dictionary Definitions of 'Disability' and 'Deformity'

For those who have the curiosity to enquire, the dictionaries are
open: as marks of national feeling and habits of thinking, speaking,
and acting, such things are not unworthy the notice of wisdom; and
to folly they may be guides, correctives, and reproof.[1]

No critical work has been done on eighteenth-century and early
nineteenth-century dictionary definitions of 'disability' and other relevant
terms, and so this Appendix will outline how the key words surrounding
disability are defined by lexicographers. The aim is to give readers a sense
of the lexical options available to the writers discussed in this study. It will
also consider the conceptual problems that derive from the current historical citations that illustrate the definitions in the *Oxford English Dictionary*,
in order to demonstrate that any definition of 'disability' must rest on a
historically theorized understanding of disability.

Deformity describes, explicitly, the aesthetic component of a bodily
impairment that may or may not be connected with function. It is most
commonly conceptualized as a set of characteristics that are the opposite of
beauty, and that are susceptible of negative evaluation. Philosophers
usually characterize deformity as something that exhibits irregularity,
disproportion, disharmony, asymmetry, and peculiarity. The importance
of the term for understanding pre-disability concepts has been vastly
underestimated in the scholarship to date.[2] Deformity is the dominant
heterogeneous category used to describe visible congenital and acquired
impairments that may or may not affect capacity. These conditions are not
always commonly associated with the word today, however. For example,
deformities (acquired, congenital, and of indeterminate origin) mentioned
in *The Times* between 1785 and 1795 range widely. The following count
as deformities: 'being one-eyed', having no teeth, dwarfism, and defects of
the skin, such as smallpox scars.[3] A 1790 advertisement for Gowland's
lotion, the treatment Mrs Clay uses for her freckles in Jane Austen's

*Persuasion*, claims that it clears 'the skin of Deformities, such as Pimples, Tetters, Ringworms, Freckles, Tan, Redness of the Nose &c. ... inducing a clear, transparent, healthy white and red'.[4] Setting aside physiological texts, discussions of deformity in the period are entirely concerned with questions of taste and aesthetics rather than of functionality, and are frequently linked to moral character. Dictionary definitions of 'deformity' are closely aligned with the philosophical discussions explored in the second part of this book.[5]

### Early Dictionary Definitions of 'Disability' and 'Disabled'

The earliest definitions of 'disability' refer solely to incapacity in general, and not specifically to people. In some of the earliest dictionaries, the word 'disability' appears to be reasonably easy to define. In 1702, John Kersey simply uses the synonym 'incapacity',[6] and Edward Cocker offers 'uncapable'.[7] Edward Phillips, in 1706, is the first to narrow the definition of 'disability' to human or other living creatures, when he defines it as 'a being unable, incapable or unfit'.[8] This definition is a preface to a legal definition of 'disability', and refers to a range of situations that can disqualify an individual from certain kinds of legal agency. The legal disqualifiers are (1) *Disability by the act of the ancestor* – i.e. being the child of a traitor; (2) *Disability by the act of the party oneself* – i.e. making oneself legally disqualified for whatever reason; (3) *Disability by act of law* – i.e. being foreign-born; and (4) *Disability by act of God* – i.e. being '*non compos mentis*, or *non sanae Memoriae* ('not in his wits, or not of a sound or disposing memory').[9] Disability in the case of mental impairment, refers to the state of being prevented from having a legal status that enabled one to function with authority or autonomy, rather than to the impairments themselves. This concurs with the modern legal uses of disability, which the *Oxford English Dictionary* (2008) defines as 'incapacity in the eye of the law, or created by the law; a restriction framed to prevent any person or class of person from sharing in duties or privileges which would otherwise be open to them; legal disqualification.

Variations on Phillips's definition persist until the mid-eighteenth century, when Benjamin Martin gives as his third sense of 'to disable', in *Lingua Britannica Reformata* (1749), the description 'to deprive of the use of one's limbs'.[10] This definition limits the sense to a particular type of function impairment, a restriction that is not excluded by the broader definition of disability as 'incapacity', but which is distinct from it. Phillips's definition of 'a being unable, incapable or unfit' was nevertheless dominant in dictionaries until the publication of Samuel Johnson's *Dictionary of the English Language* (1755–56).[11] Johnson includes the broad definition of 'disability', and also includes the legal definition. He defines 'disability' as '1. Want of power to do any thing; weakness; impotence. . . . 2. Want of proper qualifications for any purpose; legal impediment.'[12] After Johnson, the general definition of 'want of power' was dominant for the remainder of the century.[13] These definitions have some similarity to the Oxford English Dictionary definitions of 'disability' and 'disabled'.

In eighteenth- and early nineteenth-century literary usage, 'disability' is closest to our modern use of 'inability', and is used grammatically in ways that are no longer extant. For example, Lord Grondale responds mockingly to his daughter's refusal to expand on her political views, in Robert Bage's novel *Hermsprong* (1796), by saying, 'I have infinite loss in the disability. It would have edified me much to have heard the rights of daughters, and the duties of fathers, descanted upon by so fine an understanding.'[14] William Hazlitt complains, in 1825, that Jeremy Bentham 'writes as if he was allowed but a single sentence to express his whole view of a subject in'.[15] He observes further that 'Mr. Bentham has *acquired* this disability – it is not natural to him.'[16] The use of the word 'disabled' is close to our modern use of 'incapacitated'. For example, Commodore Trunnion, in Smollett's *Peregrine Pickle* (1751), is 'disabled by his infirmities'.[17] Caleb Williams uses this sense when he describes his second attempt at breaking out of prison: 'I was not however disabled as then; I was capable of exertion, to what precise extent I could not ascertain.'[18] Julian Cloudesley is 'disabled' by grief in Godwin's *Cloudesley* (1830).[19] Additionally, 'disabled' is used adjectively in the way that we use 'injured'. Commodore Trunnion has a 'disabled heel'.[20] We now tend not to use 'disabled' of individual body parts, although *OED* (2008) lists this as an occasional usage. Godwin also uses 'disabled' in a way that is close to our modern use of 'prevented'. In his *Deloraine* (1833), the dying Selina Danvers laments 'that she should be disabled from performing to the end the duties of a mother' to her surviving child.[21]

In general, dictionaries do not reference the military sense of disability, but Phillips (1706) is an exception, as he defines 'to disable' solely as 'to make unable or uncapable of, or to render unfit for Service'.[22] We see this usage in relation to Chelsea College, the hospital founded by Charles II. It was known as the 'Royal Hospital for Disabled Soldiers'.[23] Likewise, Greenwich Hospital was built for '*English Seaman as by Age, Wounds, or other Accidents, shall be disabled from further service at Sea*'.[24] I shall return to this term in a later section.

## 'Disability' and 'Disabled' in the Oxford English Dictionaries

The first two editions of the *Oxford English Dictionary* (1933, 1989), and the work on which they were based, James Murray's *A New English Dictionary* (1897), all define the word 'disability' as (1) 'Want of ability (to discharge any office or function); inability, incapacity, impotence' (earliest source 1580); (2) 'pecuniary inability' (earliest source 1624); and (3) 'Incapacity in the eye of the law' (earliest source 1641).[25] According to the third edition of the *Oxford English Dictionary* (2008), however, there are *four* main senses in which the noun 'disability' is currently used: (1a) lack of ability (to discharge any office or function); inability, incapacity; weakness; (1b) an instance of lack of ability. Chiefly in plural. Now rare; (2) '[a] physical or mental condition that limits a person's movements, senses, or activities; (as a mass noun) the fact or state of having such a condition'; (3) a legal incapacity; and (4) an inability to pay due to lack of financial means.[26] The new second sense of disability suggests that disabilities do not just result from particular bodily or mental conditions: they are also identified as the (relevant set of) bodily or mental conditions. Sense (2) identifies the 'disability' as the explanation or *cause* of the inability (the disabling condition), rather than as the inability resulting from the condition: the *effect*.[27] It is this sense that is salient in characteristically modern accounts of disability.

*OED* (2008) also suggests that the second sense of 'disability' has a history that stretches back to 1561. There are several reasons to be cautious about the pre-1899 quotations used to illustrate sense (2), however. First of all, the definition does not occur in any dictionary prior to the twentieth century, rendering its historical antecedents highly questionable. Johnson, in spite of his keenness to delineate multiple senses of incapacity, does not include anything close to sense (2). Secondly, the quotations are either ambiguous (in that the contextual material is too vague to determine whether the first and second edition sense [1] or the third edition sense [2] is evoked); misattributed (in that they more properly belong to sense [1]); or are problematic in other ways (such as evoking the specialized military usage of 'disability').

*OED* (2008) also refined the principal sense of the adjective 'disabled' into two subcategories along the same lines (the inability – sense [1] – and the condition that causes the inability – sense [2]). These definitions are accompanied by similar citation problems, and introduce further difficulties. Additionally, *OED* (2008), updated sense (2) of 'disabled' as 'Of a person: having a physical or mental condition which limits activity, movement, sensation, etc. Also occas. of a part of the body.' The earliest source for sense (2) is George Herbert's poem 'The Crosse' (1633). This citation, however, was used in previous editions of the dictionary as evidence for sense (1). It is worth looking more closely at the poem. The speaker of the poem describes an ague in his bones and in his soul that prevents him from doing God's work and which makes him 'in all a weak disabled thing'.[28] Herbert refers to the inability rather than the explanation for the inability, and so this properly belongs to sense (1). The next example, from a legal work of 1667, does the same when it refers to 'a disabled' finger being just as indicative of mutilation as any other part of the body.[29] This is followed by a quotation from Richard Cumberland's novel, *Henry* (1795), where a 'disabled man' is 'incapable' of escaping from a posse because of his sprained ankle: 'The main object with the whole posse, appeared to be that of guarding one disabled man.'[30] Here 'disabled' again refers to the inability resulting from the ankle injury, rather than to a physical condition, and so more properly belongs to sense (1). In the citations which support sense (2) of 'disability' and 'disabled', it is impossible to determine with certainty whether the inability or the explanation for the inability is being referenced in any of the citations that date before 1899.

While *OED* (2008) may have overemphasized the continuity of sense (2), it has, perhaps, underestimated the longevity of sense (3) of the adjective 'disabled'. The primary heading of this sense is 'Relating to disabled people'. This distinguishes it from the previous two senses which are categorized as 'Deprived of some ability'. Sense (3) defines 'disabled' as 'designating the status of a disabled person, esp. one recognized as disabled by the state, and who is consequently entitled to certain rights or privileges'. The first written source is 1923. A case could be made, however, that a military sense along these lines existed much earlier than the twentieth century, and, as we have seen, the Poor Law Commission used this sense of 'disabled' in the 1830s. In the case of disabled soldiers, however, it is often difficult to determine whether the physical or mental conditions, or the dismissal itself, are being referenced.

Additionally, *OED* (2008) introduced a new sense of the noun 'disabled' (sense [4b]): 'with *plural* agreement and *the* Disabled people as a class'. The earliest written source presented is from 1740. The 1740 example, however, occurs in relation to a technical point about translation, and may have resulted from the need to adapt a word that would suit a particular purpose, rather than reflect a genuine usage. The example, from Philip Doddridge, concerns a translation of Luke 14:13, in which 'the

Poor, the Disabled, the Lame, [and] the Blind' are invited to frugal entertainments.[31] The *King James Version* has 'the maimed' in place of 'the Disabled', and Doddridge explains in his notes that he has chosen a different word because 'the Signification of the [Greek] Word [ἀναπείρ-ους] is much more extensive, and indeed takes in both *the Lame*, and *the Blind*, afterwards mentioned; and may also include those, whom the Infirmities of Age have rendered helpless'.[32] This usage may well be a *hapax legomenon*. Furthermore, Doddridge refers explicitly to a group defined by their physical but not intellectual impairments, and it is difficult to see how 'the Lame' and 'the Blind' would be left out of a designation of disabled people as a class and it still retain the meaning the dictionary intends. The next citation for (4b) is from *The Times* for 9 March 1833: 'The object proposed by the petitioners … is strictly … limited to a provision of the means of existence for "the imbecile, the disabled, and the destitute".' It is not clear from the example how 'the imbecile' (which may refer to intellectual or bodily impairments) is differ-ent from 'the disabled'. Early usage of sense (4b) (disabled people as a class) is extremely rare, and the remainder of the examples in *OED* (2008) are from 1879 onwards.[33]

These new definitions raise important questions that are beyond the scope of this book, and are properly the domain of linguists and lexicog-raphers. While there are legitimate grounds to divide sense (1) from sense (2) in the modern usage, it is not certain that sense (2) has existed since 1561 in the case of 'disability', and 1633 in the case of 'disabled', given the ambiguity of the examples. The new sense (2) leaves us with questions about the historical usage. For instance, if we divide sense (2) from sense (1), do we lose a combined form of senses (1) and (2) that was used historically? These questions are important because, while Romantic-era and modern concepts of disability are related, we do not yet have a full understanding of *how* they are related.

## Defining Military Disability

The unique circumstances of disabled servicemen demand that we treat them as a distinct group from the civilian population. The word 'disability' was first used as an administrative category in the 'Act for the Reliefe of Souldiours' (1593). The act granted pensions to those who 'adventured their lives and lost their limbs or disabled their bodies, or shall hereafter adventure their lives, lose their limbs, or disable their bodies, in defence and service of Her Majesty [Queen Elizabeth I] and the State'.[34] The use of the word 'disabled' in this military sense is distinctly different from our modern usage in two ways. Firstly, it refers merely to a group of *men* who are prevented, by acquired physical, sensory, intellectual, and/or psychiatric impairments, from continuing in military service; and, secondly, these are restricted to *acquired* impairments.

The Act for the Reliefe of Souldiours required that disabled soldiers and mariners be 'relieved and rewarded to the end that they may reap the fruit of their good deservings, and others may be encouraged to perform the like endeavours'.[35] Provision for disabled servicemen was thus a reward for their labour and a reassurance to people who might think that they, or their families, would be left destitute if an injury led to the loss of a serviceman's ability to work.[36] The phrase 'good deservings' implies a moral component in this type of provision. The servicemen are, in some sense, worthy of their pensions. David Turner comments that 'the specific use of the term by those wounded in conflict meant that there was a certain degree of manly pride in claiming that one was "disabled" rather than merely "lame", establishing a firmer moral claim for assistance that was based on a strong – and in the eyes of those using the term, unambiguous – claim of functional incapacity'.[37] The nature of the moral worth, however, is left unspecified in the Act, and can take a number of different forms, as we have seen in Chapter 3.

The impairments of the serviceman were certified by his chief commander or captain, and these documents would contain descriptions of 'his hurts and services'.[38] If the soldier or mariner needed to travel back to his parish (for instance as an 'out-pensioner' – that is, someone who draws a pension but is not housed in one of the institutions for disabled soldiers, such as in Chelsea Hospital) – the treasurer of each place at which he stopped was required to give him relief until he reached his destination. If a serviceman begged for assistance, however, he could be punished, and he forfeited his entitlements.[39] According to Geoffrey Hudson, the entitlement changed in an important way in the early seventeenth century.[40] Being 'disabled' initially meant not being able to perform the job of a soldier or sailor. From the 1620s, however, being 'disabled' meant not being able to do any kind of work. Ex-servicemen began to state in their applications for relief 'that they were too disabled to work', rather than too disabled 'to fight again for king and country'.[41] The change was formalized in 1662, when disabled servicemen had to demonstrate that they were 'disabled in body for work' as part of their application for support.[42] Hudson concludes that 'the meaning of disability within the context of the ex-serviceman pension scheme became, in time, almost identical to . . .

its meaning in the parish poor relief system'.[43] Hudson concedes, however, that there was, nevertheless, a residual sense that the disabled soldier had some honorific status that separated him from civilians.

The term 'disabled' did not apply to soldiers and sailors with impairments acquired in service who continued their careers after their injuries. Horatio Nelson, for instance, did not become a disabled sailor when he became a partially sighted amputee. Nelson was a mid-career admiral when he lost an eye and an arm in the battle of Santa Cruz de Tenerife in 1797. His initial response to his injuries was concern that his career was over. His letters reveal that he saw no honour in claiming a pension. When he initially thought that he would not be able to return to work, he wrote: "'I am become ... a burthen to my friends and useless to my country'", and he asked for "'the remains of" his "carcase'" to be conveyed to England.[44] Nelson assumed that "'a left-handed admiral ... will never again be considered useful", and so he counselled himself to think about retirement: "the sooner I get to a very humble cottage the better, and make room for a sounder man to serve the State'".[45] His reputation was such, however, that after he recovered from the painful complications caused by his amputation, he went back to command. As his achievements increased, Nelson's impairments came to embody national pride. In 1805, he was celebrated in a poem on his death in which his impairments are metaphors for super-abilities.

> Oh England has lost her right-hand,
> Of NELSON her Champion bereft;
> Yet Ocean she still can command,
> And like him, beat the French with her left.[46]

Wordsworth wrote of Nelson, in his poem *Character of the Happy Warrior* (1807), that he was the person 'that every man in arms should wish to be'.[47] Nelson's exemption from being discharged or disabled was not an unusual phenomenon. Writing in the previous century, Bernard Mandeville notes, in *The Fable of the Bees* (1714), that physical ability was not required in the higher ranks of the armed services.

> As they are most commonly Men of great Age, it would be ridiculous to expect a hail Constitution and Agility of Limbs from them: So their Heads be but Active and well furnish'd, 'tis no great Matter what the rest of their Bodies are. If they cannot bear the Fatigue of being on Horseback, they may ride in Coaches, or be carried in Litters. Men's Conduct and Sagacity are never the less for being Cripples, and the best General the King of *France* has now, can hardly crawl along.[48]

As we can see, the categorization of eighteenth-century servicemen was nuanced. The level and type of function impairment associated with the military use of disablement was extremely broad, and included loss of function through ageing.

Caroline Nielsen suggests that the eighteenth-century army created 'an institutional language of impairment and disablement' of its own, and that 'disabled servicemen were viewed as a distinct group with symbolic importance to the seventeenth and eighteenth-century British nation-state'.[49] Neilsen observes that 'an individual's identification as a "soldier", "old soldier", "invalid", "veteran" or even "disabled" could depend on his contemporaries' divergent attitudes towards his regiment and service history'.[50] A 'soldier' was generally someone who did not hold officer rank. A 'discharged soldier' referred both to 'a non-commissioned man who had legally' and voluntarily left the army and to a man 'who had been forced to leave through personal injury or the dismantling of their unit'.[51] 'Veteran' was 'an honorific title, referring back to the Classical Roman understandings of twenty to thirty years of continuous military service', and so 'not all former soldiers were considered to be "veterans" by their contemporaries'.[52] The 'disabled soldier' is prevented from continuing to work as a soldier; thus the word 'disabled' is here used as an alienans adjective. One of the earliest references to a 'disabled veteran', a rare term in the eighteenth and early nineteenth centuries, is in a 1776 biography of the sister of Warwick the Kingmaker, Lady Anne Neville, who gives charity to a 'wounded and disabled Veteran'.[53] This term is likely to mean a man who is discharged from the services and who is now a veteran, though it could be the case that 'disability' is in this sense referring to 'incapacity'.

### Dictionary Definitions of 'Deformity' and Other Group Terms

Dr Johnson defines 'deformity' as: (1) 'ugliness, ill-favouredness'; (2) 'Ridiculousness; the quality of something worthy to be laughed at'; (3) 'irregularity; inordinateness'; and (4) 'Dishonour; disgrace'.[54] Nathan Bailey defines it as 'a displeasing or painful idea, which is excited in the mind on accord of some object that wants that uniformity which constitutes beauty'.[55] As for the eighteenth-century philosophical considerations of deformity, the description of the bodily configuration is intimately bound up with its evaluation or effect. The following words and phrases were first introduced into the definitions of 'deformity' and 'to deform' in the years stated: 'to disfigure' (1702),[56] 'a being ugly or mis-shapen' (1702),[57] 'out of Form' (1707),[58] 'unpleasing to the sight' (1707),[59] 'want of due Proportion' (1707),[60] 'uncomeliness' (1707),[61] 'to spoil the form or fashion of' (1713),[62] 'homely' (1715),[63] 'crooked' (1765),[64] and 'deface' (1773).[65] People with unusual deformities were often referred to in the Romantic period as 'wonders' or 'monsters'.[66] Johnson defines 'monster' as '(1) Something out of the common order of nature ... (2) Something horrible for deformity, wickedness, or mischief'.[67] Joseph Nicol Scott (1755) suggests that a 'monster' is 'an unnatural birth, or the production of a living thing, degenerating from the proper and usual disposition of parts in the species it belongs to; as when it has too many or too few members; or some of them are excessively large'.[68] The monstrous is associated with 'prodigiousness', irregularity, and the state of being 'beyond the ordinary course of nature'.[69] The word 'prodigy', as a synonym for 'monster', is present in dictionary definitions as early as 1702.[70] Lennard Davis (2000) notes that

> wonders tended to fall into the category of *lusus naturae* [a sport of nature], including giants, dwarfs, hermaphrodites, Siamese twins, hirsute women, and other kinds of anomalous births. While we now tend to consider any anomalous birth as part of the category of disability, this grouping together of birth anomalies and disability did not exist much before the nineteenth century.[71]

The relevant sense of the term 'freak' is currently defined by *OED* (in sense [4b]) as 'more fully *freak of nature* (cf. *lusus naturae*): an abnormally developed individual of any species; in recent use (*esp.* U.S.) a living curiosity exhibited in a show'.[72] The earliest written source is cited as 1847.

The other significant term in the period is 'defect'. This describes a perceived deficiency or an absence of something that may involve a function limitation or a departure from an aesthetic standard.[73] Lord Chesterfield describes a stammer, a lisp, and toothlessness as 'defects' or 'natural imperfections', that, if a man 'has a mind to it', will not 'prevent him from speaking *correctly*'.[74] Acknowledging a degree of interchangeability between 'defect' and 'deformity', Helen Deutsch and Felicity Nussbaum suggest that, in the eighteenth century, 'a debate ensued concerning the amount of slippage possible between [the] categories'.[75] They see 'defects' as inclusive of sensory impairments, whereas 'deformity' is not. Johnson defines 'defect' as '(1) Want; absence of something necessary; insufficiency; the fault opposed to superfluity ... (2) Failing ... (3) A fault; mistake; errour ... (4) Any natural imperfection; a blemish; a failure.'[76] Other eighteenth-century dictionaries are close to this definition, describing 'defect' as a 'failing' (1702),[77] 'Want; a natural Fault, Imperfection, or Blemish' (1706),[78] 'absence of something necessary' (1755),[79] 'omission' (1760),[80] and 'error' (1764).[81] 'Defect', 'lame', and 'cripple' have received some attention in recent studies.[82]

The following table is a timeline of group terms related to disability and to standardizing concepts connected with appearance and ability. It includes words associated with physical, intellectual, and emotional disabilities. The dates are derived from the *Oxford English Dictionary*, and are likely to change as new written sources are discovered and as definitions are adjusted. The list is not exhaustive, and is intended as a reference guide for identifying clusters of terms, to aid thinking about the relationships between words and their opposites, as well as an aid for word searches for those embarking on research in the field.

*Group Terms*
*(The dates of the earliest usage may change, and the list is not exhaustive)*

| Impairment | Non-impairment |
|---|---|
| Dwarf (c. 700) | Middle (early Old English, c. 500–700) [intermediate between extremes in size, stature, rank, quality] |
| Lame (c. 725) | |
| Crump (800) [deformed body or limbs] | |
| Deaf (c. 825) | |
| Halt (c. 893) | |
| Cripple (c. 950) | Strong [975–1025] |
| Lame (c. 1000) [through injury] | |
| Blind (c. 1000) | |
| Dumb (c. 1000) | |
| Feeble (c. 1175) [of the body] | Whole (c. 1200) |
| Feeble (1200) [lacking moral strength] | Hale (1200) |
| | Sound (c. 1200) |
| Palsy (c. 1250) | |
| Crooked (1290) | Proper (1225) |
| Weak (1300) [deficient in bodily strength] | Perfect (c. 1300) |
| | Order (c. 1300) |
| Purblind (1325) [completely blind] | **Beauty** (1325) |
| Impairment (1340) | |
| Maimed (1340) | |
| Imperfect (c.1340) | |
| Monster (c. 1375) | |
| Incomplete (c. 1380) | Complete (c. 1380) |

(*cont.*)

| Impairment | Non-impairment |
|---|---|
| Imperfection (c. 1380) | Able (1382) adj/vb |
| Infirmity (c. 1384) | Mete (c. 1385) |
| Impotent (1390) [non-sexual] | |
| Feeble (1393) [of the mind] | Usual (1396) |
| Defective (1398) [in general] | Ability (1398) |
| Idiot (1400) | |
| Misshapen (1400) [deformed] | |
| Delicate (1400) [of the body] | |
| Mute (1400) | Natural (1400) |
| Unnatural (1425) | Ordinary (1425) |
| Weak (1425) [wanting moral strength] | |
| Purblind (1425) [blind in one eye] | Competent (1430) |
| | Fit (c. 1440) |
| **Defect** (1450) [in a person] | Ideal (1450) [archetype] |
| Purblind (1450) [short-sighted] | Regular (1450) |
| **Deformity** (1450) | |
| Deformed (c. 1450) | |
| Extraordinary (1460) | Exemplar (1475) |
| Crook-backed (1477) | Standard (1477) |
| Stone-blind (1480) | |
| Irregular (1483) | Common (1487) |
| Sand-blind (14_) | Robust (1490) |
| **Disable** (1500) adj/vb | Natural (1500) |
| Bunch-backed (1519) | |
| Stutter (1530) | |
| Blemish (1535) | |
| Impediment (1542) [of the body] | |
| Crump-shouldered (1542) | |
| **Disability** (1545) | |
| Uncommon (1548) | |
| Imbecile (c. 1550) [of body] | |
| Club-foot (1552) | Healthy (1552) |
| Bow-legged (1552) | |
| Grotesque (1561) | |
| Hare-lip (1567) | |
| Afflicted (1574) | |
| Insane (1575) | Valetudinary (1581) [of the body] |
| Unusual (1582) | |
| Changeling (1584) | Model (1586) [exemplar] |
| Prodigy (1595) | Capable (1597) |
| Hunch-backt (1598) | Ordinary (1597) [average; of a person] |
| High-gravel blind/gravel blind (1600) | **Able-bodied** (1600) |
| Distemper (1604) [body/mind] | Ideal (1609) [Perfect] |
| Incapacity (1611) | Typical (1612) |
| Impotent (1615) [sexual] | |

(*cont.*)

| Impairment | Non-impairment |
| --- | --- |
| Deficient (1616) | |
| Disorder (1616) [of the mind] | |
| Incapable (1616) | |
| Ablepsy (1616) [physical/mental blindness] | |
| Invalid (1635/42) | |
| Distorted (1635) | |
| Disfigurement (1637) | |
| Curiosity (1645) | |
| Anomalous/anomaly (1646) | |
| Squint (1652) | |
| Effeminate (1652) [weak] | |
| Crump (1659) [hump] | |
| Crump-backed (1661) | |
| Incorrect (1672) | Norma (1676) |
| | Correct (1676) |
| Hump-backed (1681) | Correctness (1684) |
| Pockmarked (1685) | Sane (1694) [of the body] |
| Disorder (1690) [of the body] | |
| Hump-back (1697) | |
| Crump (1698) [of a person] | Epitome (1698) |
| Valetudinarian (1703) [poor health] | Correctly (1704) |
| Hunchback (1718) | Sane (1721) [of the mind] |
| Mad (1729) [as a group] | |
| **Disabled** (1740?) [as a group][1] | Model (1745) [archetype] |
| Imbecile (1755) [of the mind] | |
| Lamely (1756) [inadequately] | |
| Paralysed (1763) | |
| Diabetic (1763) | Average (1770) [mathematical] |
| Stammer (1773) | **Normal** (1777) |
| | Convention (1778) [custom/standard] |
| | Average (1803) [ordinary] |
| Incapacitated (1805) | |
| Abnormal (1817) | |
| Malformed (1817) | Norm (1821) |
| Defective (1825) [of a person] | |
| Stone-deaf (1837) | Type (1843) [model] |
| Cleft palate (1847) | Type (1847) [ideal] |
| Freak (c. 1847) | Normality (1848) |
| | Normative (1852) |
| Midget (1854) | Normalcy (1857) |
| | Conventional (1864) |
| Incompetent [as a group] (1866) | |
| Handicap (1884) | |
| Handicapped (1893) [as a group] | Competence (1895) [to function normally] |
| | Everyman (1906) [average person] |

(*cont.*)

| Impairment | Non-impairment |
| --- | --- |
| Amputee (1910) Dysfunction (1916) Gimp (1925) [United States] Hearing-impaired (1946) | |

1 Disability activists and disability studies scholars use 'nondisabled' or 'non-disabled', but these words are not in the current *OED*.

# Notes

## Introduction

1 That is, the Romantic era comes before the sense of 'disabled' that does not automatically disqualify the person so described from belonging to such-and-such a group. A 'disabled driver' would be, in the older, alienating sense of 'disabled', someone who is prevented from being a driver; in the more recent, non-alienating sense, a 'disabled driver' would be a driver with disabilities.

2 This concept is known as the 'social model' of disability, and contrasts with the 'individual' or 'medical model'. As Colin Barnes and Geof Mercer suggest, 'in the individual model, "disability" is attributed to individual pathology', whereas 'the social model interprets it as the outcome of social barriers and power relations'. Colin Barnes and Geof Mercer, *Disability* (Cambridge: Polity, 2003), 12.

3 When I use the term 'pre-disability', I use it in the sense of 'before disability'. I wish to avoid the kinds of problems that the term pre-Romanticism raised. As Morse Peckham suggests, the term pre-Romanticism 'violates a basic principle of historical scholarship' because it 'endeavors to interpret documents which began to emerge forty years before the emergence of those documents and artifacts which it is almost universally agreed are properly called Romantic' but which are 'themselves subject to interpretation'. Morse Peckham, *Romanticism and Ideology* (Hanover, NH: Wesleyan University Press, 1995), 8. Some of the concepts I identify as 'pre-disability' continue well into the modern period and become co-disability concepts.

4 My approach has some affinity with 'historical epistemology'. Lorraine Daston defines this as 'the history of categories that structure our thought, pattern our arguments and proofs, and certify our standards for explanation'. Historical epistemology, Daston argues, 'radically challenges the assumption of resemblance between ideas advanced by thinkers working within different conceptual categories'. Lorraine Daston, 'Historical Epistemology', in *Questions of Evidence: Proof, Practice, and Persuasion across the Disciplines*, ed. by James Chandler, Arnold I. Davidson, and Harry Harootunian (Chicago: University of Chicago Press, 1994), 282–9 (282 and 283). See also Michel Foucault, *The Will to Knowledge: The History of Sexuality Volume 1*, trans. by

Robert Hurley (London: Penguin, 1998); Michel Foucault, *The Use of Pleasure: The History of Sexuality Volume 2*, trans. by Robert Hurley (London: Penguin, 1992); Arnold I. Davidson, *The Emergence of Sexuality: Historical Epistemology and the Formation of Concepts* (Cambridge, MA: Harvard University Press, 2001); Lorraine Daston, 'Marvelous Facts and Miraculous Evidence in Early Modern Europe', in *Questions of Evidence: Proof, Practice, and Persuasion across the Disciplines*, ed. by James Chandler, Arnold I. Davidson, and Harry Harootunian (Chicago: University of Chicago Press, 1994), 243–74; James Chandler, 'Proving a History of Evidence', in *Questions of Evidence: Proof, Practice, and Persuasion across the Disciplines*, ed. by James Chandler, Arnold I. Davidson, and Harry Harootunian (Chicago: University of Chicago Press, 1994), 275–81.

5 Lennard J. Davis, 'Dr. Johnson, *Amelia*, and the Discourse of Disability in the Eighteenth Century', in *'Defects': Engendering the Modern Body*, ed. by Helen Deutsch and Felicity Nussbaum (Ann Arbor: University of Michigan Press, 2000), 54–74 (57).

6 Iain Hutchison, *A History of Disability in Nineteenth-Century Scotland* (Lewiston, NY: Edwin Mellen, 2007), 2.

7 Simon Dickie, *Cruelty and Laughter: Forgotten Comic Literature and the Unsentimental Eighteenth Century* (Chicago, IL: University of Chicago Press, 2011), 46. For more on the conceptual problem of disability in the period, see David M. Turner, *Disability in Eighteenth-Century England: Imagining Physical Impairment* (New York: Routledge, 2012), 16–34. For more on ancestral and analogous concepts of disability, see Rosemarie Garland Thomson, 'Introduction: From Wonder to Error – A Genealogy of Freak Discourse in Modernity', in *Freakery: Cultural Spectacles of the Extraordinary Body*, ed. by Rosemarie Garland Thomson (New York: New York University Press, 1996), 1–19; Philip K. Wilson, 'Eighteenth-Century "Monsters" and Nineteenth-Century "Freaks": Reading the Maternally Marked Child', *Literature and Medicine* 21:1 (2002): 1–25; and Paul Youngquist, *Monstrosities: Bodies and British Romanticism* (Minneapolis: University of Minnesota Press, 2003).

8 For a definition of 'first wave' and 'second wave' disability studies, see Lennard J. Davis, 'Preface to the Second Edition', and 'The End of Identity Politics and the Beginning of Dismodernism: On Disability as an Unstable Category', in *The Disability Studies Reader*, ed. by Lennard J. Davis, 2nd edn (New York: Routledge, 2006), xiii–xiv and 231–42. Davis characterizes the second wave as revisiting the foundational ideas of disability identity in 'more nuanced and complex ways' (232).

9 For example, Sandra M. Gilbert and Susan Gubar, *The Madwoman in the Attic: The Woman Writer and the Nineteenth-Century Literary Imagination* (New Haven, CT: Yale University Press, 1979); George MacLennan, *Lucid Interval: Subjective Writing and Madness in History* (Rutherford, NJ: Fairleigh Dickinson University Press, 1992); Helen Small, *Love's Madness: Medicine, the Novel and Female Insanity, 1800–1865* (Oxford: Clarendon Press, 1996); Frederick Burwick, *Poetic Madness and the Romantic Imagination* (University

Park: Pennsylvania State University Press, 1996); Ross Woodman, *Sanity, Madness, Transformation: The Psyche in Romanticism* (Toronto: University of Toronto Press, 2005); Patrick McDonagh, *Idiocy: A Cultural History* (Liverpool: Liverpool University Press, 2008); and Heather R. Beatty, *Nervous Disease in Late Eighteenth-Century Britain: The Reality of a Fashionable Disorder* (London: Pickering and Chatto, 2012).

10 In seeking to understand pre-disability group terms and concepts relevant to the period, the study also continues, although with a light touch, the historical trend that expanded the field of literary study into cultural and political history. See Gary Kelly, *The English Jacobin Novel 1780–1805* (Oxford: Clarendon Press, 1976); Marilyn Butler, *Romantics, Rebels and Reactionaries: English Literature and Its Background 1760–1830* (Oxford: Oxford University Press, 1982); Marjorie Levinson, *Wordsworth's Great Period Poems: Four Essays* (Cambridge: Cambridge University Press, 1986); David Simpson, *Wordsworth's Historical Imagination: The Poetry of Displacement* (New York: Methuen, 1987); Nicholas Roe, *Wordsworth and Coleridge: The Radical Years* (Oxford: Clarendon Press, 1988); Jon Klancher, 'English Romanticism and Cultural Production', in *The New Historicism*, ed. by H. Aram Veeser (New York: Routledge, 1989), 77–88; Alan Liu, *Wordsworth: The Sense of History* (Stanford, CA: Stanford University Press, 1989); Jon Mee, *Dangerous Enthusiasm: William Blake and the Culture of Radicalism in the 1790s* (Oxford: Clarendon Press, 1992); Nicholas Roe, *The Politics of Nature: Wordsworth and Some Contemporaries* (London: Macmillan, 1992); Gary Kelly, *Women, Writing, and Revolution, 1790–1827* (Oxford: Clarendon Press, 1993); James Chandler, *Wordsworth's Second Nature: A Study of the Poetry and Politics* (Chicago, IL: Chicago University Press, 1994). Like many others, this study also examines the case for the Romantic era as a transitional period. See Andrew McCann, *Cultural Politics in the 1790s: Literature, Radicalism and the Public Sphere* (Houndmills, Basingstoke: Macmillan, 1999); Paul Keen, *The Crisis of Literature in the 1790s: Print Culture and the Public Sphere* (Cambridge: Cambridge University Press, 2004); Miriam L. Wallace, ed., *Enlightening Romanticism, Romancing the Enlightenment: British Novels from 1750–1832* (London: Routledge, 2009); Chris Jones, *Radical Sensibility: Literature and Ideas in the 1790s* (London: Routledge, 2016).

11 *Body and Text in the Eighteenth Century*, ed. by Veronica Kelly and Dorothea von Mücke (Stanford, CA: Stanford University Press, 1994), 2.

12 Lennard J. Davis, *Enforcing Normalcy: Disability, Deafness, and the Body* (London: Verso, 1995), 2.

13 *The Body and Physical Difference: Discourses of Disability*, ed. by David T. Mitchell and Sharon L. Snyder (Ann Arbor: University of Michigan Press, 1997), 5.

14 Alan Richardson, 'Romanticism and the Body', *Literature Compass* 1 (2004): 1–14 (2).

15 See Jerome McGann, *The Poetics of Sensibility: A Revolution in Literary Style* (Oxford: Clarendon Press, 1996), 18.

16 Richardson, 'Romanticism and the Body', 12.

17 Richardson, 'Romanticism and the Body', 9.

18 For example, Laurence S. Lockridge, *The Ethics of Romanticism* (Cambridge: Cambridge University Press, 1989); and Todd F. Davis and Kenneth Womack, eds., *Mapping the Ethical Turn: A Reader in Ethics, Culture, and Literary Theory* (Charlottesville: University of Virginia Press, 2001). Some of this work was done by scholars who became central to disability studies. See Tobin Siebers, *The Ethics of Criticism* (Ithaca, NY: Cornell University Press, 1988).

19 Christoph Henke, 'Before the Aesthetic Turn: The Common Sense Union of Ethics and Aesthetics in Shaftesbury and Pope', *Anglia: Journal of English Philology* 129 (2011): 58–78 (58).

20 Lockridge, *The Ethics of Romanticism*, 9.

21 Henke, 'Before the Aesthetic Turn', 60.

22 Siebers, *The Ethics of Criticism*, 1.

23 Lockridge's study is of eight male writers, with scant mention of women writers (Dorothy Wordsworth, Austen, Wollstonecraft, and Mary Shelley appear briefly), and there is a great deal more mention of the wives of the male writers. Siebers, however, devotes a chapter to feminist criticism.

24 Michael Bradshaw and Essaka Joshua, 'Introduction', in *Disabling Romanticism: Body, Mind, and Text*, ed. by Michael Bradshaw (London: Palgrave Macmillan, 2016), 1.

25 Fuson Wang has recently asserted that disability studies has focused on theory rather than history, arguing that 'literary critics have recently taken up the challenge to historicize this decidedly ahistorical claim' that 'various forms of impairment have informed nearly all human production'. Literary disability studies has historicized its theorizing of disability since its inception in the 1990s, however. The problem has not been an ahistorical approach, but a dependency on the term 'disability'. Fuson Wang, 'The Historicist Turn of Romantic-Era Disability Studies, or *Frankenstein* in the Dark', *Literature Compass* 14.7 (2017), 1–10 (1).

26 My outline of the emergence of metanarratives is also sketched out in Bradshaw and Joshua, 'Introduction', 11–12.

27 For the view that there is a transition, see Garland Thomson, *Freakery*, 3; Davis, 'Dr. Johnson', 61–2; Helen Deutsch, 'Exemplary Aberration: Samuel Johnson and the English Canon', in *Disability Studies: Enabling the Humanities*, ed. by Sharon L. Snyder, Brenda Jo Brueggemann, and Rosemarie Garland-Thomson (New York: MLA, 2002), 198–9; and Dwight Christopher Gabbard, 'Disability Studies in the British Long Eighteenth Century', *Literature Compass* 8.2 (2011): 80–94. Gabbard summarizes the claims for this type of transition in the work of Deutsch, Felicity Nussbaum, Davis, and Garland Thomson (84). Gabbard himself views the period as transitional in the sense that the perception of disability 'shifted from serving as an outward indicator of inner vice or as divine warning – a "visual sign of deserved divine punishment for moral failings" – to viewing it as scientific pathology, as

"impersonal affliction randomly assigned throughout the population'" (Gabbard, 'Disability Studies', 84, citing Helen Deutsch and Felicity Nussbaum, eds., *'Defects': Engendering the Modern Body* (Ann Arbor: University of Michigan Press, 2000), and Davis, 'Dr. Johnson'). See also Dickie, *Cruelty and Laughter*, 88–9; and Ato Quayson, *Aesthetic Nervousness: Disability and the Crisis of Representation* (New York: Columbia University Press, 2007), 9.

28 Auguste Comte, *Introduction to Positive Philosophy*, ed. by Frederick Ferré (Indianapolis, IN: Hackett, 1988), 2.

29 Michael Oliver, *The Politics of Disablement* (London: Macmillan, 1990), 30.

30 Oliver, *The Politics of Disablement*, 30.

31 Oliver, *The Politics of Disablement*, 31.

32 Oliver, *The Politics of Disablement*, 31.

33 Garland Thomson, *Freakery*, 3.

34 Garland Thomson, *Freakery*, 3.

35 Garland Thomson, *Freakery*, 3.

36 Garland Thomson, *Freakery*, 1.

37 Rosemarie Garland Thomson, *Staring: How We Look* (Oxford: Oxford University Press, 2009), 163–4.

38 Sharon L. Snyder and David Mitchell, 'Re-engaging the Body: Disability Studies and Resistance to Embodiment', *Public Culture* 13.3 (2001): 367–89 (371).

39 This is 'disability' in the second of the 2008 *OED*'s senses. See the Appendix for more on the *Oxford English Dictionary* definitions.

40 For this view, see Stephen Pender, '"No Monsters at the Resurrection": Inside Some Conjoined Twins', *Monster Theory: Reading Culture*, ed. by Jeffrey Jerome Cohen (Minneapolis: University of Minnesota Press, 1996): 143–67 (145); Margrit Shildrick, 'The Disabled Body, Genealogy and Undecidability', *Cultural Studies* 19.6 (2005): 755–70; and Turner, *Disability in Eighteenth-Century England*, 6.

41 Pender, 'No Monsters at the Resurrection', 145.

42 Lorraine Daston and Katharine Park, *Wonders and the Order of Nature 1150–1750* (New York: Zone, 1998), 10.

43 Daston and Park, *Wonders and the Order of Nature*, 176.

44 Shildrick, 'The Disabled Body', 758.

45 Shildrick, 'The Disabled Body', 758.

46 Shildrick, 'The Disabled Body', 758.

47 William R. Paulson, *Enlightenment, Romanticism, and the Blind in France* (Princeton, NJ: Princeton University Press, 1987), 201.

48 Paulson, *Enlightenment, Romanticism, and the Blind*, 212.

49 As is the case for the prodigy-to-pathology thesis, the *recirculation* narrative highlights concepts associated with the set of bodily configurations, some of which we now categorize as disabilities. To the extent that the recirculation thesis emphasizes the synchronic complexity of the array of concepts associated with disability, my readings of the literary sources provide some limited support for a version of this thesis.

50 Irina Metzler, *Disability in Medieval Europe: Thinking about Physical Impairment during the High Middle Ages, c. 1100–1400* (London: Routledge, 2006), 9.
51 Geoffrey L. Hudson, 'Disabled Veterans and the State in Early Modern England', in *Disabled Veterans in History*, ed. by David A. Gerber (Ann Arbor: University of Michigan Press, 2012) 117–44 (134).
52 Turner, *Disability in Eighteenth-Century England*, 6.
53 Turner, *Disability in Eighteenth-Century England*, 6.
54 David M. Turner and Kevin Stagg, eds., *Social Histories of Disability and Deformity* (London: Routledge, 2006), 9.
55 Turner, *Disability in Eighteenth-Century England*, 5.
56 Turner, *Disability in Eighteenth-Century England*, 3.
57 Small, *Love's Madness*.
58 Kevis Goodman, '"Uncertain Disease": Nostalgia, Pathologies of Motion, Practices of Reading', *Studies in Romanticism* 49.2 (2010): 197–227.
59 See also Linda Austin, *Nostalgia in Transition: 1780–1917* (Charlottesville: University of Virginia Press, 2007).
60 Deborah A. Stone, *The Disabled State* (Philadelphia, PA: Temple University Press, 1984), 27.
61 Stone, *The Disabled State*, 4.
62 Stone, *The Disabled State*, 12.
63 Stone, *The Disabled State*, 13 and 23.
64 Stone, *The Disabled State*, 27.
65 Stone, *The Disabled State*, 40.
66 Stone, *The Disabled State*, 40.
67 Stone, *The Disabled State*, 50.
68 Stone, *The Disabled State*, 55.
69 Stone, *The Disabled State*, 91.
70 Stone, *The Disabled State*, 172.
71 Stone, *The Disabled State*, 188.
72 John Tidd Pratt, *A Collection of All the Statutes in Force Respecting the Relief and Regulation of the Poor, with Notes and References*, 2nd edn (London: Shaw, 1843), 417. The phrase in the Act is 'dangerous lunatic, insane person, or idiot', 417.
73 *First Annual Report of the Poor Law Commissioners for England and Wales* (London: W. Clowes, 1835), 128.
74 *First Annual Report of the Poor Law Commissioners for England and Wales*, 128.
75 *First Annual Report of the Poor Law Commissioners for England and Wales*, 128.
76 Stone, *The Disabled State*, 40–41.
77 I shall discuss this further below. *First Annual Report of the Poor Law Commissioners for England and Wales*, 128.
78 *First Annual Report of the Poor Law Commissioners for England and Wales*, 102.
79 *First Annual Report of the Poor Law Commissioners for England and Wales*, 136.
80 *First Annual Report of the Poor Law Commissioners for England and Wales*, 197.

81 *First Annual Report of the Poor Law Commissioners for England and Wales*, 128. Stone suggests, however, that 'sick' is one of the non-able-bodied categories. This also causes a problem for establishing continuity between the Poor Law Commission's use of 'disability' and the modern senses of the word.

82 Oliver, *The Politics of Disablement*, 28. See Victor Finkelstein, *Attitudes and Disabled People: Issues for Discussion* (New York: World Rehabilitation Fund, 1980). While industrialization is a partial explanation for some of the economic shifts that inform social policy surrounding welfare, Stone's thesis is not dependent on industrialization as a concept. She is concerned instead with establishing evidence for the interdependence of concepts of impairment and able-bodiedness in the legislation relating to the relief of poverty in the period before disability becomes a recognized category for welfare administration.

83 Oliver, *The Politics of Disablement*, 28.

84 Oliver, *The Politics of Disablement*, 33. Michael Oliver and Colin Barnes, *The New Politics of Disablement* (Houndmills, Basingstoke: Palgrave Macmillan, 2012), 63.

85 Oliver, *The Politics of Disablement*, 86.

86 Oliver, *The Politics of Disablement*, 35. Oliver and Barnes use the term 'people with impairments'. Oliver and Barnes, *The New Politics of Disablement*, 65.

87 Oliver, *The Politics of Disablement*, 46. Oliver and Barnes replace this with: 'the "disabled" individual as the antithesis of able-bodiedness and able-mindedness, and the medicalisation of disability became the acceptable response to a specific political and social problem'. Oliver and Barnes, *The New Politics of Disablement*, 81.

88 Oliver, *The Politics of Disablement*, 47; Oliver and Barnes, *The New Politics of Disablement*, 82.

89 Oliver, *The Politics of Disablement*, 47. Oliver and Barnes replace this with: 'individuals were rarely segregated from everyday life as a result of difference in performance'. Oliver and Barnes, *The New Politics of Disablement*, 82.

90 Oliver, *The Politics of Disablement*, 70.

91 Oliver, *The Politics of Disablement*, 84; Oliver and Barnes, *The New Politics of Disablement*, 127.

92 Oliver, *The Politics of Disablement*, 59.

93 Oliver and Barnes, *The New Politics of Disablement*, 99.

94 Oliver, *The Politics of Disablement*, 62.

95 Oliver, *The Politics of Disablement*, 62.

96 Oliver and Barnes, *The New Politics of Disablement*, 103.

97 Oliver and Barnes, *The New Politics of Disablement*, 107.

98 Katherine Gustafson, "I Never Saw Such Children': Disability, Industrialism, and Children's Advocacy in William Godwin's *Fleetwood*', *Essays in Romanticism* 24.2 (2017): 125–43.

99 Gustafson, 'I Never Saw Such Children', 126.

100 Gustafson, 'I Never Saw Such Children', 126.
101 Gustafson, 'I Never Saw Such Children', 132.
102 Gustafson, 'I Never Saw Such Children', 132.
103 Michel Foucault, *Discipline and Punish: The Birth of the Prison*, trans. by Alan Sheridan (London: Penguin, 1997), 184.
104 Davis, *Enforcing Normalcy*, 23–4.
105 Davis, *Enforcing Normalcy*, 41.
106 Davis, *Enforcing Normalcy*, 174, n. 22.
107 Samuel Taylor Coleridge, 'Selection from Mr. Coleridge's Literary Correspondence. No. 1', *Blackwood's Edinburgh Magazine* 10 (October 1821): 253–62 (257).
108 Coleridge, 'Literary Correspondence', 255.
109 Davis, *Enforcing Normalcy*, 25.
110 Davis, *Enforcing Normalcy*, 25.
111 Davis, *Enforcing Normalcy*, 25.
112 Davis, *Enforcing Normalcy*, 29.
113 Davis, *Enforcing Normalcy*, 29.
114 Davis, *Enforcing Normalcy*, 24.
115 Edmund Burke, *A Philosophical Inquiry into the Origin of Our Ideas of the Sublime and Beautiful*, ed. by Adam Phillips (Oxford: Oxford University Press, 1990), 93. My emphasis.
116 Rosemarie Garland Thomson, *Extraordinary Bodies: Figuring Physical Disability in American Culture and Literature* (New York: Columbia University Press, 1997), 8.
117 Paul Youngquist, *Monstrosities: Bodies and British Romanticism* (Minneapolis: University of Minnesota Press, 2003), xiv and xi.
118 Youngquist, *Monstrosities*, xv.
119 Youngquist, *Monstrosities*, xv.
120 Youngquist, *Monstrosities*, xxvi.
121 Youngquist, *Monstrosities*, xxix.
122 Oliver and Barnes, *The New Politics of Disablement*, 89.
123 Oliver and Barnes, *The New Politics of Disablement*, 89.
124 Oliver and Barnes, *The New Politics of Disablement*, 89.
125 Wang, 'The Historicist Turn of Romantic-Era Disability Studies', 2.
126 Colin Barnes and Geof Mercer, 'Breaking the Mould: An Introduction to Doing Disability Research', in *Doing Disability Research*, ed. by Colin Barnes and Geof Mercer (Leeds: Disability Press, 1997), 1–13 (1). Michael Oliver and Colin Barnes note that the social model was intended to be 'an analytical framework and not an empirical social theory'. Oliver and Barnes, *The New Politics of Disablement*, 54.
127 Michael Schillmeier, *Rethinking Disability: Bodies, Senses, and Things* (New York: Routledge, 2010), 113.
128 Sharon L. Snyder and David T. Mitchell, *Cultural Locations of Disability* (Chicago: University of Chicago Press, 2006), 6.
129 Snyder and Mitchell, *Cultural Locations of Disability*, 10.

130 David T. Mitchell and Sharon L. Snyder, 'Representations of Disability, History of', in *Encyclopedia of Disability*, ed. by Gary L. Albrecht, 5 vols (Thousand Oaks, CA: Sage, 2006), 3:1382–94 (1389).

131 Mitchell and Snyder, 'Representations of Disability', 3:1389.

132 Mitchell and Snyder, 'Representations of Disability', 3:1389–90.

133 Mitchell and Snyder, 'Representations of Disability', 3:1390.

134 Mitchell and Snyder, 'Representations of Disability', 3:1390.

135 Peter L. Hays, *The Limping Hero: Grotesques in Literature* (New York: New York University Press, 1971), 8. See 'Appendix Two' for a list of characters who limp in a section called 'The Hospital' (219–31). Hays includes in his study only depictions of 'real men in a reasonably realistic world, as opposed to the obviously fictitious characters of the chivalric world of romance' (8). It is worth noting that the Romantic-era examples are German: Adam Richter in Heinrich von Kleist's *The Broken Jug* (1806, 1808) and Mephisto in Goethe's *Faust* (1808).

136 Hays, *The Limping Hero*, 4.

137 *Images of the Disabled, Disabled Images*, ed. by Alan Gartner and Tom Joe (New York: Praeger, 1987).

138 Lennard J. Davis, 'Seeing the Object as in Itself It Really Is: Beyond the Metaphor of Disability', in *The Madwoman and the Blind Man: Jane Eyre, Discourse, Disability*, ed. by David Bolt, Julia Miele Rodas, and Elizabeth J. Donaldson (Columbus: Ohio State University Press, 2012), ix–xii (x).

139 Davis, 'Seeing the Object', x.

140 Davis, 'Seeing the Object', x.

141 Davis, 'Seeing the Object', x.

142 Davis, 'Seeing the Object', xi. Angela M. Smith's suggestion that we need a 'careful study of bodily metaphors', and Alice Hall's consideration of 'the importance of blindness as a metaphor, [and as a metaphor] often for writing itself', indicate that call for a theorized reconsideration of metaphor was just beginning. Angela M. Smith, *Hideous Progeny: Disability, Eugenics, and Classic Horror Cinema* (New York: Columbia University Press, 2011), 6; Alice Hall, *Literature and Disability* (New York: Routledge, 2016), 91.

143 Garland Thomson, *Extraordinary Bodies*, 5.

144 Garland Thomson, *Extraordinary Bodies*, 5.

145 Wang, 'The Historicist Turn of Romantic-Era Disability Studies', 1.

146 Wang, 'The Historicist Turn of Romantic-Era Disability Studies', 3.

147 Garland Thomson, *Extraordinary Bodies*, 140, n. 5.

148 Garland Thomson, *Extraordinary Bodies*, 7.

149 Michael Bérubé, 'Disability and Narrative', *PMLA* 120.2 (2005): 568–76 (570).

150 Bérubé, 'Disability and Narrative', 570.

151 Davis, *Enforcing Normalcy*, 106.

152 David T. Mitchell and Sharon L. Snyder, *Narrative Prosthesis: Disability and the Dependencies of Discourse* (Ann Arbor: University of Michigan Press, 2000), 47.

153 Mitchell and Snyder, *Narrative Prosthesis*, 7 and 8.
154 Mitchell and Snyder, *Narrative Prosthesis*, 8.
155 Garland Thomson, *Extraordinary Bodies*, 15.
156 Mitchell and Snyder, *Narrative Prosthesis*, 58. Much of this work builds on and challenges Erving Goffman's sociological analysis of stigma as a complex cultural exchange of multiple social identities that are '*virtual*', in the sense of being ascribed to the stigmatized, and '*actual*', in the sense of being intrinsic to the stigmatized. Erving Goffman, *Stigma: Notes on the Management of a Spoiled Identity* (New York: Simon and Schuster, 1986), 3.
157 Disability studies scholars sometimes refer to the perspective that disadvantages people with disabilities as 'ableist'. Ableism describes a range of assumptions about ability, preferences for ability and against disability (for example, conscious or unconscious bias). As Fiona Kumari Campbell observes, however, 'there is little consensus as to what practices and behaviors constitute ableism. We can, nevertheless, say that a chief feature of an ableist viewpoint is a belief that impairment or disability (irrespective of "type") is inherently negative'. Fiona Kumari Campbell, *Contours of Ableism: The Production of Disability and Abledness* (Houndmills, Basingstoke: Palgrave Macmillan, 2009), 5. Ableism creates a fiction that physical independence is derived from a body and a mind, and not from the connection between the body and mind and its context. It is a range of assumptions that constitutes a social and cultural preference for physical strength, agility, and particular kinds of beauty, and amounts to what Tobin Siebers calls an 'ideology of ability'. Tobin Siebers, *Disability Theory* (Ann Arbor: University of Michigan Press, 2008), 7. As an approach to physical disability, this perspective promotes normalcy, independence, and beauty as worthwhile categories, and eschews any sense that all people are temporarily able-bodied and interdependent, that people experience variation throughout a lifecycle, or that beauty is a culturally dependent aesthetic judgment. It also includes instructional and systemic exclusions. An ableist approach to physical disability rests on a number of acknowledged and unacknowledged assumptions about the body: (1) that disability derives solely from an individual's physical impairments; (2) that ability is in some sense an implied criterion for equal inclusion or value in a society; (3) that a body is a universal standard that exists outside of history and culture and (4) that the disabled body is in need of cure, reconstruction, or rehabilitation.
158 Rebecca Sanchez, *Deafening Modernism: Embodied Language and Visual Poetics in American Literature* (New York: New York University Press, 2015), 3.
159 Sanchez, *Deafening Modernism*, 3–4.
160 Sanchez, *Deafening Modernism*, 5.
161 Andrew Elfenbein, 'Editor's Introduction: Byron and Disability', *European Romantic Review* 12.3 (2001): 247–8 (247).
162 Elfenbein, 'Editor's Introduction', 247.

163 Rosemarie Garland Thomson, 'Byron and the New Disability Studies: A Response', *European Romantic Review* 12 (2001): 321–7 (323).
164 Youngquist, *Monstrosities*, 188.
165 Youngquist, *Monstrosities*, xxx.
166 Bradshaw and Joshua, 'Introduction', 2.
167 Bradshaw and Joshua, 'Introduction', 2.
168 See also, Michael Bradshaw, '"Its Own Concentred Recompense": The Impact of Critical Disability Studies on Romanticism', *Humanities* 8.2 (2019): 1–11.
169 Barbara M. Benedict, 'Making a Monster: Socializing Sexuality and the Monster of 1790', in *'Defects': Engendering the Modern Body*, ed. by Helen Deutsch and Felicity Nussbaum (Ann Arbor: University of Michigan Press, 2000), 127–53.
170 Wilson, 'Eighteenth-Century "Monsters" and Nineteenth-Century "Freaks"', 2; Youngquist, *Monstrosities*, 129–60.
171 Felicity Nussbaum, *The Limits of the Human: Fictions of Anomaly, Race, and Gender in the Long Eighteenth Century* (Cambridge: Cambridge University Press, 2003), 1.
172 Nussbaum, *The Limits of the Human*, 110.
173 Mark Mossman, *Disability, Representation and the Body in Irish Writing: 1800–1922* (Houndmills, Basingstoke: Palgrave Macmillan, 2009), 4.
174 Jason S. Farr, 'Sharp Minds/Twisted Bodies: Intellect, Disability, and Female Education in Frances Burney's *Camilla*', *The Eighteenth Century* 55.1 (2014): 1–17 (3).
175 Mitchell and Snyder, *Narrative Prosthesis*, 30.
176 Turner, *Disability in Eighteenth-Century England*, 3.
177 See Susan F. Bohrer, 'Harriet Martineau: Gender, Disability and Liability', *Nineteenth-Century Contexts* 25 (2003): 21–37; Maria Frawley, *Invalidism and Identity in Nineteenth-Century Britain* (Chicago, IL: University of Chicago Press, 2004); Ellen Annandale, 'Assembling Harriet Martineau's Gender and Health Jigsaw', *Women's Studies International Forum* 30.4 (2007): 355–66; and Laura A. Stef-Praun, 'Harriet Martineau's "Intellectual Nobility": Gender, Genius, and Disability', in *Harriet Martineau: Authorship, Society, and Empire*, ed. by Ella Dzelzainis and Cora Kaplan (Manchester: Manchester University Press, 2010), 38–51.
178 Heather Tilley, 'Wordsworth's Glasses: The Materiality of Blindness in Romantic Vision', in *Illustrations, Optics and Objects in Nineteenth-Century Literary and Visual Culture*, ed. by Luisa Calè and Patrizia di Bello (London: Palgrave Macmillan, 2010), 44–61 (44); and Heather Tilley, *Blindness and Writing: From Wordsworth to Gissing* (Cambridge: Cambridge University Press, 2017), 65.
179 Tilley, 'Wordsworth's Glasses', 45–6.
180 Tilley, *Blindness and Writing*, 65.

181 Tilley, 'Wordsworth's Glasses', 56. For more on Wordsworth's eye condition, see Larrissy, *The Blind and Blindness in Literature of the Romantic Period*, 102–40.

182 Paul Youngquist, 'Lyrical Bodies: Wordsworth's Physiological Aesthetics', *European Romantic Review* 10 (1999): 152–62 (152–3). See also Emily B. Stanback, 'Wordsworthian Admonishment', *The Wordsworth Circle* 44.2/3 (2013): 159–63; and Emily B. Stanback, *The Wordsworth–Coleridge Circle and the Aesthetics of Disability* (London: Palgrave Macmillan, 2016).

183 Youngquist, 'Lyrical Bodies', 159.

184 Dwight Codr, '"Her failing voice endeavoured, in vain, to articulate": Sense and Disability in the Novels of Elizabeth Inchbald', *Philological Quarterly* 87 (2008): 359–88 (360).

185 Codr, 'Her failing voice', 360.

186 Codr, 'Her failing voice', 379.

187 Deborah Needleman Armintor, *The Little Everyman: Stature and Masculinity in Eighteenth-Century English Literature* (Seattle: University of Washington Press, 2011). See also Anna Grześkowiak-Krwawicz, *Gulliver in the Land of Giants: A Critical Biography and the Memoirs of the Celebrated Dwarf Joseph Boruwlaski* (Farnham: Ashgate, 2012), and Turner, *Disability in Eighteenth-Century England*.

188 Armintor, *The Little Everyman*, 125; Kerry Duff, 'Biographies of Scale', *Disability Studies Quarterly* 25.4 (2005); Barbara M. Benedict, 'Displaying Difference: Curious Count Boruwlaski and the Staging of Class Identity', *Eighteenth-Century Life* 30.3 (2006): 78–106.

189 Duff, 'Biographies of Scale', n.p.

190 Armintor, *The Little Everyman*, 124.

191 Recent work on disability in the field of the medical humanities includes: Ross Woodman, *Sanity, Madness, Transformation: The Psyche in Romanticism* (Toronto: University of Toronto Press, 2005); Richard C. Sha, 'Towards a Physiology of the Romantic Imagination', *Configurations* 17.3 (2009): 197–226; and Tristanne Connelly and Steve Clark, eds., *Liberating Medicine: 1720–1835* (London: Pickering and Chatto, 2009). For recent work on the history of heredity and eugenics, see Jenny Davidson, *Breeding: A Partial History of the Eighteenth Century* (New York: Columbia University Press, 2009).

192 Emily B. Stanback, 'Disability and Dissent: Thelwall's Elocutionary Project', in *John Thelwall: Critical Reassessments. A Romantic Circles Praxis*, ed. by Yasmin Solomonescu (2011). https://romantic-circles.org/praxis/thelwall/HTML/praxis.2011.stanback.html

193 Davis, 'Dr. Johnson', 55.

194 Davis, 'Dr. Johnson', 55.

195 For a brief overview of other writers, see Dickie, *Cruelty and Laughter*, 88–91.

196 William Hay, 'Deformity: An Essay [1754]', in *The Works of William Hay, Esq.*, 2 vols (London: J. Nichols, 1794), 1:5–48 (12 and 5).

197 Hay, 'Deformity', 1:22. For an extensive discussion of the use of disability in comic literature, see Dickie, *Cruelty and Laughter*, 45–110.
198 For further work on Hay, see Kathleen James-Cavan, '"All in me is Nature": The Values of Deformity in William Hay's Deformity: An Essay', *Prose Studies* 27 (2005): 27–38; and Roger Lund, 'Laughing at Cripples: Ridicule, Deformity and the Argument from Design', *Eighteenth-Century Studies* 39.1 (2005): 91–114 (94).
199 Gabbard, 'Disability Studies in the British Long Eighteenth Century', 80.
200 Wang, 'The Historicist Turn of Romantic-Era Disability Studies', 1.
201 Bradshaw and Joshua, 'Introduction', 10–16); Bradshaw, 'Its Own Con-centred Recompense'.
202 Here I echo Sanchez's aims, but without the restrictions on the choice of subject matter. Sanchez sets out 'to highlight the exciting new ways deafness as a critical modality invites us to think about topics we thought we knew' and 'in so doing [to] expand literary disability studies by demonstrating the importance of the field even and especially in places where no literal deafness or disability is located'. Sanchez, *Deafening Modernism*, 31.

## 1 William Godwin and Capacity

1 William Godwin, *Fleetwood: Or, The New Man of Feeling*, ed. by Gary Handwerk and A. A. Markley (Peterborough, Ontario: Broadview, 2001), 248.
2 William Godwin, *An Enquiry Concerning Political Justice* [1793], ed. by Mark Philp, Oxford World's Classics (Oxford: Oxford University Press, 2013), 53; William Godwin, *Enquiry Concerning Political Justice and Its Influence on Morals and Happiness*, 2 vols, 2nd edn (London: G. G. and J. Robinson, 1796), 1:128; William Godwin, *Enquiry Concerning Political Justice and Its Influence on Morals and Happiness*, 2 vols, 3rd edn (London: G. G. and J. Robinson, 1798), 1:127. Here and in what follows I cite from the three main editions of Godwin's *Political Justice* (1793, 1796, and 1798), except where the statement quoted is not present in the relevant edition. This will enable the reader to note at which point in the evolution of the work particular statements entered the text and at which point they were omitted.
3 In the third edition (1798), Godwin made the servant the brother, father, or benefactor of the rescuer. The change in gender may have been significant in that the first edition's breach in chivalry (implied by choosing not to rescue a woman) may have made the example difficult to accept, and thus distracted from the moral force of the case. Raymond Preston suggests that Godwin made the servant a man 'perhaps to get rid of the imputation of lack of chivalry, and so to simplify the problem'. Raymond Preston, 'Introduction', in William Godwin, *Enquiry Concerning Political Justice*, ed. by Raymond Preston (New York: Knopf, 1926), 41–2.

4 Peter Singer, Leslie Cannold, and Helga Kuhse, 'William Godwin and the Defence of Impartialist Ethics', *Utilitas* 7.1 (1995): 67–86 (68).

5 Evan Radcliffe, 'Godwin from "Metaphysician" to Novelist: *Political Justice, Caleb Williams,* and the Tension between Philosophical Argument and Narrative', *Modern Philology* 97.4 (2000): 528–53 (529).

6 Gary Kelly, *The English Jacobin Novel 1780–1805* (Oxford: Clarendon Press, 1976), 8. I shall bring out some of the inconsistencies in Godwin's positions on physical strength later in this chapter.

7 D. H. Munro suggests that the Fénelon problem is 'inherently evil' because of the choice that is made between justice and love. Munro argues that Godwin was aiming to 'remodel the world so that that the conflict will not occur'. D. H. Munro, 'Archbishop Fénelon versus My Mother', *Australasian Journal of Psychology and Philosophy* 28.3 (1950): 154–73 (157 and 158). Susan Mendus describes Godwin as an 'impartialist . . . who is happy to accept that impartialism drives out other values, such as love and friendship'. Mendus notes the 'absurdities of thorough-going "Godwinian" impartialism', observing that Godwin's system could have been mitigated if Godwin had made a distinction between 'day to day decisions' and the 'level of principle selection'. Mendus is not concerned, however, with the consequences of Godwin's philosophy for people whose capacities are seen as limited. Susan Mendus, 'The Magic in the Pronoun My', in *Scanlon and Contractualism,* ed. by Matt Matravers (London: Frank Cass, 2003), 33–52 (34, 35–6). Lawrence Becker regards Godwinian impartialism as an example of 'the evident foolishness of following' the principle of fairness 'to its apparent conclusion'. Lawrence C. Becker, 'Impartiality and Ethical Theory', *Ethics* 101.4 (1991): 698–700 (699).

8 Don Locke, *A Fantasy of Reason: The Life and Thought of William Godwin* (London: Routledge and Kegan Paul, 1980), 170.

9 Godwin is a prime example of a writer whose views on pre-disability concepts are central to their work but which are, nonetheless, neglected by critics. Mark Philp, a notable exception, recognizes the importance of capacity to Godwin's arguments about virtue. Mark Philp, *Godwin's Political Justice* (London: Duckworth, 1986), 24–6, 85–9. Capacity-related concepts are not mentioned in Kelly, *The English Jacobin Novel;* Pamela Clemit, *The Godwinian Novel: The Rational Fictions of Godwin, Brockden Brown and Mary Shelley* (Oxford: Oxford University Press, 1993); Marilyn Butler, 'Introductory Essay', in *Burke, Paine, Godwin, and the Revolution Controversy,* ed. by Marilyn Butler (Cambridge: Cambridge University Press, 1984), 1–17; Gregory Dart, *Rousseau, Robespierre and English Romanticism* (Cambridge: Cambridge University Press, 1999); Andrew McCann, *Cultural Politics in the 1790s: Literature, Radicalism and the Public Sphere* (Houndmills: Macmillan, 1999); Jane Hodson, *Language and Revolution in Burke, Wollstonecraft, Paine, and Godwin* (Aldershot: Ashgate, 2007); and Rowland Weston, 'Chivalry, Commerce, and Generosity: Godwin on Economic Equality', *Eighteenth-Century Life* 41.2 (2017): 43–58.

10 Locke, *A Fantasy of Reason*, 1.

11 Adam Rounce, 'William Godwin: The Novel, Philosophy, and History', *History of European Ideas* 33.1 (2007): 1–8 (1).

12 Nancy E. Johnson, *The English Jacobin Novel on Rights, Property and the Law: Critiquing the Contract* (Houndmills: Palgrave Macmillan, 2004), 14.

13 William Hazlitt, *The Spirit of Age; or Contemporary Portraits*, 2nd edn (London: Henry Colburn, 1825), 29.

14 See Charles W. Roberts, 'The Influence of Godwin on Wordsworth's Letter to the Bishop of Llandaff', *Studies in Philology* 29.4 (1932): 588–606. For Wordsworth's debt to Godwin on the question of philosophical necessity, see William A. Ulmer, 'William Wordsworth and Philosophical Necessity', *Studies in Philology* 110.1 (2013): 168–98, and Nicola Trott, 'The Coleridge Circle and the "Answer to Godwin"', *Review of English Studies* 41 (1990): 212–29. Although Wordsworth was not a 'committed Godwinian', writes Alan Grob, he nonetheless 'drew upon elements from [Godwinian] associationism, the theory of moral sympathy, and ... the doctrine of rational benevolence to form a conceptual framework that would give meaning and purpose to the events in the lives of those he described'. Alan Grob, 'Wordsworth and Godwin: A Reassessment', *Studies in Romanticism* 6 (1967): 98–119 (117–18).

15 Nicholas Roe suggests that Coleridge's religious beliefs meant that 'his attitude to Godwin, Holcroft and other radical leaders was complex and sometimes critical'. Nicholas Roe, *Wordsworth and Coleridge: The Radical Years* (Oxford: Clarendon Press, 1988), 12.

16 A. A. Markley observes that 'it is important to recognize the degree to which Wollstonecraft worked to amplify Godwin's formula and the scope of the reformist novel'. A. A. Markley, 'Charlotte Smith, the Godwin Circle, and the Proliferation of Speakers in *The Young Philosopher*', in *Charlotte Smith in British Romanticism*, ed. by Jacqueline Labbe (London: Routledge, 2015), 87–99 (92).

17 Clemit, *The Godwinian Novel*, 2 and 1.

18 William Godwin, *An Enquiry Concerning Political Justice, and Its Influence on General Virtue and Happiness*, 2 vols (London: G. G. and J. Robinson, 1793), 1:81; (1796), 1:127; (1798), 1:126. My emphasis. Philp's edition of *Political Justice* (1793) does not include the marginalia.

19 Godwin, *Political Justice* (1793) 52; (1796) 1:127; (1798) 1:127. My emphasis.

20 Singer et al., 'William Godwin and the Defence of Impartialist Ethics', 75. The citation is from Samuel Parr, *A Spital Sermon, Preached at Christ Church, Upon Easter Tuesday, April 15, 1800: To Which Are Added Notes* (London: J. Mawman, 1801), 4.

21 Thomas Reid, *Essays on the Intellectual Powers of Man* (Edinburgh: John Bell and G. G. J. and J. Robinson, 1785).

22 John Bell was a significant publisher for the Scottish Enlightenment. For further comment on Reid's work see *The Edinburgh History of the Book in*

*Scotland, Volume 2: Enlightenment and Expansion 1707–1800*, ed. by Stephen W. Brown and Warren McDougall (Edinburgh: Edinburgh University Press, 2012).

23  Reid, *Intellectual Powers of Man*, 14.
24  Reid, *Intellectual Powers of Man*, 15.
25  Reid, *Intellectual Powers of Man*, 15.
26  Reid, *Intellectual Powers of Man*, 673.
27  Godwin, *Political Justice* (1796), 1:151; (1798), 1:150.
28  Godwin, *Political Justice* (1796); (1798), 2:388.
29  William Godwin, *St. Leon: A Tale of the Sixteenth Century*, ed. by William D. Brewer (Peterborough, Ontario: Broadview, 2006), 302.
30  For the *particular* sense, see Godwin, *Political Justice* (1793), 167; (1796), 1:128; (1798), 1:126–7. See also William Godwin, *Lives of the Necromancers. Or, An Account of the Most Eminent Persons in Successive Ages, Who Have Claimed for Themselves, or to Whom Has Been Imputed by Others, the Exercise of Magical Power* (London: Frederick J. Mason, 1834), viii. For the universal sense of capacity, see Godwin, *Political Justice* (1793), 33; (1796), 1:12; (1798), 1:110.
31  Godwin's uses of 'incapacity' do not concern pre-disability concepts. See William Godwin, *The History of the Life of William Pitt*, in *The Political and Philosophical Writings of William Godwin, Vol. 1: Political Writings I*, ed. by Martin Fitzpatrick (London: Pickering and Chatto, 1993), 1:35–44 (36). My emphasis.
32  Godwin, *Political Justice* (1793), 167; (1796), 1:389–90; (1798), 1:387. My emphasis. There are minor variations in the wording of the later versions.
33  Godwin, *Political Justice* (1793), 167; (1796), 1:389; (1798), 1:387.
34  Godwin swaps the phrase 'the power of exercising' for 'the option to exercise or not to exercise that capacity'. Godwin, *Political Justice* (1796), I:389; (1798), 1:387.
35  Godwin, *Political Justice* (1793), 167; (1796), 1:389; (1798), 1:387. My emphasis.
36  Godwin, *Political Justice* (1793), 167; (1796), 1:389; (1798), 1:387.
37  Godwin, *Political Justice* (1796), 1:151–2; (1798), 1:151.
38  A general good, in this instance, is something that should be promoted by all of the contributors to a society, and from which all contributors to a society benefit. General goods provide the circumstances necessary for universal happiness. Howard H. Harriott discusses the use of the public good argument in anarchist and statist accounts of social choice in the work of Godwin and others. Harriott suggests that 'a public good is one that is characterized by the fact that once it is produced, everyone can benefit, even those who did not contribute to the costs of producing that good ... A feature of public goods is that there is always the possibility of predation by non-contributors, who themselves would acknowledge the value of the good'. Howard H. Harriot, 'Defensible Anarchy?', *International Philosophical Quarterly* 33.3 (1993): 319–39 (330). There is some disagreement in the critical literature on the

extent to which Godwin is committed to maximal pleasure or happiness as a goal, and on what this terminology means. Philp suggests that 'Pleasure is an inadequate and misleading word' for Godwin's goals, even though Godwin uses it, and he argues that 'we grasp Godwin's conception better if we think of our development in terms of our gradual attainment of those excellences of our nature prescribed for us by God's providence'. Philp, *Godwin's* Political Justice, 5.

39 Godwin, *Political Justice* (1796), 2:440; (1798), 2:423.

40 'I have a right to the means of subsistence; he [another man] has an equal right.' Godwin, *Political Justice* (1796), 2:416; (1798), 2:423. 'Every man is entitled, so far as the general stock will suffice, not only to the means of being, but of well being.' Godwin, *Political Justice* (1793), 415–16.

41 'As government is a transaction in the name and for the benefit of the whole, every member of the community ought to have some share in the selection of its measures.' Godwin, *Political Justice* (1793), 91; (1796), 1:217; (1798), 1:214–15.

42 'If each do not preserve his individuality, the judgment of all will be feeble, and the progress of our common understanding inexpressibly retarded ... Nothing can be more necessary for the general benefit, than that we should divest ourselves, as soon as the proper period arrives, of the shackles of infancy; that human life should not be one eternal childhood; but that men should judge for themselves, unfettered by the prejudices of education, or the institutions of their country.' Godwin, *Political Justice* (1796), 1:238; (1798), 1:236.

43 'The perfection of the human character consists in approaching as nearly as possible to the perfectly voluntary state. We ought to be upon all occasions prepared to render a reason of [sic] our actions. We should remove ourselves to the furthest distance from the state of mere inanimate machines, acted upon by causes of which they have no understanding.' Godwin, *Political Justice* (1796), 1:69; (1798), 1:68.

44 Godwin, *Political Justice* (1793), 64; (1796), 1:144; (1798), 1:143.

45 Godwin, *Political Justice* (1793), 56; (1796), 1:135. Godwin modifies this comment in the third edition: 'it will usually be incumbent upon me, to maintain my body and mind in the utmost vigour, and in the best condition for service'. *Political Justice* (1798), 1:134.

46 Godwin, *Political Justice* (1796), 1:167; (1798), 1:166.

47 Godwin, *Political Justice* (1793), 432–3; (1796), 2:478; (1798), 2:484.

48 Godwin, *Political Justice* (1793), 56; (1796), 1:135; (1798), 1:134.

49 Godwin, *Political Justice* (1796), 1:168; (1798), 1:167. Godwin tempers this assertion in his discussion of suicide, however, when he declares that 'there are few situations that can exclude the possibility of future life, vigour, and usefulness', and he concedes that the calculation of 'whether in any instance, the recourse to a voluntary death, can overbalance the usefulness to be displayed, in twenty years of additional life' is a difficult one. Godwin, *Political Justice* (1793), 58; (1796), 1:139; (1798), 1:138; Godwin, *Political*

*Justice* (1796), 1:139–40; (1798) 1:138–9. Godwin writes substantially the same thing in different words in 1793: 'The difficulty is to decide in any instance whether the recourse to a voluntary death can overbalance the usefulness I may exert in twenty or thirty years of additional life.' Godwin, *Political Justice* (1793), 59.

50 Godwin, *Political Justice* (1793), 193; (1796), 1:437; (1798), 1:436; *Political Justice* (1793), 194; (1796), 1:437; (1798), 1:437.

51 William Godwin, *Things As They Are or The Adventures of Caleb Williams*, ed. by Maurice Hindle (London: Penguin, 1988), 19. Hereafter *Caleb Williams*.

52 Godwin, *Caleb Williams*, 97.

53 Godwin, *Caleb Williams*, 19.

54 Godwin, *Caleb Williams*, 240.

55 Godwin, *Caleb Williams*, 227.

56 Godwin, *Caleb Williams*, 238.

57 Godwin, *Political Justice* (1796), 1:152–3; (1798), 1:152. Philp cites this passage in his discussion of the ethical dimensions of the revisions of *Political Justice*. Philp is concerned solely with whether Godwin's later account of virtue includes, as it does in 1793, consideration of 'the actor's intention and the act's consequences'. Philp, *Godwin's* Political Justice, 144.

58 Chris Pierson argues that, because Godwin believes in duties rather than rights, 'the moral space that might be occupied by rights has all been gobbled up by Godwin's duties'. Chris Pierson, 'The Reluctant Pirate: Godwin, Justice, and Property', *Journal of the History of Ideas* 71.4 (2010): 569–91 (575). As Pierson points out, this is something Godwin modified in the second edition, where he introduces a theory of active and passive rights. Pierson, 'The Reluctant Pirate', 575. Pierson misses the point that Godwin's account of duty and virtue is dependent on capacity, focusing instead on Godwin's view that one's merits and virtues entitle one to social rewards.

59 Philp situates Godwin's point (about the limitations on capacity placing restrictions on duties) in the context of Godwin's debate with Richard Price over the role of intentions and consequences in determining the moral value of an act. Philp summarizes Godwin's position as challenging Price's view that 'acts which are in an absolute sense wrong are made right' if we disregard intention, with the idea that 'we are virtuous in so far as we enact that part of our absolute duty which we can recognize, given our limited intellectual, emotional and other resources'. Philp, *Godwin's* Political Justice, 25.

60 Godwin, *Political Justice* (1793), 64; (1796), 1:144; (1798), 1:143.

61 Godwin, *Political Justice* (1793), 64; (1796), 1:144; (1798), 1:143.

62 Godwin, *Political Justice* (1793), 65; (1796), 1:146; (1798), 1:145.

63 Godwin, *Political Justice* (1793), 66; (1796), 1:147; (1798), 1:146. My emphasis.

64 Godwin, *Political Justice* (1793), 66; (1796), 1:147; (1798), 1:147.

65 Godwin, *Political Justice* (1793), 282; (1796), 2:157; (1798), 2:164.

66 Godwin, *Political Justice* (1793), 65; (1796), 1:146; (1798), 1:145. My emphasis. Dr. Blick makes a similar case against the rights of man on the

basis of physical and mental inequality in Robert Bage's novel *Hermsprong* (1796). Blick finds the arguments for equality to be 'contradicted by nature, which has given us an ascending series of inequality, corporeal and mental; and plainly pointed out the way to those wise political distinctions created by birth and rank'. Robert Bage, *Hermsprong; or Man as He Is Not* [1796], ed. by Pamela Perkins (Peterborough, Ontario: Broadview, 2002), 165. Bage also engages extensively with Mary Wollstonecraft's weakness concept. See Chapter 2 for a discussion of Wollstonecraft and weakness.

67  Godwin, *Political Justice* (1793), 54; (1796), 1:129; (1798), 1:128.

68  Godwin, *Political Justice* (1793), 63.

69  Godwin, *Political Justice* (1796), 1:152; (1798), 1:151.

70  Godwin, *Caleb Williams*, 292. My emphasis.

71  Godwin, *Political Justice* (1796), 1:152; (1798), 1:151.

72  Godwin, *Political Justice* (1796), 2:152; (1798), 2:152.

73  Godwin, *Political Justice* (1796), 1:94; (1798), 1:93.

74  Nancy. J. Hirschmann, 'Freedom and (Dis)Ability in Early Modern Political Thought', in *Recovering Disability in Early Modern England*, ed. by Allison P. Hobgood and David Houston Wood (Columbus: Ohio State University Press, 2013), 167–86 (168).

75  Social contract theory describes an individual's relationship to society in terms of the overt or tacit surrender of liberties in return for an ordered, legally protected, and beneficial collective existence.

76  Martha C. Nussbaum, *Frontiers of Justice: Disability, Nationality, Species Membership* (Cambridge, MA: Belknap, 2006), 16.

77  Eva Feder Kittay, 'The Ethics of Care, Dependence, and Disability', *Ratio Juris* 24.1 (2011): 49–58 (50).

78  Kittay, 'The Ethics of Care', 51.

79  Alasdair MacIntyre, *Dependent Rational Animals: Why Human Beings Need the Virtues* (Peru, IL: Open Court, 1999), 8.

80  Godwin does not paradigmatically distinguish these groups. I have extrapolated this schema from the implied categories in Godwin's work.

81  Godwin, *Political Justice* (1793), 413; (1796), 2:412; (1798), 2:419.

82  Godwin, *Political Justice* (1796) 1:87; (1798) 1:86. *Political Justice* (1793), 71 contains a variation.

83  Godwin, *Political Justice* (1796), 1:93–4; (1798), 1:93. *Political Justice* (1793), 317 contains a variation.

84  Godwin, *Political Justice* (1796), 1:94; (1798), 1:93. My emphasis.

85  Godwin, *Political Justice* (1796), 1:69; (1798), 1:68.

86  Godwin, *Political Justice* (1793), 453; (1796), 2:511; (1798), 2:503. The source for Franklin's statement is now obscure.

87  Godwin, *Political Justice* (1793), 453; (1796), 2:511; (1798), 2:503.

88  Godwin, *Political Justice* (1793), 453.

89  Siobhan Ni Chonaill examines Godwin's perfectibility theory in the context of the population controversy of the late eighteenth century, but sees the issue of perfectibility solely in terms of extending life, and not in terms of capacity.

Siobhan Ni Chonaill, "'Why may not man one day be immortal?'": Population, Perfectibility, and the Immortality Question in Godwin's *Political
Justice*', *History of European Ideas* 33 (2007): 25–39. Adam Rounce, similarly,
does not address capacity in his discussion of Godwin's views on immortality.
Rounce, 'William Godwin: The Novel, Philosophy, and History', 7.

90 Critics have noticed the link Godwin makes between power, powerlessness,
and the production and management of bodily pain, but have not recognized
the extent of these interconnections. Scott Jeungel argues, for instance, that
for Godwin pain 'emerges as the insignia of powerlessness: the subjective
experience of pain becomes objectified in the space outside the body into its
political equivalent'. Jeungel concludes that for 'Godwin, the management of
pain *is* the government of the body, and as long as man cannot control his
susceptibility to pain, he is subject to those who can inflict it'. Godwin sees
pain as distracting the sufferer from their voluntary state. Jeungel regards
'Godwin's often derided notion of the fully realized, reasoning body' as
'seeking to make suffering answerable to cognition'. The equation of political
powerlessness and physical pain that Jeungel observes is a kind of rhetorical
intermixing that applies more broadly in Godwin's work. Scott Jeungel,
'Godwin, Lavater, and the Pleasures of Surface', *Studies in Romanticism* 35:1
(1996): 73–97 (77–8).

91 Godwin, *St. Leon*, 247.

92 Godwin, *St. Leon*, 249.

93 Godwin, *St. Leon*, 246.

94 Godwin, *Political Justice* (1793), 424; (1796), 2:454; (1798), 2:461.

95 For a fuller discussion of child labour in relation to *Fleetwood*, see Katherine
Gustafson, "'I Never Saw Such Children'": Disability, Industrialism, and
Children's Advocacy in William Godwin's *Fleetwood*', *Essays in Romanticism*
24.2 (2017): 125–43. Gustafson claims that 'the factory reform discourse in
which *Fleetwood* participated deployed the modern ability/disability paradigm even as it sought to ameliorate the actual working conditions that
would give rise to impairment' (142–3). I argue here that Godwin does not
use the term 'disability' in this way.

96 Godwin, *Fleetwood*, 157.

97 Godwin, *Fleetwood*, 161.

98 Godwin, *Fleetwood*, 156.

99 Godwin, *Fleetwood*, 151.

100 Godwin, *Fleetwood*, 148.

101 Godwin, *Fleetwood*, 157.

102 Godwin, *Fleetwood*, 150.

103 Godwin, *Fleetwood*, 273.

104 William Godwin, *Thoughts on Man: Essay II: Of the Distribution of Talents*,
in *The Political and Philosophical Writings of William Godwin*, ed. by Mark
Philp (London: Pickering and Chatto, 1993), 6:55; Godwin, *Political Justice*
(1798), 2:88. My emphasis. Note that 'the ordinary standard of man' is a
pre-normalcy concept.

105  Godwin, *Political Justice* (1793), 207–8; (1796), 2:8–9; (1798), 2:8.

106  Edmund Burke, *A Vindication of Natural Society* (London: M. Cooper, 1756), 96–7. A 'valetudinarian' is a person in poor health or an invalid. The earliest written source, according to the current *Oxford English Dictionary*, is 1703 (OED). This group term deserves further study. Sheridan uses it in *School for Scandal* (1777), 1.i.9, and it occurs in John Thelwall's *The Peripatetic* (1793). Godwin uses it in *Caleb Williams* (84, 131), *The Enquirer* (Essay 5 [1797], 227), and *St. Leon*, 150. 'Valetudinarianism' ('the tendency to be in weak health or to be much concerned about one's heath' [*OED*]) does not divide easily from other disability-related concepts.

107  Godwin, *Political Justice* (1793), 212–13; (1796), 2:18; (1798), 2:18.

108  Godwin, *Political Justice* (1793), 212–13; (1796), 2:18; (1798), 2:18.

109  William Godwin, *Mandeville*, ed. by Pamela Clemit (London: William Pickering, 1992), 6:85.

110  Godwin, *Mandeville*, 6:86.

111  Godwin, *Mandeville*, 6:88.

112  Godwin, *Mandeville*, 6:97.

113  Godwin, *Fleetwood*, 94.

114  Godwin, *Fleetwood*, 396.

115  Godwin, *Fleetwood*, 405.

116  Godwin, *Fleetwood*, 408. He echoes the argument made by Wollstonecraft in *A Vindication of the Rights of Women* (1792) that a marriage without love is a form of prostitution. Mary Wollstonecraft, 'A Vindication of the Rights of Woman', in *A Vindication of the Rights of Men, A Vindication of the Rights of Woman, An Historical and Moral View of the French Revolution*, ed. by Janet Todd (Oxford: Oxford University Press, 1993), 63–283.

117  Godwin, *St. Leon*, 55.

118  Godwin, *St. Leon*, 55.

119  Godwin, *Mandeville*, 6:34.

120  Godwin, *Mandeville*, 6:33.

121  Godwin, *Mandeville*, 6:33.

122  Godwin, *Mandeville*, 6:73.

123  Godwin, *Mandeville*, 6:76.

124  Godwin, *Mandeville*, 6:76.

125  Hebrews 12:12.

126  Godwin, *Mandeville*, 6:76.

127  Godwin, *Mandeville*, 6:76.

128  Godwin, *St. Leon*, 345–6.

129  Godwin, *St. Leon*, 150.

130  Godwin, *St. Leon*, 150.

131  Godwin, *St. Leon*, 150.

132  Godwin, *Mandeville*, 6:34.

133  Godwin, *Mandeville*, 6:25.

134  Godwin, *Mandeville*, 6:30.

135  Godwin, *Mandeville*, 6:30.

136 Godwin, *Mandeville*, 6:30.
137 Godwin, *Mandeville*, 6:206.
138 Godwin, *Mandeville*, 6:241.
139 Godwin, *Mandeville*, 6:247.
140 Godwin, *Mandeville*, 6:239.
141 Godwin, *Mandeville*, 6:246.
142 Godwin, *Political Justice* (1793), 247; *Political Justice* (1796), 2:84–5. There are variations in the second edition.
143 Godwin, *Caleb Williams*, 195.
144 Godwin, *Caleb Williams*, 203.
145 Godwin, *Caleb Williams*, 217.
146 Godwin, *Caleb Williams*, 218.
147 Godwin, *Caleb Williams*, 218.
148 Godwin, *Caleb Williams*, 219.
149 Godwin, *Caleb Williams*, 6.
150 Godwin, *Caleb Williams*, 325.
151 Godwin, *Caleb Williams*, 120.
152 Gary Handwerk, 'History, Trauma, and the Limits of the Liberal Imagination: William Godwin's Historical Fiction', in *Romanticism, History, and the Possibilities of Genre: Re-Forming Literature 1789–1837*, ed. by Tilottama Rajan and Julia M. Wright (Cambridge: Cambridge University Press, 1998), 64–85 (81).
153 Handwerk, 'History, Trauma, and the Limits of the Liberal Imagination', 70.
154 Handwerk, 'History, Trauma, and the Limits of the Liberal Imagination', 70.
155 Handwerk, 'History, Trauma, and the Limits of the Liberal Imagination', 70.
156 Handwerk, 'History, Trauma, and the Limits of the Liberal Imagination', 73.
157 Godwin, *St. Leon*, 128.
158 Godwin, *St. Leon*, 341.
159 Godwin, *St. Leon*, 341.
160 Godwin, *St. Leon*, 341.
161 Godwin, *St. Leon*, 331–2.
162 Godwin, *Mandeville*, 6:250.
163 Godwin, *Mandeville*, 6:94.
164 Godwin, *Mandeville*, 6:94.
165 Godwin, *Mandeville*, 6:298.
166 Godwin, *Caleb Williams*, 193.
167 Godwin, *Caleb Williams*, 60.
168 Godwin, *Caleb Williams*, 195.
169 Godwin, *St. Leon*, 111.
170 Godwin, *St. Leon*, 121.
171 Godwin, *St. Leon*, 292.

172 Godwin, *Caleb Williams*, 138.
173 Godwin, *Fleetwood*, 382.
174 William Godwin, *Deloraine*, ed. by Maurice Hindle (London: William Pickering, 1992), 8:218.
175 Godwin, *Caleb Williams*, 246.
176 Godwin, *Caleb Williams*, 247.
177 Godwin, *Caleb Williams*, 276.
178 Godwin, *Caleb Williams*, 282.
179 Godwin, *Caleb Williams*, 282.
180 Godwin, *Caleb Williams*, 287.
181 Godwin, *Deloraine*, 8:271.
182 Godwin, *Deloraine*, 8:271.
183 Godwin, *Deloraine*, 8:271.
184 William Godwin, *Cloudesley*, ed. by Maurice Hindle (London: William Pickering, 1992), 7:245.
185 Godwin, *Cloudesley*, 7:134–5.
186 Godwin, *Cloudesley*, 7:246.
187 Godwin, *Cloudesley*, 7:285.
188 Godwin *Caleb Williams*, 291.
189 Godwin, *Political Justice* (1793), 446; (1796), 2:498; (1798), 2:507.
190 Godwin, *Fleetwood*, 235.
191 Godwin, *Fleetwood*, 385.
192 Godwin, *Fleetwood*, 327.
193 Godwin, *Fleetwood*, 326.
194 Godwin, *Fleetwood*, 320.
195 Godwin, *Deloraine*, 8:43.
196 Godwin, *Deloraine*, 8:43. Godwin, *Deloraine*, 8:92, 95, 107, and 105–6.
197 Godwin, *Deloraine*, 8:75.
198 Colin Carman suggests that there is a homosexual subtext in the novel. He reads Casimir as a 'fetishist, an asexual bachelor, [and] a closeted homosexual' who is 'incapable of heterosexual love and intimacy'. Colin Carman, 'Godwin's *Fleetwood*, Shame and the Sexuality of Feeling', *Nineteenth-Century Prose* 41 (2014): 225–54 (245).
199 Godwin, *Fleetwood*, 281.
200 Godwin, *Fleetwood*, 273.
201 The effigy scene in *Fleetwood* is prefigured by another doll-scene that connects mind–body alienation with the misuse of capacities. Godwin devotes an entire chapter to bullying, in which Withers, a partially sighted student, is duped by a puppet he thinks is the Master of the college. The college bucks treat Withers 'as the weakest, the absurdist, and the most despicable of mankind'. Godwin, *Fleetwood*, 89. Although Withers has received a great deal of critical attention for such a minor character, his sight impairment is rarely if ever mentioned.
202 Steven Bruhm, 'William Godwin's *Fleetwood*: The Epistemology of the Tortured Body', *Eighteenth-Century Life* 16.2 (1992): 25–43 (36).

203 Bruhm, 'William Godwin's *Fleetwood*', 37.

204 Bruhm, 'William Godwin's *Fleetwood*', 37.

205 Bruhm, 'William Godwin's *Fleetwood*', 37.

206 Mona Scheuermann, 'The Study of Mind: The Later Novels of William Godwin', *Forum for Modern Language Studies* 19.1 (1983): 16–30 (19).

207 Godwin, *Fleetwood*, 387.

208 Godwin, *Political Justice* (1796), 1:40; (1798), 1:39.

209 For a more extensive discussion of Godwin's engagement with Lavater, see Jeungel, 'Godwin, Lavater, and the Pleasures of Surface'.

210 Godwin, *Political Justice* (1796), 1:38; (1798), 1:37.

211 Godwin, *Political Justice* (1796), 1:38; (1798), 1:37.

212 Godwin, *Political Justice* (1796), 1:46; (1798), 1:45.

213 Godwin, *Political Justice* (1796), 1:38; (1798), 1:37. Jeungel notices the echoes of Locke in this passage: 'It is crucial to note that this "correspondence" between moral character and somatic legibility – [is] framed here in Lockean metaphors of "sketch", "impress", and "inscription".' 'Godwin, Lavater, and the Pleasures of Surface', 77.

214 Godwin, *Political Justice* (1796), 1:457; (1798), 1:457.

215 John Caspar Lavater, *Essays on Physiognomy*, trans. by Henry Hunter, 3 vols (London: John Murray, 1789), 1:140 and 142.

216 Godwin, *Political Justice* (1793), 128; (1796), 1:312; (1798), 1:310. The 1793 version has 'only' in place of 'most'.

217 For a fuller discussion of the role of physiognomy in the reading of bodies in Godwin's fictional characters, see Jeungel, 'Godwin, Lavater, and the Pleasures of Surface'. Jeungel describes Falkland as 'a body fixed in the penetrating gaze of the physiognomist' (80). Jeungel does not, however, consider the aesthetics of deformity or monstrosity.

218 Godwin, *Caleb Williams*, 329.

219 Godwin, *St. Leon*, 391.

220 Godwin, *Cloudesley*, 7:134.

221 Godwin, *St. Leon*, 355.

222 *Caleb Williams* includes various scenes depicting the taunting of people with incapacities and deformities. Tyrrel, for instance, refers disparagingly to Falkland's 'diminutive and dwarfish' body, and believes that his bookishness and lack of physical vigour even have the potential to damage the physical strength of the nation. Godwin, *Caleb Williams*, 22. Collins, as narrator, comments that Tyrrel thought that '[a] nation of such animals would have no chance with a single regiment of the old English votaries of beef and pudding. ... It was impossible that people could seriously feel any liking for such a ridiculous piece of goods as this outlandish foreign-made Englishman'. Godwin, *Caleb Williams*, 22. Godwin frequently pays attention to height in the portraits of his characters. Falkland is introduced as a 'man of small stature with an extreme delicacy of form and appearance' who is 'in the autumn and decay of his vigour'. Godwin, *Caleb Williams*, 13. Falkland's small stature is presented as a defect, but this is offset aesthetically by the

proportions of his body and his deportment: 'though his stature was small, his person had an air of uncommon dignity'. Godwin, *Caleb Williams*, 12.

223 See Chapter 6 for a discussion of Mary Shelley's understanding of the relationship between deformity and monstrosity.

224 Godwin, *St. Leon*, 119.

225 Godwin, *St. Leon*, 429.

226 Godwin, *Political Justice* (1793), 246; (1796), 2:84; (1798), 2:86; *St. Leon*, 406; *Mandeville*, 146; *Deloraine*, 10.

227 Godwin, *Mandeville*, 6:26.

228 Godwin, *Mandeville*, 6:25.

229 Godwin, *Mandeville*, 6:25.

230 Godwin, *Mandeville*, 6:25.

231 Godwin, *Political Justice* (1793), 63.

232 Godwin, *Thoughts on Man*, 6:56.

233 Godwin, *Thoughts on Man*, 6:53. See Paula Findlen for a discussion of *lusus naturae* as an aesthetic term in the eighteenth century. Paula Findlen, 'Jokes of Nature and Jokes of Knowledge: The Playfulness of Scientific Discourse in Early Modern Europe', *Renaissance Quarterly* 43.2 (1990): 292–331 (318).

234 Godwin, *Thoughts on Man*, 6:53.

235 Godwin, *Thoughts on Man*, 6:53.

236 Jeungel, 'Godwin, Lavater, and the Pleasures of Surface', 76.

237 Elizabeth Hamilton, *Memoirs of Modern Philosophers*, ed. by Claire Grogan (Peterborough, Ontario: Broadview, 2000), 209. My emphasis.

238 Nussbaum, *Frontiers of Justice*, 75.

239 Nussbaum, *Frontiers of Justice*, 77, 78.

240 Nussbaum, *Frontiers of Justice*, 75.

241 Nussbaum, *Frontiers of Justice*, 75.

242 Godwin, *Political Justice* (1798), 1:330; (1796), 1:330. The second edition has a variation.

243 Godwin, *Political Justice* (1796), 1:38; (1798), 1:37.

244 There is no equivalent modern term for ableism in the case of the aesthetic use of deformity. I suggest 'deformism' to indicate the assumption that the aesthetic component of a bodily impairment has necessarily negative connotations.

245 I use 'inclusive' to mean taking account of disability or pre-disability concepts and incorporating them into social structures alongside able-bodied and able-minded groups in a manner that is either egalitarian (i.e. treating people the same) or accommodating (i.e. treating people in a manner that accounts for difference but does not make difference a reason to exclude).

246 'It is not the man of great stature or vigorous make that outstrips his fellow in understanding' as 'children of all sizes and forms indifferently become wise'. Godwin, *Political Justice* (1796), 1:40; (1798), 1:39.

## 2 Invigorating Women

1 Mary Wollstonecraft, 'A Vindication of the Rights of Woman', in *A Vindication of the Rights of Men, A Vindication of the Rights of Woman, An Historical and Moral View of the French Revolution*, ed. by Janet Todd (Oxford: Oxford University Press, 1993), 63–283 (136).

2 Wollstonecraft, 'Rights of Woman', 136.

3 Wollstonecraft, 'Rights of Woman', 136.

4 I shall not always reiterate that Wollstonecraft writes mainly of middle- and high-ranking white women and will use the term 'women' to stand for this. It is not my intention, nor is it Wollstonecraft's, to suggest that the experiences of these women are to be understood as the experiences of women of all ranks or races. Eva Badowska calls what I term the culturally feminine woman the 'model woman'. I use a different term so as to avoid conflating the ideal with the typical. See Eva Badowska, 'The Anorexic Body of Liberal Feminism: Mary Wollstonecraft's *A Vindication of the Rights of Woman*', in *Mary Wollstonecraft and the Critics 1788–2001*, ed. by Harriet Devine Jump, 2 vols (London: Routledge, 2002), 2:320–40 (327).

5 Douglas C. Baynton, 'Disability and the Justification of Inequality in American History', in *The New Disability History: American Perspectives*, ed. by Paul K. Longmore and Laura Umansky (New York: New York University Press, 2001), 33–57 (43).

6 Baynton, 'Disability and the Justification of Inequality', 43.

7 Baynton, 'Disability and the Justification of Inequality', 43.

8 For discussion of Wollstonecraft's implied misogyny, see especially Susan Gubar, 'Feminist Misogyny: Mary Wollstonecraft and the Paradox of "It Takes One to Know One"', in *Mary Wollstonecraft and the Critics 1788–2001*, ed. by Harriet Devine Jump, 2 vols (London: Routledge, 2002), 2:146–65. This was first published in *Feminist Studies* 20.3 (1994): 453–73. Gubar criticizes Wollstonecraft for making femininity feel 'like a malady' (149). See also Miriam Brody, 'The Vindication of the Writes of Women: Mary Wollstonecraft and Enlightenment Rhetoric', in *Feminist Interpretations of Mary Wollstonecraft*, ed. by Maria J. Falco (University Park: Pennsylvania State University Press, 1996), 105–23.

9 For a discussion of Wollstonecraft's homophobic and misogynist agenda, see Claudia Johnson, *Equivocal Beings: Politics, Gender, and Sentimentality in the 1790s – Wollstonecraft, Radcliffe, Burney, Austen* (Chicago, IL: University of Chicago Press, 1995), 23–46.

10 Baynton, 'Disability and the Justification of Inequality', 43.

11 Wollstonecraft, 'Rights of Woman', 111.

12 Laurie Finke, in her exploration of Wollstonecraft's philosophical discourse, notes a flexibility in the way Wollstonecraft slips between rational and emotional discourses. Finke identifies words such as 'melancholy', 'depressed', 'sighed', 'misery', 'weak and wretched' as belonging to a 'gothic intensity' that often contradicts the 'rational disinterestedness' of the openings of

Wollstonecraft's sentences. Laurie A. Finke, 'A Philosophic Wanton: Language and Authority in Wollstonecraft's *Vindication of the Rights of Woman*', in *Mary Wollstonecraft and the Critics 1788–2001*, ed. by Harriet Devine Jump, 2 vols (London: Routledge, 2002), 2:1–21 (8).

13  Wollstonecraft, 'Rights of Woman', 87.

14  Mary Wollstonecraft, 'An Historical and Moral View of the Origin and Progress of the French Revolution', in *The Works of Mary Wollstonecraft*, ed. by Janet Todd, Marilyn Butler, and Emma Rees-Mogg, 7 vols (London: Pickering and Chatto, 2004), 6:289.

15  See Nancy Hirschmann for a full discussion of the relationship between freedom and disability in Locke. Nancy. J. Hirschmann, 'Freedom and (Dis)Ability in Early Modern Political Thought', in *Recovering Disability in Early Modern England*, ed. by Allison P. Hobgood and David Houston Wood (Columbus: Ohio State University Press, 2013), 167–86.

16  John Locke, *An Essay Concerning Human Understanding*, ed. by Peter H. Nidditch (Oxford: Oxford University Press, 1975), 2.21.11:239.

17  Locke is concerned with the problem of whether voluntary actions are compatible with necessary ones. He argues that people are not free when doing or not-doing does not follow from volition. E. J. Lowe suggests that Locke's examples of voluntary action under necessity do not stand up to scrutiny, 'for even according to Locke's own doctrines it appears that we should say that the first example (that of the man in the locked room) is not a case of *action under necessity* and that the second example (that of the paralytic) is not a case of *voluntary action*. What may have obscured Locke's vision are the complications arising from the fact that the first example turns on an *omission* and the second on a *prevention*'. E. J. Lowe, 'Necessity and the Will in Locke's Theory of Action', *History of Philosophy Quarterly* 3.2 (1986): 149–63 (158). See also Michael Jacovides, 'Locke's Construction of the Idea of Power', *Studies in History of Philosophy and Science* 34 (2003): 329–50 (349).

18  According to Helen Thompson, Wollstonecraft argues that women 'are as incapable of forced virtue as Locke's contractarian sons'. Helen Thompson, *Ingenuous Subjection: Compliance and Power in the Eighteenth-Century Domestic Novel* (Philadelphia: University of Pennsylvania Press, 2005), 23. Susan James observes that Wollstonecraft 'seems to conceive of rights as effective powers to act', as in 'what women are actually capable of doing', and that this builds 'on a republican conception of liberty'. Susan James, 'Mary Wollstonecraft's Conception of Rights', in *The Social and Political Philosophy of Mary Wollstonecraft*, ed. by Sandrine Bergès and Alan Coffee (Oxford: Oxford University Press, 2016), 148–65 (154).

19  Wollstonecraft, 'Rights of Woman', 101.

20  Wollstonecraft, 'Rights of Woman', 95.

21  Wollstonecraft, 'Rights of Woman', 90.

22  Wollstonecraft, 'Rights of Woman', 87.

23  Wollstonecraft, 'Rights of Woman', 91.

24 Wollstonecraft, 'Rights of Woman', 148.
25 Wollstonecraft, 'Rights of Woman', 115 and 88. My emphasis.
26 Mary Wollstonecraft ('W.Q'), 'On Poetry, and Our Relish for the Beauties of Nature', *The Monthly Magazine* 3 (April 1797), 279–82.
27 Wollstonecraft, 'On Poetry, and Our Relish for the Beauties of Nature', 281.
28 Eliza Fenwick, *Secresy; or, The Ruin on the Rock*, ed. by Isobel Grundy (Peterborough, Ontario: Broadview, 1998), 74.
29 Fenwick, *Secresy*, 93.
30 Fenwick, *Secresy*, 174 and 64.
31 Fenwick, *Secresy*, 104.
32 Fenwick, *Secresy*, 103.
33 Fenwick, *Secresy*, 69.
34 Tim Milnes and Kerry Sinanan argue that it is 'in Romantic literature and thought that "sincerity" and "authenticity" are fused – and thereby trans-formed – for the first time'. Tim Milnes and Kerry Sinanan, eds., *Romanticism, Sincerity, and Authenticity* (London: Palgrave Macmillan, 2010), 2. They suggest that it is Romanticism's self-reflexivity that makes it 'more than just the historical space or critical medium in which this fusion occurs', and it is because Romanticism is concerned 'with history and intensely – sometimes *cripplingly* – conscious of its own becoming' that it is 'the problematic *form* through which modernity understands itself as self-inaugurating'. Milnes and Sinanan, *Romanticism, Sincerity, and Authenticity*, 2. My emphasis. I comment later in this chapter on the extensive use of 'crippling' metaphors in the critical reception of Wollstonecraft's work. Although Wollstonecraft is mentioned in their study only once (in relation to Godwin's assessment of *Mary* as having been based on feelings of 'the truest and most exquisite class'), sincerity is an important part of Wollstonecraft's work. Milnes and Sinanan, *Romanticism, Sincerity, and Authenticity*, 10.
35 Wollstonecraft, 'Rights of Woman', 222.
36 Wollstonecraft, 'Rights of Woman', 222.
37 Wollstonecraft, 'Rights of Woman', 226.
38 Wollstonecraft, 'Rights of Woman', 222 and 120.
39 Mary Wollstonecraft, *A Short Residence in Sweden, Norway and Denmark and William Godwin, Memoirs of the Author of 'The Rights of Woman'*, ed. by Richard Holmes (London: Penguin, 1987), 192.
40 Wollstonecraft, *A Short Residence*, 192.
41 Wollstonecraft, 'An Historical and Moral View of the Origin and Progress of the French Revolution', 6:235.
42 Mary Wollstonecraft, 'Letter on the Character of the French Nation', in *The Works of Mary Wollstonecraft*, ed. by Janet Todd, Marilyn Butler, and Emma Rees-Mogg, 7 vols (London: Pickering and Chatto, 2004), 6:440–46 (446).
43 Wollstonecraft, 'Rights of Woman', 227.
44 Badowska, 'The Anorexic Body of Liberal Feminism', 320–21.

45 Mary Wollstonecraft, *Original Stories from Real Life; With Conversations, Calculated to Regulate the Affections, and Form the Mind to Truth and Goodness* (London: J. Johnson, 1788), 85 and 82.
46 Badowska, 'The Anorexic Body of Liberal Feminism', 329.
47 Badowska, 'The Anorexic Body of Liberal Feminism', 326.
48 Badowska, 'The Anorexic Body of Liberal Feminism', 321.
49 Badowska, 'The Anorexic Body of Liberal Feminism', 334.
50 Wollstonecraft, 'An Historical and Moral View of the Origin and Progress of the French Revolution', 6:74.
51 Wollstonecraft, 'An Historical and Moral View of the Origin and Progress of the French Revolution', 6:74.
52 Wollstonecraft, 'An Historical and Moral View of the Origin and Progress of the French Revolution', 6:74. Carol Poston notes that 'in Wollstonecraft women actually *are* the food … often "literally standing dishes" to that gluttony'. Carol Poston, 'Mary Wollstonecraft and "The Body Politic"', in *Feminist Interpretations of Mary Wollstonecraft*, ed. by Maria J. Falco (University Park: Pennsylvania State University Press, 1996), 85–104 (90).
53 Wollstonecraft, 'An Historical and Moral View of the Origin and Progress of the French Revolution', 6:80.
54 Wollstonecraft, *A Short Residence*, 166.
55 Wollstonecraft, *A Short Residence*, 167.
56 Wollstonecraft, *A Short Residence*, 167.
57 Wollstonecraft, 'Rights of Woman', 242.
58 Wollstonecraft, 'Rights of Woman', 217.
59 Wollstonecraft, 'Rights of Woman', 85.
60 John Milton, 'Paradise Lost', in *The Complete Poetry and Essential Prose of John Milton*, ed. by William Kerrigan, John Rumrich, and Stephen M. Fallon (New York: The Modern Library, 2007), 10:891–2.
61 Robert Jungman, 'Eve as a "Fair Defect" in Milton's *Paradise Lost*, Book 10', *The Explicator* 65.4 (2007): 204–6 (206).
62 Wollstonecraft, 'Rights of Woman', 124.
63 Wollstonecraft, 'Rights of Woman', 100. My emphasis.
64 Wollstonecraft, 'Rights of Woman', 124.
65 Wollstonecraft, 'Rights of Woman', 88.
66 Wollstonecraft, 'Rights of Woman', 107.
67 Wollstonecraft, 'Rights of Woman', 107.
68 Wollstonecraft, 'Rights of Woman', 105.
69 Wollstonecraft, 'Rights of Woman', 107.
70 Wollstonecraft, 'Rights of Woman', 107.
71 Wollstonecraft, 'Rights of Woman', 192–3.
72 Burke, *A Philosophical Enquiry*, 100.
73 Burke, *A Philosophical Enquiry*, 100.
74 Burke, *A Philosophical Enquiry*, 105.
75 Burke, *A Philosophical Enquiry*, 106.

76 Mary Wollstonecraft, 'A Vindication of the Rights of Men [1790]', in *A Vindication of the Rights of Men, A Vindication of the Rights of Woman, An Historical and Moral View of the French Revolution*, ed. by Janet Todd, Oxford World's Classics (Oxford: Oxford University Press, 1993), 3–62 (45).
77 Wollstonecraft, 'Rights of Men', 45.
78 Wollstonecraft, 'Rights of Woman', 87.
79 Wollstonecraft, 'Rights of Woman', 87.
80 Wollstonecraft, 'Rights of Woman', 261 and 88.
81 Wollstonecraft, 'Rights of Woman', 261.
82 Wollstonecraft, 'Rights of Woman', 84–5.
83 Wollstonecraft, 'Rights of Woman', 87.
84 Wollstonecraft, 'Rights of Woman', 85.
85 'Strengthen the female mind by enlarging it, and there will be an end to blind obedience.' Wollstonecraft, 'Rights of Woman', 90. Blindness is the most common impairment that Wollstonecraft uses figuratively, and she most often uses it to describe an unquestioning submission to power. Monsters are almost as common in her work, and are used figuratively to stand for tyranny or irrationality.
86 Wollstonecraft, 'Rights of Woman', 90.
87 Wollstonecraft, 'Rights of Woman', 103.
88 Wollstonecraft, 'Rights of Woman', 266.
89 Wollstonecraft, 'Rights of Woman', 218.
90 Wollstonecraft, 'Rights of Woman', 256.
91 Wollstonecraft, 'Rights of Woman', 95.
92 Wollstonecraft, 'Rights of Woman', 256–7. Ruth Abbey incorrectly summarizes Wollstonecraft's position in the following way: 'while women's socialization renders them weak and dependent, it does not render them helpless'. Ruth Abbey, 'Back to the Future: Marriage as Friendship in the Thought of Mary Wollstonecraft', *Hypatia* 14.3 (1999): 78–95 (85). Wollstonecraft calls women helpless on several occasions. For example, 'the education of the rich tends to render them [women] vain and helpless'. 'Rights of Woman', 73. 'I have seldom seen much compassion excited by the helplessness of females, unless they were fair.' 'Rights of Woman', 230.
93 Wollstonecraft, 'Rights of Woman', 94.
94 Wollstonecraft, 'Rights of Woman', 228.
95 Mary Wollstonecraft, *Mary and The Wrongs of Woman*, ed. by Gary Kelly, Oxford World's Classics (Oxford: Oxford University Press, 1998), 1.
96 Wollstonecraft, *Mary*, 5 and 11.
97 Wollstonecraft, *Mary*, 2.
98 Wollstonecraft, *Mary*, 2.
99 Wollstonecraft, *Mary*, 2. Claudia Johnson notes that 'Eliza's asthenia [lack of strength] is marked out for particular abuse'. Johnson, *Equivocal Beings*, 50.
100 Wollstonecraft, *Mary*, 3.
101 Wollstonecraft, *Mary*, 6.

102 Wollstonecraft, *Mary*, 4.
103 Wollstonecraft, *Mary*, 6. G. J. Barker-Benfield notices a slightly different, though related, situation in Wollstonecraft's unfinished tale 'The Cave of Fancy' (1787). In the tale, a sage, Sagestus, adopts a young woman who is the only survivor of a shipwreck. He calls her Sagesta and devotes himself to her education. Sagesta narrates the story of the melancholy she experiences after the loss of the man she loves. Barker-Benfield suggests that Sagesta 'is really unhappy but her husband interprets that as sensibility. Consequently she pretends her real symptom is false'. G. J. Barker-Benfield, 'Mary Wollstonecraft's Depression and Diagnosis: The Relation between Sensibility and Women's Susceptibility to Nervous Disorders', *Psychohistory Review* 13.4 (1985): 15–31 (17).
104 Wollstonecraft, *Mary*, 6.
105 Wollstonecraft, *Mary*, 6.
106 Wollstonecraft, *Mary*, 1.
107 Mary Poovey, *The Proper Lady and the Woman Writer: Ideology as Style in the Works of Mary Wollstonecraft, Mary Shelley, and Jane Austen* (Chicago, IL: University of Chicago Press, 1984); Adriana Craciun, 'Violence against Difference: Mary Wollstonecraft and Mary Robinson', in *Making History: Textuality and the Forms of Eighteenth Century Culture*, ed. by Greg Clingham (Lewisburg, PA: Bucknell University Press, 1998), 111–41; Finke, 'A Philosophic Wanton', 1–2; Catherine Packham, *Eighteenth-Century Vitalism: Bodies, Cultures, Politics* (London: Palgrave Macmillan, 2012), 53.
108 Poovey, *The Proper Lady*, 63.
109 Poovey, *The Proper Lady*, 69. Barbara Taylor argues that applying the label 'feminist' to Wollstonecraft is anachronistic and risks the assimilation of 'Wollstonecraft's ideas to those of her successors'. Barbara Taylor, *Mary Wollstonecraft and the Feminist Imagination* (Cambridge: Cambridge University Press, 2003), 12. Claudia Johnson notes that 'the feminist agenda of the *Vindication of the Rights of Woman* cannot … be discussed apart from its larger republican agenda'. Johnson, *Equivocal Beings*, 23.
110 Poovey, *The Proper Lady*, 64.
111 Craciun, 'Violence against Difference, 126.
112 Craciun, 'Violence against Difference', 132.
113 Craciun, 'Violence against Difference', 128.
114 Craciun, 'Violence against Difference', 129. Ashley Tauchert argues that Wollstonecraft's pre-maternal writing contains a 'displaced account of female-embodied same-sex desire in Athenic mode'. Ashley Tauchert, *Mary Wollstonecraft and the Accent of the Feminine* (Houndmills, Basingstoke: Palgrave Macmillan, 2002), 13. Tauchert defines the Athenic mode as the 'appropriation of masculinist subjectivity' by 'women under patriarchy'. Tauchert, *Mary Wollstonecraft and the Accent of the Feminine*, 8. She styles Wollstonecraft as an 'Athenic writer' who repudiates 'the castrated maternal body, establishing an imaginary transgendering of her own body in order to write at all'. Tauchert, *Mary Wollstonecraft and the Accent of the Feminine*, 13.

Wollstonecraft's '"one sex" scale of corporeal potential towards a single standard of virtue allows the writing subject to state an Athenic claim'. Tauchert, *Mary Wollstonecraft and the Accent of the Feminine*, 72.

115 Craciun, 'Violence against Difference', 124.
116 Craciun, 'Violence against Difference', 123.
117 Finke, 'A Philosophic Wanton', 10.
118 Finke, 'A Philosophic Wanton', 14.
119 Wendy Gunther-Canada, 'Mary Wollstonecraft's "Wild Wish": Confounding Sex in the Discourse on Political Rights', in *Feminist Interpretations of Mary Wollstonecraft*, ed. by Maria J. Falco (University Park: Pennsylvania State University Press, 1996), 61–83 (75).
120 Rosemarie Garland Thomson, 'Integrating Disability, Transforming Feminist Theory', *National Women's Studies Association Journal* 14.3 (2002): 1–32 (9).
121 Packham, *Eighteenth-Century Vitalism*, 10.
122 Packham, *Eighteenth-Century Vitalism*, 11.
123 Packham, *Eighteenth-Century Vitalism*, 54.
124 Packham, *Eighteenth-Century Vitalism*, 53.
125 Packham, *Eighteenth-Century Vitalism*, 53.
126 Packham, *Eighteenth-Century Vitalism*, 53.
127 Packham, *Eighteenth-Century Vitalism*, 56.
128 Packham, *Eighteenth-Century Vitalism*, 56.
129 For a discussion of female vigour and bourgeois ideology, see Poovey, *The Proper Lady*; and Barker-Benfield, 'Mary Wollstonecraft's Depression and Diagnosis'.
130 For a discussion of the distinction between individualism and independence, see Alan M. S. Coffee, 'Freedom as Independence: Mary Wollstonecraft and the Grand Blessing of Life', *Hypatia* 29.4 (2014): 908–24.
131 Poovey, *The Proper Lady*, 63.
132 Poovey, *The Proper Lady*, 62.
133 Poovey, *The Proper Lady*, 109.
134 Barker-Benfield, 'Mary Wollstonecraft's Depression and Diagnosis', 19.
135 Gary Kelly notes that 'Wollstonecraft's insistence on vigorous exercise for females goes beyond most conduct books and participates in the *embourgeoisement* of the female body – the appropriation or construction of the female body for middle-class culture'. Gary Kelly, *Revolutionary Feminism: The Mind and Career of Mary Wollstonecraft* (New York: St Martin's, 1992), 30.
136 Barker-Benfield, 'Mary Wollstonecraft's Depression and Diagnosis', 20, citing Lawrence Stone, *The Family, Sex and Marriage in England, 1500–1800* (New York: Harper and Row, 1977), 353.
137 G. J. Barker-Benfield, 'Mary Wollstonecraft: Eighteenth-Century Commonwealthwoman', in *Mary Wollstonecraft and the Critics 1788–2001*, ed. by Harriet Devine Jump, 2 vols (London: Routledge, 2002), 39–59. First published in *Journal of the History of Ideas* 50.1 (1989): 95–115.

138 Angela Keane, 'Mary Wollstonecraft's Imperious Sympathies: Population, Maternity and Romantic Individualism', in *Body Matters: Feminism, Textuality, Corporeality*, ed. by Avril Horner and Angela Keane (Manchester: Manchester University Press, 2000), 29–57 (30).

139 Keane, 'Mary Wollstonecraft's Imperious Sympathies', 35.

140 Keane, 'Mary Wollstonecraft's Imperious Sympathies', 30.

141 Keane, 'Mary Wollstonecraft's Imperious Sympathies', 31.

142 Keane, 'Mary Wollstonecraft's Imperious Sympathies', 30.

143 Keane, 'Mary Wollstonecraft's Imperious Sympathies', 38.

144 Keane, 'Mary Wollstonecraft's Imperious Sympathies', 39.

145 Gubar, 'Feminist Misogyny'; Taylor, *Mary Wollstonecraft and the Feminist Imagination*; and Johnson, *Equivocal Beings*.

146 Gubar, 'Feminist Misogyny', 149.

147 Gubar, 'Feminist Misogyny', 149.

148 Gubar, 'Feminist Misogyny', 150.

149 Gubar, 'Feminist Misogyny', 154.

150 Taylor, *Mary Wollstonecraft and the Feminist Imagination*, 13.

151 Craciun, 'Violence against Difference', 129.

152 Johnson, *Equivocal Beings*, 31.

153 Johnson, *Equivocal Beings*, 41.

154 Poovey, *The Proper Lady*, 48. My emphasis.

155 Poovey, *The Proper Lady*, 110. My emphasis.

156 Poovey, *The Proper Lady*, 105. My emphasis.

157 Barker-Benfield, 'Mary Wollstonecraft's Depression and Diagnosis', 18. My emphasis.

158 Johnson, *Equivocal Beings*, 28. My emphasis.

159 Badowska, 'The Anorexic Body of Liberal Feminism', 325.

160 Wollstonecraft, 'Rights of Woman', 74.

161 Badowska, 'The Anorexic Body of Liberal Feminism', 335.

162 Anon., '*A Vindication of the Rights of Woman*', *The Critical Review* 5 n.s. (June 1792): 132–41 (141).

163 Anon., 'Review of *Historical . . . View . . . of The French Revolution*', *The New Annual Register*, 1794, 221–2. Cited in *Mary Wollstonecraft and the Critics 1788–2001*, ed. by Harriet Devine Jump, 2 vols (London: Routledge, 2002), 1:79; Anon., 'Review of *Historical . . . View . . . of The French Revolution*', *Monthly Review* 16 n.s. (1795): 393–402 (394). Gary Kelly has characterized Wollstonecraft's writing as exhibiting 'a vigorous, various, "nervous" style, thought at the time to be characteristic of genius', and engaging 'in flights of the elevated and sublime'. Kelly, *Revolutionary Feminism*, 111. More recently, Catherine Packham has commented on 'the particular strenuousness of [Wollstonecraft's] writing' with its 'ungainly but effortful repetitions, exclamations, and expostulations'. Packham, *Eighteenth-Century Vitalism*, 57.

164 Anon., 'Review of *Historical . . . View . . . of The French Revolution*', *Monthly Review*, 402.

165 Hannah Mather Crocker, *Observations on the Real Rights of Women, with Their Appropriate Duties, Agreeable to Scripture, Reason and Common Sense* (Boston: Printed for the Author, 1818), 41.

166 Chris Pierson, 'The Reluctant Pirate: Godwin, Justice, and Property', *Journal of the History of Ideas* 71.4 (2010): 569–91 (576). My emphasis.

167 Craciun, 'Violence against Difference', 122.

168 Wollstonecraft, 'Rights of Woman', 73.

169 Wollstonecraft recalls that 'at fifteen I resolved never to marry for interested motives, or to endure a life of dependence'. Mary Wollstonecraft, letter to William Godwin, 4 September 1796, in *Collected Letters of Mary Wollstonecraft*, ed. by Ralph M. Wardle (Ithaca, NY: Cornell University Press, 1979), 345.

170 Coffee, 'Freedom as Independence', 908.

171 Coffee, 'Freedom as Independence', 909.

172 Coffee, 'Freedom as Independence', 910.

173 Coffee, 'Freedom as Independence', 910.

174 Lena Halldenius, *Mary Wollstonecraft and Feminist Republicanism: Independence, Rights and the Experience of Unfreedom* (London: Pickering and Chatto, 2015), 20.

175 Halldenius, *Mary Wollstonecraft and Feminist Republicanism*, 24.

176 Halldenius, *Mary Wollstonecraft and Feminist Republicanism*, 24–5.

177 Caroline Franklin notes the class dimensions to Wollstonecraft's approach to independence (which I here include in the concept of *social* independence). See Caroline Franklin, *Mary Wollstonecraft: A Literary Life* (Houndmills, Basingstoke: Palgrave Macmillan, 2004), 140.

178 Wollstonecraft, 'Rights of Woman', 111.

179 Wollstonecraft, 'Rights of Woman', 227.

180 Coffee notes that 'independence of mind is most closely associated with virtue, and civil independence with equality'. Coffee, 'Freedom as Independence', 913.

181 Wollstonecraft, 'Rights of Woman', 128.

182 Wollstonecraft, 'Rights of Woman', 92.

183 Wollstonecraft, 'Rights of Woman', 118.

184 Wollstonecraft, 'Rights of Woman', 86.

185 Wollstonecraft, 'Rights of Woman', 128.

186 Wollstonecraft, 'Rights of Woman', 128. Mary Poovey notes that, like Wollstonecraft, Burke 'associates energy with the bourgeoisie and a sort of decorous indolence with the aristocracy. Explicitly, he allies himself with the latter, but the nature of his images and the contradictions in his argument have led Isaac Kramnick, very understandably, to suspect some ambivalence'. Poovey, *The Proper Lady*, 255, n. 18. See Isaac Kramnick, *The Rage of Edmund Burke: Portrait of an Ambivalent Conservative* (New York: Basic Books, 1977), 143–68.

187 Wollstonecraft, 'Rights of Men', 15.

188 G. J. Barker-Benfield calls Wollstonecraft's justification for the education of women on the grounds of them needing healthy minds and bodies for child-rearing 'the most effective argument for education reform', and, ironically, one which involved 'women thereby adapting their own demands to the most fundamental of arguments against them', 27. He suggests that this argument 'would remain so throughout the next century'. Barker-Benfield, 'Mary Wollstonecraft's Depression and Diagnosis', 27. Ashley Tauchert argues that, in attempting to assert that virtue is independent of gender, Wollstonecraft makes virtue dependent on 'an individual's corporeal strength and health', and inevitably spends a great deal of time 'worrying over sexual difference'. Tauchert, *Mary Wollstonecraft and the Accent of the Feminine*, 77.

189 Wollstonecraft, *Mary*, frontispiece.

190 Jean-Jacques Rousseau, *Julie, or The New Heloise. Letters of Two Lovers Who Live in a Small Town at the Foot of the Alps. The Collected Writings of Rousseau*, 14 vols, trans. by Philip Stewart and Jean Vaché (Hanover, NH: Dartford College Press, 1997), 6:249. My emphasis. The italicized lines are a translation of Wollstonecraft's epigraph.

191 Wollstonecraft, *Mary*, 29.

192 Wollstonecraft, *Mary*, 13.

193 Wollstonecraft, *Mary*, 19.

194 Wollstonecraft, *Mary*, 8.

195 Wollstonecraft, *Mary*, 12.

196 Wollstonecraft, *Mary*, 32.

197 Mary Hays, *The Victim of Prejudice*, ed. by Eleanor Ty, 2nd edn (Peterborough, Ontario: Broadview, 1998), 5.

198 Hays, *The Victim of Prejudice*, 24.

199 Hays, *The Victim of Prejudice*, 24–5.

200 Hays, *The Victim of Prejudice*, 5.

201 Hays, *The Victim of Prejudice*, 14.

202 Hays, *The Victim of Prejudice*, 170. My emphasis.

203 Mary Hays, 'Improvements Suggested in Female Education [1797]', in *The Victim of Prejudice*, 232–5 (234). My emphasis.

204 Thomas Holcroft, *Anna St. Ives. The Novels and Selected Plays of Thomas Holcroft*, ed. by W. M. Verhoeven, 5 vols (London: Pickering and Chatto, 2007), 2:119.

205 Holcroft, *Anna St. Ives*, 2:97.

206 Holcroft, *Anna St. Ives*, 2:125. There is a brief discussion of 'the powerful agency of "energy of mind"' in Patricia Meyer Spacks, 'Energies of Mind: Plot's Possibilities in the 1790s', *Eighteenth-Century Fiction* 1.1 (1988): 37–52 (39).

207 Elizabeth Hamilton, *Memoirs of Modern Philosophers*, ed. by Claire Grogan (Peterborough, Ontario: Broadview, 2000), 70.

208 Hamilton, *Memoirs of Modern Philosophers*, 70.

209 Hamilton, *Memoirs of Modern Philosophers*, 154.

210 Hamilton, *Memoirs of Modern Philosophers*, 345.
211 Critics have noticed Wollstonecraft's preoccupation with inauthenticity. See, for example, Barker-Benfield, 'Mary Wollstonecraft's Depression and Diagnosis', 17; Poston, 'Wollstonecraft and "The Body Politic"', 99.
212 Wollstonecraft, 'Rights of Woman', 192–3. My emphasis.
213 Wollstonecraft, *Mary*, 28.
214 Wollstonecraft, *Mary*, 25.
215 Wollstonecraft, *Mary*, 25.
216 Wollstonecraft, *Mary*, 24.
217 Wollstonecraft, *Mary*, 34.
218 Wollstonecraft, *Mary*, 34.
219 Wollstonecraft, *Mary*, 35.
220 Following Ruth Abbey, Alan Coffee argues that 'although mutual reliance is consistent with Wollstonecraft's conception of independence, it would not be accurate, as is sometimes suggested, to substitute the term *interdependence* in order to dissociate the concept [of independence] from any potentially individualistic connotations'. Coffee, 'Freedom as Independence', 911. See Abbey, 'Back to the Future', 79. The *OED* defines 'interdependence' as 'mutual dependence'. I use the term 'interdependence' to mean mutual reliance. Coffee's caution over the term 'interdependence', probably arises from a need to understand Wollstonecraft's weakness rhetoric as consonant with her discussion of illness. I suggest keeping the term 'interdependence', as Wollstonecraft treats authentic illness as a separate case from culturally derived weakness.
221 Wollstonecraft, *Mary*, 9.
222 Wollstonecraft, *Mary*, 5.
223 Wollstonecraft, *Mary*, 20.
224 Wollstonecraft, *Mary*, 42.
225 Wollstonecraft, *Mary*, 31.
226 Wollstonecraft, *Mary*, 64.
227 Wollstonecraft, *Mary*, 31.
228 Wollstonecraft, *Mary*, 34.
229 Wollstonecraft, *Mary*, 64.
230 Wollstonecraft, *Mary*, 61.
231 Wollstonecraft, *Original Stories*, xiii.
232 Wollstonecraft draws on her own experiences as a governess in these tales. She perhaps means Mrs Mason to be a portrait of herself through the allusion of the work of the mason in crafting stone (stone-craft).
233 Wollstonecraft, *Original Stories*, 77.
234 Wollstonecraft, *Original Stories*, 78.
235 The tale of honest Jack is possibly recalled in the tale of Griffith the sailor in Mary Robinson's *Walsingham* (1797).
236 Wollstonecraft, *Original Stories*, 78.
237 Mary Wollstonecraft, 'Thoughts on the Education of Daughters [1787]', in *The Works of Mary Wollstonecraft*, ed. by Janet Todd, Marilyn Butler, and

Emma Rees-Mogg, 7 vols (London: Pickering and Chatto, 2004), 4:2–49 (33).

238 Wollstonecraft, *Original Stories*, 58.
239 Wollstonecraft, 'Rights of Woman', 257.
240 Wollstonecraft, *Original Stories*, 59.
241 Wollstonecraft, *Original Stories*, 257.
242 Burke, *A Philosophical Enquiry*, 101.
243 Wollstonecraft, 'Rights of Woman', 257. Note the echo of Mary Shelley's *Frankenstein* here. 'I had selected his features as beautiful.' Mary Shelley, *Frankenstein: The Original 1818 Text*, ed. by D. L. Macdonald and Kathleen Scherf, 2nd edn (Peterborough, Ontario: Broadview, 2005), 85.
244 Wollstonecraft, 'Rights of Woman', 81.
245 Wollstonecraft, 'Rights of Woman', 230.
246 Wollstonecraft, *Original Stories*, 68.
247 Wollstonecraft, *Original Stories*, 68.
248 Mary Wollstonecraft, 'Elements of Morality for the Use of Children [1790]', in *The Works of Mary Wollstonecraft*, ed. by Janet Todd, Marilyn Butler, and Emma Rees-Mogg, 7 vols (London: Pickering and Chatto, 2004), 2:3–210 (103).
249 'Man dürfe auch nicht gleich einen Menschen wegen eines oder des andern Fehlers verspotten, denn er könne dem ohngeachtet noch viel Gutes an sich haben.' Christian Gotthilf Salzmann, *Moralisches Elementarbuch: nebst einer Anleitung zum nützlichen Gebrauch desselben*, 2 vols (Leipzig: Siegfried Lebrecht Crusius, 1785), 1:189. I am grateful to Eleoma Bodammer for the English translation.
250 Wollstonecraft, *Original Stories*, 64. The story is similar to that of Lady Aubrey in Mary Robinson's *Walsingham*. Lady Aubrey's 'beautiful features were changed and distorted, and the mirror which reflected her deformity looked like the fiat of total annihilation'. Lady Aubrey, however, pursues a more destructive course than Wollstonecraft's smallpox survivor. Mary Robinson, *Walsingham; or the Pupil of Nature*, ed. by Julie A. Shaffer (Peterborough, Ontario: Broadview, 2003), 54.
251 Wollstonecraft, *Original Stories*, 63.
252 Wollstonecraft, *Original Stories*, 64.
253 Wollstonecraft, *Original Stories*, 64.
254 Wollstonecraft, 'Rights of Woman', 105.
255 Wollstonecraft, 'An Historical and Moral View of the French Revolution', 6: 17.
256 Garland Thomson, 'Integrating Disability', 21.
257 Garland Thomson, 'Integrating Disability', 28.
258 Garland Thomson, 'Integrating Disability 3.
259 Garland Thomson, 'Integrating Disability', 2.
260 Garland Thomson, 'Integrating Disability', 5 and 4.
261 Garland Thomson, 'Integrating Disability', 5 and 4.

262 Wollstonecraft's arguments persist into twentieth-century feminist thought. Garland Thomson cites Iris Marion Young's statement on modern misogynistic cultures: 'women in a sexist society are physically handicapped'. Iris Marion Young, *Throwing Like a Girl and Other Essays in Feminist Philosophy and Social Theory* (Bloomington: Indiana University Press, 1990), 153. See Garland Thomson, 'Integrating Disability', 6.

263 Garland Thomson, 'Integrating Disability', 9.

# 3 Wordsworth's 'The Discharged Soldier' and the Question of Desert

1 John Gibson Lockhart, *Memoirs of the Life of Sir Walter Scott*, 10 vols (Boston: Houghton, Mifflin, 1901), 3:60.

2 Lockhart, *Memoirs of the Life of Sir Walter Scott*, 3:60.

3 Lockhart, *Memoirs of the Life of Sir Walter Scott*, 3:60.

4 Lockhart, *Memoirs of the Life of Sir Walter Scott*, 3:60.

5 See David M. Engel, 'Origin Myths: Narratives of Authority, Resistance, Disability, and Law', *Law and Society Review* 27.4 (1993): 785–826; Corbett Joan O'Toole, 'Disclosing Our Relationships to Disabilities', *Disability Studies Quarterly* 33.2 (2013); Rosemarie Garland Thomson, 'The Story of My Work: How I Became Disabled', *Disability Studies Quarterly* 34.2 (2014). Many modern life narratives also address the issue of responding to questions about the origins of a disability. See, for example, Harilyn Rousso, *Don't Call Me Inspirational: A Disabled Feminist Talks Back* (Philadelphia, PA: Temple University Press, 2013).

6 Engel, 'Origin Myths', 821.

7 Engel, 'Origin Myths', 821.

8 Engel, 'Origin Myths', 823.

9 Engel, 'Origin Myths', 788 and 791.

10 Engel, 'Origin Myths', 821.

11 Engel, 'Origin Myths', 785.

12 Engel, 'Origin Myths', 822. Engel is careful to point out that he is not concerned with the truth value of these accounts, merely that they are repeatedly present.

13 See the Appendix for an account of the military sense of 'disabled' current in the Romantic period.

14 Joel Feinberg, *Doing and Deserving: Essays in the Theory of Responsibility* (Princeton, NJ: Princeton University Press, 1970), 74–5.

15 Engel is not concerned with desert claims in these stories, but the examples he uses clearly demonstrate that the parents are concerned with desert.

16 Oliver Goldsmith, 'The Distresses of a Common Soldier', *The British Magazine* 1, June 1760, 369–72 (370). This was reprinted with some changes as Letter CXIX in Goldsmith's *Citizen of the World* (1762). Later editions circulated through the magazines and in collections of essays under different

titles. See, for example, Anon., 'The Story of a Disabled Soldier', *The New London Magazine*, March 1793, 127–30; Anon., 'The Disabled Soldier', in *Satirical, Humourous, and Familiar Pieces of Prose* (Manchester: G. Nicholson, 1796), 1–6; and Anon., 'The Disabled Soldier', *The Literary Mirror* 1, 11 June 1808, 65.

17 Henry Mackenzie, *The Man of Feeling*, ed. by Maureen Harkin (Peterborough, Ontario: Broadview, 2005), 106.

18 Robert Bage, *Mount Henneth, A Novel*, 2 vols (London: T. Lowndes, 1782), 2:84. Although Morgan is in sailor's garb, the story is given the title '*The Soldier's* STORY'. Morgan has been disqualified from applying for an army pension on the grounds that was temporarily employed before he made his claim. Bage, *Mount Henneth*, 2:93–4.

19 Goldsmith, 'The Distresses of a Common Soldier', 370.

20 Goldsmith, 'The Distresses of a Common Soldier', 370.

21 Bage, *Mount Henneth*, 2:92.

22 William Combe, *The Philosopher in Bristol* [1775] (Dublin: T. Jackson, 1784), 19.

23 Shelly Kagan outlines a theory of comparative desert and a theory of non-comparative desert in *The Geometry of Desert* (Oxford: Oxford University Press, 2012).

24 Goldsmith, 'The Distresses of a Common Soldier', 369.

25 Goldsmith, 'The Distresses of a Common Soldier', 369.

26 Goldsmith, 'The Distresses of a Common Soldier', 372.

27 Mackenzie, *The Man of Feeling*, 114.

28 Daniel James Ennis, *Enter the Press-Gang: Naval Impressment in Eighteenth-Century British Literature* (Newark: University of Delaware Press, 2002), 130.

29 Henry Sidgwick. *The Methods of Ethics*, 2nd edn (Indianapolis: Hackett, 1907), 284, n. 1.

30 Goldsmith, 'The Distresses of a Common Soldier', 369.

31 Mackenzie, *The Man of Feeling*, 117.

32 Combe, *The Philosopher in Bristol*, 23.

33 Goldsmith, 'The Distresses of a Common Soldier', 372.

34 Mackenzie, *The Man of Feeling*, 112.

35 Bage, *Mount Henneth*, 2:86 and 2:96.

36 Combe, *The Philosopher in Bristol*, 20.

37 Mackenzie, *The Man of Feeling*, 116.

38 Bage, *Mount Henneth*, 2:86.

39 William Wordsworth, '[*The Discharged Soldier*] (edited from MS; composed late January 1798)', in *Romanticism: An Anthology*, 2nd edn, ed. by Duncan Wu (Oxford: Blackwell, 1998), 273–7. The poem was originally intended for *The Recluse*, but was reworked for *The Prelude*. The title was given to the poem by later editors. The discharged soldier may also be a 'disabled' soldier, on the grounds that his impairments may have caused his departure from the services, but this is kept vague.

40 Although it is customary to refer to the speaker as Wordsworth, I will refer to him as a male speaker or narrator in order to preserve some neutrality on the question of whether the poet is speaking about himself. When the poem is part of *The Prelude* it is more definitely about Wordsworth, but for the sake of consistency I will continue to use speaker or narrator in this context too.

41 James H. Averill, *Wordsworth and the Poetry of Human Suffering* (Ithaca, NY: Cornell University Press, 1980), 142.

42 Averill, *Wordsworth and the Poetry of Human Suffering*, 144.

43 See, for example, Yu Liu, 'The Politics of Compassion', *English Language Notes* 37.4 (2000): 52–61; Nancy Yousef, 'Wordsworth, Sentimentalism, and the Defiance of Sympathy', *European Romantic Review* 17.2 (2006): 205–13; Francis O'Gorman, 'Wordsworth and Touch', *English* 58 (2009): 4–23; Simon Parkes, 'Wooden Legs and Tales of Sorrow Done: The Literary Broken Soldier of the Late Eighteenth Century', *Eighteenth-Century Studies* 39 (2013): 191–207; Turner, *Disability in the Eighteenth Century*, 73–7.

44 Matthew C. Brennan, '"The Ghastly Figure Moving at My Side": The Discharged Soldier as Wordsworth's Shadow', *Wordsworth Circle* 18.1 (1987): 19–23 (21).

45 Brennan, 'The Ghastly Figure Moving at My Side', 19; Warren Stephenson, 'Wordsworth and the Stone of Night', *The Wordsworth Circle* 13.4 (1982): 175–8.

46 Stephenson, 'Wordsworth and the Stone of Night', 176.

47 Brennan, 'The Ghastly Figure Moving at My Side', 19.

48 Simon Bainbridge, *British Poetry and the Revolutionary and Napoleonic Wars: Visions of Conflict* (Oxford: Oxford University Press, 2003), 89.

49 Mark Offord, *Wordsworth and the Art of Philosophical Travel* (Cambridge: Cambridge University Press, 2016), 82.

50 Offord, *Wordsworth and the Art of Philosophical Travel*, 82.

51 Adam Potkay, *Wordsworth's Ethics* (Baltimore, MD: Johns Hopkins University Press, 2012), 10.

52 Beth Darlington, 'Wordsworth and the Alchemy of Healing', *The Wordsworth Circle* 29.1 (1998): 52–60 (55).

53 Brennan, 'The Ghastly Figure Moving at My Side', 19.

54 Yousef, 'Wordsworth, Sentimentalism, and the Defiance of Sympathy', 206.

55 Yousef, 'Wordsworth, Sentimentalism, and the Defiance of Sympathy', 206.

56 Yousef, 'Wordsworth, Sentimentalism, and the Defiance of Sympathy', 211.

57 William Richey, 'The Rhetoric of Sympathy in Smith and Wordsworth', *European Romantic Review* 13.4 (2002): 427–43 (438). Richey's comment relates to Wordsworth's poem 'Simon Lee', a poem about civilian impairment, but it sums up neatly the conclusions that critics come to about Wordsworth's 'The Discharged Soldier', and it is intended to broadly describe Wordsworth's approach.

58 Wordsworth may have been influenced by Godwin's interest in desert. Gregory Claeys explores Godwin's theories of justice (according to merit and need) extensively in 'The Effects of Property on Godwin's Theory of

Justice', *Journal of the History of Philosophy* 22.1 (1984): 81–101. See especially 82–3 and 91.

59 It is worth noting here that Wordsworth modifies this line in later versions.

60 Potkay, *Wordsworth's Ethics*, 32.

61 Stone finds this sense of inadequacy again in Wordsworth's 'A Night-Piece', and uses this poem as evidence that we should not see the opening of 'The Discharged Soldier' as unsettling. C. F. Stone, 'Narrative Variation in Wordsworth's Versions of "The Discharged Soldier"', *Journal of Narrative Technique* 4 (1974): 32–44 (34–5).

62 Wordsworth, '[*The Discharged Soldier*]', l. 17. Wordsworth alters the cause of his tiredness dramatically in the version that appears as part of *The Prelude* (1850). In this version, the speaker, instead of being a busy man in search of a restorative view, suggests that he is exhausted, not from work, but from 'a round of strenuous idleness' caused by rowing on the lake, and staying up late with friends. The narrator is, in 1850, unworthy in a way that he is not in the earlier version, and his unworthiness gains a moral connotation. This hints that the poet will explore desert claims, and that he will not see them as a necessary condition for a received good. William Wordsworth, *The Prelude: The Four Texts (1978, 1799, 1805, 1850)*, ed. by Jonathan Wordsworth (London: Penguin, 1995), 1850, 4.378.

63 Wordsworth, '[*The Discharged Soldier*]', l. 1.

64 Wordsworth, '[*The Discharged Soldier*]', l. 2.

65 Wordsworth, '[*The Discharged Soldier*]', l. 6.

66 Wordsworth, '[*The Discharged Soldier*]', l. 6.

67 Wordsworth, '[*The Discharged Soldier*]', l. 9.

68 Wordsworth, '[*The Discharged Soldier*]', l. 12.

69 Wordsworth, '[*The Discharged Soldier*]', l. 18.

70 Wordsworth, '[*The Discharged Soldier*]', l. 34.

71 Wordsworth, '[*The Discharged Soldier*]', ll. 34–5. Wordsworth, who enjoyed playing on words, may hint again at halting, though the use of the word 'pause' at the end of an enjambed line.

72 Mackenzie, *The Man of Feeling*, 105.

73 Mackenzie, *The Man of Feeling*, 105.

74 Mackenzie, *The Man of Feeling*, 105.

75 Mackenzie, *The Man of Feeling*, 106.

76 Mackenzie, *The Man of Feeling*, 107.

77 Mackenzie, *The Man of Feeling*, 105.

78 Mackenzie, *The Man of Feeling*, 105.

79 Mackenzie, *The Man of Feeling*, 105.

80 Wordsworth, '[*The Discharged Soldier*]', l. 124.

81 Wordsworth, '[*The Discharged Soldier*]', l.38.

82 Wordsworth, '[*The Discharged Soldier*]', l. 84.

83 Wordsworth, '[*The Discharged Soldier*]', ll. 130–37.

84 Wordsworth, '[*The Discharged Soldier*]', l. 82. Wordsworth later changes this to 'self-blame' (1805, 4.432; 1850, 4.408). He explores this feeling of self-

reproach again in his fourth poem on the naming of places – a poem that contains an encounter with a peasant figure. The speaker of this poem mistakes the peasant for an idle man who wastes good harvesting time; but when the speaker sees his face, he realizes that the man is weak and 'worn down / By sickness, gaunt and lean, with sunken cheeks / And wasted limbs, his legs so long and lean / That for my single self I looked at them, / Forgetful of the body they sustained'. The speaker's mistake changes his own happy day 'To serious musing and to self-reproach'. Wordsworth, 'IV A narrow girdle of rough stones and crags', in *The Major Works*, ed. by Stephen Gill (Oxford: Oxford University Press, 2000), 203–5, ll. 64–8 and l. 76. I am grateful to an anonymous reader for pointing out the relevance of this poem. According to Gill, *Poems on the Naming of Places* 'were composed between December 1799 and October 1800', and so is close in time to 'The Discharged Soldier'. *The Major Works*, 697, n. 199.

85  David Bromwich, *Disowned by Memory: Wordsworth's Poetry of the 1790s* (Chicago, IL: University of Chicago Press, 1998), 9.

86  Wordsworth, '[*The Discharged Soldier*]', l. 38.

87  This image would later come to have Frankensteinian connotations. William Wordsworth, *Wordsworth's Tract on the Convention of Cintra [Published 1809] With Two Letters of Wordsworth Written in the Year 1811 Now Republished*, ed. by A. V. Dicey (London: Humphrey Milford, 1915), 97. *The Convention of Cintra* is Wordsworth's most extensive piece of writing on desert and justice.

88  Wordsworth, *The Convention of Cintra*, 99.

89  Wordsworth, '[*The Discharged Soldier*]', ll. 43–5.

90  Wordsworth, '[*The Discharged Soldier*]', l. 50.

91  Wordsworth, '[*The Discharged Soldier*]', l. 49.

92  Wordsworth, '[*The Discharged Soldier*]', l. 47.

93  The qualities in parentheses are assumptions that we can make from non-explicit claims.

94  Wordsworth, *The Prelude* (1850), 4.422.

95  Wordsworth, '[*The Discharged Soldier*]', l. 137.

96  Wordsworth, '[*The Discharged Soldier*]', l. 99.

97  Wordsworth, '[*The Discharged Soldier*]', l. 113. My emphasis.

98  Wordsworth, '[*The Discharged Soldier*]', l. 58. My emphasis.

99  Wordsworth, '[*The Discharged Soldier*]', ll. 121–2. My emphasis.

100  Wordsworth, '[*The Discharged Soldier*]', ll. 44–5. My emphasis.

101  Wordsworth, '[*The Discharged Soldier*]', l. 69. My emphasis.

102  Wordsworth, '[*The Discharged Soldier*]', ll. 141–4. My emphasis.

103  Wordsworth, '[*The Discharged Soldier*]', l. 78.

104  Wordsworth, '[*The Discharged Soldier*]', ll. 91–2.

105  Wordsworth, '[*The Discharged Soldier*]', l. 96.

106  Wordsworth, '[*The Discharged Soldier*]', l. 11.

107  Wordsworth, '[*The Discharged Soldier*]', l. 112.

108  Wordsworth, '[*The Discharged Soldier*]', l. 134.

109 Wordsworth, *The Convention of Cintra*, 6.
110 Wordsworth, '[*The Discharged Soldier*]', l. 111.
111 Wordsworth, '[*The Discharged Soldier*]', ll. 151–2.
112 Wordsworth, '[*The Discharged Soldier*]', l. 153.
113 Wordsworth, *The Prelude* (1798), l. 170; (1805), 4.504; (1850), 4.469. Matthew Brennan suggests that the poet resolves what he sees as the speaker's contempt for the soldier in the later versions through a more direct expression of sympathy, when he lingers at the door of the cottage before he seeks with 'quiet heart' his 'distant home' (1805, 4.504; 1850, 4.469). This later stance, Brennan asserts, represents Wordsworth's assimilation of the shadow and therefore the re-establishment of his psychological equilibrium. By dint of his 'outward appearance', which Brennan describes as 'dreamlike and nightmarish', the soldier 'correlates to a previously hidden or repressed aspect of Wordsworth's psyche'. Brennan, 'The Ghastly Figure Moving at My Side', 19.
114 Wordsworth, *The Prelude* (1798), ll. 154–5; (1805), 4.488–9; (1850), 4.453–4.
115 Wordsworth, '[*The Discharged Soldier*]', l. 165.
116 Wordsworth, *The Prelude* (1805), 4.456.
117 Wordsworth, *The Prelude* (1805), 4.458–9.
118 Wordsworth, '[*The Discharged Soldier*]', l. 113.
119 Wordsworth, *The Prelude* (1805), 4.486–7.
120 Wordsworth, '[*The Discharged Soldier*]', l. 153.
121 Wordsworth, *The Prelude* (1805), 4.497.
122 Wordsworth, *The Prelude* (1805), 4.487.
123 Wordsworth, *The Prelude* (1850), 4.426.
124 Wordsworth, *The Prelude* (1850), 4.450–52.
125 Wordsworth, *The Prelude* (1850), 4.453.
126 Wordsworth, *The Prelude* (1850), 4.462.
127 Wordsworth, '[*The Discharged Soldier*]', ll. 5, 25–6.
128 Wordsworth, '[*The Discharged Soldier*]', l. 158.
129 Wordsworth, '[*The Discharged Soldier*]', l. 157.
130 Wordsworth, '[*The Discharged Soldier*]', ll. 159–60.
131 Wordsworth, '[*The Discharged Soldier*]', l. 156.
132 Wordsworth, *The Prelude* (1805), 4.491–2; (1850), 4.456–7.
133 Wordsworth, '[*The Discharged Soldier*]', ll. 162–3; *The Prelude* (1805), 4.494–5; (1850), 4.459–60.
134 Mark Offord calls him a 'soldier-beggar', but the speaker does not treat him as a beggar. Offord, *Wordsworth and the Art of Philosophical Travel*, 82.
135 We see something of Wordsworth's further thinking on this in the Preface to the second edition of *Lyrical Ballads* (1802), where he introduces the term 'rational sympathy' to describe the directness of expression needed in poetry. A poet 'must express himself as other men express himself' in order to 'excite rational sympathy'. William Wordsworth, 'Preface (1802)', *Lyrical Ballads*, ed. by Michael Mason (London: Longman, 1992), 55–87 (79).

136 Wordsworth, '[*The Discharged Soldier*]', l. 16; *The Prelude* (1805), 4.380.
137 Wordsworth, '[*The Discharged Soldier*]', ll. 166–70.
138 Adam Smith, *The Theory of Moral Sentiments* (London: A. Millar, 1759), 8.
139 *The Prose Works of William Wordsworth*, ed. by W. J. B. Owen and Jane Worthington Smyser, 3 vols (Oxford: Clarendon Press, 1974), 2.49–62 (57).
140 Offord, *Wordsworth and the Art of Philosophical Travel*, 61. I have argued contrary to this that altruism does not follow a *quid pro quo* contract.
141 I make a distinction here between receiving charity and begging.
142 See Robert F. Drake, 'A Critique of the Role of Traditional Charities', in *Disability and Society: Emerging Issues and Insights*, ed. by Len Barton (London: Longman, 1996), 147–66; Chris Hanvey and Terry Philpot, eds., *Sweet Charity: The Role and Workings of Voluntary Organizations* (London: Routledge, 1996); John Swain, Sally French, and Colin Cameron, *Controversial Issues in a Disabling Society* (Buckingham: Open University Press, 2003); and Paul Longmore, *Telethons: Spectacle, Disability, and the Business of Charity* (Oxford: Oxford University Press, 2016).
143 Tom Shakespeare, *Disability Rights and Wrongs* (London: Routledge, 2006), 155.
144 Ellen L. Barton, 'Textual Practices of Erasure: Representations of Disability and the Founding of the United Way', in *Embodied Rhetorics: Disability in Language and Culture*, ed. by James C. Wilson and Cynthia Lewiecki-Wilson (Carbondale, IL: Southern Illinois University Press, 2001), 169–99 (172).
145 Barton, 'Textual Practices of Erasure', 196.

## 4 Picturesque Aesthetics

1 Percy Shelley, 'A Defence of Poetry', in *Percy Bysshe Shelley: The Major Works*, ed. by Zachary Leader and Michael O'Neill (Oxford: Oxford University Press, 2003), 674–701 (698). My emphasis.
2 Percy Shelley, *The Letters of Percy Bysshe Shelley*, ed. by Roger Ingpen, 2 vols (London: Isaac Pitman, 1909), 2:859.
3 Shelley, 'A Defence of Poetry', 698.
4 Tobin Siebers, *Disability Aesthetics* (Ann Arbor: University of Michigan Press, 2010), 3 and 19.
5 Siebers, *Disability Aesthetics*, 19.
6 The beauty–deformity binary has a long history, stretching back through Platonic traditions that see evil as the privation of good.
7 David Hume, *Treatise of Human Nature* (1738), ed. by Ernest C. Mossner (London: Penguin, 1985), 349.
8 Edmund Burke, *A Philosophical Enquiry into the Origin of Our Ideas of the Sublime and Beautiful*, ed. by Adam Phillips (Oxford: Oxford University Press, 1990), 94.
9 Francis Hutcheson, *An Inquiry into the Original of Our Ideas of Beauty and Virtue* [1725], 2nd edn (London: J. Darby, A. Bettesworth, F. Fayram, J. Pemberton, C. Rivington, J. Hooke, F. Clay, J. Batley, and E. Symon, 1726), Treatise I, sect. VI, art. 1.

10 Anthony Ashley Cooper [Lord Shaftesbury], *Characteristics of Men, Manners, Opinions, Times*, ed. by Lawrence E. Klein (Cambridge: Cambridge University Press, 1999), 415.

11 Joseph Addison and Richard Steele, *The Spectator*, ed. by Donald Bond, 5 vols (Oxford: Oxford University Press, 1965), 3:566.

12 Hume, *Treatise of Human Nature*, 353.

13 Hume, *Treatise of Human Nature*, 353.

14 As Miles Rind notes, 'eighteenth-century thinkers commonly defined taste . . . as the faculty of perceiving what is beautiful with pleasure'. Miles Rind, 'The Concept of Disinterestedness in Eighteenth-Century British Aesthetics', *Journal of the History of Philosophy* 40.1 (2002): 67–87 (86–7).

15 Richard Glausner and Anthony Savile, 'Aesthetic Experience in Shaftesbury', *Proceedings of the Aristotelian Society* 76 (2002): 25–74 (25).

16 Jerome Stolnitz, 'On the Origins of "Aesthetic Disinterestedness"', *Journal of Aesthetics and Art Criticism* 20.2 (1961): 131–43 (134). For an account of disinterestedness in Shaftesbury, Addison, Hutcheson, and Alison, see Rind, 'The Concept of Disinterestedness in Eighteenth-Century British Aesthetics'. Rind argues that these authors have a concept of taste rather than of the aesthetic, and that the concept of taste *'does not contain the concept of disinterestedness as a defining element'* before Kant (86). According to Rind, Shaftesbury's account is of 'a disinterested pleasure' that occurs 'independent of any prospect of advantage arising from the object' (86).

17 Shaftesbury, *Characteristics*, 408. Christoph Henke describes this process as 'perception–apprehension–reflection'. Christoph Henke, 'Before the Aesthetic Turn: The Common Sense Union of Ethics and Aesthetics in Shaftesbury and Pope', *Anglia: Journal of English Philology* 129 (2011): 58–78 (67).

18 Henke takes this to mean that Shaftesbury believes there is 'a universal sense of beauty, sublimity, and their opposites, independent of subjective preferences'. Henke, 'Before the Aesthetic Turn', 67.

19 Richard Glausner and Anthony Savile argue that Shaftesbury would agree with the view that beauty is 'a quality that things possess independently of our aesthetic experiences'. Glausner and Savile, 'Aesthetic Experience in Shaftesbury', 29.

20 Shaftesbury, *Characteristics*, 274.

21 Shaftesbury, *Characteristics*, 65.

22 Shaftesbury, *Characteristics*, 59.

23 Shaftesbury, *Characteristics*, 277.

24 James Chandler, *An Archeology of Sympathy: The Sentimental Mode in Literature and Cinema* (Chicago: University of Chicago Press, 2013), 240.

25 See Hutcheson, *An Inquiry into the Original of Our Ideas of Beauty and Virtue*, Treatise I, sect. I, art. 7.

26 Carolyn Korsmeyer describes Hutcheson as 'not wholly at ease with subjectivism'. Carolyn Korsmeyer, 'The Two Beauties: A Perspective on Hutcheson's Aesthetics', *Journal of Aesthetics and Art Criticism* 38.2 (1979): 145–51 (149).

27 Hutcheson, *An Inquiry into the Original of Our Ideas of Beauty and Virtue*, Treatise I, sect. I, art. 17. For more on the distinctions between the two types of beauty, see Korsmeyer, 'The Two Beauties'.

28 Hutcheson, *An Inquiry into the Original of Our Ideas of Beauty and Virtue*, Treatise I, sect. II, art. 3.

29 Hutcheson, *An Inquiry into the Original of Our Ideas of Beauty and Virtue*, Treatise II, sect. IV, art. 1.

30 Hutcheson, *An Inquiry into the Original of Our Ideas of Beauty and Virtue*, Treatise I, sect. IV, art. 1.

31 Hutcheson, *An Inquiry into the Original of Our Ideas of Beauty and Virtue*, Treatise I, sect. VI, art. 1.

32 I am in agreement with Emily Michael, who notes that while '[George] Dickie and [Carolyn] Korsmeyer both claim that for Hutcheson the idea of beauty can be identified as the perception of pleasure … Hutcheson regularly speaks of the experience of beauty as *accompanied* or *joined* by pleasure, suggesting that pleasure arises in conjunction with or as a result of an idea of beauty'. Emily Michael, 'Francis Hutcheson on Aesthetic Perception and Aesthetic Pleasure', *British Journal of Aesthetics* 24.3 (1984): 241–55 (214).

33 Hutcheson, *An Inquiry into the Original of Our Ideas of Beauty and Virtue*, Treatise I, sect. VI, art. 1.

34 Hutcheson, *An Inquiry into the Original of Our Ideas of Beauty and Virtue*, Treatise I, sect. VI, art. 2.

35 Hutcheson, *An Inquiry into the Original of Our Ideas of Beauty and Virtue*, Treatise I, sect. VI, art. 2.

36 See Hutcheson, *An Inquiry into the Original of Our Ideas of Beauty and Virtue*, Treatise I, sect. VI, art. 2.74 and Treatise II, sect. VI, art. 3.251.

37 Hume, *Treatise of Human Nature*, 350.

38 David Hume, 'Of the Standard of Taste', in *Moral Philosophy*, ed. by Geoffrey Sayre-McCord (Indianapolis, IN: Hackett, 2006), 345–60 (347).

39 Hume, 'Of the Standard of Taste', 347.

40 Hume, *Treatise of Human Nature*, 350. Given Hume's view that deformity is a subjective property – the pain caused in an observer by a given object – it is an analytic or definitional matter for him that deformity has a negative association. Subjectivists do not have to accept this evaluation of deformity, however. A judgement that an object is deformed may naturally result in a judgement that there is something negative about the object; but it need not. The evaluative appraisal of an object can itself be a subjective or an objective matter.

41 Michelle Mason discusses some of this ambiguity in 'Moral Prejudice and Aesthetic Deformity: Rereading Hume's "Of the Standard of Taste"', *Journal of Aesthetics and Art Criticism* 59.1 (2001): 59–71.

42 David Hume, *Four Dissertations* (London: A. Millar, 1757), 220.

43 Paddy Bullard notes that Burke also engages with Shaftesbury in this treatise. Paddy Bullard, *Edmund Burke and the Art of Rhetoric* (Cambridge: Cambridge University Press, 2011), 86.

44 Burke, *A Philosophical Enquiry*, 15.

45 Burke, *Philosophical Enquiry*, 1.

46 Burke, *Philosophical Enquiry*, 23.

47 Burke, *Philosophical Enquiry*, 1.

48 Burke, *Philosophical Enquiry*, 84.

49 Burke, *Philosophical Enquiry*, 85.

50 Burke, *Philosophical Enquiry*, 93.

51 Burke, *Philosophical Enquiry*, 108.

52 Burke, *Philosophical Enquiry*, 93.

53 William Gilpin, *An Essay on Prints* (London: J. Robson, 1768), xii.

54 William Gilpin, *Three Essays: On Picturesque Beauty; On Picturesque Travel; and On Sketching Landscape: To Which Is Added a Poem, on Landscape Painting* (London: R. Blamire, 1792), 3.

55 William Gilpin, *Observations, Relative Chiefly to Picturesque Beauty, Made in the Year 1772*, 2 vols (London: R. Blamire, 1786), 2:139; Gilpin, *Three Essays*, 14, 15–16.

56 William Gilpin, *Observations on Several Parts of the Counties of Cambridge, Norfolk, Suffolk, and Essex; Also on Several Parts of North Wales; Relative Chiefly to Picturesque Beauty in Two Tours, the Former Made in the Year 1769. The Latter in the Year 1773* (London: T. Cadell and W. Davies, 1809), 122.

57 Gilpin, *Observations, Relative Chiefly to Picturesque Beauty*, 2:44.

58 Gilpin, 'On Landscape Painting, A Poem', in *Three Essays*, 9. The poem is bound at the end of the volume, and the page numbers restart at the beginning of the poem.

59 William Gilpin, *Observations on the River Wye, and Several Parts of South Wales, &c. Relative Chiefly to Picturesque Beauty; Made in the Summer of the Year 1770* (London: R. Blamire, 1786); Gilpin, *Observations, Relative Chiefly to Picturesque Beauty*; Gilpin, *Three Essays*; and Gilpin, *Observations on Several Parts of the Counties of Cambridge*.

60 Gilpin, *Three Essays*, iii.

61 Gilpin, *Three Essays*, 4, 9.

62 Gilpin, *Three Essays*, 3.

63 Gilpin, *Three Essays*, 10–11.

64 Gilpin, *An Essay on Prints*, xii.

65 Gilpin, *Observations on Several Parts of the Counties of Cambridge*, 168–9.

66 Gilpin, *Observations on the River Wye*, 33.

67 Gilpin, *Observations on the River Wye*, 35.

68 Gilpin, *Observations on the River Wye*, 34.

69 Gilpin, *Observations on the River Wye*, 33.

70 Gilpin, *Observations on the River Wye*, 35.

71 Gilpin, *Observations, Relative Chiefly to Picturesque Beauty*, 2:44.

72 Gilpin, *Observations on the River Wye*, 36.

73 Gilpin, *Observations on the River Wye*, 36.

74 Gilpin, *Observations on the River Wye*, 36.

75 Gilpin, *Observations on the River Wye*, 36.

76 Gilpin, *Observations on the River Wye*, 37. The woman's palsy is assumed to be the result of her living conditions, but the story does not elaborate on whether the woman has told the travellers this.

77 Gilpin, *Observations on the River Wye*, 36.

78 Gilpin, *Observations on the River Wye*, 36.

79 Uvedale Price, *An Essay on the Picturesque, as Compared with the Sublime and the Beautiful; and, on the Use of Studying Pictures, for the Purpose of Improving Real Landscape* (London: J. Robson, 1794), 42 n.

80 Price, *An Essay on the Picturesque*, 76–7.

81 Price, *An Essay on the Picturesque*, 76 and 51.

82 Price, *An Essay on the Picturesque*, 169.

83 Price, *An Essay on the Picturesque*, 43.

84 Price, *An Essay on the Picturesque*, 76.

85 Price, *An Essay on the Picturesque*, 86.

86 Price, *An Essay on the Picturesque*, 163.

87 Price, *An Essay on the Picturesque*, 175.

88 Price, *An Essay on the Picturesque*, 176.

89 Price, *An Essay on the Picturesque*, 178–9. The quotation is from Dryden's *Absalom and Achitophel* (1681), l. 164.

90 Price, *An Essay on the Picturesque*, 179.

91 Price, *An Essay on the Picturesque*, 90.

92 Price, *An Essay on the Picturesque*, 173.

93 Price, *An Essay on the Picturesque*, 168. My emphasis.

94 Price, *An Essay on the Picturesque*, 70.

95 Price, *An Essay on the Picturesque*, 71.

96 Price, *An Essay on the Picturesque*, 138.

97 Price, *An Essay on the Picturesque*, 101 n. and 102 n.

98 Uvedale Price, *A Dialogue on the Distinct Characters of the Picturesque and the Beautiful in Answer to the Objections of Mr. Knight* (London: J. Robson, 1801), 118.

99 Price, *A Dialogue*, 119.

100 Price, *An Essay on the Picturesque*, 172.

101 William Hazlitt, 'Essay XXXII. On the Picturesque and Ideal. A Fragment', in *The Selected Writings of William Hazlitt*, ed. by Duncan Wu, 9 vols (London: Pickering and Chatto, 1998), 6:284–7 (284).

102 Rosemarie Garland Thomson, 'The Politics of Staring: Visual Rhetorics of Disability in Popular Photography', in *Disability Studies: Enabling the Humanities*, ed. by Sharon L. Snyder, Brenda Jo Brueggemann, and Rosemarie Garland Thomson (New York: MLA, 2002), 56–75 (57).

103 Hazlitt, 'On the Picturesque and Ideal', 6:285.

104 William Hazlitt, 'On Imitation', in *The Complete Works of William Hazlitt*, ed. by P. P. Howe, 22 vols (London: J. M. Dent, 1930–34), 4:72–7 (73–4).

105 Addison, *The Spectator*, 3:541.

106 Addison, *The Spectator*, 3:541.

107 Richard Payne Knight, *An Analytical Inquiry into the Principles of Taste*, 3rd edn (London: Luke Hansard, T. Payne, and J. White, 1806), 154.
108 Knight, *An Analytical Inquiry*, 142–3.
109 Knight, *An Analytical Inquiry*, 172.
110 Knight, *An Analytical Inquiry*, 207.
111 Knight, *An Analytical Inquiry*, 9.
112 Knight, *An Analytical Inquiry*, 152.
113 See, for example, Richard Payne Knight, *The Landscape: A Didactic Poem in Three Books*, 2nd edn (London: W. Bulmer, 1794), 22 n. The note is not in the first edition.
114 Knight, *An Analytical Inquiry*, 13–14. In Knight's work, beauty, when used to describe virtue, is not used in a special figurative sense, but in the same sense as the beauty of objects and people.
115 Knight, *An Analytical Inquiry*, 73.
116 Knight, *An Analytical Inquiry*, 73.
117 In 1794, Price comes close to anticipating Knight's idea about the effect of aesthetic distancing on the appreciation of deformity. He comments that 'he who has been used to admire such picturesque ugliness in painting, will from the same causes look with pleasure (for we have no other word to express the degree or character of that sensation) at the original in nature; and one cannot think slightly of the power and advantage of that art which makes its admirers often gaze with such delight on some antient lady, as with the help of a little vanity might perhaps lead her to mistake the motive'. Price, *An Essay on the Picturesque*, 174–5.
118 Burke, *A Philosophical Enquiry*, 45. Burke may well be referring to Addison.
119 Addison, *The Spectator*, 3:566.
120 Addison, *The Spectator*, 3:567.
121 Addison, *The Spectator*, 3:546.
122 Addison, *The Spectator*, 3:546.
123 Addison, *The Spectator*, 3:567.
124 Burke, *A Philosophical Enquiry*, 17.
125 Burke, *A Philosophical Enquiry*, 45.
126 Byron includes an interesting use of the dunghill image in connection with deformity in his play *The Deformed Transformed*. The protagonist, Arnold, compares his soul inhabiting his deformed body with a gem in a dunghill that has been set in gold: 'as the dunghill may conceal a gem / Which is now set in gold, as jewels should be'. Lord Byron, *The Deformed Transformed; A Drama* (London: J. and H. L. Hunt, 1824).
127 Knight, *An Analytical Inquiry*, 200.
128 Knight's note is reproduced, inaccurately, in Price's *A Dialogue*, and the inaccuracy caused further irritation for Knight.
129 Price, *A Dialogue*, 82.
130 Price, *A Dialogue*, 128.
131 Price, *A Dialogue*, 130–31.

132 Price, *A Dialogue*, 132–3.

133 Price, *A Dialogue*, 135.

134 Price, *A Dialogue*, 135–6. Price briefly satirizes his own commitment to naturally aged buildings by having Seymour suggest that Hamilton (Price) would require the parson's daughter to have aged like a building in order to be truly picturesque. Price also hints at his own analogy, in *An Essay on the Picturesque* (1794), between the 'painted old woman' in make-up and the white-washed cottage (137–8).

135 Price, *A Dialogue*, 136.

136 Knight, *An Analytical Inquiry*, 206.

137 Knight, *An Analytical Inquiry*, 205.

138 Knight, *An Analytical Inquiry*, 206.

139 Knight, *An Analytical Inquiry*, 206–7.

140 Knight, *An Analytical Inquiry*, 206.

141 Knight, *An Analytical Inquiry*, 207.

142 Knight, *An Analytical Inquiry*, 185–6.

143 Price, *A Dialogue*, 136.

144 Knight, *An Analytical Inquiry*, 205.

145 Knight, *An Analytical Inquiry*, 202–4.

146 Joseph Farington, *The Farington Diary*, ed. by James Grieg, vol. 4 (20 September 1806 to 7 January 1808) (New York: George H. Doran, 1924), 4:31.

147 William Wordsworth, *The Letters of William and Dorothy Wordsworth, A Supplement of New Letters*, ed. by Alan G. Hill (Oxford: Clarendon Press, 1993), 8:102.

148 Uvedale Price, *Essays on the Picturesque as Compared with the Sublime and Beautiful; and On the Use of Studying Pictures for the Purpose of Improving Real Landscape*, 3 vols (London: J. Mawman, 1810), 3:392.

149 Price, *Essays on the Picturesque*, 3:392.

150 Price, *Essays on the Picturesque*, 3:392.

151 Price, *Essays on the Picturesque*, 3:393.

152 Price, *Essays on the Picturesque*, 3:393.

153 Price, *Essays on the Picturesque*, 3:393. Here Price slightly misquotes Knight, who writes 'sexual and social sympathies', and no doubt adds to Knight's annoyance.

154 Siebers, *Disability Aesthetics*, 3.

155 Samuel Taylor Coleridge, *The Complete Poetical Works of Samuel Taylor Coleridge*, ed. by E. H. Coleridge (Oxford: Clarendon Press, 2000), ll. 253, 224.

156 Josiah Conder, 'Coleridge's "Christabel"', *The Eclectic Review* (1816), 565–6 (566).

157 Gilpin, *Three Essays*, 7.

158 Anne Janowitz, 'The Romantic Fragment', in *A Companion to Romanticism*, ed. by Duncan Wu (Oxford: Blackwell, 1999), 442–51 (443).

159 Janowitz, 'The Romantic Fragment', 449.

160 William Wordsworth, 'Preface (1802)', *Lyrical Ballads*, ed. by Michael Mason (London: Longman, 1992), 55–87 (82).

## 5 Relational Deformity in Frances Burney's *Camilla*

1 The questioning of the fixity of aesthetic value in *Camilla* is part of what Kristen Pond sees as an extensive destabilization of 'acts of interpretation, both for characters who attempt to read others within the novel and for readers attempting to read the novel itself'. Kristen Pond, '"Fairest Observers" and "Restless Watchers": Contested Sites of Epistemology in Frances Burney's *Camilla*', *Studies in the Novel* 50.3 (2018): 315–35 (316).

2 Melissa Pino, 'Burney's *Evelina* and Aesthetics in Action', *Modern Philology* 108.2 (2010): 263–303 (267).

3 Pino, 'Burney's *Evelina* and Aesthetics in Action', 268.

4 Pino, 'Burney's *Evelina* and Aesthetics in Action', 268.

5 Pino, 'Burney's *Evelina* and Aesthetics in Action', 267.

6 G. Gabrielle Starr, 'Burney, Ovid, and the Value of the Beautiful', *Eighteenth-Century Fiction* 24.1 (2011): 77–104 (78).

7 For Burney's interest in other philosophical questions, see Preben Mortensen, 'Shaftesbury and the Morality of Art Expression', *Journal of the History of Ideas* 55.4 (1994): 631–50. Mortensen uses Burney's *Cecilia* in his study of Shaftesbury to make the case that one's 'interest' and one's desire may be different. He cites Burney's usage as typical: 'interest and inclination are eternally at strife'. Burney, cited in Mortensen, 'Shaftesbury and the Morality of Art Expression', 633.

8 Burke's *A Philosophical Enquiry* would have given Burney indirect access to Shaftesbury, Addison, Hutcheson, and Hume. Edmund Burke, *A Philosophical Enquiry into the Origin of Our Ideas of the Sublime and Beautiful*, ed. by Adam Phillips (Oxford: Oxford University Press, 1990).

9 The first edition of the novel notes that Burke bought five sets. Frances Burney, *Camilla or a Picture of Youth*, ed. by Edward A. Bloom and Lillian D. Bloom (Oxford: Oxford University Press, 1999), x.

10 Around half of the early reviews mention Eugenia, but none discusses her deformity in any depth. Eugenia and Camilla are the two heroines, but early opinion was divided over Eugenia's importance. The *English Review* describes Eugenia as '*properly* the heroine of the tale'; but the *Monthly Review* sees her as 'an interesting under-part of the story'. Anon., 'Art. XXV. Camilla; or, A Picture of Youth. By the Author of Evelina and Cecilia', *English Review* 28 (1796): 178–80 (180); [William Enfield and George E. Giffiths], 'Art. IX. Camilla; or, A Picture of Youth. By the Author of Evelina and Cecilia', *Monthly Review* 21 (October 1796): 156–63 (158).

11 Burney, *Camilla*, 293.

12 Burney, *Camilla*, 50.

13 Burney, *Camilla*, 293.

14 Burney, *Camilla*, 286.
15 Burney, *Camilla*, 280.
16 Burney, *Camilla*, 300.
17 Burney, *Camilla*, 562.
18 Burney, *Camilla*, 565.
19 Burney, *Camilla*, 566.
20 Burney, *Camilla*, 577.
21 Burney, *Camilla*, 905.
22 Burney, *Camilla*, 905.
23 Burney, *Camilla*, 302. Either Burney or Mr Tyrold misattributes this reference to Addison.
24 Joseph Addison and Richard Steele, *The Spectator*, ed. by Donald Bond, 5 vols (Oxford: Oxford University Press, 1965), 1.74. Neither Addison's essays on taste (which appeared in *The Spectator* as 'The Pleasures of the Imagination' in 1712) nor Steele's essays on deformity are philosophical in a strict sense, but they are engaged with the philosophical debates, and Addison's essays certainly influence these debates. The essays are an early response to Shaftesbury's *Characteristics*. Both Shaftesbury and Addison are also sources for Mark Akenside's *The Pleasures of the Imagination* (1744/1772), a poem which draws heavily on Plato, Locke, and Hutcheson, and which features briefly in *Camilla*. Burney has the beautiful Mrs Berlinton miss a raffle because she is 'in the midst of Akenside's Pleasures of the Imagination, and could not tear herself away from them'. Burney, *Camilla*, 474. We know from Burney's diaries that she, with her friend Mr Fairly, read Akenside, alongside extracts from Locke, in July and August of 1788. She describes her 'imagination' as 'amply gratified' by Akenside's 'very, very charming poem'. Frances Burney, *Diary and Letters of Madame D'Arblay (1778–1840)*, ed. by Charlotte Barrett and Austin Dobson, 6 vols (London: Macmillan, 1905), 4:65, 4:72.
25 Burney, *Camilla*, 287.
26 Burney, *Camilla*, 30.
27 Burney, *Camilla*, 379.
28 Burney, *Camilla*, 120.
29 Echoing Godwin, Julia Epstein writes that 'Eugenia's literal entrapment in her deformed body and imprisonment in the house arrest . . . are only two of the kinds of prisons that enclose Burney's women in *Camilla*.' Julia Epstein, *The Iron Pen: Frances Burney and the Politics of Women's Writing* (Bristol: Bristol Classical Press, 1989), 147. Rebecca Garden reads illness and deformity in the novel as a punishment for 'excesses of female freedom and power', and for social mixing beyond 'the healthy private life on the family estates'. Rebecca Garden, 'Illness and Inoculation: Narrative Strategies in Frances Burney's *Camilla*', ed. by Marcelline Block and Angela Laflen (Newcastle upon Tyne: Cambridge Scholars, 2010), 64–94 (65 and 69).
30 Burney, *Camilla*, 10.
31 Burney, *Camilla*, 10.
32 Burney, *Camilla*, 891.

33 Burney, *Camilla*, 142.
34 Burney, *Camilla*, 537.
35 Burney, *Camilla*, 133.
36 Burney, *Camilla*, 23.
37 Margaret Doody, *Frances Burney: The Life in the Works* (New Brunswick, NJ: Rutgers University Press, 1988), 261.
38 Burney, *Camilla*, 404.
39 Burney, *Camilla*, 406.
40 Burney, *Camilla*, 365.
41 Burney, *Camilla*, 579. Margaret Doody recognizes that Eugenia's 'double deformity', as an educated deformed woman, is a 'decontaminating reversal' of the usual 'satiric trope' of the learned lady. Doody, *Frances Burney*, 242–3. In 'associating the horror at learned ladies with the old vulgar outcry at a crippled body', Doody recognizes the author's compassion: 'the author makes us reject both reactions as crude, inhumane, and archaic'. Doody, *Frances Burney*, 243. Felicity Nussbaum views Eugenia as a 'gender anomaly', whose 'disability . . . empower[s] her to escape the usual trivial femininities'. Felicity Nussbaum, *The Limits of the Human: Fictions of Anomaly, Race, and Gender in the Long Eighteenth Century* (Cambridge: Cambridge University Press, 2003), 125. Sara Salih also uses the term 'gender anomaly' to describe Eugenia. Salih equates Eugenia's acquisition of deformities with a 'loss of femininity'. Sara Salih, '*Camilla* and *The Wanderer*', in *The Cambridge Companion to Frances Burney*, ed. by Peter Sabor (Cambridge: Cambridge University Press, 2007), 39–53 (41).
42 Burney, *Camilla*, 592.
43 Burney, *Camilla*, 589.
44 Burney, *Camilla*, 748.
45 Burney, *Camilla*, 46.
46 Burney, *Camilla*, 905.
47 Burney, *Camilla*, 905. Diane Harris suggests that, 'after enduring her uncle's clumsy attempts to reshape her reality through language, Eugenia creates for herself a textual body which reflects her inner beauty in a way that her misshapen physical body cannot'. Harris calls Eugenia's education a form of 'bibliotherapy'. Diane Harris, 'Eugenia's Escape: The Written Word in Frances Burney's *Camilla*', *Lumen* 17 (1998): 151–64 (151 and 157).
48 Burney, *Camilla*, 51.
49 Burney, *Camilla*, 905.
50 Anthony Ashley Cooper [Lord Shaftesbury], *Characteristics of Men, Manners, Opinions, Times*, ed. by Lawrence E. Klein, Cambridge Texts in the History of Philosophy (Cambridge: Cambridge University Press, 1999), 323.
51 Shaftesbury, *Characteristics*, 65.
52 Shaftesbury, *Characteristics*, 63.
53 Burney, *Camilla*, 308. Barry McCrea notes that Burney does not outline a standard of beauty, only its effect in this scene: 'we never learn what the imbecile looked like'. Barry McCrea, *Frances Burney and Narrative Prior to*

*Ideology* (Newark: University of Delaware Press, 2013), 37. I suggest, however, that the description does include the standard of beauty, and couples this with an account of its negation.

54  Burney, *Camilla*, 309.

55  Burney, *Camilla*, 310. Nussbaum reads the description of the unnamed woman as 'racialized' on account of the description of her becoming 'almost black in the face' while demanding a shilling. Nussbaum, *The Limits of the Human*, 128.

56  Burney, *Camilla*, 310. The reviewers in the *Monthly Review* commented that 'the meeting with the beautiful idiot, as contributed by Eugenia's father, furnishes an admirable lesson on beauty; and the picture of idiocy is a striking one: but we are not sure that it is sufficiently distinct from that of madness'. [Enfield and Griffiths], 'Art. IX', 158. Claudia Johnson suggests that the woman's condition is indicative of a quality that is demanded of Camilla and Eugenia, commenting that 'insensibility is actually what is required' of them. Claudia Johnson, *Equivocal Beings: Politics, Gender, and Sentimentality in the 1790s – Wollstonecraft, Radcliffe, Burney, Austen* (Chicago, IL: Chicago University Press, 1995), 154. Camilla is also referred to as mad on several occasions. For example, *Camilla*, 608, 612, 621. The unnamed madwoman/idiot is seen by Rebecca Garden as a 'treatment' that will inoculate Eugenia 'against the violent self-recognition' that she encountered with the market women. Garden, 'Illness and Inoculation', 75.

57  Burney, *Camilla*, 310.

58  Burney, *Camilla*, 311.

59  Burney, *Camilla*, 311. Ignoring Mr Tyrold's lesson on vanity, George Haggerty argues that Eugenia learns 'self-love' in this scene 'by means of a careful hierarchy of debility that places her above a raving lunatic if implicitly below her lovely and affectionate sister'. George E. Haggerty, *Unnatural Affections: Women and Fiction in the Later 18th Century* (Bloomington: Indiana University Press, 1998), 143.

60  Burney, *Camilla*, 311.

61  Andrea Haslanger, 'From Man-Machine to Woman-Machine: Automata, Fiction, and Femininity in Dibdin's *Hannah Hewit* and Burney's *Camilla*', *Modern Philology* 111.4 (2014): 788–817 (813).

62  Nussbaum, *The Limits of the Human*, 128.

63  Doody, *Frances Burney*, 404, n. 54.

64  Sarah Scott, *Millenium Hall*, ed. by Gary Kelly (Peterborough, Ontario: Broadview, 1995), 72. The use of the word 'standard' here is additional evidence for moving beyond normalcy as the sole normative concept. Scott's female refuge was echoed a few years later in Lady Mary Hamilton's *Munster Village* (1778), though without the idea of the separation of deformity from its negative associations.

65  Sara Coleridge, 'On the Disadvantages Resulting from the Possession of Beauty', in *Sara Coleridge: A Victorian Daughter: Her Life and Essays*, ed. by

Bradford Keyes Mudge (New Haven, CT: Yale University Press, 1989), 187–200 (187).

66 Coleridge, 'On the Disadvantages Resulting from the Possession of Beauty', 193.

67 Coleridge, 'On the Disadvantages Resulting from the Possession of Beauty', 190.

68 'M' [Mary Wollstonecraft], 'Art, VI. *Camilla; or A Picture of Youth*. By the Author of Evelina and Cecilia', *The Analytical Review* (August 1796): 142–8 (145). This review was identified as Wollstonecraft's work in Joseph A. Grau, *Fanny Burney: An Annotated Bibliography* (New York: Garland, 1981), 27.

69 'M' [Mary Wollstonecraft], 'Art, VI.', 145.

70 Charles Burney, *Memoirs of Doctor Burney*, ed. by Madame D'Arblay, 3 vols (London: Edward Moxon, 1832), 1:184.

71 Charles Burney, *Memoirs of Doctor Burney*, ed. by Madame D'Arblay, 3 vols (London: Edward Moxon, 1832), 1:187.

72 David Hartley, *Observations on Man, His Frame, His Duty, and His Expectations*, 2 vols (London: Charles Hitch and Stephen Austen, 1749), 447.

73 Barry McCrea suggests that the opening of *Camilla* 'it would seem, should point to standards' of beauty, but it describes 'no physical features', and concentrates on the effects of beauty instead. McCrea, *Frances Burney and Narrative Prior to Ideology*, 36.

74 Burney, *Camilla*, 10.

75 Burney, *Camilla*, 11.

76 Burney, *Camilla*, 11.

77 Burney, *Camilla*, 15.

78 Burney, *Camilla*, 15.

79 Burney, *Camilla*, 102.

80 Burney, *Camilla*, 102.

81 Burney, *Camilla*, 102.

82 Burney, *Camilla*, 15, 191. Haslanger presents Indiana as an example of 'the female mind/body problem', where beauty and intellect are opposed in the way they affect a woman's chances on the marriage market. Haslanger notes that word 'automaton' refers in this period to 'mindless, repetitive behaviour', as well as to non-human models (as is evidenced above in my discussion of Ruffigny in Godwin's *Fleetwood*). She observes, further, that 'both senses of the word attach primarily to women', and that 'the strong association between the automaton and femininity, which emerges in the 1770s ... reaches its peak in the 1790s'. Haslanger, 'From Man-Machine to Woman-Machine', 811 and 788.

83 Burney, *Camilla*, 233.

84 Burney, *Camilla*, 817. It is no accident that in Book 4, chapter 8, the Tyrold family attends a performance of *Othello*.

85 Burney, *Camilla*, 690.

86 Burney, *Camilla*, 714.

87 Burney, *Camilla*, 714–15.
88 Burney, *Camilla*, 19, 32.
89 Shaftesbury, *Characteristics*, 414.
90 Shaftesbury, *Characteristics*, 416.
91 Shaftesbury, *Characteristics*, 65.
92 Shaftesbury sees goodness in a person or animal as the harmonious interaction between the creature and the external system to which it belongs: an appropriate social interaction is good, and an action which benefits the species is good.
93 Burney, *Camilla*, 50–51.
94 Burney, *Camilla*, 373.
95 Burney, *Camilla*, 754.
96 Burney, *Camilla*, 794.
97 Burney, *Camilla*, 149.
98 Burney, *Camilla*, 912.
99 Burney, *Camilla*, 913.
100 For 'lameness', see Burney, *Camilla*, 64, 439, and 566. For 'lame', see Burney, *Camilla*, 77, 91, and 277. 'Lame' is one of the oldest words connected with disability (*OED* c. 725). For more on the terms 'lame' and 'cripple', see Simon Dickie, *Cruelty and Laughter: Forgotten Comic Literature and the Unsentimental Eighteenth Century* (Chicago, IL: University of Chicago Press, 2011), 54, 60, 68, 81, and 96. For Dickie's account of Burney's cruel judgements on the personal appearances of her acquaintances, see 84–5.
101 Burney, *Camilla*, 468.
102 Burney, *Camilla*, 289. Were Eugenia to need unimpaired mobility for work, as Jemima does in Wollstonecraft's novel *Maria* (1798), she would be at a disadvantage.
103 Burney, *Camilla*, 64.
104 Carol Ann Howells, '"The Proper Education of A Female... Is Still To Seek": Childhood and Girls' Education in Fanny Burney's *Camilla; or, A Picture of Youth*', *British Journal for Eighteenth-Century Studies* 7.2 (1984): 191–8 (193).
105 David E. Shuttleton, *Smallpox and the Literary Imagination 1660–1820* (Cambridge: Cambridge University Press, 2007), 135.
106 Jason Farr, 'Sharp Minds/Twisted Bodies: Intellect, Disability, and Female Education in Frances Burney's *Camilla*', *The Eighteenth Century* 55.1 (2014): 1–17 (3).
107 Nussbaum, *The Limits of the Human*, 18.
108 Nussbaum, *The Limits of the Human*, 121.
109 Nussbaum, *The Limits of the Human*, 121.
110 Nussbaum, *The Limits of the Human*, 121.
111 Nussbaum, *The Limits of the Human*, 121.
112 Nussbaum, *The Limits of the Human*, 121.

113 Nussbaum, *The Limits of the Human*, 125.
114 Nussbaum, *The Limits of the Human*, 127.
115 Nussbaum, *The Limits of the Human*, 127.
116 Nussbaum, *The Limits of the Human*, 121.
117 Nussbaum, *The Limits of the Human*, 132.
118 Felicity Nussbaum reads the enclosure in *Millenium Hall* as a 'feminotopia'. Felicity Nussbaum, 'Feminotopias: The Pleasures of "Deformity" in Mid-Eighteenth-Century England', in *The Body and Physical Difference: Discourses of Disability*, ed. by David T. Mitchell and Sharon L. Snyder (Ann Arbor: University of Michigan Press, 1997), 161–73. Alice Hall notes that '"to crip" or "to queer" is to question and to subvert dominant cultural expectations about heteronormativity and/or able-bodiedness in fresh new ways'. Alice Hall, *Literature and Disability* (New York: Routledge, 2016), 45. The term 'criptopia' is my own.
119 Johnson, *Equivocal Beings*, 152.
120 Nussbaum, *The Limits of the Human*, 121.
121 Farr, 'Sharp Minds/Twisted Bodies', 3.
122 Burney, *Camilla*, 776.

## 6 Monstrous Sights

1 William Wordsworth, 'Illustrated Books and Newspapers', in William Wordsworth, *Poetical Works*, ed. by Thomas Hutchinson, rev. by Ernest de Selincourt (Oxford: Oxford University Press, 1981), 383.
2 William H. Galperin, *The Return of the Visible in British Romanticism* (Baltimore, MD: Johns Hopkins University Press, 1993), 3.
3 Sophie Thomas, *Romanticism and Visuality: Fragments, History, Spectacle* (New York: Routledge, 2008), 4.
4 Deformities in their physiological sense can be congenital or acquired. See, for example, John Sheldon, *An Essay on the Fracture of the Patella or Kneepan. Containing a New and Efficacious Method of Treating That Accident, by Which the Deformity and Lameness That Arise from the Old and Common Mode of Treatment, Are Avoided. With Observations on the Fracture of the Olecranon* (London: J. Johnson, P. Elmsley, T. Cadell, E. and C. Dilly, G. G. G. J. and J. Robinson, and J. Robson, 1789). For more on the physiological study of monsters, see Lorraine Daston and Katharine Park, *Wonders and the Order of Nature 1150–1750* (New York: Zone, 1998), especially chapter 5. For a usage of deformity and monstrosity in a physiological sense, see for example Adam Smith's comment: 'Monsters ... or what is perfectly deformed, are always most singular and odd, and have the least resemblance to the generality of the species to which they belong. And thus the beauty of each species, though in one sense the rarest of all things ... yet in another is the most common.' Adam Smith, *The Theory of Moral Sentiments* (London: A. Millar, 1759), 381–2.

5 Chris Baldick expresses uncertainty over whether it is appropriate for critics to refer to the creature as a 'monster', but settles on the frequency of the use of the term in the novel as the deciding factor in using it. He notes that the creature is referred to as a monster '27 times'. Chris Baldick, *In Frankenstein's Shadow* (Oxford: Clarendon Press, 1987), 10, n. 1. Abigail Six and Hannah Thompson use the same list, noting that 'monster' is the term most often applied to the creature, 'appearing 27 times, ahead of "fiend", "daemon", "creature", "wretch", "devil", "being", and "ogre"'. Abigail Lee Six and Hannah Thompson, 'From Hideous to Hedonist: The Changing Face of the Nineteenth-Century Monster', in *The Ashgate Research Companion to Monsters and the Monstrous*, ed. by Asa Simon Mittman and Peter J. Dendle (Farnham: Ashgate, 2012), 237–55 (239, n. 7). Jared Richman offers a different reckoning, suggesting that 'the term "monster" appears twenty-five times'. Jared Richman, 'Monstrous Elocution: Disability and Passing in *Frankenstein*', *Essays in Romanticism* 25.2 (2018): 187–207 (189). According to my count, in the 1818 edition, the creature is referred to as a 'monster' thirty-five times, and once as 'monstrous'. In the 1831 edition, the creature is described as a 'monster' thirty-six times, and as 'monstrous' once. Justine uses the term 'monster' once of herself, and Elizabeth uses it once of men or of mankind. Mary Shelley, *Frankenstein: The Original 1818 Text*, ed. by D. L. Macdonald and Kathleen Scherf, 2nd edn (Peterborough, Ontario: Broadview, 2005), 113 and 120. The latter references are in both editions. Some scholars have made a choice to refer to the character with neutral terminology (e.g. the creature), as I do here, except when citing or discussing the derogatory terms. Pejorative terms for bodily difference, no matter how frequently used, should be employed with at least an acknowledgement that they are derogatory. The novel uses other descriptive words for the creature (fiend, daemon, wretch, devil, being, ogre), but these are relatively self-explanatory. Unless otherwise stated, quotations from *Frankenstein* are from Macdonald and Scherf.

6 James Chandler, *An Archeology of Sympathy: The Sentimental Mode in Literature and Cinema* (Chicago, IL: University of Chicago Press, 2013), 243.

7 Shelley, *Frankenstein*, 86.

8 Shelley, *Frankenstein*, 139.

9 P. B. Shelley, 'On Frankenstein', *Athenaeum*, 10 November 1832, 730.

10 Peter Brooks, 'What Is a Monster? (According to *Frankenstein*)', in *Frankenstein: New Casebooks*, ed. by Fred Botting (Houndmills, Basingstoke: Macmillan, 1995), 81–106 (100).

11 Brooks, 'What Is a Monster?', 83.

12 Brooks, 'What Is a Monster?', 96.

13 Brooks, 'What Is a Monster?', 100.

14 It is particularly important to consider eighteenth-century and early nineteenth-century definitions of monstrosity in this context, as the field has been dominated by early modern definitions, such as that of Francis Bacon.

15 Edmund Burke, *A Philosophical Enquiry into the Origin of Our Ideas of the Sublime and Beautiful*, ed. by Adam Phillips (Oxford: Oxford University Press, 1990), 90.

16 Burke, *A Philosophical Enquiry*, 143.

17 Denise Gigante argues, contrary to this, that aesthetics and science merge at the turn of the nineteenth century: 'the aesthetic category of monstrosity intersected with natural philosophy around the turn of the nineteenth century, transforming the idea of the monster as a static deformity or collection of poorly assembled parts into a distinctly Romantic, vitalist conception of monstrosity as too much life. Linked to process rather than to product, to formative power rather than malformation, the objectified monster gave way to a monstrous vitality that was frightening in its unbounded purpose'. Denise Gigante, *Life: Organic Form and Romanticism* (New Haven, CT: Yale University Press, 2009), 210.

18 Burke, *A Philosophical Enquiry*, 90.

19 Burke, *A Philosophical Enquiry*, 143.

20 Burke, *A Philosophical Enquiry*, 143.

21 Burke, *A Philosophical Enquiry*, 94.

22 Burke, *A Philosophical Enquiry*, 93.

23 Shelley, *Frankenstein*, 85.

24 Shelley, *Frankenstein*, 240.

25 Burke, *A Philosophical Enquiry*, 109. Denise Gigante dismisses the idea that the creature's appearance makes him an 'object of sublimity', arguing that, although Burke associates ugliness with the sublime aesthetic when it is accompanied by qualities that terrify, 'the principal factor of sublime experience – being elevated from terror to a comprehension of greatness – is absent from Victor's experience'. Denise Gigante, 'Facing the Ugly: The Case of *Frankenstein*', *English Literary History* 67 (2000): 565–87 (575).

26 Burke, *A Philosophical Enquiry*, 108–9.

27 The creature is not the only character who is described as ugly, though he is the only sublime *and* ugly character. Elizabeth Lavenza describes Manon, the 'ugly sister' of 'the pretty Miss Mansfield', as having married M. Duvillard, 'a rich banker'. Elizabeth provides the expected explanation in the case of 'the very lively pretty Frenchwoman, Madame Tavernier', who is about to marry a younger man, but omits to provide a reason why the 'ugly sister' attracts a banker. Shelley, *Frankenstein*, 94.

28 Shelley, *Frankenstein*, 240.

29 Shelley, *Frankenstein*, 85.

30 Burke, *A Philosophical Enquiry*, 94.

31 Shelley, *Frankenstein*, 155.

32 Baldick, *In Frankenstein's Shadow*, 11.

33 Six and Thompson, 'From Hideous to Hedonist', 238.

34 Six and Thompson, 'From Hideous to Hedonist', 237.

35 Six and Thompson, 'From Hideous to Hedonist', 237.

36 Six and Thompson, 'From Hideous to Hedonist', 237.

37 John Block Friedman, 'Foreword', in *The Ashgate Research Companion to Monsters and the Monstrous*, ed. by Asa Simon Mittman and Peter J. Dendle (Farnham, Surrey: Ashgate, 2012), xxv–xxxix (xv).

38 Patricia MacCormack, 'Posthuman Teratology', in *The Ashgate Research Companion to Monsters and the Monstrous*, ed. by Asa Simon Mittman and Peter J. Dendle (Farnham: Ashgate, 2012), 293–309 (294).

39 Denise Gigante has fleshed out the use of the term 'ugly' as distinct from deformity, for instance. Gigante, 'Facing the Ugly', 575. My own article places the novel in the context of the use of blindness and sight in eighteenth-century concepts of historiography. Essaka Joshua, "'Blind Vacancy": Sighted Culture and Voyeuristic Historiography in Mary Shelley's *Frankenstein*', *European Romantic Review* 22.1 (2011): 49–69.

40 David T. Mitchell and Sharon L. Snyder, *Narrative Prosthesis: Disability and the Dependencies of Discourse* (Ann Arbor: University of Michigan Press, 2000), 132. For Paul Youngquist, the creature's retaliation for his stigmatization is a 'response to the regulatory force of the norm of the proper body'. The creature takes 'vengeance on the bodies that the norm so invisibly advantages'. Paul Youngquist, *Monstrosities: Bodies and British Romanticism* (Minneapolis: University of Minnesota Press, 2003), 53 and 55.

41 Mitchell and Snyder, *Narrative Prosthesis*, 58. Much of this work builds on and challenges Erving Goffman's sociological analysis of stigma as a complex cultural exchange of multiple social identities that are '*virtual*', in the sense of being ascribed to the stigmatized, and '*actual*', in the sense of being intrinsic to the stigmatized. Erving Goffman, *Stigma: Notes on the Management of a Spoiled Identity* (New York: Simon and Schuster, 1986), 3.

42 Julia Miele Rodas, 'Autistic Voice and Literary Architecture in Mary Shelley's *Frankenstein*', in *Disabling Romanticism*, ed. by Michael Bradshaw (London: Palgrave Macmillan, 2016), 169–90 (173).

43 William D. Brewer, 'Mary Shelley on the Therapeutic Value of Language', in *Critical Essays on Mary Wollstonecraft Shelley* (New York: G. K. Hall, 1998), 152–65 (163).

44 Fuson Wang, 'The Historicist Turn of Romantic-Era Disability Studies, or *Frankenstein* in the Dark', *Literature Compass* 14.7 (2017): 1–10 (7).

45 Wang, 'The Historicist Turn of Romantic-Era Disability Studies', 2.

46 Six and Thompson, 'From Hideous to Hedonist', 240.

47 Francis Bacon, 'Of Deformity' (1597), in *Lord Bacon's Essays, or Counsels Moral and Civil*, trans. by William Willimot, 2 vols (London: H. Parson, J. Brotherton and W. Meadows, A. Bettesworth, S. Ballard, R. Gosling, and C. King, 1720), 271–3.

48 Bacon, 'Of Deformity', 271.

49 Bacon, 'Of Deformity', 272.

50 Bacon, 'Of Deformity', 271.

51 Shelley, *Frankenstein*, 139.

52 For example, when Victor comments on his father's 'cursory glance' and uninformed dismissal of his reading of Cornelius Agrippa, he says that, if

his father had taken the time to explain or read Agrippa, 'It is even possible, that the train of my ideas would never have received the fatal impulse that led to my ruin.' Shelley, *Frankenstein*, 68.

53 Shelley, 'On Frankenstein', 730.

54 Erasmus Darwin, *Zoonomia; or, The Laws of Organic Life*, 2 vols (London: J. Johnson, 1794–96), 1:501.

55 Maureen N. McLane, *Romanticism and the Human Sciences: Poetry, Population, and the Discourse of the Species* (Cambridge: Cambridge University Press, 1996), 100. Elizabeth Dolan suggests that Victor 'conceptualizes the creature as a different species'. Elizabeth Dolan, *Seeing Suffering in Women's Literature of the Romantic Era* (Aldershot: Ashgate, 2008), 59.

56 The 1823 (Thomas) edition adds a sentence to the creation scene in which Victor describes 'the contortions that ever and anon convulsed & deformed his un-human features', but this addition did not reach the 1831 edition. Mary Wollstonecraft Shelley, *Frankenstein: or, The Modern Prometheus. The 1818 Text*, ed. by James Rieger (Chicago, IL: University of Chicago Press, 1974), 52. McLane comments that this is perhaps an attempt 'to establish immediately the difference in species being'. McLane, *Romanticism and the Human Sciences*, 88. Several of McLane's claims about the concepts used to describe the creature are based on evidence from annotations of the 1823 edition that were never published. For example, McLane cites the reference to 'un-human features', and Walton's comment that 'if what we saw was an optical delusion, it was the most perfect and wonderful recorded in the history of nature'. *Frankenstein*, ed. Rieger, 18. We may want to be cautious about building a case on ideas that the author rejected.

57 Shelley, *Frankenstein*, 82.

58 Shelley, *Frankenstein*, 168.

59 McLane, *Romanticism and the Human Sciences*, 90.

60 Shelley, *Frankenstein*, 161.

61 Shelley, *Frankenstein*, 168.

62 Shelley, *Frankenstein*, 190.

63 See Erasmus Darwin's definition quoted above. Darwin, *Zoonomia*, 1:501.

64 Shelley, *Frankenstein*, 126. David Marshall suggests that the creature may be regarded as a monster on the grounds of him merely resembling a human being. David Marshall, *The Surprising Effects of Sympathy: Marivaux, Diderot, Rousseau, and Mary Shelley* (Chicago, IL: University of Chicago Press, 1988), 208.

65 Friedman, 'Foreword', xvii.

66 Baldick, *In Frankenstein's Shadow*, 8.

67 Anne K. Mellor, *Mary Shelley: Her Life, Her Fiction, Her Monsters* (New York: Routledge, 1989), 63.

68 Richman, 'Monstrous Elocution', 191. See Jeffrey A. Brune and Daniel J. Wilson, eds., *Disability and Passing: Blurring the Lines of Identity* (Philadelphia, PA: Temple University Press, 2013).

69 McLane, *Romanticism and the Human Sciences*, 84.

70 McLane, *Romanticism and the Human Sciences*, 85.
71 Jenny Davidson notes that the issue of 'whether the human race was indeed a single species ... or whether the races represented different species of men' was 'a particularly pressing question for eighteenth-century commentators' such as Henry Home, Lord Kames, scientists such as William Lawrence and John Gregory. Jenny Davidson, *Breeding: A Partial History of the Eighteenth Century* (New York: Columbia University Press, 2009), 92.
72 Shelley, *Frankenstein*, 94.
73 Shelley, *Frankenstein*, 57.
74 H. L. Malchow, 'Frankenstein's Monster and Images of Race in Nineteenth-Century Britain', *Past & Present* 139 (1993): 90–130 (90).
75 John Clement Ball, 'Imperial Monstrosities: *Frankenstein*, the West Indies, and V. S. Naipaul', *ARIEL: A Review of International Literature* 32.3 (2001): 31–58 (36).
76 Ball, 'Imperial Monstrosities', 39.
77 Laurence Lipking cautions us to remain aware of a 'liberal consensus' that results in a selective reading of *Frankenstein* in his challenge to critics who see Victor as an oppressor and his creature as a victim. Lipking composes a laundry list of items that appear in selective readings. 'Item: Frankenstein is a degenerate offspring of a dysfunctional family; Not Worth Mentioning: every character in the book loves and admires him ... Item: Frankenstein's abandonment of his Creature is an act of unforgivable irresponsibility; Not Worth Mentioning: the Creature murders a small child and frames an innocent woman for the crime.' Lipking argues that readers should feel ambivalent about 'who fills the role of hero or villain'. Laurence Lipking, '*Frankenstein* the True Story; or, Rousseau Judges Jean-Jacques', in Mary Shelley, *Frankenstein: The 1818 Text*, ed. by J. Paul Hunter (New York: W. W. Norton: 1996): 313–31 (319, 317, and 319).
78 Bruce Wyse, '"The Human Senses Are Insurmountable Barriers": Deformity, Sympathy, and Monster Love in Three Variations on *Frankenstein*', in *Global Frankensteins*, ed. by Carol Margaret Davison and Marie Mulvey-Roberts (Cham, Switzerland: Palgrave Macmillan, 2018), 75–90 (77).
79 Amy Viadli, 'Seeing What We Know: Disability and Theories of Metaphor', *Journal of Literary and Cultural Disability Studies* 4.1 (2010): 33–54 (42).
80 Mary Poovey, 'My Hideous Progeny: Mary Shelley and the Feminization of Romanticism', *PMLA* 95 (1980): 332–47 (337).
81 Poovey, 'My Hideous Progeny', 337.
82 Shelley, *Frankenstein*, 31.
83 Shelley, 'On *Frankenstein*', cited in Six and Thompson, 'From Hideous to Hedonist', 240.
84 Six and Thompson, 'From Hideous to Hedonist', 240.
85 Six and Thompson, 'From Hideous to Hedonist', 240.
86 Six and Thompson, 'From Hideous to Hedonist,' 240.
87 Dean Franco, 'Mirror Images and Otherness in Mary Shelley's *Frankenstein*', *Literature and Psychology* 44 (1998): 80–95 (89).

88 Franco, 'Mirror Images and Otherness', 90.
89 Franco, 'Mirror Images and Otherness', 89. James Heffernan suggests that the silencing of the creature in the film versions of *Frankenstein* 'forces us to face the monster's physical repulsiveness'. James Heffernan, 'Looking at the Monster: *Frankenstein* and Film', *Critical Inquiry* 24 (1997): 133–58 (136).
90 Baldick *In Frankenstein's Shadow*, 10.
91 Baldick, *In Frankenstein's Shadow*, 16.
92 Fred Botting, 'Reflections of Excess: *Frankenstein*, the French Revolution and Monstrosity', in *Reflections of Revolution: Images of Romanticism*, ed. by Alison Yarrington and Kelvin Everest (London: Routledge, 1993), 28–38 (28).
93 Lee Sterrenburg, 'Mary Shelley's Monster: Politics and Psyche in *Franken-stein*', in *The Endurance of Frankenstein: Essays on Mary Shelley's Novel*, ed. by George Levine and U. C. Knoepflmacher (Berkeley: University of California Press, 1979), 143–71. See also Warren Montag, '"The Workshop of Filthy Creation": A Marxist Reading of *Frankenstein*', in Mary Shelley, *Franken-stein*, ed. by Johanna M. Smith. Case Studies in Contemporary Criticism (Boston: Bedford, 1992), 300–311 (300).
94 Sandra M. Gilbert and Susan Gubar, *The Madwoman in the Attic: The Woman Writer and the Nineteenth-Century Literary Imagination* (New Haven, CT: Yale University Press, 1984), 241. Barbara Johnson argues against these interpretations, suggesting that monstrosity 'is so incompatible with femininity that Frankenstein cannot even complete the female companion that his creature so eagerly awaits'. Barbara Johnson, 'My Monster/ My Self', *Diacritics* 12 (1982): 2–10 (7).
95 Alan Bewell, 'An Issue of Monstrous Desire: *Frankenstein* and Obstetrics', *Yale Journal of Criticism* 2 (1988): 105–28 (112).
96 Bewell, 'An Issue of Monstrous Desire', 116.
97 Thomas, *Romanticism and Visuality*, 2.
98 W. J. T. Mitchell, *Picture Theory: Essays in Verbal and Visual Representation* (Chicago, IL: University of Chicago Press, 1994), 16.
99 Mitchell, *Picture Theory*, 16.
100 Mitchell, *Picture Theory*, 12.
101 See Rosemarie Garland Thomson, 'The Politics of Staring: Visual Rhetorics of Disability in Popular Photography', in *Disability Studies: Enabling the Humanities*, ed. by Sharon L. Snyder, Brenda Jo Brueggemann, and Rosemarie Garland Thomson (New York: MLA, 2002), 56–75; and Rosemarie Garland Thomson, *Staring: How We Look* (New York: Oxford University Press, 2009). Garland Thomson draws on Foucault in her theorizing of looking both in the context of identity formation and as part of science. She comments that 'scientific observation and its twin, medical diagnosis, require sustained, intense looking that is imagined as untainted by the viewer's subjectivity'. Garland Thomson, *Staring*, 28. Additionally, Paul Youngquist engages with Foucault when he describes Victor Frankenstein's creature's retaliation for his stigmatization as a 'response to the regulatory force of the

norm of the proper body'. The creature takes 'vengeance on the bodies that the norm so invisibly advantages'. Youngquist, *Monstrosities*, 55.

102 Garland Thomson, 'The Politics of Staring', 56.

103 Garland Thomson, 'The Politics of Staring', 57.

104 Garland Thomson, *Staring*, 46.

105 Garland Thomson, 'The Politics of Staring', 56.

106 Jenny Sager, working on early modern drama and modern cinema, notes that in the early modern period the term 'spectacle', in theology, politics, poetry, and drama, referred to 'a person or object capable of inciting horror, contempt or admiration'. It is 'the sight of a strange or unfamiliar thing or person [such as the Queen], which incites speculation'. Using Philip Fisher's idea of the unfamiliar as a varied form of the familiar, Sager defines 'wonder' as 'the shock of the new' that means that 'the audience needs to make what was strange familiar'. Sighted people who are caught up in spectacle, Fisher argues, rely on their memories to understand the visual rhetoric at work in a particular scene. Just as plays carry with them what Sager calls 'the burden of their theatrical past[,] . . . so people who become spectacles carry with them a visual context'. Jenny Sager, *The Aesthetics of Spectacle in Early Modern Drama and Modern Cinema: Robert Greene's Theatre of Attractions* (Basingstoke: Palgrave Macmillan, 2013), 29, 30, 47, and 48. See Philip Fisher, *Wonder, the Rainbow, and the Aesthetics of Rare Experiences* (London: Harvard University Press, 1998).

107 Garland Thomson, 'The Politics of Staring', 56.

108 Lennard J. Davis, *Enforcing Normalcy: Disability, Deafness, and the Body* (London: Verso, 1995), 129.

109 Garland Thomson, *Staring*, 28.

110 Galperin, *The Return of the Visible in British Romanticism*, 23.

111 Galperin, *The Return of the Visible in British Romanticism*, 23.

112 Galperin, *The Return of the Visible in British Romanticism*, 31. Galperin echoes here M. H. Abrams's seminal study *The Mirror and the Lamp: Romantic Theory and the Critical Tradition* (London: Oxford University Press, 1953), which traces the literary development from neoclassical imitation to romantic expression.

113 William Wordsworth, *The Prelude: The Four Texts (1798, 1799, 1805, 1850)*, ed. by Jonathan Wordsworth (London: Penguin, 1995), (1805), 5.470–73.

114 Wordsworth, *The Prelude* (1805), 5.473.

115 Wordsworth, *The Prelude* (1805), 5.475–7.

116 Galperin, *The Return of the Visible in British Romanticism*, 23.

117 Galperin, *The Return of the Visible in British Romanticism*, 111.

118 Galperin claims, further, that this response 'is also a response to the contradiction that *is romanticism*'. Galperin, *The Return of the Visible in British Romanticism*, 23.

119 Galperin, *The Return of the Visible in British Romanticism*, 111.

120 Cynthia Chase, 'The Accidents of Disfiguration: Limits to the Literal and Rhetorical Reading in Book V of "The Prelude"', *Studies in Romanticism* 18.4 (1979): 547–65 (557).

121 Geoffrey Hartman observes that 'the landscape of fairy story and romance ... had anticipated such terrors; that ghastly face was, therefore, a poetic rather than soul-debasing spectacle. This imaginative literature continues the child's "natural" maturation by keeping it from being plunged too quickly into the adult world'. Geoffrey Hartman, *Wordsworth's Poetry 1787–1814* (New Haven, CT: Yale University Press, 1971), 232.

122 Galperin, *The Return of the Visible in British Romanticism*, 127.

123 Wordsworth, *The Prelude* (1805), 7.600; (1850), 7.633. The second sight reference evokes, for Edward Larrissy, the connection 'between blindness and bardic vision which would have been automatic for a contemporary reader'. Edward Larrissy, *The Blind and Blindness in Literature of the Romantic Period* (Edinburgh: Edinburgh University Press, 2007), 128.

124 Wordsworth, *The Prelude* (1805), 7.620–21; (1850), 7.648–9.

125 Galperin, *The Return of the Visible in British Romanticism*, 121.

126 Galperin, *The Return of the Visible in British Romanticism*, 121.

127 Galperin, *The Return of the Visible in British Romanticism*, 124. In his reading of 'autobiographical discourse as a discourse of self-restoration', Paul de Man points out that 'figures of deprivation, maimed men, drowned corpses, blind beggars, children about to die, that appear throughout *The Prelude* are figures of Wordsworth's own poetic self'. Paul de Man, 'Autobiography as De-facement', *Modern Language Notes* 94.5 (1979): 919–30 (925 and 924). The idea of Wordsworth's perception of himself as a blind beggar (his perceiving I) is consistent with recent readings of blindness in *The Prelude* that focus on Wordsworth's own experiences of eye disease and his fears of becoming blind.

128 Neil Hertz, 'The Notion of Blockage in the Literature of the Sublime', in *The End of the Line: Essays on Psychoanalysis and the Sublime* (New York: Columbia University Press, 1985), 62–84 (84).

129 Galperin, *The Return of the Visible in British Romanticism*, 111.

130 Galperin, *The Return of the Visible in British Romanticism*, 121.

131 Abrams, *The Mirror and the Lamp*, 58.

132 Abrams, *The Mirror and the Lamp*, 69.

133 Abrams, *The Mirror and the Lamp*, 68.

134 Abrams, *The Mirror and the Lamp*, 57.

135 Abrams, *The Mirror and the Lamp*, 59.

136 Abrams, *The Mirror and the Lamp*, 59.

137 Garland Thomson, *Staring*, 185.

138 The first name of Monsieur De Lacey is not mentioned in the text and so I shall refer to him as De Lacey or Monsieur De Lacey. This character is frequently referred to in reductionist terms as 'the blind De Lacey', 'old De Lacey', and 'blind old De Lacey'. See McLane, *Romanticism and the Human*

*Sciences*, 101; Larrissy, *The Blind and Blindness in the Literature of the Romantic Period*, 188; Eileen Hunt Botting, *Frankenstein and the Rights of the Child* (Philadelphia: University of Pennsylvania Press, 2018), 119; Richman, 'Monstrous Elocution', 207; Ellen J. Goldner, 'Monstrous Body, Tortured Soul: *Frankenstein* at the Juncture between Discourses', in *Genealogy and Literature*, ed. by Lee Quinby (Minneapolis: University of Minnesota Press, 1995), 28–47 (35).

139  I depart here from Elizabeth Dolan's view that the creature's diseased eyes and fear of contagion prevent 'Victor from looking at his creature compassionately'. Dolan, whose interests are in the medical humanities, invokes 'the history of the contagious disease ophthalmia' as a context for understanding Shelley's view of the interplay between sensibility and sight. 'Fear of contagion', she suggests, 'limits the viewer's ability to see both suffering and individual subjectivity in "the other".' Dolan, *Seeing Suffering*, 52, 50, and 50. Heather Tilley suggests that 'fear of contagion might limit the viewer's ability to see both suffering and individual subjectivity in "the other"', and asserts that Wordsworth's sense of 'dislocation' as a poet as originates in ophthalmia. Heather Tilley, *Blindness and Writing: From Wordsworth to Gissing* (Cambridge: Cambridge University Press, 2018), 46.

140  Shelley, *Frankenstein*, 50.
141  Shelley, *Frankenstein*, 51.
142  Shelley, *Frankenstein*, 51.
143  Shelley, *Frankenstein*, 53.
144  Shelley, *Frankenstein*, 58.
145  Shelley, *Frankenstein*, 58.
146  Shelley, *Frankenstein*, 58.
147  Shelley, *Frankenstein*, 60.
148  Shelley, *Frankenstein*, 61.
149  Shelley, *Frankenstein*, 231.
150  Shelley, *Frankenstein*, 230.
151  Shelley, *Frankenstein*, 231.
152  Shelley, *Frankenstein*, 232.
153  Shelley, *Frankenstein*, 240.
154  Shelley, *Frankenstein*, 240.
155  Shelley, *Frankenstein*, 242.
156  Shelley, *Frankenstein*, 235.
157  Shelley, *Frankenstein*, 78.
158  The vision of other characters similarly turns negative during periods of grief or distress. Elizabeth's vision changes after Justine's erroneous conviction for murdering William; she says: 'I no longer see the world and its works as they before appeared to me. Before, I looked upon the accounts of vice and injustice, that I read in books or heard from others, as tales of ancient days, or imaginary evils ... but now ... men appear to me as monsters thirsting for each other's blood.' After Clerval's death, Victor sees around him 'nothing but a dense and frightful darkness, penetrated by no light but the

glimmer of two eyes that glared upon me. Sometimes they were the expressive eyes of Henry, languishing in death, the dark orbs nearly covered by the lids, and the long lashes that fringed them; sometimes it was the watery clouded eyes of the monster, as I first saw them in the chamber of Ingolstadt'. Victor's vision has changed so intensely in this moment that he can only focus on eyes themselves. Shelley, *Frankenstein*, 119–20 and 206.

159 Shelley, *Frankenstein*, 59.
160 Galperin, *The Return of the Visible in British Romanticism*, 111.
161 Shelley, *Frankenstein*, 57.
162 Walton uses several metaphors that evoke painting. The friend Walton seeks will look with sense, affection, and perspective (*'keeping'*). Shelley, *Frankenstein*, 53. Walton also characterizes his inability to think about the potential failure of the voyage as not being able to look at 'the reverse of the picture'. Shelley, *Frankenstein*, 55.
163 Shelley, *Frankenstein*, 57.
164 Shelley, *Frankenstein*, 59.
165 Shelley, *Frankenstein*, 204.
166 Shelley, *Frankenstein*, 89–90.
167 Shelley, *Frankenstein*, 86.
168 Shelley, *Frankenstein*, 85.
169 Shelley, *Frankenstein*, 85.
170 Shelley, *Frankenstein*, 86. Victor is not sure at this point in the narrative whether the creature had retained language, and adds that he 'might have spoken, but I did not hear'. Shelley, *Frankenstein*, 86.
171 Shelley, *Frankenstein*, 86.
172 Garland Thomson, *Staring*, 41.
173 'grin, v.2.' *OED Online* (Oxford: Oxford University Press, 2018). Accessed 8 September 2018.
174 'grin, v.2.' *OED Online*.
175 Shelley, *Frankenstein*, 86.
176 Phoebe C. Ellsworth, J. Merrill Carlsmith, and Alexander Henson, 'The Stare as a Stimulus to Flight in Human Subjects: A Series of Field Experiments', *Journal of Personality and Social Psychology* 21.3 (1972): 301–11 (311).
177 Shelley, *Frankenstein*, 240.
178 Shelley, *Frankenstein*, 86 and 85. Like the word 'grin', the word 'wretch' is ambiguous. It either expresses sympathy or is a term of abuse. '2.a. One who is sunk in deep distress, sorrow, misfortune, or poverty; a miserable, unhappy, or unfortunate person; a poor or hapless being.' '3.a. A vile, sorry, or despicable person; one of opprobrious or reprehensible character; a mean or contemptible creature.' 'wretch, n. and adj.' *OED Online* (Oxford University Press, 2018). Accessed 8 September 2018. The ambiguity lends itself to the doubleness in this scene (beauty/deformity; death/life).
179 Shelley, *Frankenstein*, 85.

180 James Chandler reads *Frankenstein* as a literalization of Adam Smith's account of the possibility of sympathizing with the 'deformed and mangled carcass' of a slain man. Smith, Chandler observes, 'does not imagine such physical deformity as an obstacle to sympathetic identification'. Chandler, *An Archeology of Sympathy*, 245, citing Adam Smith's *The Theory of Moral Sentiments*.

181 Shelley, *Frankenstein*, 139.

182 Shelley, *Frankenstein*, 139.

183 Shelley, *Frankenstein*, 166.

184 Shelley, *Frankenstein*, 130.

185 I explore how 'Shelley's novel includes a pervasive set of metaphors connected with sight and blindness' and how it 'problematizes both our understanding of the tensions between sight and sightlessness, and the pervasive historiographies with which the novel engages' in Joshua, 'Blind Vacancy', 50.

186 Larrissy, *The Blind and Blindness in Literature of the Romantic Period*, 188.

187 Larrissy, *The Blind and Blindness in Literature of the Romantic Period*, 188–9.

188 Larrissy, *The Blind and Blindness in Literature of the Romantic Period*, 188.

189 Larrissy, *The Blind and Blindness in Literature of the Romantic Period*, 2.

190 Tobin Siebers, *Disability Theory* (Ann Arbor: University of Michigan Press, 2008), 112.

191 Siebers, *Disability*, 112.

192 Shelley, *Frankenstein*, 159.

193 For example, Eileen Hunt Botting comments that De Lacey's 'blindness frees his judgment of prejudice'. Botting, *Frankenstein and the Rights of the Child*, 124.

194 Shelley, *Frankenstein*, 75.

195 For an exploration of blindness in eighteenth-century art, see Georgina Cole, 'Rethinking Vision in Eighteenth-Century Paintings of the Blind', in *Art as Visual Epistemology*, ed. Harald Klinke (Newcastle upon Tyne: Cambridge Scholars, 2014), 47–64 (62).

196 Poovey, 'My Hideous Progeny', 337.

197 Richman, 'Monstrous Elocution,' 205.

198 Richman, 'Monstrous Elocution,' 207.

199 Tobin Siebers, 'Disability as Masquerade', *Literature and Medicine* 23.1 (2004): 1–22 (5).

200 Shelley, *Frankenstein*, 159.

201 Shelley, *Frankenstein*, 158. James Holman alludes to himself as gaining a kind of political neutrality as a blind Englishman in Napoleonic France. Although he is 'surrounded by a people, to me, strange, invisible, and incomprehensible', he remarks that he is treated as a 'citizen of the world', and his blindness removes some of the obstacles that an English traveller would have experienced at this time. James Holman, *The Narrative of a Journey Undertaken in the Years 1819, 1820, & 1821, through France* (London: F. C. and J. Rivington, 1822), 3.

202 Shelley, *Frankenstein*, 159.
203 Shelley, *Frankenstein*, 157.
204 Shelley, *Frankenstein*, 157.
205 Shelley, *Frankenstein*, 222.
206 Shelley, *Frankenstein*, 312.
207 Shelley, *Frankenstein*, 207.
208 Shelley, *Frankenstein*, 172. My emphasis.
209 Larrissy explores this aspect of the cultural history of blindness in depth in *The Blind and Blindness in Literature of the Romantic Period*, 2–35.
210 McLane, *Romanticism and the Human Sciences*, 101.
211 Shelley, *Frankenstein*, 127.
212 Shelley, *Frankenstein*, 127.
213 Shelley, *Frankenstein*, 126.
214 Shelley, *Frankenstein*, 167.
215 Shelley, *Frankenstein*, 167.
216 Shelley, *Frankenstein*, 89.
217 Shelley, *Frankenstein*, 167. My emphasis.
218 Shelley, *Frankenstein*, 167.
219 Shelley, *Frankenstein*, 167.
220 See Davis, *Enforcing Normalcy*, 143. See also Mark Mossman, 'Acts of Becoming: Autobiography, *Frankenstein*, and the Postmodern Body', *Postmodern Culture* 11.3 (2001): 1–12; Wang, 'The Historicist Turn of Romantic-Era Disability Studies'; and Gilbert and Gubar, *The Madwoman in the Attic*, 239.
221 Richman, 'Monstrous Elocution', 188 and 189. Richman cites Joshua, 'Blind Vacancy'; Mossman, 'Acts of Becoming'; and Wang, 'The Historicist Turn of Romantic-Era Disability Studies', as disability studies accounts of the visual.
222 Thomas, *Romanticism and Visuality*, 3.
223 Thomas, *Romanticism and Visuality*, 7.
224 Kate Flint, *The Victorians and the Visual Imagination* (Cambridge: Cambridge University Press, 2000), 2.
225 Davis, *Enforcing Normalcy*, 129.
226 Like Galperin, Davis draws on Freud in his argument that the disabled body is *unheimlich*. Davis suggests that the disabled body is perceived as 'the familiar gone wrong'. Davis, *Enforcing Normalcy*, 140 and 141. Larrissy echoes this sentiment in his description of the blind beggar as 'an overdetermined hieroglyph of social damage'. *The Blind and Blindness*, 128.
227 Thomas, *Romanticism and Visuality*, 20.
228 Flint, *The Victorians and the Visual Imagination*, 2.
229 Elizabeth Dolan, for instance, suggests that the creature's 'physical appearance prevents him from receiving' a 'level of acceptance', rather than raising the possibility that stigma works relationally. Dolan, *Seeing Suffering*, 50.
230 Heffernan, 'Looking at the Monster', 157–8.
231 Wang, 'The Historicist Turn of Romantic-Era Disability Studies', 3.

232 Wang, 'The Historicist Turn of Romantic-Era Disability Studies', 5.
233 Brooks, 'What Is a Monster?', 83–4.
234 Wang, 'The Historicist Turn of Romantic-Era Disability Studies', 10.

## Conclusion

1 Helen Deutsch argues for the eighteenth century as a 'period suspended' between religious and scientific understandings of disability, and as a period 'torn in its representations of disability between two ideas of agency – one divine and insurmountable, one human and exceptional'. Helen Deutsch, 'Exemplary Aberration: Samuel Johnson and the English Canon', in *Disability Studies: Enabling the Humanities*, ed. by Sharon Snyder, Brenda Jo Brueggemann, and Rosemarie Garland-Thomson (New York: MLA, 2002), 197–210 (198–9).

2 Some proponents of the *prodigy-to-pathology* thesis use a range of terms in their discussion of the evolution of disability. For example, Rosemary Garland Thomson refers to 'disability', 'freaks', 'prodigious monsters', and 'terata' in her account of the movement from the theological phase to the scientific. Rosemarie Garland Thomson, 'Introduction: From Wonder to Error – A Genealogy of Freak Discourse in Modernity', in *Freakery: Cultural Spectacles of the Extraordinary Body*, ed. by Rosemarie Garland Thomson (New York: New York University Press, 1996), 1–19 (3).

3 Stephen Pender suggests that the 'status of the monstrous' as portentous did not stop in the early modern period, but recirculated in later centuries. Stephen Pender, '"No Monsters at the Resurrection": Inside Some Conjoined Twins', in *Monster Theory: Reading Culture*, ed. by Jeffrey Jerome Cohen (Minneapolis: University of Minnesota Press, 1996), 143–67 (145). William Paulson argues for a similar recirculation of ideas on blindness in French literature. We may see in *Frankenstein* further support for Paulson's claims about the circulation of philosophical, sentimental, visionary, and romantic discourses on blindness.

4 Deborah Stone, *The Disabled State* (Philadelphia, PA: Temple University Press, 1984), 13 and 50.

5 Jane Austen, *Pride and Prejudice*, ed. by James Kinsley (Oxford: Oxford University Press, 2004), 29. My emphasis.

## Appendix  Dictionary Definitions of 'Disability' and 'Deformity'

1 Thomas Holcroft, *Travels from Hamburg, through Westphalia, Holland, and the Netherlands, to Paris*, 2 vols (London: Richard Phillips, 1804), 2:97.

2 Although it is extensively discussed in the eighteenth and early nineteenth centuries, deformity has also been largely excluded from recent studies of the aesthetics of the period. Peter Kivy's *The Seventh Sense*, for example, does not deal in depth with deformity, despite deformity being an important part of

Hutcheson's aesthetics. Peter Kivy, *The Seventh Sense: Francis Hutcheson and Eighteenth-Century Aesthetics* (Oxford: Oxford University Press, 2003). *The Stanford Encyclopedia of Philosophy* contains an entry on 'beauty' but not one on 'deformity'. Timothy Costelloe's *The British Aesthetic Tradition: From Shaftesbury to Wittgenstein* (Cambridge: Cambridge University Press, 2013) does not include discussion of deformity. Similarly, the critical editions of important philosophical texts often do not reference deformity in the index.

3 Anon., *The Times* 1 July 1785; 13 September 1793; 14 November 1786; 8 February 1788.

4 Anon., 'Dr. Gowland's Vegetable Lotion', *The Times*, 5 May 1790, 1. 'Tetters' are pustular eruptions of the skin (*OED* [2008]).

5 Dictionaries of literary terms, critical theory, and encyclopedias have recently begun to include disability. See Janet K. Boles and Diane Long Hoeveler, eds, 'Women with Disabilities', *Historical Dictionary of Feminism*, 2nd edn (Lanham, MD: Scarecrow, 2004); Nicole Markotić, 'Disability Studies', in *The Johns Hopkins Guide to Literary Theory and Criticism*, ed. by Michael Groden et al. (Baltimore, MD: Johns Hopkins University Press, 2008); Rosemarie Garland Thomson, 'Physical Disability', in Elizabeth Kowaleski Wallace, ed., *Encyclopedia of Feminist Literary Theory* (Abingdon, Oxon: Routledge, 2009); Peter Auger, 'Disability Studies', in *The Anthem Dictionary of Literary Terms and Theory* (London: Anthem, 2010); and J. A. Cuddon, 'Disability Studies', in *A Dictionary of Literary Terms and Literary Theory*, 5th edn, rev. by M. A. R. Habib (Oxford: Wiley-Blackwell, 2013). For recent dictionaries, handbooks, and encyclopedias of Romanticism with no entries on disability studies, see Paul Baines, Julian Ferraro, and Pat Rogers, eds., *The Wiley-Blackwell Encyclopedia of Eighteenth-Century Writers and Writing 1660–1789* (Oxford: Wiley-Blackwell, 2011); Frederick Burwick, *The Encyclopedia of Romantic Literature* (Oxford: Wiley-Blackwell, 2012); Joel Faflak and Julia M. Wright, *A Handbook of Romanticism Studies* (Oxford: Wiley-Blackwell, 2012); and Paul Varner, *Historical Dictionary of Romanticism in Literature* (London: Rowman and Littlefield, 2015). For recent dictionaries of literary terms and literary theory that do not include entries on disability studies, see Chris Baldick, ed., *The Oxford Dictionary of Literary Terms*, 4th edn (Oxford: Oxford University Press, 2015).

6 John Kersey, *A New English Dictionary* (London: Henry Bonwicke and Robert Knaplock, 1702).

7 In 1715, Edward Cocker added 'not able to perform' to 'uncapable' to his revised edition. Edward Cocker, *Cocker's English Dictionary* (London: A. Back and A. Bettesworth, 1704); Edward Cocker, *Cocker's English Dictionary* (London: T. Norris and A. Bettesworth, 1715).

8 Edward Phillips, *New World of Words, or Universal English Dictionary*, 6th edn, rev. by John Kersey (London: J. Phillips and J. Taylor, 1706).

9 Phillips, *New World of Words* (1706).

10 [Thomas Blount], *Glossographia Anglicana Nova; Or, a Dictionary* (London: D. Brown, T. Goodwin, J. Walthoe, M. Newborough, J. Nicholson, B. Took, D. Midwinter, and F. Coggan, 1707); John Kersey, *Dictionarium*

*Anglo-Britannicum* (London: J. Wilde, H. Rhodes, and J. Taylor, 1708); John Kersey, *A New English Dictionary* (London: Robert Knaplock, R. and J. Bonwicke, 1713); Elisha Coles, *An English Dictionary* (London: F. Collins, R. Bonwicke, 1713); Cocker, *Cocker's English Dictionary*, 1715; Elisha Coles, *An English Dictionary* (London: F. Collins, R. Bonwicke, 1717); Nathan Bailey, *An Universal English Dictionary* (London: E. Bell, J. Darby. A. Bettesworth, F. Fayram, J. Pemberton, J. Hooke, C. Rivington, F. Clay, J. Batley, F. Symon et al., 1724); Nathan Bailey, *Dictionarium Britannicum* (London: T. Cox, 1730); John Kersey, *A New English Dictionary* (London: Robert Knaplock, R. and J. Bonwicke, 1731); John Kersey, *A New English Dictionary* (London: J. and J. Bonwicke and H. Knaplock, 1739); Benjamin Martin, *Lingua Britannica Reformata* (London: J. Hodges et al., 1749); John Kersey, *A New Classical English Dictionary*, 7th edn (Dublin: S. Powell, 1757); John Kersey, *A New English Dictionary* (London: L. Hawes, W. Clarke, R. Collins, S. Crowder, S. Bladen, R. Baldwin, W. Woodfall, 1772).

11  Phillips, *New World of Words* (1706).

12  Samuel Johnson, *A Dictionary of the English Language*, 2nd edn, 2 vols (London: W. Strahan, 1755). Johnson defines 'to disable' as '1. To deprive of natural force; to weaken; to crush. . . . 2. To impair; to diminish. . . . 3. To make unactive. . . . 4. To deprive of usefulness or efficacy. . . . 5. To exclude as wanting proper qualifications.'

13  There are variations on it in John Marchant, *A New Complete English Dictionary* (London: J. Fuller, 1760); Nathan Bailey, *A Universal Etymological Dictionary of the English Language* (Edinburgh: printed for the proprietors, 1764); Francis Allen, *A Complete English Dictionary* (London: J. Wilson and J. Fell, 1765); Anne Fisher, *An Accurate New Spelling Dictionary* (London: Hawes, Clarke, Collins, G. Robinson, E. Stevens, and T. Slack, 1773); Anne Fisher, *An Accurate New Spelling Dictionary* (London: G. G. J. and J. Robinson and T. Slack, 1784); Anne Fisher, *An Accurate New Spelling Dictionary* (London: G. Robinson, W. Nicoll, and S. Hodgson, 1788); John Bentick, *The Spelling and Explanatory Dictionary of the English Language* (London: Thomas Carnan, 1786); Stephen Jones, *A General Pronouncing and Explanatory Dictionary of the English Language* (London: Vernor, Hood; J. Cuthel, Ocilvy, Lackington, Allen, 1797); Thomas Browne, *The Union Dictionary* (London: J. W. Myers, 1800).

14  Robert Bage, *Hermsprong; Or Man as He Is Not*, 3 vols (London: Minerva, 1796), 3:69.

15  William Hazlitt, *The Spirit of Age; or Contemporary Portraits*, 2nd edn (London: Henry Colburn, 1825), 23.

16  Hazlitt, *The Spirit of Age*, 24.

17  Tobias Smollett, *The Adventures of Peregrine Pickle*, ed. by James L. Clifford and Paul-Gabriel Boucé, Oxford World's Classics (Oxford: Oxford University Press, 1983), 153.

18  William Godwin, *Things as They Are or The Adventures of Caleb Williams*, ed. by Maurice Hindle (London: Penguin, 1988), 213.

19 William Godwin, *Cloudesley* [1830], ed. by Maurice Hindle (London: William Pickering, 1992), 7:242.
20 Smollett, *Peregrine Pickle*, 38.
21 William Godwin, *Deloraine* [1833], ed. by Maurice Hindle (London: William Pickering, 1992), 8:188.
22 Phillips, *New World of Words* (1706).
23 Edward Chamberlayne and John Chamberlayne, *Angliae Notitia: or the Present State of England, with Divers Remarks upon the Ancient State Therof* (London: S. Smith, B. Walford, T. Goodwin, M. Wooton, B. Tooke, T. Leigh, D. Midwinter, 1704), 420.
24 Chamberlayne and Chamberlayne, *Angliae Notitia*, 422.
25 James Murray, ed., *A New English Dictionary on Historical Principles*, 10 vols (Oxford: Clarendon Press, 1897); *The Oxford English Dictionary*, 12 vols (Oxford: Clarendon Press, 1933); *Oxford English Dictionary*, 2nd edn (Oxford: Oxford University Press, 1989).
26 *Oxford English Dictionary*, 3rd edn (Oxford: Oxford University Press, 2008).
27 Put in terms of the social model of disability, sense (2) would be the cause of the impairment, rather than the disability.
28 George Herbert, 'The Crosse', in *The Works of George Herbert*, ed. by F. E. Hutchison (Oxford: Clarendon Press, 1941), 164–5 (165), ll. 17–18.
29 Sense (2) of 'disabled' allows for a malfunctioning body part, but this sense overlaps with sense (1) and so is difficult to isolate.
30 Richard Cumberland, *Henry*, 4 vols (London: Charles Dilly, 1795), 1:152.
31 Philip Doddridge, *The Family Expositor*, 2 vols (London: John Wilson, 1740), 2:147.
32 Doddridge, *The Family Expositor*, 2:147, n. i.
33 I have been unable to find an eighteenth-century example of sense (4b).
34 *Papers Illustrative of the Origin and Early History of the Royal Hospital at Chelsea* (London: George E. Eyre and William Spottiswoode, 1872), 5.
35 *Papers Illustrative of the Origin and Early History of the Royal Hospital at Chelsea*, 5.
36 Geoffrey Hudson points out that these pensions were intended to keep demobilized soldiers in order, and to prevent 'former servicemen, [who were] destitute, [and] maimed' from begging in the streets. They were also 'a practical preventative measure against desertion, [and] evasion of impressment'. Geoffrey L. Hudson, 'Disabled Veterans and the State in Early Modern England', in *Disabled Veterans in History*, ed. by David L. Gerber (Ann Arbor: University of Michigan Press, 2012), 117–44 (119).
37 David Turner, *Disability in Eighteenth-Century England: Imagining Physical Impairment* (New York: Routledge, 2012), 21.
38 Francis Grose, *Military Antiquities Respecting a History of the English Army from the Conquest to the Present Time*, 2 vols (London: T. Egerton, 1801), 2:85.

39 Grose, *Military Antiquities*, 2:86.
40 Hudson, 'Disabled Veterans and the State in Early Modern England', 128.
41 Hudson, 'Disabled Veterans and the State in Early Modern England', 128.
42 Cited in Hudson, 'Disabled Veterans and the State in Early Modern England', 129.
43 Hudson, 'Disabled Veterans and the State in Early Modern England', 128.
44 Quoted in Robert Southey, *The Life of Nelson* (London: George Routledge, 1886), 110.
45 Quoted in Southey, *The Life of Nelson*, 110.
46 Anon., 'On the Death of Lord Nelson', *The Times*, 23 November 1805, 3.
47 William Wordsworth, *The Major Works*, ed. by Stephen Gill (Oxford: Oxford University Press, 2000), 320 (l. 2).
48 Bernard Mandeville, *The Fable of the Bees: Or, Private Vices, Publick Benefits*, 2nd edn (London: Edmund Parker, 1723), 121.
49 Caroline Louise Nielsen, 'The Chelsea Out-Pensioners: Image and Reality in Eighteenth-Century and Early Nineteenth-Century Social Care', PhD Diss. (University of Newcastle, August 2014), 13.
50 Nielsen, 'The Chelsea Out-Pensioners', 17.
51 Nielsen, 'The Chelsea Out-Pensioners', xi.
52 Nielsen, 'The Chelsea Out-Pensioners', xi. Nielsen's is the only historical study of eighteenth-century disabled soldiers to include an account of literature and to acknowledge a disability studies perspective. David Gerber's *Disabled Veterans in History* does not spend much time on the Romantic period, though it is a revisionist account theorized in ways that reflect recent work in disability studies.
53 Alexander Bicknell, *The History of Lady Anne Neville, Sister to the Great Early of Warwick*, 2 vols (London: T. Cadell, 1776), 1:164–5.
54 Johnson, *A Dictionary of the English Language* (1755)
55 Bailey, *Dictionarium Britannicum* (1730).
56 Kersey, *A New English Dictionary* (1702).
57 Kersey, *A New English Dictionary* (1702).
58 Blount, *Glossographia Anglicana Nova* (1707).
59 Blount, *Glossographia Anglicana Nova* (1707).
60 Blount, *Glossographia Anglicana Nova* (1707).
61 John Bullokar, *The English Expositor Improv'd* (London: A. and J. Churchill, 1707).
62 Kersey, *A New English Dictionary* (1713).
63 Cocker, *Cocker's English Dictionary* (1715).
64 Allen, *A Complete English Dictionary* (1765).
65 Fisher, *An Accurate New Spelling Dictionary* (1773).
66 For more on 'monsters', see *Monster Theory: Reading Culture*, ed. by Jeffrey Jerome Cohen (Minneapolis: University of Minnesota Press, 1996); Paul Youngquist, *Monstrosities: Bodies and British Romanticism* (Minneapolis: University of Minnesota Press, 2003); and Asa Simon Mittman and Peter J. Dendle, *The Ashgate Research Companion to Monsters and the Monstrous*

(Farnham: Ashgate, 2012). For more on 'wonders', see Lorraine Daston and Katharine Park, *Wonders and the Order of Nature 1150–1750* (New York: Zone, 1998).

67 Johnson, *A Dictionary of the English Language* (1755).
68 Joseph Nicol Scott, *A New Universal Etymological Dictionary* (London: T. Osborne and J. Shipton; J. Hodges; R. Baldwin; W. Johnston, and J. Ward, 1755).
69 Nicol Scott, *A New Universal Etymological Dictionary* (1755).
70 Kersey, *A New English Dictionary* (1702).
71 Davis, 'Dr. Johnson', 59. For more on *lusus naturae* see Paula Findlen, 'Jokes of Nature and Jokes of Knowledge: The Playfulness of Scientific Discourse in Early Modern Europe', *Renaissance Quarterly* 43.2 (1990): 292–331.
72 The entry for 'freak' has only been partially updated since 1898.
73 See Helen Deutsch and Felicity Nussbaum, 'Introduction', in *'Defects': Engendering the Modern Body* (Ann Arbor: University of Michigan Press, 2000), 1–28.
74 Philip Dormer Stanhope [Earl of Chesterfield], 'Elegance of Expression', *Principles of Politeness, and of Knowing the World*, ed. by John Trussler, 8th edn (London: J. Bell, 1778), 29–34 (29).
75 Deutsch and Nussbaum, 'Introduction', in *'Defects'*, 2.
76 Johnson, *A Dictionary of the English Language* (1755).
77 Kersey, *A New English Dictionary* (1702).
78 Phillips, *The New World of English Words* (1706).
79 Nicol Scott, *A New Universal Etymological Dictionary*.
80 Marchant, *A New Complete English Dictionary* (1760).
81 Bailey, *A Universal Etymological Dictionary of the English Language* (1764).
82 See, for example, Deutsch and Nussbaum, *'Defects'*; Simon Dickie, *Cruelty and Laughter: Forgotten Comic Literature and the Unsentimental Eighteenth Century* (Chicago, IL: University of Chicago Press, 2011), 45–110; David M. Turner, *Disability in Eighteenth-Century England: Imagining Physical Impairment* (New York: Routledge, 2012), 16–34; and Katherine Schaap Williams, '"More Legs than Nature Gave Thee": Performing the Cripple in *The Fair Maid of the Exchange*', *English Literary History* 82.2 (2015): 491–519.

# Bibliography

## PRIMARY

Addison, Joseph, and Richard Steele. *The Spectator.* 5 vols. Ed. Donald Bond. Oxford: Clarendon Press, 1965.

Allen, Francis. *A Complete English Dictionary: Containing an Explanation of All the Words Made Use of in the Common Occurrences of Life, or in the Several Arts and Sciences.* London: J. Wilson and J. Fell, 1765. Gale. Eighteenth Century Collections Online.

Anon. *The Times.* 1 July 1785. *Times Digital Archive: 1785–1985.*

*The Times.* 14 November 1786. *Times Digital Archive: 1785–1985.*

*The Times.* 8 February 1788. *Times Digital Archive: 1785–1985.*

'Dr. Gowland's Vegetable Lotion.' *The Times.* 5 May 1790. 1. *Times Digital Archive: 1785–1985.*

'*A Vindication of the Rights of Woman.*' *The Critical Review.* 5 n.s. June (1792): 132–41.

'The Story of a Disabled Soldier.' *The New London Magazine.* March 1793. 127–30.

*The Times.* 13 September 1793. *Times Digital Archive: 1785–1985.*

'Review of *Historical . . . View . . . of the French Revolution.*' *The New Annual Register,* 1794. 221–2. In *Mary Wollstonecraft and the Critics 1788–2001.* Ed. Harriet Devine Jump. 2 vols. London: Routledge, 2002.

'Review of *Historical . . . View . . . of the French Revolution.*' *Monthly Review.* 16 n.s. (1795): 393–402.

'The Disabled Soldier.' In *Satirical, Humourous, and Familiar Pieces of Prose.* Manchester: G. Nicholson, 1796. 1–6.

'Art. XXV. *Camilla; or, A Picture of Youth.* By the Author of Evelina and Cecilia.' *English Review* 28 (1796): 178–80. Gale. Eighteenth Century Collections Online.

'On the Death of Lord Nelson.' *The Times.* 23 November 1805. 3. *Times Digital Archive: 1785–1985.*

'The Disabled Soldier.' *The Literary Mirror.* 1 (11 June 1808): 65.

Austen, Jane. *Pride and Prejudice.* Ed. James Kinsley. Oxford: Oxford University Press, 2004.

Bacon, Francis. 'Of Deformity.' In *Lord Bacon's Essays, or Counsels Moral and Civil*. Trans. William Willimot. 2 vols. London: H. Parson, J. Brotherton and W. Meadows, A. Bettesworth, S. Ballard, R. Gosling, and C. King, 1720. 271–73.

Bage, Robert. *Mount Henneth, A Novel*. 2 vols. London: T. Lowndes, 1782.

*Hermsprong; Or Man as He Is Not*. 3 vols. London: Minerva, 1796. Gale. Eighteenth Century Collections Online.

*Hermsprong; Or Man as He Is Not*. Ed. Pamela Perkins. Peterborough, Ontario: Broadview, 2002.

Bailey, Nathan. *An Universal English Dictionary: Comprehending the Derivations of the Generality of Words in the English Tongue*. London: E. Bell, J. Darby. A. Bettesworth, F. Fayram, J. Pemberton, J. Hooke, C. Rivington, F. Clay, J. Batley, F. Symon et al., 1724. Gale. Eighteenth Century Collections Online.

*Dictionarium Britannicum: Or a More Compleat Universal Etymological English Dictionary Than any Extant. Containing Not Only the Words, and Their Explication; But Their Etymologies*. London: T. Cox, 1730. Gale. Eighteenth Century Collections Online.

*A Universal Etymological Dictionary of the English Language. Comprehending the Derivations of the Generality of Words in the English Tongue, Either Antient or Modern*. Edinburgh: printed for the proprietors, 1764. Gale. Eighteenth Century Collections Online.

Bentick, John. *The Spelling and Explanatory Dictionary of the English Language*. London: Thomas Carnan, 1786. Gale. Eighteenth Century Collections Online.

Bicknell, Alexander. *The History of Lady Anne Neville, Sister to the Great Early of Warwick*. 2 vols. London: T. Cadell, 1776. Gale. Eighteenth Century Collections Online.

Blount, Thomas. *Glossographia Anglicana Nova: Or, A Dictionary*. London: D. Brown, T. Goodwin, J. Walthoe, M. Newborough, J. Nicholson, B. Took, D. Midwinter, and F. Coggan, 1707. Eighteenth Century Collections Online.

Browne, Thomas. *The Union Dictionary, Containing All That Is Truly Useful in the Dictionaries of Johnson, Sheridan, and Walker*. London: J. W. Myers, 1800. Gale. Eighteenth Century Collections Online.

Bullokar, John. *The English Expositor Improv'd*. London: A. and J. Churchill, 1707. Gale. Eighteenth Century Collections Online.

Burke, Edmund. *A Vindication of Natural Society: Or, a View of the Miseries and Evils Arising to Mankind from Every Species of Artificial Society. In a Letter to Lord \*\*\*\* by a Late Noble Writer*. London: M. Cooper, 1756.

*A Philosophical Enquiry into the Origin of Our Ideas of the Sublime and Beautiful*. Ed. Adam Phillips. Oxford: Oxford University Press, 1990.

Burney, Charles. *Memoirs of Doctor Burney*. Ed. Madame D'Arblay. 3 vols. London: Edward Moxon, 1832.

Burney, Frances. *Diary and Letters of Madame D'Arblay (1778–1840)*. Ed. *Memoirs of Doctor Burney*. 3 vols. London: Edward Moxon, 1832.
Ed. Charlotte Barrett and Austin Dobson. 6 vols. London: Macmillan, 1905. *Camilla or A Picture of Youth*. Ed. Edward A. Bloom and Lillian D. Bloom. Oxford World's Classics. Oxford: Oxford University Press, 1999.

Byron, Lord George Gordon. *The Deformed Transformed: A Drama*. London: J. and H. L. Hunt, 1824.

Chamberlayne, Edward, and John Chamberlayne. *Angliae Notitia: Or the Present State of England, with Divers Remarks upon the Ancient State Thereof.* London: S. Smith, B. Walford, T. Goodwin, M. Wooton, B. Tooke, T. Leigh, D. Midwinter, 1704.

Cocker, Edward. *Cocker's English Dictionary: Interpreting the Most Refined and Difficult Words*. London: A. Back and A. Bettesworth, 1704. Gale. Eighteenth Century Collections Online.
*Cocker's English Dictionary, Containing an Explanation of the Most Refined and Difficult Words and Terms in Divinity, Philosophy, Law, Physick, Mathematicks, Navigation, Husbandry, Military Discipline, and Other Arts and Sciences: And the Derivation of Them from the Hebrew, Greek, Latin, Italian, Spanish, French, and Other Languages*. London: T. Norris, A. Bettesworth, 1715. Gale. Eighteenth Century Collections Online.

Coleridge, Samuel Taylor. 'Selection from Mr. Coleridge's Literary Correspondence. No. 1.' *Blackwood's Edinburgh Magazine*. 10 (October 1821): 253–62.
*The Complete Poetical Works of Samuel Taylor Coleridge*. 2 vols. Ed. Ernest Hartley Coleridge. Oxford: Clarendon Press, 2000.

Coleridge, Sara. 'On the Disadvantages Resulting from the Possession of Beauty.' In *Sara Coleridge: A Victorian Daughter: Her Life and Essays*. Ed. Bradford Keyes Mudge. New Haven, CT: Yale University Press, 1989. 187–200.

Coles, Elisha. *An English Dictionary, Explaining the Difficult Terms That Are Used in Divinity, Husbandry, Physic, Philosophy, Law, Navigation, Mathematicks, and Other Arts and Science*. London: F. Collins, R. Bonwicke, 1713. Gale. Eighteenth Century Collections Online.
*An English Dictionary, Explaining the Difficult Terms That Are Used in Divinity, Husbandry, Physic, Philosophy, Law, Navigation, Mathematicks, and Other Arts and Science*. London: F. Collins, R. Bonwicke, 1717. Gale. Eighteenth Century Collections Online.

Combe, William. *The Philosopher in Bristol [1775]*. Dublin: T. Jackson, 1784.

Comte, Auguste. *Introduction to Positive Philosophy*. Ed. Frederick Ferré. Indianapolis, IN: Hackett, 1988.

Conder, Josiah. 'Coleridge's "Christabel".' *The Eclectic Review* (1816): 565–6.

Cooper, Anthony Ashley. [Lord Shaftesbury]. *Characteristics of Men, Manners, Opinions, Times*. Ed. Lawrence E. Klein. Cambridge Texts in the History of Philosophy. Cambridge: Cambridge University Press, 1999.

Crocker, Hannah Mather. *Observations on the Real Rights of Women, with Their Appropriate Duties, Agreeable to Scripture, Reason and Common Sense.* Boston, MA: Printed for the Author, 1818.

Cumberland, Richard. *Henry.* 4 vols. London: Charles Dilly, 1795.

Darwin, Erasmus. *Zoonomia; Or, The Laws of Organic Life.* 2 vols. London: J. Johnson, 1794–96.

Doddridge, Philip. *The Family Expositor.* 2 vols. London: John Wilson, 1740.

[Enfield, William, and George E. Giffiths]. 'Art. IX. *Camilla; or, A Picture of Youth.* By the Author of *Evelina* and *Cecilia.*' *Monthly Review* 21 (October 1796): 156–63.

Farington, Joseph. *The Farington Diary.* Ed. James Grieg, 4 (20 September 1806 to 7 January 1808). New York: George H. Doran, 1924.

Fenwick, Eliza. *Secresy; Or, The Ruin on the Rock.* Ed. Isobel Grundy. Peterborough, Ontario: Broadview, 1998.

*First Annual Report of the Poor Law Commissioners for England and Wales.* London: W. Clowes, 1835.

Fisher, Anne. *An Accurate New Spelling Dictionary, and Expositor of the English Language.* London: Hawes, Clarke, and Collins, G. Robinson, E. Stevens, and T. Slack, 1773. Gale. Eighteenth Century Collections Online.

*An Accurate New Spelling Dictionary, and Expositor of the English Language.* London: G. G. J. and J. Robinson and T. Slack, 1784. Gale. Eighteenth Century Collections Online.

*An Accurate New Spelling Dictionary, and Expositor of the English Language.* London: G. Robinson, W. Nicoll, and S. Hodgson, 1788. Gale. Eighteenth Century Collections Online.

Fisher, Philip *Wonder, the Rainbow, and the Aesthetics of Rare Experiences.* London: Harvard University Press, 1998.

Gilpin, William. *An Essay on Prints.* London: J. Robson, 1768.

*Observations on the River Wye, and Several Parts of South Wales, &c. Relative Chiefly to Picturesque Beauty; Made in the Summer of the Year 1770.* London: R. Blamire, 1782.

*Observations, Relative Chiefly to Picturesque Beauty, Made in the Year 1772.* 2 vols. London: R. Blamire, 1786.

*Three Essays: On Picturesque Beauty; On Picturesque Travel; and On Sketching Landscape: To Which Is Added a Poem, on Landscape Painting.* London: R. Blamire, 1792.

*Observations on Several Parts of the Counties of Cambridge, Norfolk, Suffolk, and Essex; Also on Several Parts of North Wales; Relative Chiefly to Picturesque Beauty in Two Tours, The Former Made in the Year 1769. The Latter in the Year 1773.* London: T. Cadell and W. Davies, 1809.

Godwin, William. *An Enquiry Concerning Political Justice, and Its Influence on General Virtue and Happiness.* 2 vols. London: G. G. and J. Robinson, 1793.

*Enquiry Concerning Political Justice and Its Influence on Morals and Happiness.* 2 vols. 2nd edn. London: G. G. and J. Robinson, 1796. Gale. Eighteenth Century Collections Online.

*Enquiry Concerning Political Justice and Its Influence on Morals and Happiness.* 2 vols. 3rd edn. London: G. G. and J. Robinson, 1798. Gale. Eighteenth Century Collections Online.

*Lives of the Necromancers. Or, an Account of the Most Eminent Persons in Successive Ages, Who Have Claimed for Themselves, or To Whom Has Been Imputed by Others, the Exercise of Magical Power.* London: Frederick J. Mason, 1834.

*Enquiry Concerning Political Justice.* Ed. Raymond Preston. New York: Knopf, 1926.

*Things as They Are or the Adventures of Caleb Williams.* Ed. Maurice Hindle. London: Penguin, 1988.

*Mandeville.* Ed. Pamela Clemit. London: William Pickering, 1992. Vol. 6 of *Collected Novels and Memoirs of William Godwin.* Gen. ed. Mark Philp. 9 vols. London: William Pickering, 1992.

*Cloudesley.* Ed. Maurice Hindle. London: William Pickering, 1992. Vol. 7 of *Collected Novels and Memoirs of William Godwin.* Gen. ed. Mark Philp. 9 vols. London: William Pickering, 1992.

*Deloraine.* Ed. Maurice Hindle. London: William Pickering, 1992. Vol. 8 of *Collected Novels and Memoirs of William Godwin.* Gen. ed. Mark Philp. 9 vols. London: William Pickering, 1992.

*The History of the Life of William Pitt.* In *The Political and Philosophical Writings of William Godwin.* Vol. 1: Political Writings I. Ed. Martin Fitzpatrick. London: Pickering and Chatto, 1993.

*Thoughts on Man: Essay II: Of the Distribution of Talents.* In *The Political and Philosophical Writings of William Godwin.* Vol. 6. Romanticism Redefined. Ed. Mark Philp. London: Pickering and Chatto, 1993.

*Fleetwood: Or, The New Man of Feeling.* Ed. Gary Handwerk and A. A. Markley. Peterborough, Ontario: Broadview, 2001.

*St. Leon: A Tale of the Sixteenth Century.* Ed. William D. Brewer. Peterborough, Ontario: Broadview, 2006.

*An Enquiry Concerning Political Justice.* Ed. Mark Philp. Oxford World's Classics. Oxford: Oxford University Press, 2013.

Goldsmith, Oliver. 'The Distresses of a Common Soldier.' *The British Magazine.* 1, June 1760, 369–72.

Grose, Francis. *Military Antiquities Respecting a History of the English Army from the Conquest to the Present Time.* 2 vols. London: T. Egerton, 1801.

Hamilton, Elizabeth. *Memoirs of Modern Philosophers.* Ed. Claire Grogan. Peterborough, Ontario: Broadview, 2000.

Hartley, David. *Observations on Man, His Frame, His Duty, and His Expectations.* 2 vols. London: Charles Hitch and Stephen Austen, 1749.

Hay, William. 'Deformity: An Essay.' In *The Works of William Hay, Esq.* 2 vols. London: J. Nichols, 1794.

Hays, Mary. *The Victim of Prejudice.* Ed. Eleanor Ty. 2nd edn. Peterborough, Ontario: Broadview, 1998.

Hazlitt, William. *The Spirit of Age; or Contemporary Portraits*. 2nd edn. London: Henry Colburn, 1825.

'On Imitation.' In *The Complete Works of William Hazlitt*. Ed. P. P. Howe. 21 vols. London: J. M. Dent, 1930–34. 4: 72–7.

'Essay XXXII. On the Picturesque and Ideal. A Fragment.' In *The Selected Writings of William Hazlitt*. 9 vols. Ed. Duncan Wu. London: Pickering and Chatto, 1998. 6: 284–7.

Herbert, George. *The Works of George Herbert*. Ed. F. E. Hutchison. Oxford: Clarendon Press, 1941.

Holcroft, Thomas. *Travels from Hamburg, through Westphalia, Holland, and the Netherlands, to Paris*. 2 vols. London: Richard Phillips, 1804.

*Anna St. Ives*. In *The Novels and Selected Plays of Thomas Holcroft*. Ed. W. M. Verhoeven. 5 vols. London: Pickering and Chatto, 2007.

Holman, James. *The Narrative of a Journey Undertaken in the Years 1819, 1820, & 1821, through France, Italy, Savoy, Switzerland, Parts of Germany Bordering on the Rhine, Holland, and the Netherlands; Comprising Incidents That Occurred to the Author, Who Has Long Suffered under a Total Deprivation of Sight; With Various Points of Information Collected on His Tour*. London: F. C. and J. Rivington, 1822. Googlebooks.

Hume, David. *Four Dissertations*. London: A. Millar, 1757. Gale. Eighteenth Century Collections Online.

*A Treatise of Human Nature*. Ed. Ernest C. Mossner. London: Penguin, 1985.

'Of the Standard of Taste.' In *Moral Philosophy*. Ed. Geoffrey Sayre-McCord. Indianapolis: Hackett, 2006. 345–60.

Hutcheson, Francis. *An Inquiry into the Original of Our Ideas of Beauty and Virtue; in Two Treatises. I. Concerning Beauty, Order, Harmony, Design. II. Concerning Moral Good and Evil*. 2nd edn. London: J. Darby, A. Bettesworth, F. Fayram, J. Pemberton, C. Rivington, J. Hooke, F. Clay, J. Batley, and E. Symon, 1726.

Johnson, Samuel. *A Dictionary of the English Language*. 2nd edn. 2 vols. London: W. Stahan, 1755. Gale. Eighteenth Century Collections Online.

Jones, Stephen. *A General Pronouncing and Explanatory Dictionary of the English Language*. London: Vernor, Hood; J. Cuthel, Ocilvy, Lackington, Allen, 1797. Gale. Eighteenth Century Collections Online.

Kersey, John. *A New English Dictionary; Or, Compleat Collection of the Most Proper and Significant Words, Commonly Used in the Language; With a Short and Clear Exposition of Difficult Words and Terms of Art*. London: Henry Bonwicke and Robert Knaplock, 1702. Gale. Eighteenth Century Collections Online.

*Dictionarium Anglo-Britannicum; Or, a General English Dictionary, Comprehending a Brief, But Emphatical and Clear Explication of All Sorts of Difficult Words*. London: J. Wilde, H. Rhodes, and J. Taylor, 1708. Gale. Eighteenth Century Collections Online.

*A New English Dictionary*. London: Robert Knaplock and R. and J. Bonwicke, 1713. Gale. Eighteenth Century Collections Online.

*A New English Dictionary.* London: Robert Knaplock and R. and J. Bonwicke, 1731. Gale. Eighteenth Century Collections Online.

*A New English Dictionary.* London: J. and J. Bonwicke and H. Knaplock, 1739. Gale. Eighteenth Century Collections Online.

*A New Classical English Dictionary, Or, a Complete Collection of the Most Proper and Significant Words, and Terms of Art, Commonly Used in the Language.* 7th edn. Dublin: S. Powell, 1757. Gale. Eighteenth Century Collections Online.

*A New English Dictionary.* London: L. Hawes, W. Clarke, R. Collins, S. Crowder, S. Bladen, R. Baldwin, W. Woodfall, 1772. Gale. Eighteenth Century Collections Online.

Knight, Richard Payne. *The Landscape: A Didactic Poem in Three Books. Addressed to Uvedale Price, Esq.* 2nd edn. London: W. Bulmer, 1794.

*An Analytical Inquiry into the Principles of Taste.* 3rd edn. London: Luke Hansard, T. Payne, and J. White, 1806.

Lavater, Johann Caspar. *Essays on Physiognomy.* Trans. Henry Hunter. 3 vols. London: John Murray, 1789.

Locke, John. *An Essay Concerning Human Understanding.* Ed. Peter H. Nidditch. Oxford: Oxford University Press, 1975.

Lockhart, John Gibson. *Memoirs of the Life of Sir Walter Scott.* 10 vols. Boston, MA: Houghton, Mifflin, 1901.

Mackenzie, Henry. *The Man of Feeling.* Ed. Maureen Harkin. Peterborough, Ontario: Broadview, 2005.

Mandeville, Bernard. *The Fable of the Bees: Or, Private Vices, Publick Benefits.* 2nd edn. London: Edmund Parker, 1723. Gale. Eighteenth Century Collections Online.

Marchant, John. *A New Complete English Dictionary.* London: J. Fuller, 1760. Gale. Eighteenth Century Collections Online.

Martin, Benjamin. *Lingua Britannica Reformata: Or, a New English Dictionary.* London: J. Hodges et al., 1749.

Milton, John. 'Paradise Lost.' In *The Complete Poetry and Essential Prose of John Milton.* Ed. William Kerrigan, John Rumrich, and Stephen M. Fallon. New York: The Modern Library, 2007. 293–697.

Murray, James. Ed. *A New English Dictionary on Historical Principles; Founded Mainly on the Materials Collected by the Philological Society.* 10 vols. Oxford: Clarendon Press, 1897.

Nicol Scott, Joseph. *Universal Etymological Dictionary.* London: T. Osborne and J. Shipton; J. Hodges; R. Baldwin; W. Johnston, and J. Ward, 1755. Gale. Eighteenth Century Collection Online.

*The Oxford English Dictionary, Being a Corrected Reissue with an Introduction, Supplement, and Bibliography of a New English Dictionary on Historical Principles Founded Mainly on the Materials Collected by the Philological Society.* 12 vols. Oxford: Clarendon Press, 1933.

*The Oxford English Dictionary.* 2nd edn. Oxford: Oxford University Press, 1989. Online version 2015.

*Oxford English Dictionary.* 3rd edn. Oxford: Oxford University Press, 2008. Online version 2015.

*Papers Illustrative of the Origin and Early History of the Royal Hospital at Chelsea.* London: George E. Eyre and William Spottiswoode, 1872.

Parr, Samuel. *A Spital Sermon, Preached at Christ Church, upon Easter Tuesday, April 15, 1800: To Which Are Added Notes.* London: J. Mawman, 1801. Hathi Trust.

Phillips, Edward. *New World of Words, Or Universal English Dictionary.* 6th edn. Rev. John Kersey. London: J. Phillips and J. Taylor, 1706. Gale. Eighteenth Century Collections Online.

Pratt, John Tidd. *A Collection of All the Statutes in Force Respecting the Relief and Regulation of the Poor, With Notes and References.* 2nd edn. London: Shaw, 1843.

Price, Uvedale. *An Essay on the Picturesque, as Compared with the Sublime and the Beautiful; and, on the Use of Studying Pictures, for the Purpose of Improving Real Landscape.* London: J. Robson, 1794.

  *A Dialogue on the Distinct Characters of the Picturesque and the Beautiful in Answer to the Objections of Mr. Knight.* London: J. Robson, 1801.

  *Essays on the Picturesque as Compared with the Sublime and Beautiful; and On the Use of Studying Pictures for the Purpose of Improving Real Landscape.* 3 vols. London: J. Mawman, 1810.

Reid, Thomas. *Essays on the Intellectual Powers of Man.* Edinburgh: John Bell and G. G. J. and J. Robinson, 1785. Googlebooks.

Robinson, Mary. *Walsingham; or the Pupil of Nature.* Ed. Julie A. Shaffer. Peterborough, Ontario: Broadview, 2003.

Rousseau, Jean-Jacques. *Emile or On Education.* Trans. Allan Bloom. London: Penguin, 1991.

  *Julie, or The New Heloise. Letters of Two Lovers Who Live in a Small Town at the Foot of the Alps. The Collected Writings of Rousseau.* 14 vols. Trans. Philip Stewart and Jean Vaché. Hanover, NH: Dartford College Press, 1997. Vol. 6.

Salzmann, Christian Gotthilf. *Moralisches Elementarbuch: nebst einer Anleitung zum nützlichen Gebrauch desselben.* 2 vols. Leipzig: Siegfried Lebrecht Crusius, 1785.

Scott, Sarah. *Millenium Hall.* Ed. Gary Kelly. Peterborough, Ontario: Broadview, 1995.

Sheldon, John. *An Essay on the Fracture of the Patella or Kneepan. Containing a New and Efficacious Method of Treating That Accident, by Which the Deformity and Lameness That Arise from the Old and Common Mode of Treatment, Are Avoided. With Observations on the Fracture of the Olecranon.* London: J. Johnson, P. Elmsley, T. Cadell, E, and C, Dilly, G. G. G. J. and J. Robinson, and J. Robson, 1789.

Shelley, Mary. *Frankenstein: or, The Modern Prometheus. The 1818 Text.* Ed. James Rieger. Chicago, IL: University of Chicago Press, 1974.

*Frankenstein; Or the Modern Prometheus [1818]*. Ed. D. L. Macdonald and Kathleen Scherf. 2nd edn. Peterborough, Ontario: Broadview, 1999.

*Frankenstein: The Original 1818 Text*. Ed. D. L. Macdonald and Kathleen Scherf. 2nd edn. Peterborough, Ontario: Broadview, 2005.

*Frankenstein: The 1818 Text*. Ed. J. Paul Hunter. 2nd edn. New York: Norton, 2012.

Shelley, P. B. 'On Frankenstein.' *Athenaeum*. 10 November 1832. 730.

*The Letters of Percy Bysshe Shelley*. 2 vols. Ed. Roger Ingpen. London: Isaac Pitman, 1909.

'A Defence of Poetry.' *Percy Bysshe Shelley: The Major Works*. Ed. Zachary Leader and Michael O'Neill. Oxford: Oxford University Press, 2003. 674–701.

Smith, Adam. *The Theory of Moral Sentiments*. London: A. Millar, 1759.

Smollett, Tobias *The Adventures of Peregrine Pickle*. Ed. James L. Clifford and Paul-Gabriel Boucé. Oxford World's Classics. Oxford: Oxford University Press, 1983.

Southey, Robert. *The Life of Nelson*. London: George Routledge, 1886.

Stanhope, Philip Dormer. [Earl of Chesterfield]. *Principles of Politeness, and of Knowing the World*. Ed. John Trussler. 8th edn. London: J. Bell, 1778.

Wollstonecraft, Mary. *Original Stories from Real Life; With Conversations, Calculated to Regulate the Affections, and Form the Mind to Truth and Goodness*. London: J. Johnson, 1788. Gale. Eighteenth Century Collections Online.

'M' [Mary Wollstonecraft]. 'Art, VI. Camilla; or A Picture of Youth. By the Author of Evelina and Cecilia.' *The Analytical Review* (August 1796): 142–8.

('W.Q') 'On Poetry, and Our Relish for the Beauties of Nature.' *The Monthly Magazine* 3 (April 1797): 279–82.

*Collected Letters of Mary Wollstonecraft*. Ed. Ralph M. Wardle. Ithaca, NY: Cornell University Press, 1979.

*A Short Residence in Sweden, Norway and Denmark and William Godwin, Memoirs of the Author of 'The Rights of Woman'*. Ed. Richard Holmes. London: Penguin, 1987.

*A Vindication of the Rights of Men, A Vindication of the Rights of Woman, An Historical and Moral View of the French Revolution*. Ed Janet Todd. Oxford World's Classics. Oxford: Oxford University Press, 1993.

*Mary and The Wrongs of Woman*. Ed. Gary Kelly. Oxford World's Classics. Oxford: Oxford University Press, 1998.

'Elements of Morality for the Use of Children.' In *The Works of Mary Wollstonecraft*. Ed. Janet Todd, Marilyn Butler, and Emma Rees-Mogg. 7 vols. London: Pickering and Chatto, 2004. Electronic edition. 2: 3–210.

'Thoughts on the Education of Daughters.' In *The Works of Mary Wollstonecraft*. Ed. Janet Todd, Marilyn Butler, and Emma Rees-Mogg. 7 vols. London: Pickering and Chatto, 2004. Electronic edition. 4: 2–49.

'An Historical and Moral View of the Origin and Progress of the French Revolution and the Effect It Has Produced in Europe.' In *The Works of Mary Wollstonecraft*. Ed. Janet Todd, Marilyn Butler, and Emma Rees-Mogg. 7 vols. London: Pickering and Chatto, 2004. Electronic edition. 6: 2–235.

'Letter on the Character of the French Nation.' In *The Works of Mary Wollstonecraft*. Ed. Janet Todd, Marilyn Butler, and Emma Rees-Mogg. 7 vols. London: Pickering and Chatto, 2004. Electronic edition. 6: 440–46.

Wordsworth, William. *The Prose Works of William Wordsworth*. Ed. W. J. B. Owen and Jane Worthington Smyser. 3 vols. Oxford: Clarendon Press, 1974.

*Poetical Works*. Ed. Thomas Hutchinson. Rev. Ernest de Selincourt. Oxford: Oxford University Press, 1981.

'Preface (1802).' *Lyrical Ballads*. Ed. Michael Mason. London: Longman, 1992. 55–87.

*The Letters of William and Dorothy Wordsworth, A Supplement of New Letters*. Ed. Alan G. Hill. Vol. 8. Oxford: Clarendon Press, 1993.

*The Prelude: The Four Texts (1798, 1799, 1805, 1850)*. Ed. Jonathan Wordsworth. London: Penguin, 1995.

'[The Discharged Soldier] (edited from MS; composed late January 1798).' In *Romanticism: An Anthology*. Ed. Duncan Wu. 2nd edn. Oxford: Blackwell, 1998. 273–7.

*The Major Works*. Ed. Stephen Gill. Oxford: Oxford University Press, 2000.

*Wordsworth's Tract on the Convention of Cintra [Published 1809] with Two Letters of Wordsworth Written in the Year 1811 Now Republished*. Ed. A. V. Dicey. London: Humphrey Milford, 1915. Hathi Trust.

## SECONDARY

Abbey, Ruth. 'Back to the Future: Marriage as Friendship in the Thought of Mary Wollstonecraft.' *Hypatia*. 14.3 (1999): 78–95.

Abrams, M. H. *The Mirror and the Lamp: Romantic Theory and the Critical Tradition*. London: Oxford University Press, 1953.

Annandale, Ellen. 'Assembling Harriet Martineau's Gender and Health Jigsaw.' *Women's Studies International Forum*. 30.4 (2007): 355–66.

Armintor, Deborah Needleman. *The Little Everyman: Stature and Masculinity in Eighteenth-Century English Literature*. Seattle: University of Washington Press, 2011.

Auger, Peter. *The Anthem Dictionary of Literary Terms and Theory*. London: Anthem, 2010.

Austin, Linda. *Nostalgia in Transition: 1780–1917*. Charlottesville: University of Virginia Press, 2007.

Averill, James H. *Wordsworth and the Poetry of Human Suffering*. Ithaca, NY: Cornell University Press, 1980.

Badowska, Eva. 'The Anorexic Body of Liberal Feminism: Mary Wollstonecraft's *A Vindication of the Rights of Woman.*' In *Mary Wollstonecraft and the Critics 1788–2001.* Ed. Harriet Devine Jump. 2 vols. London: Routledge, 2002. 2: 320–40.

Baldick, Chris. *In Frankenstein's Shadow: Myth, Monstrosity, and Nineteenth-Century Writing.* Oxford: Clarendon Press, 1987.

Ed. *The Oxford Dictionary of Literary Terms.* 4th edn. Oxford: Oxford University Press, 2015.

Ball, John Clement. 'Imperial Monstrosities: *Frankenstein*, the West Indies, and V. S. Naipaul.' *ARIEL: A Review of International Literature.* 32.3 (2001): 31–58.

Bainbridge, Simon. *British Poetry and the Revolutionary and Napoleonic Wars: Visions of Conflict.* Oxford: Oxford University Press, 2003.

Baines, Paul, Julian Ferraro, and Pat Rogers. Eds. *The Wiley-Blackwell Encyclopedia of Eighteenth-Century Writers and Writing 1660–1789.* Oxford: Wiley-Blackwell, 2011.

Barker-Benfield, G. J. 'Mary Wollstonecraft's Depression and Diagnosis: The Relation between Sensibility and Women's Susceptibility to Nervous Disorders.' *Psychohistory Review.* 13.4 (1985): 15–31.

'Mary Wollstonecraft: Eighteenth-Century Commonwealthwoman.' In *Mary Wollstonecraft and the Critics 1788–2001.* Ed. Harriet Devine Jump. 2 vols. London: Routledge, 2002. 2: 39–59.

Barnes Colin, and Geof Mercer. 'Breaking the Mould: An Introduction to Doing Disability Research.' In *Doing Disability Research.* Ed Colin Barnes and Geof Mercer. Leeds: Disability Press, 1997. 1–13.

*Disability.* Cambridge: Polity, 2003.

Barton, Ellen L. 'Textual Practices of Erasure: Representations of Disability and the Founding of the United Way.' In *Embodied Rhetorics: Disability in Language and Culture.* Ed. James C. Wilson and Cynthia Lewiecki-Wilson. Carbondale: Southern Illinois University Press, 2001. 169–99.

Baynton, Douglas C. 'Disability and the Justification of Inequality in American History.' In *The New Disability History: American Perspectives.* Ed. Paul K. Longmore and Laura Umansky. New York: New York University Press, 2001. 33–57.

Beatty, Heather R. *Nervous Disease in Late Eighteenth-Century Britain: The Reality of a Fashionable Disorder.* London: Pickering and Chatto, 2012.

Becker, Lawrence C. 'Impartiality and Ethical Theory.' *Ethics.* 101.4 (1991): 698–700.

Benedict, Barbara M. 'Making a Monster: Socializing Sexuality and the Monster of 1790.' In *'Defects': Engendering the Modern Body.* Ed. Helen Deutsch and Felicity Nussbaum. Ann Arbor: University of Michigan Press, 2000. 127–53.

'Displaying Difference: Curious Count Boruwlaski and the Staging of Class Identity.' *Eighteenth-Century Life.* 30.3 (2006): 78–106.

Berkowitz, Gerald. *David Garrick: A Reference Guide.* Boston, MA: G. K. Hall, 1980.

Bérubé, Michael. 'Disability and Narrative.' *PMLA.* 120.2 (2005): 568–76.

Bewell, Alan. 'An Issue of Monstrous Desire: *Frankenstein* and Obstetrics.' *Yale Journal of Criticism.* 2 (1988): 105–28.

Bohrer, Susan F. 'Harriet Martineau: Gender, Disability and Liability.' *Nineteenth-Century Contexts.* 25 (2003): 21–37.

Boles, Janet K., and Diane Long Hoeveler. Eds. *Historical Dictionary of Feminism.* 2nd edn. Lanham, MD: Scarecrow, 2004.

Bolt, David. *The Metanarrative of Blindness: A Rereading of Twentieth-Century Anglophone Writing.* Ann Arbor: University of Michigan Press, 2014.

Botting, Eileen Hunt. *Frankenstein and the Rights of the Child.* Philadelphia: University of Pennsylvania Press, 2018.

Botting, Fred. 'Reflections of Excess: *Frankenstein*, the French Revolution and Monstrosity.' In *Reflections of Revolution: Images of Romanticism.* Ed. Alison Yarrington and Kelvin Everest. London: Routledge, 1993. 28–38.

Bradshaw, Michael. Ed. *Disabling Romanticism: Body, Mind, Text.* Michael Bradshaw. London: Palgrave Macmillan, 2016.

'"Its Own Concentred Recompense": The Impact of Critical Disability Studies on Romanticism.' *Humanities.* 8.2 (2019): 1–11.

Bradshaw, Michael, and Essaka Joshua. 'Introduction.' In *Disabling Romanticism: Body, Mind, and Text.* Ed. Michael Bradshaw. London: Palgrave Macmillan, 2016. 1–27.

Brennan. Matthew C. '"The Ghastly Figure Moving at My Side": The Discharged Soldier as Wordsworth's Shadow.' *Wordsworth Circle.* 18.1 (1987): 19–23.

Brewer, William D. 'Mary Shelley on the Therapeutic Value of Language.' In *Critical Essays on Mary Wollstonecraft Shelley.* New York: G. K. Hall, 1998. 152–65.

Brody, Miriam. 'The Vindication of the Writes of Women: Mary Wollstonecraft and Enlightenment Rhetoric.' In *Feminist Interpretations of Mary Wollstonecraft.* Ed. Maria J. Falco. University Park: Pennsylvania State University Press, 1996. 105–23.

Bromwich, David. *Disowned by Memory: Wordsworth's Poetry of the 1790s.* Chicago, IL: University of Chicago Press, 1998.

Brooks, Peter. 'What Is a Monster? (According to Frankenstein).' In *Frankenstein. New Casebooks.* Ed. Fred Botting. Houndmills, Basingstoke: Macmillan, 1995. 81–106.

Brown, Stephen W., and Warren McDougall. Eds. *The Edinburgh History of the Book in Scotland. Volume 2: Enlightenment and Expansion 1707–1800.* Edinburgh: Edinburgh University Press, 2012.

Bruhm, Steven. 'William Godwin's *Fleetwood*: The Epistemology of the Tortured Body.' *Eighteenth-Century Life.* 16.2 (1992) 25–43.

Brune, Jeffrey A., and Daniel J. Wilson. Eds. *Disability and Passing: Blurring the Lines of Identity.* Philadelphia, PA: Temple University Press, 2013.

Bullard, Paddy. *Edmund Burke and the Art of Rhetoric*. Cambridge: Cambridge University Press, 2011.

Burwick, Frederick. *Poetic Madness and the Romantic Imagination*. University Park: Pennsylvania State University Press, 1996.

*The Encyclopedia of Romantic Literature*. Oxford: Wiley-Blackwell, 2012.

Butler, Marilyn. *Romantics, Rebels and Reactionaries: English Literature and Its Background 1760–1830*. Oxford: Oxford University Press, 1982.

*Burke, Paine, Godwin, and the Revolution Controversy*. Ed. Marilyn Butler. Cambridge English Prose Texts. Cambridge: Cambridge University Press, 1984. 1–17.

Carman, Colin. 'Godwin's *Fleetwood*, Shame and the Sexuality of Feeling.' *Nineteenth-Century Prose*. 41 (2014): 225–54.

Chandler, James. *Wordsworth's Second Nature: A Study of the Poetry and Politics*. Chicago, IL: Chicago University Press, 1984.

'Proving a History of Evidence.' In *Questions of Evidence: Proof, Practice, and Persuasion across the Disciplines*. Ed. James Chandler, Arnold I. Davidson, and Harry Harootunian. Chicago, IL: University of Chicago Press, 1994. 275–81.

*An Archeology of Sympathy: The Sentimental Mode in Literature and Cinema*. Chicago, IL: University of Chicago Press, 2013.

Chase, Cynthia. 'The Accidents of Disfiguration: Limits to the Literal and Rhetorical Reading in Book V of "The Prelude".' *Studies in Romanticism*. 18.4 (1979): 547–65.

Claeys, Gregory. 'The Effects of Property on Godwin's Theory of Justice.' *Journal of the History of Philosophy*. 22.1 (1984): 81–101.

Clemit, Pamela. *The Godwinian Novel: The Rational Fictions of Godwin, Brockden Brown and Mary Shelley*. Oxford: Oxford University Press, 1993.

Codr, Dwight. '"Her failing voice endeavoured, in vain, to articulate": Sense and Disability in the Novels of Elizabeth Inchbald.' *Philological Quarterly*. 87 (2008): 359–388.

Coffee, Alan M. S. 'Freedom as Independence: Mary Wollstonecraft and the Grand Blessing of Life.' *Hypatia*. 29.4 (2014): 908–24.

Cohen, Jeffrey Jerome. Ed. *Monster Theory: Reading Culture*. Minneapolis: University of Minnesota Press, 1996.

Cole, Georgina. 'Rethinking Vision in Eighteenth-Century Paintings of the Blind.' In *Art as Visual Epistemology*. Ed. Harald Klinke. Newcastle upon Tyne: Cambridge Scholars, 2014. 47–64.

Connelly, Tristanne, and Steve Clark. Eds. *Liberating Medicine: 1720–1835*. London: Pickering and Chatto, 2009.

Costelloe, Timothy. *The British Aesthetic Tradition: From Shaftesbury to Wittgenstein*. Cambridge: Cambridge University Press, 2013.

Craciun, Adriana. 'Violence against Difference: Mary Wollstonecraft and Mary Robinson.' In *Making History: Textuality and the Forms of Eighteenth Century Culture*. Ed. Greg Clingham. Lewisburg, PA: Bucknell University Press, 1998. 111–41.

Cuddon, J. A. A. *Dictionary of Literary Terms and Literary Theory*. 5th edn. Rev. M. A. R. Habib. Oxford: Wiley-Blackwell, 2013.

Darlington, Beth. 'Two Early Texts: *A Night-Piece* and *The Discharged Soldier*.' In *Bicentenary Wordsworth Studies in Memory of John Alban Finch*. Ed. Jonathan Wordsworth Ithaca, NY: Cornell University Press, 1970. 425–48.

'Wordsworth and the Alchemy of Healing.' *The Wordsworth Circle*. 29.1 (1998) 52–60.

Dart, Gregory. *Rousseau, Robespierre and English Romanticism*. Cambridge: Cambridge University Press, 1999.

Daston, Lorraine. 'Marvelous Facts and Miraculous Evidence in Early Modern Europe.' In *Questions of Evidence: Proof, Practice, and Persuasion across the Disciplines*. Ed. James Chandler, Arnold I. Davidson, and Harry Harootunian. Chicago, IL: University of Chicago Press, 1994. 243–74.

'Historical Epistemology.' In *Questions of Evidence: Proof, Practice, and Persuasion across the Disciplines*. Ed. James Chandler, Arnold I. Davidson, and Harry Harootunian. Chicago, IL: University of Chicago Press, 1994. 282–9.

Daston, Lorraine, and Katharine Park. *Wonders and the Order of Nature 1150–1750*. New York: Zone, 1998.

Davidson, Arnold I. *The Emergence of Sexuality: Historical Epistemology and the Formation of Concepts*. Cambridge, MA: Harvard University Press, 2001.

Davidson, Jenny. *Breeding: A Partial History of the Eighteenth Century*. New York: Columbia University Press, 2009.

Davis, Lennard J. *Enforcing Normalcy: Disability, Deafness, and the Body*. London: Verso, 1995.

'Dr. Johnson, *Amelia*, and the Discourse of Disability in the Eighteenth Century.' In *'Defects': Engendering the Modern Body*. Ed. Helen Deutsch and Felicity Nussbaum. Ann Arbor: University of Michigan Press, 2000. 54–74.

Ed. *The Disability Studies Reader*. 2nd edn. New York: Routledge, 2006.

'Seeing the Object as in Itself It Really Is: Beyond the Metaphor of Disability.' *The Madwoman and the Blindman: Jane Eyre, Discourse, Disability*. Ed. David Bolt, Julia Miele Rodas, and Elizabeth J. Donaldson. Columbus: Ohio University Press, 2012. ix–xii.

Davis, Todd F., and Kenneth Womack. Eds. *Mapping the Ethical Turn: A Reader in Ethics, Culture, and Literary Theory*. Charlottesville: University of Virginia Press, 2001.

De Man, Paul. 'Autobiography as De-facement.' *Modern Language Notes*. 94.5 (1979): 919–30.

Deutsch, Helen. 'Exemplary Aberration: Samuel Johnson and the English Canon.' In *Disability Studies: Enabling the Humanities*. Ed. Sharon Snyder, Brenda Jo Brueggemann and Rosemarie Garland-Thomson. New York: MLA, 2002. 197–210.

Deutsch, Helen, and Felicity Nussbaum. Eds. *'Defects': Engendering the Modern Body*. Ann Arbor: University of Michigan Press, 2000.

Dickie, Simon. *Cruelty and Laughter: Forgotten Comic Literature and the Unsentimental Eighteenth-Century.* Chicago, IL: University of Chicago Press, 2011.

Dolan, Elizabeth A. *Seeing Suffering in Women's Literature of the Romantic Era.* Aldershot: Ashgate, 2008.

Doody, Margaret Anne. *Frances Burney: The Life in the Works.* New Brunswick, NJ: Rutgers University Press, 1988.

Drake, Robert F. 'A Critique of the Role of Traditional Charities.' In *Disability and Society: Emerging Issues and Insights.* Ed. Len Barton. Longman Sociology Series. London: Longman, 1996. 147–66.

Duff, Kerry. 'Biographies of Scale.' *Disability Studies Quarterly.* 25.4 (2005).

Elfenbein, Andrew. 'Editor's Introduction. Byron and Disability.' *European Romantic Review.* 12:3 (2001): 247–8.

Ellsworth, Phoebe C., J. Merrill Carlsmith, and Alexander Henson. 'The Stare as a Stimulus to Flight in Human Subjects: A Series of Field Experiments.' *Journal of Personality and Social Psychology.* 21.3 (1972), 301–11.

Engel, David M. 'Origin Myths: Narratives of Authority, Resistance, Disability, and Law.' *Law and Society Review.* 27.4 (1993): 785–826.

Ennis, Daniel James. *Enter the Press-Gang: Naval Impressment in Eighteenth-Century British Literature.* Newark: University of Delaware Press, 2002.

Epstein, Julia. *The Iron Pen: Frances Burney and the Politics of Women's Writing.* Bristol: Bristol Classical Press, 1989.

Faflak, Joel, and Julia M. Wright. *A Handbook of Romanticism Studies.* Oxford: Wiley-Blackwell, 2012.

Farr, Jason S. 'Sharp Minds/Twisted Bodies: Intellect, Disability, and Female Education in Frances Burney's *Camilla.' The Eighteenth Century.* 55.1 (2014): 1–17.

Feinberg, Joel. *Doing and Deserving: Essays in the Theory of Responsibility.* Princeton, NJ: Princeton University Press, 1970.

Findlen, Paula. 'Jokes of Nature and Jokes of Knowledge: The Playfulness of Scientific Discourse in Early Modern Europe.' *Renaissance Quarterly.* 43:2 (1990): 292–331.

Finke, Laurie A. 'A Philosophic Wanton: Language and Authority in Wollstonecraft's *Vindication of the Rights of Woman.'* In *Mary Wollstonecraft and the Critics 1788–2001.* Ed. Harriet Devine Jump. 2 vols. London: Routledge, 2002. 2: 1–21.

Finkelstein, Victor. *Attitudes and Disabled People: Issues for Discussion.* New York: World Rehabilitation Fund, 1980.

Fisher, Philip. *Wonder, the Rainbow, and the Aesthetics of Rare Experiences.* London: Harvard University Press, 1998.

Flint, Kate. *The Victorians and the Visual Imagination.* Cambridge: Cambridge University Press, 2000.

Franco, Dean. 'Mirror Images and Otherness in Mary Shelley's *Frankenstein.' Literature and Psychology.* 44 (1998): 80–95.

Franklin, Caroline. *Mary Wollstonecraft: A Literary Life.* Houndmills, Basingstoke: Palgrave Macmillan, 2004.

Frawley, Maria. '"A Prisoner to the Couch": Harriet Martineau, Invalidism and Self-Representation.' In *The Body and Physical Difference: Discourses of Disability.* Ed. David T. Mitchell and Sharon L. Snyder. Ann Arbor: University of Michigan Press, 1997.

*Invalidism and Identity in Nineteenth-Century Britain.* Chicago, IL: University of Chicago Press, 2004.

Friedman, John Block. 'Foreword.' In *The Ashgate Research Companion to Monsters and the Monstrous.* Ed. Asa Simon Mittman and Peter J. Dendle. Farnham: Ashgate, 2012. xv–xxxix.

Foucault, Michel. *The Use of Pleasure: The History of Sexuality Volume 2.* Trans. Robert Hurley. London: Penguin, 1992.

*Discipline and Punish: The Birth of the Prison.* Trans. Alan Sheridan. London: Penguin, 1997.

*The Will to Knowledge: The History of Sexuality Volume 1.* Trans. Robert Hurley. London: Penguin, 1998.

Gabbard, Dwight Christopher. 'Disability Studies in the British Long Eighteenth Century.' *Literature Compass.* 8.2 (2011): 80–94.

Galperin, William H. *The Return of the Visible in British Romanticism.* Baltimore, MD: Johns Hopkins University Press, 1993.

Garden, Rebecca. 'Illness and Inoculation: Narrative Strategies in Frances Burney's *Camilla.*' In *Gender Scripts and Medicine and Narrative.* Ed. Marcelline Block and Angela Laflen. Newcastle upon Tyne: Cambridge Scholars, 2010. 64–94.

Garland Thomson, Rosemarie. Ed., *Freakery: Cultural Spectacles of the Extraordinary Body.* New York: New York University Press, 1996.

*Extraordinary Bodies: Figuring Physical Disability in American Culture and Literature.* New York: Columbia University Press, 1997.

'Byron and the New Disability Studies: A Response.' *European Romantic Review.* 12 (2001): 321–7.

'Integrating Disability, Transforming Feminist Theory.' *National Women's Studies Association Journal.* 14.3 (2002): 1–32.

'The Politics of Staring: Visual Rhetorics of Disability in Popular Photography.' In *Disability Studies: Enabling the Humanities.* Ed. Sharon L. Snyder, Brenda Jo Brueggemann, and Rosemarie Garland Thomson. New York: MLA, 2002. 56–75.

*Staring: How We Look.* Oxford: Oxford University Press, 2009.

'The Story of My Work: How I Became Disabled.' *Disability Studies Quarterly.* 34.2 (2014).

Gartner, Alan, and Tom Joe. Eds. *Images of the Disabled, Disabled Images.* New York: Praeger, 1987.

Gigante, Denise. 'Facing the Ugly: The Case of *Frankenstein.*' *English Literary History.* 67 (2000): 565–87.

*Life: Organic Form and Romanticism.* New Haven, CT: Yale University Press, 2009.

Gilbert, Sandra, and Susan Gubar. *The Madwoman in the Attic: The Woman Writer and the Nineteenth-Century Imagination.* New Haven, CT: Yale University Press, 1979.

Glausner, Richard, and Anthony Savile. 'Aesthetic Experience in Shaftesbury.' *Proceedings of the Aristotelian Society* 76 (2002): 25–74.

Goffman, Erving. *Stigma: Notes on the Management of a Spoiled Identity.* New York: Simon and Schuster, 1986.

Goldner, Ellen J. 'Monstrous Body, Tortured Soul: *Frankenstein* at the Juncture between Discourses.' In *Genealogy and Literature.* Ed. Lee Quinby. Minneapolis: University of Minesota Press, 1995. 28–47.

Goodman, Kevis. '"Uncertain Disease": Nostalgia, Pathologies of Motion, Practices of Reading.' *Studies in Romanticism.* 49.2 (2010): 197–227.

Grau, Joseph A. *Fanny Burney: An Annotated Bibliography.* New York: Garland, 1981.

Grob, Alan. 'Wordsworth and Godwin: A Reassessment.' *Studies in Romanticism.* 6 (1967): 98–119.

Grześkowiak-Krwawicz, Anna. *Gulliver in the Land of Giants: A Critical Biography and the Memoirs of the Celebrated Dwarf Joseph Boruwlaski.* Farnham: Ashgate, 2012.

Gubar, Susan. 'Feminist Misogyny: Mary Wollstonecraft and the Paradox of "It Takes One to Know One".' In *Mary Wollstonecraft and the Critics 1788–2001.* Ed. Harriet Devine Jump. 2 vols. London: Routledge, 2002. 2: 146–65.

Gunther-Canada, Wendy. 'Mary Wollstonecraft's "Wild Wish": Confounding Sex in the Discourse on Political Rights.' In *Feminist Interpretations of Mary Wollstonecraft.* Ed. Maria J. Falco. University Park: Pennsylvania State University Press, 1996. 61–83.

Gustafson, Katherine. '"I Never Saw Such Children": Disability, Industrialism, and Children's Advocacy in William Godwin's *Fleetwood.' Essays in Romanticism.* 24.2 (2017): 125–43.

Haggerty, George E. *Unnatural Affections: Women and Fiction in the Later 18th Century.* Bloomington: Indiana University Press, 1998.

Hall, Alice. *Literature and Disability.* New York: Routledge, 2016.

Halldenius, Lena. *Mary Wollstonecraft and Feminist Republicanism: Independence, Rights and the Experience of Unfreedom.* London: Pickering and Chatto, 2015.

Handwerk, Gary. 'History, Trauma, and the Limits of the Liberal Imagination: William Godwin's Historical Fiction.' In *Romanticism, History, and the Possibilities of Genre: Re-forming Literature 1789–1837.* Ed. Tilottama Rajan and Julia M. Wright. Cambridge: Cambridge University Press, 1998. 64–85.

Hanvey, Chris, and Terry Philpot. Eds. *Sweet Charity: The Role and Workings of Voluntary Organizations.* London: Routledge, 1996.

Harris, Diane. 'Eugenia's Escape: The Written Word in Frances Burney's *Camilla.*' *Lumen.* 17 (1998): 151–64.

Harriott, Howard H. 'Defensible Anarchy?' *International Philosophical Quarterly.* 33.3 (1993): 319–39.

Hartman, Geoffrey. *Wordsworth's Poetry 1787–1814.* New Haven, CT: Yale University Press, 1971.

Haslanger, Andrea. 'From Man-Machine to Woman-Machine: Automata, Fiction, and Femininity in Dibdin's *Hannah Hewit* and Burney's *Camilla.*' *Modern Philology.* 111.4 (2014): 788–817.

Hays, Peter L. *The Limping Hero: Grotesques in Literature.* New York: New York University Press, 1971.

Heffernan, James. 'Looking at the Monster: *Frankenstein* and Film.' *Critical Inquiry.* 24 (1997): 133–58.

Henke, Christoph. 'Before the Aesthetic Turn: The Common Sense Union of Ethics and Aesthetics in Shaftesbury and Pope.' *Anglia: Journal of English Philology.* 129 (2011): 58–78.

Hertz, Neil. 'The Notion of Blockage in the Literature of the Sublime.' In *The End of the Line: Essays on Psychoanalysis and the Sublime.* New York: Columbia University Press, 1985. 62–84.

Hirschmann, Nancy J. 'Freedom and (Dis)Ability in Early Modern Political Thought.' In *Recovering Disability in Early Modern England.* Ed. Allison P. Hobgood and David Houston Wood. Columbus: Ohio State University Press, 2013. 167–86.

Hodson, Jane. *Language and Revolution in Burke, Wollstonecraft, Paine, and Godwin.* Aldershot, Hampshire: Ashgate, 2007.

Howells, Carol Ann. '"The Proper Education of a Female... Is Still to Seek": Childhood and Girls' Education in Fanny Burney's *Camilla; Or, A Picture of Youth.*' *British Journal for Eighteenth-Century Studies.* 7.2 (1984): 191–8.

Hudson, Geoffrey L. 'Disabled Veterans and the State in Early Modern England.' In *Disabled Veterans in History.* Ed. David L. Gerber. Ann Arbor: University of Michigan Press, 2012. 117–44.

Hutchison, Iain. *A History of Disability in Nineteenth-Century Scotland.* Lewiston, NY: Edwin Mellen, 2007.

Jacovides, Michael. 'Locke's Construction of the Idea of Power.' *Studies in History of Philosophy and Science.* 34 (2003): 329–50.

James, Susan. 'Mary Wollstonecraft's Conception of Rights.' In *The Social and Political Philosophy of Mary Wollstonecraft.* Ed. Sandrine Bergès and Alan Coffee. Oxford: Oxford University Press, 2016. 148–65.

James-Cavan, Kathleen. '"All in me is Nature": The Values of Deformity in William Hay's *Deformity: An Essay.*' *Prose Studies* 27 (2005): 27–38.

Janowitz, Anne. 'The Romantic Fragment.' In *A Companion to Romanticism.* Ed. Duncan Wu. Oxford: Blackwell, 1999. 442–51.

Jeungel, Scott. 'Godwin, Lavater, and the Pleasures of Surface.' *Studies in Romanticism.* 35:1 (1996): 73–97.

Johnson, Barbara. 'My Monster/My Self.' *Diacritics.* 12 (1982): 2–10.

Johnson, Claudia. *Equivocal Beings: Politics, Gender, and Sentimentality in the 1790s – Wollstonecraft, Radcliffe, Burney, Austen.* Chicago, IL: University of Chicago Press, 1995.

Johnson, Nancy E. *The English Jacobin Novel on Rights, Property and the Law: Critiquing the Contract.* Houndmills, Basingstoke: Palgrave Macmillan, 2004.

Jones, Chris. *Radical Sensibility: Literature and Ideas in the 1790s.* London: Routledge, 2016.

Joshua, Essaka. '"Blind Vacancy": Sighted Culture and Voyeuristic Historiography in Mary Shelley's *Frankenstein.*' *European Romantic Review.* 22.1 (2011): 49–69.

Jump, Harriet Devine. Ed. *Mary Wollstonecraft and the Critics 1788–2001.* 2 vols. London: Routledge, 2002.

Jungman, Robert. 'Eve as a "Fair Defect" in Milton's Paradise Lost, Book 10.' *The Explicator.* 65.4 (2007): 204–6.

Kagan, Shelly. *The Geometry of Desert.* Oxford: Oxford University Press, 2012.

Keen, Paul. *The Crisis of Literature in the 1790s: Print Culture and the Public Sphere.* Cambridge: Cambridge University Press, 2004.

Keane, Angela. 'Mary Wollstonecraft's Imperious Sympathies: Population, Maternity and Romantic Individualism.' In *Body Matters: Feminism, Textuality, Corporeality.* Ed. Avril Horner and Angela Keane. Manchester: Manchester University Press, 2000. 29–57.

Kelly, Gary. *The English Jacobin Novel 1780–1805.* Oxford: Clarendon Press, 1976.

   *Revolutionary Feminism: The Mind and Career of Mary Wollstonecraft.* New York: St. Martin's, 1992.

   *Women, Writing, and Revolution, 1790–1827.* Oxford: Clarendon Press, 1993.

Kelly, Veronica, and Dorothea von Mücke. Eds. *Body and Text in the Eighteenth Century.* Stanford, CA: Stanford University Press, 1994.

Kittay, Eva Feder. 'The Ethics of Care, Dependence, and Disability.' *Ratio Juris.* 24.1 (2011): 49–58.

Kivy, Peter. *The Seventh Sense: A Study of Francis Hutcheson and Eighteenth-Century Aesthetics.* 2nd edn. Oxford: Clarendon Press, 2003.

Klancher, Jon. 'English Romanticism and Cultural Production.' In *The New Historicism.* Ed. H. Aram Veeser. New York: Routledge, 1989. 77–88.

Korsmeyer, Carolyn. 'The Two Beauties: A Perspective on Hutcheson's Aesthetics.' *Journal of Aesthetics and Art Criticism.* 38.2 (1979): 145–51.

Kowaleski Wallace, Elizabeth. Ed. *Encyclopedia of Feminist Literary Theory.* Abingdon: Routledge, 2009.

Kramnick, Isaac. *The Rage of Edmund Burke: Portrait of an Ambivalent Conservative.* New York: Basic, 1977.

Kumari Campbell, Fiona. *Contours of Ableism: The Production of Disability and Ableness.* Houndmills, Basingstoke: Palgrave Macmillan, 2009.

Larrissy, Edward. *The Blind and Blindness in Literature of the Romantic Period.* Edinburgh: Edinburgh University Press, 2007.

Levinson, Marjorie. *Wordsworth's Great Period Poems: Four Essays*. Cambridge: Cambridge University Press, 1986.

Lipking, Laurence. '*Frankenstein* the True Story; or, Rousseau Judges Jean-Jacques.' In Mary Shelley. *Frankenstein: The 1818 Text*. Ed. J. Paul Hunter. New York: W. W. Norton, 1996. 313–31.

Liu, Alan. *Wordsworth: The Sense of History*. Stanford, CA: Stanford University Press, 1989.

Liu, Yu. 'The Politics of Compassion.' *English Language Notes*. 37.4 (2000): 52–61.

Locke, Don. *A Fantasy of Reason: The Life and Thought of William Godwin*. London: Routledge and Kegan Paul, 1980.

Lockridge, Laurence S. *The Ethics of Romanticism*. Cambridge: Cambridge University Press, 1989.

Longmore, Paul. *Telethons: Spectacle, Disability, and the Business of Charity*. Oxford: Oxford University Press, 2016.

Lowe, E. J. 'Necessity and the Will in Locke's Theory of Action.' *History of Philosophy Quarterly*. 3.2 (1986): 149–63.

Lund, Roger. 'Laughing at Cripples: Ridicule, Deformity and the Argument from Design.' *Eighteenth-Century Studies*. 39.1 (2005): 91–114.

MacCormack, Patricia. 'Posthuman Teratology.' In *The Ashgate Research Companion to Monsters and the Monstrous*. Ed. Asa Simon Mittman and Peter J. Dendle. Farnham: Ashgate, 2012. 293–309.

MacIntyre, Alasdair. *Dependent Rational Animals: Why Human Beings Need the Virtues*. Peru, IL: Open Court, 1999.

MacLennan, George. *Lucid Interval: Subjective Writing and Madness in History*. Rutherford, NJ: Fairleigh Dickinson University Press, 1992.

Malchow, H. L. 'Frankenstein's Monster and Images of Race in Nineteenth-Century Britain.' *Past & Present*. 139 (1993): 90–130.

Markley, A. A. 'Charlotte Smith, the Godwin Circle, and the Proliferation of Speakers in *The Young Philosopher*.' In *Charlotte Smith in British Romanticism*. Ed. Jacqueline Labbe. London: Routledge, 2015. 87–99.

Markotić, Nicole. 'Disability Studies.' In *The Johns Hopkins Guide to Literary Theory and Criticism*. Ed. Michael Groden et al. Baltimore, MD: Johns Hopkins University Press, 2008.

Marshall, David. *The Surprising Effects of Sympathy: Marivaux, Diderot, Rousseau, and Mary Shelley*. Chicago, IL: University of Chicago Press, 1988.

Mason, Michelle. 'Moral Prejudice and Aesthetic Deformity: Rereading Hume's "Of the Standard of Taste".' *Journal of Aesthetics and Art Criticism*. 59.1 (2001): 59–71.

McCann, Andrew. *Cultural Politics in the 1790s: Literature, Radicalism and the Public Sphere*. Houndmills, Basingstoke: Macmillan, 1999.

McCrea, Barry. *Frances Burney and Narrative Prior to Ideology*. Newark: University of Delaware Press, 2013.

McDonagh, Patrick. *Idiocy: A Cultural History*. Liverpool: Liverpool University Press, 2008.

McGann, Jerome. *The Poetics of Sensibility: A Revolution in Literary Style*. Oxford: Clarendon Press, 1996.

McLane, Maureen N. *Romanticism and the Human Sciences: Poetry, Population, and the Discourse of the Species*. Cambridge: Cambridge University Press, 1996.

Mee, Jon. *Dangerous Enthusiasm: William Blake and the Culture of Radicalism in the 1790s*. Oxford: Clarendon Press, 1992.

Mellor, Anne K. *Mary Shelley, Her Life, Her Fiction, Her Monsters*. New York, Routledge, 1989.

Mendus, Susan, 'The Magic in the Pronoun My.' In *Scanlon and Contractualism*. Ed. Matt Matravers. London: Frank Cass, 2003. 33–52.

Metzler, Irina. *Disability in Medieval Europe: Thinking about Physical Impairment during the High Middle Ages, c. 1100–1400*. London: Routledge, 2006.

Michael, Emily. 'Francis Hutcheson on Aesthetic Perception and Aesthetic Pleasure.' *British Journal of Aesthetics*. 24.3 (1984): 241–55.

Milnes, Tim, and Kerry Sinanan. Eds. *Romanticism, Sincerity, and Authenticity*. London: Palgrave Macmillan, 2010.

Mitchell, David T., and Sharon L. Snyder. Eds. *The Body and Physical Difference: Discourses of Disability*. Ann Arbor: University of Michigan Press, 1997.

*Narrative Prosthesis: Disability and the Dependencies of Discourse*. Ann Arbor: University of Michigan Press, 2000.

'Representations of Disability, History of.' In *Encyclopedia of Disability*. Ed. Gary L. Albrecht. 5 vols. Thousand Oaks, CA: Sage, 2006. 3: 1382–94.

Mitchell, W. J. T. *Picture Theory: Essays in Verbal and Visual Representation*. Chicago, IL: University of Chicago Press, 1994.

Mittman, Asa Simon, and Peter J. Dendle. Eds. *The Ashgate Research Companion to Monsters and the Monstrous*. Farnham: Ashgate, 2012.

Montag, Warren. '"The Workshop of Filthy Creation": A Marxist Reading of *Frankenstein*.' In Mary Shelley. *Frankenstein*. Ed. Johanna M. Smith. Case Studies in Contemporary Criticism. Boston, MA: Bedford, 1992. 300–311.

Mortensen, Preben. 'Shaftesbury and the Morality of Art Expression.' *Journal of the History of Ideas*. 55.4 (1994): 631–50.

Mossman, Mark. 'Acts of Becoming: Autobiography, *Frankenstein*, and the Postmodern Body.' *Postmodern Culture*. 11.3 (2001): 1–12.

*Disability, Representation and the Body in Irish Writing: 1800–1922*. Houndmills, Basingstoke: Palgrave Macmillan, 2009.

Munro, D. H. 'Archbishop Fénelon versus My Mother.' *Australasian Journal of Psychology and Philosophy*. 28.3 (1950): 154–73.

Ni Chonaill, Siobhan. '"Why may not man one day be immortal?": Population, Perfectibility, and the Immortality Question in Godwin's *Political Justice*.' *History of European Ideas*. 33 (2007): 25–39.

Nielsen, Caroline Louise. 'The Chelsea Out-Pensioners: Image and Reality in Eighteenth-Century and Early Nineteenth-Century Social Care.' PhD Diss. University of Newcastle. August 2014.

Nussbaum, Felicity. 'Feminotopias: The Pleasures of "Deformity" in Mid-Eigh-teenth-Century England.' In *The Body and Physical Difference: Discourses of Disability*. Ed. David T. Mitchell and Sharon L. Snyder. Ann Arbor: University of Michigan Press, 1997. 161–73.

*The Limits of the Human: Fictions of Anomaly, Race, and Gender in the Long Eighteenth Century*. Cambridge: Cambridge University Press, 2003.

Nussbaum, Martha C. *Frontiers of Justice: Disability, Nationality, Species Member-ship*. Cambridge, MA: Belknap, 2006.

Offord, Mark. *Wordsworth and the Art of Philosophical Travel*. Cambridge: Cam-bridge University Press, 2016.

O'Gorman, Francis. 'Wordsworth and Touch.' *English*. 58 (2009): 4–23.

Oliver, Michael. *The Politics of Disablement*. London: Macmillan, 1990.

Oliver, Michael, and Colin Barnes. *The New Politics of Disablement*. Houndmills, Basingstoke: Palgrave Macmillan, 2012.

O'Toole, Corbett Joan. 'Disclosing Our Relationships to Disabilities.' *Disability Studies Quarterly*. 33.2 (2013).

Packham, Catherine. *Eighteenth-Century Vitalism: Bodies, Cultures, Politics*. Lon-don: Palgrave Macmillan, 2012.

Parkes, Parkes. 'Wooden Legs and Tales of Sorrow Done: The Literary Broken Soldier of the Late Eighteenth Century.' *Eighteenth-Century Studies*. 39 (2013): 191–207.

Paulson, William R. *Enlightenment, Romanticism, and the Blind in France*. Prin-ceton, NJ: Princeton University Press, 1987.

Peckham, Morse. *Romanticism and Ideology*. Hanover, NH: Wesleyan University Press, 1995.

Pender, Stephen. '"No Monsters at the Resurrection": Inside Some Conjoined Twins.' *Monster Theory: Reading Culture*. Ed. Jeffrey Jerome Cohen. Min-neapolis: University of Minnesota Press, 1996. 143–67.

Philp, Mark. *Godwin's Political Justice*. London: Duckworth, 1986.

Pierson, Chris. 'The Reluctant Pirate: Godwin, Justice, and Property.' *Journal of the History of Ideas*. 71.4 (2010): 569–91.

Pino, Melissa. 'Burney's *Evelina* and Aesthetics in Action.' *Modern Philology*. 108.2 (2010): 263–303.

Pond, Kristen. '"Fairest Observers" and "Restless Watchers": Contested Sites of Epistemology in Frances Burney's *Camilla*.' *Studies in the Novel*. 50.3 (2018): 315–35.

Poovey, Mary. 'My Hideous Progeny: Mary Shelley and the Feminization of Romanticism.' *PMLA*. 95 (1980): 332–47.

*The Proper Lady and the Woman Writer: Ideology as Style in the Works of Mary Wollstonecraft, Mary Shelley, and Jane Austen*. Chicago, IL: University of Chicago Press, 1984.

Poston, Carol H. 'Mary Wollstonecraft and "The Body Politic".' In *Feminist Interpretations of Mary Wollstonecraft*. Ed. Maria J. Falco. University Park: Pennsylvania State University Press, 1996. 85–104.

Potkay, Adam. *Wordsworth's Ethics.* Baltimore, MD: Johns Hopkins University Press, 2012.

Quayson, Ato. *Aesthetic Nervousness: Disability and the Crisis of Representation.* New York: Columbia University Press, 2007.

Radcliffe, Evan. 'Godwin from "Metaphysician" to Novelist: *Political Justice, Caleb Williams,* and the Tension between Philosophical Argument and Narrative.' *Modern Philology.* 97.4 (2000): 528–53.

Richardson, Alan. 'Romanticism and the Body.' *Literature Compass.* 1 (2004): 1–14.

Richey, William. 'The Rhetoric of Sympathy in Smith and Wordsworth.' *European Romantic Review.* 13.4 (2002): 427–43.

Richman, Jared. 'Monstrous Elocution: Disability and Passing in *Frankenstein.*' *Essays in Romanticism.* 25.2 (2018): 187–207.

Rind, Miles. 'The Concept of Disinterestedness in Eighteenth-Century British Aesthetics.' *Journal of the History of Philosophy.* 40.1 (2002): 67–87.

Roberts, Charles W. 'The Influence of Godwin on Wordsworth's Letter to the Bishop of Llandaff.' *Studies in Philology.* 29.4 (1932): 588–606.

Rodas, Julia Miele. 'Autistic Voice and Literary Architecture in Mary Shelley's *Frankenstein.*' In *Disabling Romanticism.* Ed. Michael Bradshaw. London: Palgrave Macmillan, 2016. 169–90.

Roe, Nicholas. *Wordsworth and Coleridge: The Radical Years.* Oxford: Clarendon Press, 1988.

  *The Politics of Nature: Wordsworth and Some Contemporaries.* London: Macmillan, 1992.

Rousso, Harilyn. *Don't Call Me Inspirational: A Disabled Feminist Talks Back.* Philadelphia, PA: Temple University Press, 2013.

Rounce, Adam. 'William Godwin: The Novel, Philosophy, and History.' *History of European Ideas.* 33.1 (2007): 1–8.

Sager, Jenny. *The Aesthetics of Spectacle in Early Modern Drama and Modern Cinema: Robert Greene's Theatre of Attractions.* Basingstoke: Palgrave Macmillan, 2013.

Salih, Sara. '*Camilla* and *The Wanderer.*' In *The Cambridge Companion to Frances Burney.* Ed. Peter Sabor. Cambridge: Cambridge University Press, 2007.

Sanchez, Rebecca. *Deafening Modernism: Embodied Language and Visual Poetics in American Literature.* New York: New York University Press, 2015.

Scheuermann, Mona. 'The Study of Mind: The Later Novels of William Godwin.' *Forum for Modern Language Studies.* 19.1 (1983): 16–30.

Schillmeier, Michael. *Rethinking Disability: Bodies, Senses, Things.* New York: Routledge, 2010.

Sha, Richard C. 'Towards a Physiology of the Romantic Imagination.' *Configurations.* 17.3 (2009): 197–226.

Shakespeare, Tom. *Disability Rights and Wrongs.* London: Routledge, 2006.

Shildrick, Margrit. 'The Disabled Body, Genealogy and Undecidability.' *Cultural Studies.* 19.6 (2005): 755–70.

Shuttleton, David E. *Smallpox and the Literary Imagination 1660–1820.* Cambridge: Cambridge University Press, 2007.

Sidgwick, Henry. *The Methods of Ethics.* 2nd edn. Indianapolis, IN: Hackett, 1907.

Siebers, Tobin. *The Ethics of Criticism.* Ithaca, NY: Cornell University Press, 1988.

'Disability as Masquerade.' *Literature and Medicine.* 23.1 (2004): 1–22.

*Disability Theory.* Ann Arbor: University of Michigan Press, 2008.

*Disability Aesthetics.* Ann Arbor: University of Michigan Press, 2010.

Simpson, David. *Wordsworth's Historical Imagination: The Poetry of Displacement.* New York: Methuen, 1987.

Singer, Peter, Leslie Cannold, and Helga Kuhse. 'William Godwin and the Defence of Impartialist Ethics.' *Utilitas.* 7.1 (1995): 67–86.

Six, Abigail Lee, and Hannah Thompson. 'From Hideous to Hedonist: The Changing Face of the Nineteenth-Century Monster.' In *The Ashgate Research Companion to Monsters and the Monstrous.* Ed. Asa Simon Mittman and Peter J. Dendle. Farnham: Ashgate, 2012. 237–55.

Small, Helen. *Love's Madness: Medicine, the Novel and Female Insanity, 1800–1865.* Oxford: Clarendon Press, 1996.

Smith, Angela M. *Hideous Progeny: Disability, Eugenics, and Classic Horror Cinema.* New York: Columbia University Press, 2011.

Snyder, Sharon L., and David T. Mitchell. 'Re-engaging the Body: Disability Studies and Resistance to Embodiment.' *Public Culture.* 13.3 (2001): 367–90.

*Cultural Locations of Disability.* Chicago, IL: University of Chicago Press, 2006.

Snyder, Sharon L., Brenda Jo Brueggemann, and Rosemarie Garland Thomson. Eds. *Disability Studies: Enabling the Humanities.* New York: MLA, 2002.

Spacks, Patricia Meyer. 'Energies of Mind: Plot's Possibilities in the 1790s.' *Eighteenth-Century Fiction.* 1.1 (1988): 37–52.

Stanback, Emily B. 'Disability and Dissent: Thelwall's Elocutionary Project.' In *John Thelwall: Critical Reassessments.* A Romantic Circles Praxis Volume. Ed. Yasmin Solomonescu, 2011. https://romantic-circles.org/praxis/thelwall/HTML/praxis.2011.stanback.html

'Wordsworthian Admonishment.' *The Wordsworth Circle.* 44.2/3 (2013): 159–63.

*The Wordsworth–Coleridge Circle and the Aesthetics of Disability.* London: Palgrave Macmillan, 2016.

Starr, G. Gabrielle. 'Burney, Ovid, and the Value of the Beautiful.' *Eighteenth-Century Fiction.* 24.1 (2011): 77–104.

Stephenson, Warren. 'Wordsworth and the Stone of Night.' *The Wordsworth Circle.* 13.4 (1982): 175–8.

Stolnitz, Jerome. 'On the Origins of "Aesthetic Disinterestedness".' *Journal of Aesthetics and Art Criticism.* 20.2 (1961): 131–43.

Stone, C. F. 'Narrative Variation in Wordsworth's Versions of "The Discharged Soldier".' *Journal of Narrative Technique.* 4 (1974): 32–44.

Stone, Deborah A. *The Disabled State.* Philadelphia, PA: Temple University Press, 1984.

Stef-Praun, Laura A. 'Harriet Martineau's "Intellectual Nobility": Gender, Genius, and Disability.' In *Harriet Martineau: Authorship, Society, and Empire.* Ed. Ella Dzelzainis and Cora Kaplan. Manchester: Manchester University Press, 2010. 38–51.

Sterrenburg, Lee. 'Mary Shelley's Monster: Politics and Psyche in *Frankenstein.*' In *The Endurance of Frankenstein: Essays on Mary Shelley's Novel.* Ed. George Levine and U. C. Knoepflmacher. Berkeley: University of California Press, 1979. 143–71.

Swain, John, Sally French, and Colin Cameron. *Controversial Issues in a Disabling Society.* Buckingham: Open University Press, 2003.

Tauchert, Ashley. *Mary Wollstonecraft and the Accent of the Feminine.* Houndmills, Basingstoke: Palgrave Macmillan, 2002.

Taylor, Barbara. *Mary Wollstonecraft and the Feminist Imagination.* Cambridge: Cambridge University Press, 2003.

Tilley, Heather. 'Wordsworth's Glasses: The Materiality of Blindness in Romantic Vision.' In *Illustrations, Optics and Objects in Nineteenth-Century Literary and Visual Culture.* Ed. Luisa Calè and Patrizia di Bello. London: Palgrave Macmillan, 2010. 44–61.

*Blindness and Writing: From Wordsworth to Gissing.* Cambridge: Cambridge University Press, 2018.

Thomas, Sophie. *Romanticism and Visuality: Fragments, History, Spectacle.* New York: Routledge, 2008.

Thompson, Helen. *Ingenuous Subjection: Compliance and Power in the Eighteenth-Century Domestic Novel.* Philadelphia, PA: University of Pennsylvania Press, 2005.

Trott, Nicola. 'The Coleridge Circle and the "Answer to Godwin".' *Review of English Studies.* 41 (1990): 212–29.

Turner, David M. *Disability in Eighteenth-Century England: Imagining Physical Impairment.* Routledge Studies in Modern British History. New York: Routledge, 2012.

Ulmer, William A. 'William Wordsworth and Philosophical Necessity.' *Studies in Philology.* 110.1 (2013): 168–98.

Varner, Paul. *Historical Dictionary of Romanticism in Literature.* London: Rowman and Littlefield, 2015.

Viadli, Amy. 'Seeing What We Know: Disability and Theories of Metaphor.' *Journal of Literary and Cultural Disability Studies.* 4.1 (2010): 33–54.

Wallace, Miriam L. Ed. *Enlightening Romanticism, Romancing the Enlightenment: British Novels from 1750–1832.* London: Routledge, 2009.

Wang, Fuson. 'The Historicist Turn of Romantic-Era Disability Studies, or *Frankenstein* in the Dark.' *Literature Compass.* 14.7 (2017): 1–10.

Weston, Rowland. 'Chivalry, Commerce, and Generosity: Godwin on Economic Equality.' *Eighteenth-Century Life*. 41.2 (2017): 43–58.

Williams, Katherine Schaap. '"More Legs than Nature Gave Thee": Performing the Cripple in the Fair Maid of the Exchange.' *English Literary History*. 82.2 (2015): 491–519.

Wilson, Philip K. 'Eighteenth-Century "Monsters" and Nineteenth-Century "Freaks": Reading the Maternally Marked Child.' *Literature and Medicine*. 21.3 (2002): 1–25.

Woodman, Ross. *Sanity, Madness, Transformation: The Psyche in Romanticism*. Toronto: University of Toronto Press, 2005.

Wyse, Bruce. '"The Human Senses Are Insurmountable Barriers": Deformity, Sympathy, and Monster Love in Three Variations on *Frankenstein*.' In *Global Frankensteins*. Ed Carol Margaret Davison and Marie Mulvey-Roberts. Cham, Switzerland: Palgrave Macmillan, 2018. 75–90.

Young, Iris Marion. *Throwing Like a Girl and Other Essays in Feminist Philosophy and Social Theory*. Bloomington: Indiana University Press, 1990.

Youngquist, Paul. 'Lyrical Bodies: Wordsworth's Physiological Aesthetics.' *European Romantic Review*. 10 (1999): 152–62.

*Monstrosities: Bodies and British Romanticism*. Minneapolis: University of Minnesota Press, 2003.

Yousef, Nancy. 'Wordsworth, Sentimentalism, and the Defiance of Sympathy.' *European Romantic Review*. 17.2 (2006): 205–13.

# Index

# CAMBRIDGE STUDIES IN ROMANTICISM

*General Editor*
JAMES CHANDLER, *University of Chicago*